Action Explorations

Action
Explorations

Using Psychodramatic Methods
in Non-Therapeutic Settings

Edited by Adam Blatner

*a parallax
production*

To my family, who made this book possible:
my wife Allee, my daughter Alisa,
and my son David who picked up the reins.

Action Explorations: Using Psychodramatic Methods in Non-Therapeutic Settings

Published by Parallax Productions / 63p.com LLC
Seattle, Washington USA
web: *www.parallax.productions*
email: *info@parallax.productions*

ISBN 978-1-7335520-0-4 (*paper*)
ISBN 978-1-7335520-1-1 (*ebook*)

Cover artwork: "Angles Grid" © Sarah Benson
Book Design: David Blatner
Project Lead and Production Manager: David Blatner
Copy Editors: Allee Blatner and Alisa Piette

Typeset in FreightText Pro Book (designed by Joshua Darden)
and FF Enzo (designed by Tobias Kvant).

Contents

For All Humankind

Adam Blatner
Edited by Allee Blatner and David Blatner

Many people feel constantly under pressure, as though everything they say or do is a final, graded performance: "No mistakes allowed!" What if there were another way?

Now let's say someone created a system of social and interpersonal tools that we could use in both personal and professional interactions. And what if those tools empower us to experiment, explore, and even make mistakes — correcting them, right in the moment and with the help with others?!

Of course, we *do* have these tools, but unfortunately they have long been buried in the confines of therapeutic settings. Psychodrama, created by the psychiatrist J.L. Moreno, M.D. (1889–1972) contains a cornucopia of techniques to aid in these sorts of interpersonal issues. Moreno and his wife and professional partner, Zerka Toeman Moreno, were acutely aware of the power and value of these methods and believed they should eventually be applied to a far wider audience.

This has been a rallying cry in my own work for over 50 years. Even though I am a psychiatrist and certified Trainer, Educator and Practitioner in Psychodrama, my intention has always been to offer these skills to everyone. And as we'll see throughout this book, these methods can be (and are!) used for improving business relationships, social justice, education, and even spiritual endeavors. They can be used to enable greater reflection, lasting self-empowerment, and more vibrant, happier lives.

However, for reasons I'll discuss in a moment, I propose we shed the moniker "psychodrama" or even "psychodramatic techniques" when referring to this valuable tool box. The umbrella term I prefer is: *Action Explorations*.

Using action explorations, individuals and groups are empowered to explore their attitudes and behaviors, offering a chance to play through a possible interaction as a scene in an improvised story. Once an idea is enacted, many more resources are available for an individual or a group.

In a way, that's what science does, too: Turn ideas into experiments where they can be tried out, even repeated while changing variables. As an eminent physicist noted, "Science advances only by making all possible mistakes . . . the main thing is to make the mistakes as fast as possible and to recognize them."[1] Yet those risking this kind of experiential learning are protected by psychodrama's special setting, a "stage" on which to explore, safely, and with an audience committed to support rather than rejection.

From Patient to Person

For over 45 years as a clinical psychiatrist, I treated patients both with medicines that ease or alleviate symptoms and with various forms of psychotherapy. Gradually my main interest has shifted from treating those suffering from mental illness to focusing on the exciting potential for these approaches to increase mental flexibility, deepen self-awareness, amplify communications, and enhance socio-emotional problem-solving for everyone. As Moreno said in his seminal book, *Who Shall Survive*, "a truly therapeutic procedure cannot have less an objective than the whole of mankind." Everyone!

The world is ripe for this innovation. A shift in the decision making process is occurring—from a 20th century goal of "get it right" (as if some authority knew what that was) to a 21st century openness to the need for collaboration, creative alternatives and a synthesis of ideas. Action explorations offers a way to systematically open our minds, explore new options and apply them to personal and community challenges. Instead of traditional brainstorming or exhaustive rational analysis, we can use improvisation for re-visioning and dramatic simulations with groups of people to invite options to "come out of left field."

Improvisation is the activity that engenders an attitude and readiness of mind with which to support the opportunity for spontaneity—which is the very heart of creativity—to emerge and offer its invaluable gifts.

It's worth noting that many human anxieties and troubles are impossible to work out rationally. People have long come to terms with death, hardship and losses, not through rational talk, but through the arts. Intractable problems can be better managed by not having to make logical sense of the experience, but rather through rituals and enactments with others who can empathize and confirm that some things just don't make any sense. Once again, even in non-therapeutic settings, action explorations can be applied successfully.

---

1   Wheeler, John A., quoted in John P. Wiley, Jr. "Phenomena, Comment, and Notes." *Smithsonian*, 1981, August, p. 26.

Action Exploration Techniques

As I've said previously, action explorations are the tools or techniques used in psychodrama psychotherapy but adapted and expanded to be used outside of the purely therapeutic context. Let's look at what some of those methods are.

In psychodrama psychotherapy, instead of lying on a couch or sitting in a chair, the patient is encouraged by the therapist/"director" to enact scenes or situations from their own life problems. As the saying goes: "Don't just talk about it. Get up and show it." The dynamic of making the situation "pretend"—which is part of drama— makes use of the element of play. That is, providing a category of action which resembles a scene from a play or story immediately imparts the feeling that says "this doesn't really count," since it is being "made up." People are more open to experimenting when it's "pretend play," rather than paralyzed by fear of a mistake that will have overwhelming consequences.

These techniques often involve a group—though not just a passive audience who await entertainment or even instruction, but in a sense, they join in co-producing the action. The "audience" is the source of the protagonist and supporting players; and later on, they may switch roles to complement the exploration. At the end of the scene, they share with the protagonist, and sometimes the sharing can take as much or even more time than the action!

An area or "stage" is designated as a space within which what happens is played. (Not "a play" in the sense of a theatrical performance, but rather play/not-count/just pretend/as-if.) However, the action moves between on- and off-stage: The person exploring a scene (traditionally called the "protagonist") is offered an opportunity to step out of the story to reconsider what has happened. The director and group members can talk about what might be done next so that the situation can be explored even more effectively. In this sense, the stage is an area for experimentation, a laboratory.

The point is to use the dramatic context to generate "role distance"—a way to figuratively step back and reflect on our own actions. This taking a break from the action subtly builds up the internal role of mediator—helping people develop a master self-identity that has the perspective of a "more conscious chooser."

Dialog is used in these enactments. The participants can say something aloud, experience how it sounds and feels, and then experiment saying it another way; even directing supporting players to try new dialog in order to experience what different effects it creates in a scene.

For example, the director might allow a scene to play out, then say:

> **Director (D):** Cut. Joe, what did you think
> of the way you played that role?

> **Joe (J):** I don't know. I guess I said what I felt.

D: (*to group*) What did you think?

Group member: I think it was weak. He could have said that far more forcefully and it would make his point much stronger.

D: (*to Joe*) What do you think?

J: Yeah, now that you mention it, maybe they didn't know how I really felt.

D: Okay, well, let's try it again. Take it from where you come into the room.

Scene repeats and Joe re-enters.

Role distance is an essential component of imaginative play and the basis for the most natural way to learn. Role playing, or simulation training, has applications in many types of learning where more complex understanding and interpersonal development is needed—from the rehearsal of a speech or presentation to exploring business options, from new skills training in management to anti-bully behavior for middle school kids.

Action explorations offer a vast repertoire of component techniques such as role-taking, role reversal (experiencing one's actions from another person's point of view), role distancing (shifting from actor to self-observation), improvising, amplifying, exaggerating, replaying (a chance to do it again, a different way), and doubling (expressing deeper levels of self-disclosure). With so many options, wide-ranging and complex issues can be explored and integrated.

All these techniques (and more) are a bridge to a new level of thinking, communicating, and problem-solving—more inclusive of right brain emotionality, vulnerability, unspoken needs, social sensitivity, intuition, and imagination. By balancing left-brain language formulation and reasoning with the evanescent and intuitive right-brain, we can construct a more richly textured and thereby more easily remembered schema or framework that is conducive to further refinement. Equally important to these methods is the experience of grounding the conceptual/hypothetical/remembered experience with bodily action. This core principle allows a person to literally "feel-into" how old, new or possible behaviors will affect their memories and future interactions while receiving the validation of the group members.

The use of the metaphor of drama or story—that is, life as a series of scenes played by various actors—allows for an expansion into a context of discussion. The profound and extensive influence of the non-rational is openly recognized, and these elements are worked with in compassionate and adaptive ways rather than discounting them. There is an overall benefit of helping that which is unconscious move towards consciousness. It also weaves in a recognition of the artistic, aesthetic, poetic, mythic, and other dimensions that are not irrational so much as trans-rational. They are not forced to be reduced to language or rationality.

In fact, in action explorations, there is a conscious agreement to explore the pre-conscious realm, the parts of the mind that protest, whine, fume, cringe, and behave in a less mature, more childish fashion. It turns out that these feelings are like two sides of a coin: one half of what these parts say is transparently immature and unrealistic; but the other half often contains important information that needs to be woven back into the discourse. Action explorations allows a more nuanced type of discernment, investigating the potential for redemption of disowned parts of oneself—the proverbial baby that should not be thrown out with the bathwater, or the "shadow" that yearns for integration with the whole self.

Rather than overcoming, controlling, or forcefully dominating the non-rational elements of our own minds, action explorations seek to negotiate with them, integrate them, and find creative syntheses that direct their energies.

Why "Action Explorations"

As previously mentioned, although these techniques are rooted in the valuable history of psychodrama, I prefer the name "action explorations" for several of reasons.

On the one hand, the prefix "psycho" is too easily conflated by the general public with "psychotic" or "psychopathic," as in the 1960 Alfred Hitchcock thriller *Psycho*. Another unfortunate popular association is with traditional "psychoanalysis," which not only has become significantly less useful in recent years, but moreover uses almost diametrically opposite methodologies.

On the other hand, the word "drama" itself has shifted in its semantic associations over the past 50 years. Drama used to include comedy—think of the two symbolic masks representing both tears and laughter. But more recently "drama" has come to indicate something that will scare you or touch your heart to the point of tears. The term implies a "heavy" or disturbing story line.

More simply, most people have a general association to the word "drama" with its most pervasive form, which is traditional theatre:

- scripted by a playwright
- directed by a "director" who has his or her own interpretation or approach rather than working from what the actors have to say
- performed by professional or amateur actors who audition for the role and then memorize and rehearse the script to some level of perfection
- acted fairly consistently before an audience that is expected to remain observers rather than participants

In contrast, action explorations expect the participants to improvise the situation that is most relevant to them, is facilitated rather than directed, and includes a more fluid audience who may even generate supporting players for the subject of exploration.

So, at least for most non-clinical settings (such as business, education, or social groups), the term psychodrama has had an uphill battle toward understanding and acceptance. Many of us in this field have tossed around a variety of descriptive phrases, such as creativity enhancement, action methods, reality practice, enhanced simulations, applied improvisation, and life enlargement. However, the term I have come to appreciate the most is "action explorations." The public understands the idea much more easily and is intrigued by what it offers.

After all, *exploring in action* is what children do as they grow and learn to be human beings in their society, through the activity called play. It is through similar—though perhaps more structured—action explorations that we all can continue to grow, learn, and develop our human capabilities!

The Tools of Change

Tools aren't just material things, like hammers or coffee makers; they also can be the way a task is managed, the techniques used. In this sense, psychodrama is a complex of tools for thinking and communicating about feelings and relationships.[2] Just as the telephone, television, and the Internet added the dimensions of immediacy and visual connection to the technology of writing, so psychodrama adds the dimensions of space, action, non-linear time, and imagination to the more conventional "technology" of rational verbal discussion. These added dimensions allow for improvisation, alternative scenarios, shifting roles and points of view, opportunities for replay, and other elements which offer new avenues toward insight and self-reflection.

And just as electrical carpentry tools can be used to build a wide range of things, big and small, so too psycho-social tools may be used for a remarkably wide range of purposes. Powerful tools, however, must be applied cautiously— and psychodrama must also be used judiciously, with safety as an important consideration. In addition, tools cannot substitute for the good judgment of the craftsperson. There are many operations in both carpentry and working with people—such as planning the project, selection of the participants, and organizing the procedures—in which technique is secondary.

Continuing with the analogy, a good tool finds many applications beyond its original function. Writing was at first a tool simply for accounting; poetry came later. The computer was designed as a calculator before growing into its potential for "information processing." Similarly, psychotherapy's tools have also expanded far beyond the clinical context and have come to be used

---

2   Blatner, Adam. (1992). Theoretical principles underlying creative arts therapies. *The Arts in Psychotherapy*, 18, 405–409.

in business and other cultural institutions, popularized for the general reader, and spread in many other ways.

Clearly, psychodrama's tools can also be applied outside its traditional context, to many other areas: education, business, organizational development, experiential education, self-help groups, empathy development, management and personnel training, *in situ* interventions on the playground or on the streets, in religious retreats, as part of personal growth programs, community building, creating more meaningful celebrations or rituals, the arts, and even just for pure recreation.[3]

Thus, the audience for this book is anyone who wants to acquire new tools to help themselves, their families and friends, their community, social and spiritual groups. This includes students in many fields of learning, business and management trainers, public service representatives, teachers of many disciplines, performers and other creative artists, and the list goes on.

What the World Needs Next

This quote by the futurologist Alvin Toffler feels particularly relevant and prescient:

> *The illiterate of the 21st century will not be those who cannot read and write, but those who cannot learn, unlearn, and relearn.*

I suggest that action explorations is among the best ways to help people with this new kind of literacy, offering personal and interpersonal tools for exploring and developing new habits of action and thought. Action explorations addresses the need for problem solving and innovation by integrating three things that most folks are afraid to do: improvise, enact, and collaborate creatively (using "yes and" rather than "no but").

Also, there is an important dimension of psychodramatic technique that the word "exploration" points to: The use of imagination. The human forebrain is unique in the animal kingdom in that it can consider "what if I were to act this way?" Ultimately, the basis of all action explorations work is "what if?" Humans can imagine multiple futures: What might be? What could be? And even what could have been? In other words, problem solving and re-thinking in whatever context they occur can greatly benefit from psychodramatic techniques that enable exploration outside of habitual and ordinary reality.

In this 21st century, it's time to shift from the ethos of confrontation, aggression, and win/lose thinking to that of peacemaking, negotiating, and mediating to work out differences. I believe this cannot be attained without a critical mass of people learning new ways of thinking and behaving, something

---

3 Blatner, Adam & Blatner, Allee. (1997), *The Art of Play*, Brunner/Mazel.

like action explorations. For example, consider Moreno's concept of encounter, which invites people to care enough to reverse roles, to do the work of imagining and enacting what it's really like to be the other person ("to walk a mile in another's shoes" as the saying goes). This is empathy, and nothing less than an operationalizing of the Golden Rule.[4]

Similarly, when people spend a fair amount of time doing action explorations, they begin to think more like being *all* the components of a play—actors, playwrights, directors, producers and audiences. The practice in shifting perspective among all of the different roles and viewpoints develops the capacity for self-reflection and stepping outside of one's habitual and familiar stance. This ability is an important component in psychological maturation. The benefits, then, go beyond merely solving the problem at hand: the component skills develop one's mental flexibility, social interactivity, and social interactivity.

Schools and community organizations can use role-playing for cultivating the kinds of "emotional intelligence" skills described by Daniel Goleman,[5] skills which are fast becoming indispensable for coping with the challenges of everyday life. Businesses and organizations of all sorts can apply these tools to enable their workforce to rapidly problem-solve and adapt in a rapidly changing world.

Once again, I am not dismissing the important place of the use of psychodramatic methods in psychotherapy—which was a major foundation for my own work as a psychiatrist and on the faculty of medical schools from the 1960s through 2016. My earlier books were targeted for psychotherapists, in whatever discipline they practiced—including creative arts therapists and psychodramatists who worked with patients. My wife, Allee, and I taught "Practical Applications of Psychodramatic Methods" as a day-long course for ten years at the American Psychiatric Association Annual Conferences. We were passionate about the immense value of these tools in psychotherapy. Again, this re-naming to "action explorations" is a re-branding of sorts, a re-thinking of the wider applications of psychodrama, beyond the medical.

I am happy to report that there are many people doing this important work, and I have asked a number of them to contribute to this book. The authors of the chapters have developed and extended the techniques from psychodrama, drama therapy, improvisation, social justice, and allied approaches into a wide range of applications represented by their work.

However, if you are considering using these tools to attempt the more complex scenarios presented in this book, you will need to be trained in the various disciplines represented by the authors. One cannot learn these approaches through "cookbook" reading, any more than one can learn music or surgery solely from a text.

---

4 Bischof, Ledford J. (1966). "Are We Climbing Jacob's Ladder?" *Group Psychotherapy*.
5 Goleman, Daniel. (1998) *Working with Emotional Intelligence*. New York: Bantam.

My excitement in creating this book is broader and deeper than any one of the specific applications in this book. I want to excite you to consider where you can use these interpersonal and intrapersonal tools in many areas of your own life, relationships, work, and communities. I want to also encourage you to seek out teachers of these kinds of methods. They are offering workshops and classes all over the world.

J.L. Moreno envisioned, in his work *Who Shall Survive*, "If the future of mankind can be 'planned,' then conscious evolution through training of spontaneity opens a new vista for the development of the human race." His words point to the need for action explorations, in combination with all the other psychological and social technologies being developed, to facilitate a new, potentially achievable goal: the conscious, intentional transformation of consciousness itself.

It is my deepest hope that this book and the invaluable tools presented will help many of you to make your own life and work more successful, joyful, and accessible to many more people. As Moreno would have wanted: "for the good of all humankind!"

Adam Blatner

Adam Blatner, M.D., TEP, is a retired psychiatrist and Trainer of Psychodrama. He is a former Associate Professor of Psychiatry at The University of Louisville School of Medicine and Texas A&M University School of Medicine. Adam has written books and articles in the field of psychodrama, drama therapy and the creative arts in therapy. He is internationally recognized as an authority on the theory and practice of psychodrama. Adam has championed the place of the arts in healing and health for over 50 years through his writings, teachings at conferences and mentoring students all over the world. He is author of the basic text in psychodrama *Acting*-In, many articles and chapters, and the books *Foundations of Psychodrama*, *Interactive Improvisation*, and co-author *The Art of Play*.

Section I

Action Explorations in Business and Organizations

Using Action Methods in Coaching

Marilyn S. Feinstein

I hear and I forget; I see and I remember; I do and I understand.
—Confucius

Like many living in the New York area, 9/11 was a defining moment for me. Loss for some and survival guilt for others (not at the scene at the time) was ubiquitous. I gained a new career perspective. Trained at NYU as an LCSW therapist, I was hired by several corporations to help employees deal with the aftermath of terror and slaughter of 3,000 lives.

A large accounting firm in Stamford, CT, lost many employees in their Twin Towers office on that beautiful September day in 2001. The Head of HR hired me to help the Stamford employees, many who, she said, "were in shock and tremendous grief." A memo circulated: "*a therapist* will be available in Room 101." No one showed the whole day. I offered to return the next day, if a different memo could circulate, with an invitation for 1:1 sessions in Rm 502 to learn an easy relaxation exercise. The company had me at their Stamford site for 3 weeks. Each person who entered the room longed to relax and unload their stress. Behind closed doors, each opened up and processed their feelings (grief, anger, *etc*) and sense of loss.

Here was a profound example of how marketing something in 2 different ways produced very different results. I was the same person with the same training. The message behind the "no shows" the first day, sadly lent itself to the still lingering stigma around therapy. One must be crazy/sick to seek therapy. Yet, taking a break to learn an easy relaxation exercise—who wouldn't want that?

That reframe/marketing lesson informed my decision to get certified in Personal and Executive Coaching at *The College of Executive Coaching,* (headed by a Psychologist) and expand my practice. I now offer therapy and coaching.

The history of recorded coaching dates back to ancient China, in which coaching, 陪導 (*pei dao*), meant *journeying together, one inch at a time.* The word *coach* stems from actual movement. In the 1550s, a carriage maker in the Hungarian village, Kocs, devised a *kocsi,* the ultimate in comfort. The modern coach serves as the metaphorical vehicle, safely carrying the person from his/her beginning (point A) to desired outcome (point B).[1] Today, coaching is seen as a partnership between coach and individual. Hargrove speaks of the coach as a "thinking partner."[2]

In coach training, I saw how coaching implemented so many therapeutic concepts and techniques, *just packaged differently!* Literature contrasting coaching with psychotherapy often paints differences in black and white, shedding therapy in a pejorative light. There are more than 400 therapies, yet the marketing of coaching tends to refer to therapy through the lens of one—psychoanalysis (not practiced much anymore). Coaching and therapy have more in common than differences, including: the focus is client centered; facilitating another's learning, positive psychology centered on the client's strengths vs deficits; helping clients examine irrational beliefs keeping them from accomplishing their goals; reframing ways to view a situation; engaging the client's intrinsic motivation to change behavior; motivational interviewing—guides the client to explore his/her ambivalence; present centered, using solution rather than problem talk; miracle question, *"Imagine your desired future is here. What would be the first thing you'd do that's different?"*[3]

Therapy has always included elements of coaching. Coaching is present, future and goal oriented, nested in a larger frame of the many forms of therapeutic styles it has adopted. Both disciplines use similar techniques, focused within their respective scope of practice. Coaches incorporate therapeutic techniques within the context of coaching, while psychotherapists may use coaching techniques within the context of psychotherapy. The *International Coaching Federation (ICF)* Code of Ethics mandates that ICF coaches must, in their contracting with clients, make a clear distinction between coaching and psychotherapy. An ICF coach must refer the client to another psychotherapist, even if he/she like myself has the training to do both therapy and coaching. However, a mental health professional, also an ICF credentialed

---

1 Hargove R. *Masterful Coaching. 3rd ed.* (2008). San Francisco, CA: Jossey-Bass

2 Ibid.

3 Feinstein, M.S. and Feinstein, R. E. (2017). *Health coaching.* In (Eds.) Feinstein, R.E., Connolly, J.V., and Feinstein, M.S. *Integrating Behavioral Health and Primary Care.* New York, NY: Oxford University Press.

coach, entering a psychotherapy agreement with a client, has wide latitude to use coaching techniques.[4]

While offering training certification through coach training schools, and accreditation through organizations, like *The International Coaching Federation,* the coaching profession doesn't yet require licensing. Coaching, by no means new, has become in vogue — a go to for personal and professional development.

Why Action Exploration?

Adam Blatner, M.D., has used and written prodigiously about action methods developed by Jacob L. Moreno, M.D., and others. He developed the term action exploration, an umbrella approach for the many experiential methods used to provide a safe, laboratory setting[5] for personal/professional development. Grounded in principles of creativity and play, improvisation and role theory, these exploration methods help clients achieve new perspectives of themselves and others. This approach "allows for more integration of mind and body, thinking and acting, reason and emotion, and other dualities that tend not to be included in ordinary discussion."[6] Practical application of this dynamic recipe not only helps clients learn and problem solve, but can serve as an agent of change in their lives.

Following are coaching cases using action methods of applied improvisation, role reversal and active use of guided imagery: 1) to help improve a business relationship with a prospect in sales; 2) an executive explores his ambivalence about staying or leaving his company; 3) the executive navigates a specific way to give notice; and 4) an athlete develops a way to get into *the zone* for peak performance.

Using Role Play Reversal in the Corporate Environment

When working for a Fortune 500 sales/marketing company, I called on an organization not using our products. My goal was to develop a relationship which could potentially lead to doing business. My contact — the purchasing agent, low on the organizational chart in terms of decision making. I didn't quite understand the affectionate moniker given to him, *Attila the Hun,* until I first met him. Traveling with my manager, I saw *Attila* viciously put down our company. He seemed narcissistic, devaluing everyone. Each time I called on him, we seemed to go through a painful ritual. After opening social pleasantries, I asked about his organization and was shot down. I wondered how I would develop a working relationship with this man. His behavior certainly couldn't

---

4   Ibid.

5   Blatner, A. (2012) *Action Explorations: An Inclusive Category* Accessed 7-5-18 from *blatner.com*

6   Ibid.

help me grasp what document and information processing issues his organization might have. He seemed to have a good time in his tirade, and I felt our conversations were totally unproductive. During my 3rd visit, as he began his devaluing rant, I stood up and said:

> **Sales Executive (Me):** "Let's trade places."

> **Prospect:** "What?"

> **Me:** "You sit in my seat, play my role, and I'll sit in yours, playing yours. Not only take on each other's body posture, mannerisms, but also the viewpoint and underlying reasoning of each other."

I walked around his desk. Incredulously, he stood up, and exchanged seats/roles with me, yet continued to rail at me, (as if *I* were still playing the sales role), to which I interjected,

> **Me:** "Uh, uh, uh . . . you're not sitting where I am now. You're sitting in that chair, representing the sales company. Speak from that role and how your product(s) could satisfy our organization's needs."

Perhaps to demonstrate he could rise to my challenge, he proceeded to tell me, *as if* he represented the sales company, specifically how their products could help this organization. In so doing, he revealed issues the organization had been having. This information had never been shared with anyone from our company.

Playing his role as purchasing agent, I started to criticize this sales person's company for being way too expensive. As sales executive, he detailed how equipment not designed with quality, often had a much bigger failure rate, with implications of down time, lost productivity, *etc.*, and could cost the organization a lot more in the long run. In effect, he articulated the concept of the *cost of quality* vs poor quality, the supposed cheaper product would cost more in total cost of ownership (adding consumable costs, breakdown costs and loss of productivity), while quality products at the outset seeming more expensive, could be a much better value, at ultimately a lower cost.[7]

From reversing roles with me, the purchasing agent revealed how my company might help his organization: 1) using our quality products with true value; 2) through the total cost of ownership our quality products might actually work within their operating costs.

Still in the purchasing agent role, I stood and said, "Well, that's interesting. I'll have to think about that." I extended my hand and thanked the man

---

7 Reeve, T and Everdene, B. *Applying Total Cost of Ownership to Sustainability Purchasing.* Sustainability Purchasing Network. Accessed 6-20-18 from *www.buysmartbc.com*

playing the sales executive. Now as myself, I suggested we shake ourselves out (de-role) and return to our original seats. I moved away from his desk and resumed my authentic sales executive role. I commended him for bringing out some profound ideas about value, and shared how I could better appreciate *his* position (in his organization). How could he possibly recommend "the most expensive products?" I wondered aloud to what extent those in the upper ranks understood his perception of value. He smiled and said he found the exercise to be revealing. "This was interesting. I look forward to exploring this idea of value more with you."

I shared this visit with management at my company. To a person, they were flabbergasted. No one in years had been able to move the needle, even a little bit, in improving communication with this man, let alone develop a relationship. They found the process profound, as they understood how it provided an *experiential* way for each party to better understand the other, *as if truly standing in each others shoes.* We discussed how we might have misunderstood this man (perceiving him as *Attila the Hun*) and his actions in the past. This action method of *reciprocal role reversal* between the two of us allowed us to "correct biased perceptions."[8]

All those years of this man putting our company down in meetings. Sitting in his seat allowed me to understand that it might have been just easier in the past for him to cut the conversation off with representatives of our company. If he believed his management would shoot him down for recommending the most expensive products, that night jeopardize his position in the organization. Yet, in playing the role of sales executive, he beautifully articulated why quality products ultimately make good business sense in terms of not just performance, but are actually more cost effective in the end. By switching roles, we had each switched our *perceptual positions.* By taking on the other's position, not only were we both able to "see, feel and think through the other person's being,"[9] but through the spontaneity of the process, look at the situation differently.[10]

Healthy relationships and alignment with others promotes potential win-win transactions, which make for good business.[11] Empathy is needed "to push past 1st meetings and make sustainable business relationships that will last

8   Kellermann, P.F. *Role reversal in psychodrama. In Psychodrama Since Moreno: Innovations in Theory and Practice.* (Eds.) Holmes, P., Karp, M. and Watson, M. 1994 Routledge: New York, NY

9   Howie, P. *Philosophy of Life: J. L. Moreno's revolutionary philosophical underpinnings of psychodrama, and group psychotherapy.* In *Group: The Journal of the Eastern Group Psychotherapy Society,* Volume 36.2, Summer, 2012 pp. 135–146.

10   Kellerman, P.F. (1994) *Role reversal in psychodrama.*

11   Tuten, L. and Urban, J. *An Expanded Model of Business-to-Business Partnership Formation and Success. Industrial Marketing Management.* Vol. 30, Issue 2. Feb. 2001, pp 149–164.

for years."[12] *The action technique of role reversal* was so powerful in the above experience, disarming defenses and dismantling walls created[13] between our organizations. Some of its many benefits coming out of our meeting:

- shifted the perspective, so we better understood each other from the other's view
- helped answer questions re: other participant's thought process and reasoning. The prospect absolutely understood the details of his organization's document processing issues much better than me
- allowed us to see the impact we had on each other—there seemed to be more of a feeling of mutual respect
- helped his organization and my company, previously at an impasse, get unstuck
- helped to further the business relationship.

Using Action Methods in Executive Coaching

The precipitant for John, a 41 year old seeking coaching ("Why now?"), was a "wake up call" from his doctor. John's blood pressure was off the charts. Though a young man in his early 40s, he had a family history of heart disease. He was a big man at 6′6″ tall, weighing 300 lbs. Growing up, he engaged in all sorts of sports, but now worked non-stop, and became a "couch potato." He was so exhausted working as a Project Manager for a media company, that he'd come home, have dinner with his wife and 2 year old son, then snack while finishing unanswered customer emails. Any time remaining was spent vegging out in front of the TV. Exhausted, he had no energy left to connect with his wife or young son.

John said he felt out of alignment, and that his goal was to improve his work/life balance. He felt ambivalent about his job, and wanted to explore whether he should stay, or go work for another company in the same industry. The CEO of his current company had given him a $500 bonus, a merit increase, and publicly praised him, saying he was their MVP. While the other company offered less pay, it was purported to have a culture of collaboration, and encouraged personal growth and upward movement, which his current company did not. I invited him to *actively* look at both sides of his ambivalence with his job.

---

12 Stephenson, A. *The Most Important Sales Skill: Empathy*. 6-19-14. *www.tlsasalestraining.com*, Accessed 5-25-18.

13 Blatner, A. *Action Explorations*. (2012)

Using the action method, known as the *empty chair* technique.[14] I guided him through a *representational* role reversal with himself.[15]

- John sat in one chair taking the stance—wanting to stay, speaking to the part of himself (sitting in the empty chair) that wants to leave.
- He switched chairs—taking the stance—wanting to leave, speaking to the part of himself sitting in the empty chair, that wanted to stay.

By externalizing his internal dialogue and separating his two inner "voices," John was better able to appreciate his competing internal demands.[16]

The client seemed to have quite an "AHA" moment, saying the *empty chair* exercise helped him sort out both sides of how he felt, better than just evaluating the pros and cons in his head, and that it helped him make peace with leaving. He had been feeling guilty, as he had been singled out as the company's MVP, and had just received a $500 bonus plus merit increase they hadn't paid out the previous year.

Then John said he wanted to explore giving notice in such a respectful way, that he'd be welcomed back sometime— *"Who knows? Maybe even to run the company!"*

I invited him to use the *empty chair* exercise in a *reciprocal* way[17] (between himself and another), to explore what might happen if he gave his notice and his company tried to get him to stay.

John sat in chair "A" as himself, giving his resignation to his boss (imagining boss sitting in the empty chair "B"); then switched chairs and sat in chair "B," playing the role of his boss (using mannerisms and speaking like his boss) asking John *"what would it take for you to stay with us?"* The client found these action exercises so eye opening, commenting on how he kept having "aha" moments." Earlier, he had felt guilty about leaving. Since he had taken on so much, how would they pick up the pieces if he left? He remembered that when he first started working there, he had received no training whatsoever, and had to find his own way. He also realized that his health was deteriorating by staying. While management vowed they would bring in more resources, he felt that was just lip service. He decided there was no amount of money they could throw at him to stay.

John arrived at his next coaching session, all smiles.

---

14   Blatner, A *The "empty chair" technique*. (2018). Words and images from the Mind of Adam Blatner. Accessed 6-28-18 www.blatner.com

15   Kellerman, P.F. (1994) *Role reversal in psychodrama*. Ibid.

16   Blatner, A. (2012) *Action Explorations*. Ibid.

17   Kellerman, P.F. (1994) *Role reversal in psychodrama*. Ibid.

John: "I went in to my manager's office to give my resignation. You're not going to believe it, but the meeting went almost identical to that *empty chair* exercise I did in your office last week. My manager lauded my work, reminding me I was their MVP, and offered to raise my salary with more bonuses if I stayed. It wasn't even tempting, because I realized that not only was the company's culture not going to change, but that it would make it very difficult for me to achieve my goal of having a healthy work/life balance. I respectfully declined the offer, saying I wanted to move in a different direction in my career. As I got up, my manager reached out his hand and wished me well. That night the CEO of the company called and did his best to change my mind. When he realized I was resolved to move on, he said, 'John, you're a class act. Anytime you want to come back, our door is always open.' I thanked him and thought, some day I might just do that—run the company the way I know it can operate and flourish."

John switched companies. He was pleasantly surprised to see how his new company's culture really espoused teamwork and encouraged their employees to "have a life." Even though initially he was making less money, John felt it offered him a career path where he could move up the ladder. Most important, it allowed him to more easily create healthy boundaries around himself and his family.

In his executive coaching, John had used the action technique of the *empty chair* in 2 ways: 1) to explore both sides of his ambivalence of whether to stay or leave; and 2) as a behavioral rehearsal to help him prepare for an upcoming encounter with another person,[18] in this case, giving notice to his manager.

Using Guided Imagery in Peak Performance Coaching with Athletes

I coached a 14 year-old superstar in basketball on mental toughness. Brian loved to play, and often was the top shooter in competition. As soon as he made the All Star Team though, he stopped shooting. When he got the ball, he quickly passed it off to his teammates. His father asked me to coach him as soon as possible, as the All Star Game was scheduled to play in four days.

When we met, I was impressed with Brian's poise.

C(oach): "What changed in your desire to shoot baskets?"

---

18   Blatner, A. (2012) Ibid.

B(rian): "I'm passing the ball as soon as I get it, because I don't want to let my teammates down. Then I really feel bad, because I can hear my coach shouting, 'Shoot, shoot. For God's sake, shoot!'

C: "So you also feel you're letting down your coach?" Brian nodded yes.

Fears in athletes of letting down teammates, coach, *etc.* is a common anxiety related to the fear of negative social evaluation,[19] particularly when one's self-worth is linked to one's accomplishments.[20] For many athletes, athletic success is a major source of recognition and self-esteem.[21] Brian's fear of letting others down precipitated his cautious play (*"better to pass the ball, than make a mistake"*). The need for social approval, especially for adolescents, can cause athletes to perform worse — and then feeds into a negative feedback loop — causing a self-fulfilling prophecy. The need for social approval is in direct opposition to three of the most salient actions necessary for creating *the zone* for peak performance in sports:

- Total Immersion on the task at hand — described concentration as the capacity to exert mental effort on a task while ignoring distractions. Poor focus directs attention away from beneficial information and onto cues that distract athletes from these processes.[22]
- Focus in the here and now, rather than the future outcome.
- Have Fun.

C: "Brian, what kind of mental preparation do you do before competing?"

B: "None. Just physical."

I offered to share an additional warm up he could do on a regular basis, even before getting to the gym. Beginning with deep abdominal breathing, I took him through the *relaxation body scan* (progressively relax each part of the

19   Passer, M. W. (1983). "Fear of failure, fear of evaluation, perceived competence, and self-esteem in competitive-trait-anxious children." *Journal of Sport Psychology*, 5(2), 172–188.

20   Covington, M.V. 1992. *Making the Grade: A Self-Worth Perspective on Motivation and School Reform*. New York, NY. Cambridge University Press

21   Martin, J.J. and Gill, D.L. The relationships among competitive orientation, sport-confidence, self-efficacy, anxiety, and performance. *Journal of Sport and Exercise Psychology*. 1991, 13, 149–159

22   Baghurst, T., Thierry, G. and Holder, T. Evidence for a relationship between attentional styles and effective cognitive strategies during performance. *Athletic Insight: The Online Journal of Sport Psychology* Vol. 6; Issue 1. 2004.

body by letting go of any tension felt in each of those muscles; a variant of progressive muscle relaxation, without first tensing the muscles). While in a relaxed state, I asked Brian to tell me of an animal in the wild that spoke to him of confidence, assertiveness and focus. Concepts like confidence and focus in sports can be tapped by using an animal metaphor.[23]

> **B:** "I think lions are so cool. Their focus is so intense — they lock in, not allowing anything to sway them from going after what they want."

> **C:** Hmmm. They lock in. Okay. Brian, let's play a game, I like to call *The Magic As If*.

Stanislavski's *Magic If* describes an ability to imagine oneself in a set of fictional circumstances and to envision the consequences of finding oneself facing that situation in terms of action.[24]

> **C:** "I invite you to pretend — *as if* you are a lion in the wild. Set the scene . . . you're in the African Savannah — feel the hot sand under your paws . . . the scorching sun on your back. It's so hot, you might prefer to sleep by day and hunt at night . . ."

> (silence)

> **C:** "Let's say you're awake now as the sun is setting and you're hungry. Feel free to physically explore — *as if* you're lying in the bush; *as if* you're preparing to set out and stalk your prey."

With his eyes still closed, Brian crouched on the floor, *as if* in wait.

> **C:** "While you're waiting for the sun to set, to more easily stalk your prey, talk with me as the lion."

(I chose not to ask him gender questions about his lion, since the females tend to do the bulk of hunting).

> **C:** "As night falls, you and the rest of the pride slink through the high wheat colored grass and spot some gazelles. You pounce and miss. Do you look around, worried what the other lions will think?"

> **B:** (laughing) *"No."*

---

23 Gallan, D. *The Big Cat Whisperer: What Elite Sport Can Learn from the Wild* 4-16-15. assessed 6-12-18 from *www.conqagroup.com*

24 Stanislavski, Constantin; Elizabeth Reynolds Hapgood, translator. *An Actor Prepares*, (New York: Theatre Arts Books, 1936, translation 1948).

C: "Why not?'

B: "Because I'm hungry!"

C: "Ah . . . You're hungry. "What do you do next?"

B: "I attack again. In fact, I continue, until we take something substantial down to eat."

Brian had taken on the persona in this relaxed state of the confident and assertive, lion. Before bringing him out of the trance of relaxation, using classical conditioning, I *anchored*[25] Brian's lion experience of *laser focus* by giving him the suggestion that he would continue to act *as if* he were the lion when playing basketball; that he would *lock in* (the phrase he used) and be so focused on working with his team to take down their prey — in this case, shoot baskets. I counted backwards out loud, from five to one, helping him reorient himself (not as the lion) back to the present. I suggested he continue to de-role by getting up, stretching out and then sitting as himself.

C: "How was that for you?"

B: "I felt as if I were in the tall grass; the intense heat during the day; cooler air as dusk fell; I could smell the animals around me. It was weird. While I could feel the desert sand under my paws, at the same time, it was like I was standing to the side watching myself, crouched as the lion."

Research shows 3 kinds of visualizations:

- as if watching oneself;
- from one's eyes looking out, kinesthetically recreating the feelings of the movements;
- combination of the two.[26]

B: "I can't believe what I just did. Aside from playing sports, I've never felt comfortable with people watching me, like in a play. I actually forgot you were in the room — and this is your office!"

C: "Makes a lot of sense. Earlier you said lions were so cool, because their focus is so intense — they lock in and don't allow anything to sway them from going after what they want."

---

25 Livingston, K. Anchoring and Post Hypnotic suggestions. *www.hypnosis101.com* accessed 6-12-18

26 Sutton, J. Memory before the game: switching perspectives in imagining and remembering sport and movement. *Journal of Mental Imagery* 36 (1/2): 85–95 2012

We talked about the *process of guided* imagery[27] in which he first began with a deep sense of relaxation. Then he entered a state of "public solitude"—a sense of privacy.[28]

> **C:** "Stansilavski spoke of 3 circles of concentration/attention:[29] 1st circle—an internal focus of thoughts, feelings and sensations; 2nd circle—external sphere of focus on the task at hand; for the lion—working with the pride to take down their prey; for you as basketball player, working with your team to repeatedly get the ball down the court and in the hoop; and 3rd circle—external focus—spectators/audience, what your peers think of you—to which you said you had no awareness of what your fellow lions thought of you when you missed."
>
> **B:** "Wow. That's right. I didn't."
>
> **C:** "What else did you experience?"
>
> **B:** "That was so fun!! Like I was playing."
>
> **C:** "Playing is fun, isn't it? Tell me more about having fun while playing basketball?"
>
> **B:** "Well it is, but only when I focus on just playing—you know, not worried about winning or losing, and what others might think of me if I miss the basket."
>
> **C:** "Hmm—just focus on as if you were the lion?"
>
> **B:** He nods "yes."

"The art of play refers to both an attitude and practice in everyday life . . ."[30] The act of *playing* sports is one of many areas of expression in which playfulness can occur.[31] Yet, so often the focus (unconscious as well as conscious) is on distractions, like the outcome of winning vs losing, the score, opponent's rankings/ratings, *etc.*, letting peers, coaches, parents down—again focus on outcome) drain the fun out of the sense of play when playing sports.

> **C:** "Anything else, Brian?"

---

27   Runco, M.A. (2014) *Creativity. 2nd Edition*. Academic Press: Waltham, Mass.

28   Stanislavski, C. (1936, translation 1948). *An Actor Prepares*.

29   Ibid.

30   Blatner, A.B. and Blatner, A.B. (1997) *The Art of Play: Helping Adults Reclaim Imagination a and Spontaneity*. Brunner/Mazel, Inc.: New York, N.Y.

31   Sapora, A.V., (1961). *The Theory of Play and Recreation. 3rd Ed*. The Ronald Press: New York, NY

B: "Yeah, I've heard top athletes talk a lot about that zone thing . . . you know . . . like playing on all 4 cylinders, where you feel you can do no wrong. I've felt that way sometimes, playing basketball. It's weird, but I actually felt that way today, playing this *As If* game."

C: "Sounds like fun — "playing this game.""

B: "Hmmm. Yeah — playing. Is that why so many star athletes talk about how they practice this imaging thing?"

C: "Yup. So many top athletes play what some call, their *mini movies* — in a relaxed state, they rehearse their actual competitive routines in their mind. Vividly imaging an activity with your senses actually activates areas of the brain involved when physically performing that activity. The brain doesn't know the difference between what is real and what is imagined.[32]

B: "You mean, I can practice without having to be on the court?"

C: "It's the next best thing. Begin with the deep breathing, just as you did here; progressively relax each part of your body by letting go of any tension you're feeling in those muscles. Then step into the role of the lion you created — seeing yourself and feeling yourself lock in, as you play basketball with your teammates.. You can do this every night before going to sleep. After practicing this guided imagery during the day (never when driving), de-role from the lion and bring yourself back into your own self by counting backwards from 5–1, after which you suggest to yourself that you will be wide awake, more alert and very very relaxed. "

B: "Wow. This is really cool. I'm going to practice this every day and at night before I go to sleep."

Brian was quite effective at redefining his role[33]—not as a performer to be judged by his peers, but as a lion, with an unfailing purpose — to eat for

---

32 Letswaart, M., Butler, A.J., Jackson, P.L., and Edwards, M.G. Editorial: mental practice: clinical and experimental research in imagery and action observation. *Frontiers in Human Neuroscience*. Vol. 9: 2015

33 Blatner, A. The role of the meta-role: an integrative element in psychology. In *Psychodrama: Advances in Theory and Practice*. Eds., Baim, C., Burmeister, J. and Maciel, M. Taylor and Francis, Inc.: New York, NY 2007.

survival. His ability to reframe his role allowed him to have a laser focus on the task at hand.

Two days later, I got a call from Brian's father.

Father: "What did you tell Brian in that coaching session? He was like a different player."

C: "You'll have to ask Brian."

Father: "I've never seen him play like that. He was the top shooter in the All Star Game! Brian absolutely came alive, and what's more, seemed to be having the time of his life! . . . His focus . . . He was so transfixed . . . He was playing like an animal!"

Action techniques are very effective in coaching. They provide a laboratory and safe space to explore more integration of mind and body, thinking and acting, reason and emotions, thereby engaging both left and right hemispheres of the brain,[34] as they foster:

- empathy and the ability to see/understand situations from the perspectives of others involved;
- the capacity to better understand oneself and work through ambivalence;
- work through and rehearse how one might want to have an encounter with someone in the future;
- *play* with a guided imagery in an experiential way to develop laser focus on the task at hand, an important element for an athlete to create *the zone* for peak performance.

While each presenting situation could have been approached through traditional coach/client conversation, exploration through experiential action methods quickly produced the desired client outcomes.

---

34 Hug, E. A neuroscience perspective of psychodrama. In *Psychodrama: Advances in Theory and Practice*. Eds., Baim, C., Burmeister, J. and Maciel, M. Taylor and Francis, Inc.: New York, N.Y. 2007.

Marilyn S. Feinstein

Marilyn S. Feinstein, ACC, LCSW, USPTA, received her MSW from NYU and trained in Psychodrama with Gene Eliasoph. She has an Advanced Certification in Personal and Executive Coaching from the College of Executive Coaching; and is accredited with the International Coaching Federation.

Marilyn worked 9.5 yrs for Xerox Corporation, achieving President's Club. She's a USPTA Tennis Pro, and coaches athletes in all sports on how to engage one's Inner Champion when competing. She and her mother, Tybie (recipient of Lifetime Achievement Award in Table Tennis), are writing a book, *You Don't Have to Be the Best to Beat the Best: How Your Inner Champion Can Create The Zone for Peak Performance in Sports and Life.* An Equity actress, Marilyn received her MFA in Acting from The Yale School of Drama, and has worked with greats, like Barbra Streisand.

Publications Include: *Integrating Behavioral Health and Primary Care.* (2017, Eds. Feinstein, Connolly, and Feinstein; Oxford University Press, NY), in which the Feinsteins also contributed the chapter, "Health Coaching in Integrated Care." In 2001, they contributed "Psychotherapy for Health and Lifestyle Change" to Session Psychotherapy in Practice. New York: John Wiley and Sons, Inc. They created a one-person comic/drama, *Got Any Change?* that Marilyn performed at The George E. Reed Heart Center, Westchester, NY; Hartford Hospital, CT; and Cape Cod.

She continues to see clients in therapy and coaching, and uses her integrated background of corporate, sports, acting, and clinical training to speak and give interactive workshops/seminars in Personal and Professional development.

The Unspoken in Teamwork

Applying Action Methods for the Benefit of Organizations and Their Teams

Norbert Apter

- How can the Action Methods of J.L. Moreno best be employed when facilitating teams, especially where unspoken issues exist?
- How to detect and pay attention to these issues?
- What key-role needs to be maintained?
- How to ensure that people can feel secure about speaking out?

These are the basic questions we will ask ourselves in this chapter. Following an introduction on the applications of Action Methods in the work environment and a reminder of the challenges involved in accompanying teams where tensions are present (which is often the case), the reader will be taken step by step through the process of preparation, action and follow-up in facilitating the emergence of the unsaid and the unspoken using the J.L. Moreno method.

In particular, I will describe here a technique I created in 2007: the Delayed Dialogue. The Delayed Dialogue is a "reality practice," whose main objectives are to reinforce the dynamics of constructive communication and to create a secure environment where unspoken issues can emerge and be expressed.

J.L. Moreno's method is based on "Let's show/demonstrate" rather than "Let's talk about it." His theory and practice stimulate creativity, through action and interaction, and actively promote change by soliciting both the right brain and left-brain functions. *The Action Methods* are the pedagogical, formative and social applications of J.L. Moreno's methodology. Their goal is to foster individual and/or team professional development. These "visual and role-based approaches"[1] have two main components:

- Training: *Expanding skills* on personal, professional, social and academic levels
- Facilitating: *Activating dynamics and dynamism* within the individual and the team.

Such professional training and / or team coaching is carried out in a stimulating interactive environment which develops and deepens, through action, 6 lines of integration: (1) to *express*, (2) to *experiment* and to *explore*, and (3) to *exercise* different behavior and approaches to tasks; thus everyone can (4) more easily *elaborate* options, (5) *evaluate* possibilities and *acquire* deeper insight (6) enabling them to *evolve* towards the desired objectives. The combination of these 6 channels of dynamic integration facilitates the transformation of the knowledge aquired as well as the awareness gained into new skills that are directly applicable to everyday professional life.[2]

In Switzerland and in Europe, our[3] experience of more than 25 years in humanistic Action Methods shows that the world of work finds attractive and beneficial these seminars in the course of which everyone gets actively involved. Most participants in training seminars or facilitation sessions are rightly aware that the active experience[4] promoted by the method is an essential asset for professional development. Referring to[5] Kate Hudgins defines "active experiencing" as "the ability to both experience the self in the present moment, while simultaneously being able to self-reflect and make meaning of that experiencing."[6]

Indeed, J.L. Moreno's method produces almost simultaneously immersion and hindsight. This 'immersion-hindsight', combined with the Multiple Intelligence[7] solicited by 'putting into action' (demonstration), are the two key-springs of achieving enhanced awareness. It has been shown that not only professionals, but also (top) managers, HR professionals and politicians particularly appreciate this "light and intense" way of not only raising awareness, but also and above all of producing desired changes. Almost systematically over the years, thanks to J.L. Moreno's method, a Collective Intelligence has emerged

---

1 BPA, 2018
2 Apter, 2011
3 The team from l'Institut ODeF cf. *www.odef.ch*
4 Active experiencing
5 Gendlin, 1996
6 Hudgins, 2007, p.181
7 Gardner, 1983

and this has given rise to convincing results, developing both knowledge and efficiency.

This has been confirmed in our work in a diversity of fields:

- in the Public Sector: Finance, heritage, management, police (*etc.*) as well as in medico-psycho-social and educational Institutions.
- for municipalities, departmental managers, elected representatives and their teams.
- in private companies: banks, law firms, transport and haulage, specialized technology, telecommunications, micro informatics, security services, *etc.*
- International organizations (ILO, CERN, UNAIDS, IOM, WMO, *etc.*) and humanitarian organizations (ICRC, MONUC, MSF, OECD, UNICEF, *etc.*).[8]

Ultimately, Action Methods can benefit all actors in society: either as a pedagogical and formative method, or as a technique for facilitating and support of the teams' operational and relational process. It is this second application that we will develop here.

Facilitating Teams: The Challenges

Dealing with Tensions

Working on the dynamics within a team is not easy and requires real discernment. As Abraham Maslow could have stated, every team and every professional aspires to a feeling of belonging, of self-esteem, of accomplishment, in short a sense of fulfillment,[9] at least as much as circumstances permit.

In today's world, as a consequence of increasingly demanding workloads and working conditions, many professionals and many teams live under constant pressure. Moreover, the focus on tasks and performance is often made at the expense of consideration given to relationships. Subsequently, this can have a negative impact on the two key dimensions of professional activity, Tasks and

---

8 International and Humanitarian Organizations mentioned in this article: CERN: European Organization for Nuclear Research; ICRC : International Committee of the Red Cross; ILO : International Labour Organization; IOM : International Organization for Migrants; MONUC : United mission in R.D. Congo; MSF : Médecins Sans Frontières; OECD : Organisation for Economic Co-operation and Development; WMO : World Meteorological Organization; UNAIDS : United Nations Organization aiming at ending AIDS; UNICEF : United Nations Organization protecting children around the world.

9 Maslow, 1972

Relations.[10] Stress becomes the rule—or at least the undesirable effect . . . with damaging repercussions. This phenomena is becoming increasingly frequent:

- The 2014–2016 Job Stress Index, created by Promotion Santé Suisse, shows that nearly 25% of employees in Switzerland are stressed and feel exhausted, with consequent health problems and reduced productivity.[11]
- In its report "Stress at Work, a Collective Challenge," the International Labour Organization notes the serious—if not to say alarming—impact of stress on physical and mental health, on productivity, and of course on the high economic costs of work-related stress.[12]

Although this is often overlooked, when we use the word stress what we mean is "tension." When working on the dynamics of a team the facilitator is thus confronted not only with the tensions within the team itself but also internal and external conflicts that have sometimes been grafted onto them. This is nothing out of the ordinary, especially given that it's unusual for teams to regularly take the time to step back and reflect on workaday concerns. However, this regular examination of current problematic issues, as a measure of collective hygiene, allows the development of realistic and creative options that can help solve the difficulties that accumulate over time. Increased wellbeing and performance is thus enhanced for the benefit of each and everyone and thereby for the whole organization. Unfortunately this practice is not part of our corporate culture. Instead, requests for assistance (usually punctual) appear only when the team has been or has begun to be destabilized by increasing tensions and conflict.

It is therefore imperative that the outside professional appointed to do the work of facilitation and reconsolidation for the team should carefully assess the situation beforehand. This is an essential step that allows them to evaluate whether or not they have the skills required for the task in order to avoid a situation where they may be overwhelmed by events and / or end up playing the double role of fire-starter and fire-fighter.

Essentially it is necessary on the one hand to examine the relational and operational condition of the team and on the other to determine the type of action that needs to be undertaken. In my article "Team Caring, Team Building, or Team Mediation?"[13] dealing with this initial evaluation I point out that each

---

10 Bales, 1953

11 ATS, 2018, Jan.27

12 ILO, 2016

13 Apter, 2016

Level of Conflicting Tension (LCT) corresponds to a specific type of support response, *i.e.* on a scale of 0 to 10:

- Team Caring, when the team is in good shape (LCT between O and 3)
- Team Building, when the team is unstable and tense (LCT between 4 and 6)
- Team Mediation, when tensions dominate (LCT between 7 and 10).

For each situation, the basic indicators, the basic axiom and its corollaries, as well as the transversal objectives and the means to be implemented must be differentiated and used accordingly. The same is true of the requisite skills and the ways they are deployed.

Facilitating a team where the LCT exceeds 4–5 requires precaution: the Facilitator should be trained — and at ease — in areas such as group work (their developments, dynamics, *etc.*), team animation and team leadership, as well as the management of difficult or very difficult situations (team problem solving, conflict management, crisis intervention, team mediation, *etc.*).

These skills will undoubtedly be needed in (very) delicate situations where there are risks of implosion/explosion. They will allow the facilitator to be in a secure, non-pressured position enabling them to broach with the team the conflicting issues present both from the point of view of tasks and that of relationships.

Dealing with the Unspoken

Even when a team is functioning well, everything is not necessarily 'out in the open.' These hidden, *unsaid* issues pose a priori no major problems. If the opportunity is given to the members of the team to take a step back from their daily work and develop their communication, these *unsaid* issues can emerge and lead to a renewal of collaboration. On the other hand, when the level of conflicting tension (LCT) rises to rates between 4 and 6, security and trust can diminish rapidly and the *unsaid* becomes the *unspoken*. The co-existing presence of the need to speak out and to address tensions is set against the fear of upsetting the status quo thereby creating an inherent contradiction. "Clans" are formed, insinuation and innuendo develop, and little by little clashes increase in number and strength.

If a procedure for the resolution of problems and conflicts is not put into place and a resumption of the constructive dialogue is not facilitated, the situation deteriorates and the LCT increases: what was unspoken becomes markedly unexpressed, even inexpressible. Everything becomes mixed up and confused, heightened sensitivity leads to heightened, open aggressiveness . . . along with the development of habitual power games. A situation that appeared at one point to be "potentially resolvable" degenerates into explosive/ implosive and violent verbal exchanges: a "war" has broken out.

The table below illustrates the main warning signals that, in my experience, are displayed by teams when what may become a "tidal wave sweeping everything in its path" gradually builds up.

	LCT 0 – 3 Unsaid	LCT 4 – 6 Unspoken	LCT 7 – 10 Unexpressed
Judgement	'Improvements are possible'	Not positive, more and more negative	Condemning
Relation to the system	Educational or cultural norms (or customs)	Personal and/or subgroups' visible loyalties	Painful and irritating double binds
Emotional drive	No active need nor obstacle for dialogue	Fear of dialogue and of 'making it worse'	'Fed up with frustration and fear; urge for ventilation'
Attitude	Lack of assertiveness	(High) ambivalence	'Much too risky to express oneself'
Basic positioning	'Not hiding . . . but not saying'	'Matters are obvious and should be guessed'	Issues are hidden or thrown into each other's face
Relation to information	'Information is not essential'	Info retention = power gains	Power games
Internal weight	'Not a problem', 'Tolerable'	(very) Difficult internal and/or external conflicts	'Unbearable' internal and/or external conflicts
Level of suffering	Low level suffering – if any at all	Suffering from tensions and conflicts	High level suffering from the 'war' that is taking place

Table 1: Indicators of the unsaid, unspoken and unexpressed within a team
Adapted from the author's lecture at the opening session of the 9th Baltic
Moreno Days in 2016 in Kaunas (Lithuania).

These signals are usually cries for help (sometimes clumsily expressed or 'disguised') which need to be heard and to which we must give the most constructive attention.

It should be noted that when the LCT is between 7 and 10, distress is very high and Team Mediation becomes necessary. This may entail beginning with individual interviews, subgroup and / or pair mediation sessions, and/ or sessions with the whole team. In my professional practice there have been many occasions when I have found that Humanistic Action Methods are an undeniable asset in such a process of conflict resolution. However, this is not the subject of this chapter, here we will maintain our focus on situations with a (lowered) LCT, between 4 and 6.

In a team where tensions, conflicts and lulls alternate, how can we prevent communication blockages, power games and uncontrolled aggressiveness (*etc.*) from taking hold and precipitating hostility within the team to the point where "war" breaks out? What alternatives can be offered?

Facilitating: a Key Role

Calling in a third party external to the team is usually the most appropriate option. In this context, the Action Methods professional who has experience in conflict management can be an effective resource in the process of easing the relational and operational state of the team: they are an expert in their field, and their methodology enables them to reactivate gradually, through action, the Multiple Intelligence of each individual, as well as the Collective Intelligence of the team, leading to a transformation of the conflicts. On the other hand, this professional — fully trained to deal with collective challenges — does not 'know' and cannot 'act' in place of the team; They do not "know" nor can they "seek or bring" solutions to the difficulties and problems that are present. It is up to the team to do so. Indeed, each member of the team is an expert on the situation: their experience of the problems encountered, their knowledge of the field and their perception of possible solutions are likely to give rise to realistic and effective contributions. When pooled, individual intelligences can combine creatively and constructively into a Collective Intelligence, the potential for satisfactory results for everyone is all the greater, as long as the work atmosphere allows this! Hence the emphasis in Humanistic Action Methods on the role of the Facilitator.

This key role of the Facilitator is aimed at creating a relational environment of security and trust that promotes communication, constructive and creative dialogue, leading to the professional development of each and everyone. This role was best defined by Carl R. Rogers, founder of the Person Centered Approach. For Rogers, in order to make defensive-aggressive positioning unnecessary (which in a tense team is the *sine qua non* for a resumption of dialogue), the Facilitator must promote three attitudes[14] and gradually introduce them together into the situation as a whole:

- *the unconditional positive regard of each and everyone as a complex human being*, thereby promoting mutual recognition[15]
- *Empathy*, seeking to understand others in a genuine and sensitive way; this is the essential component to really listening to each person's perceptions[16]
- *Congruence*, the way to express what is to be said respectfully and in one's own terms;[17] this promotes the Encounter between I and You, of such vital importance to Martin Buber and J. L. Moreno[18]

These attitudes, when all three gradually develop within a group, facilitate the resolution of tensions and conflicts.[19] Especially if the creativity that the Moreno method promotes is part of the picture.

Safely Bringing Out the Unspoken

While not expressing issues may be a choice, the unspoken is an indirect mode of communication. Though silent, it can be 'high volume', it is certainly frustrating and painful, leading to a continuous poisoning of relationships. The more unspoken practice takes hold, the more it seems too risky or pointless to say anything. Obviously, in such situations which are sometimes (very) emotionally charged, the Emotional Intelligence[20] of the facilitator and the intra- and interpersonal skills that flow from them greatly contribute to securing the process of dealing with these issues.

Thus, the greatest caution is necessary in the way in which a team is assisted towards the expression of unspoken issues. In my experience, three steps are necessary:

- *Prepare the ground for the expression of the unspoken*: set up several complete cycles of team facilitation sessions, which makes it possible for the team to express what they are unable to talk about.
- *Use Delayed Dialogue*, a technically "simple," safe and structured 'reality practice' that gives the individual and the group a way to express themselves.

---

14 Rogers, 1980, 1984,1986
15 Bozarth & Wilkins, 2001
16 Bohart & Greenberg, 1997
17 Wyatt, 2001
18 Buber, 1970, Moreno, 1964
19 Kirschenbaum & Land Henderson, 2001
20 Goleman, 1995

- *Provide follow-up* to refine, improve and anchor the renewal of perspectives.

This three-step strategy, requiring the constant activation of the role of the Facilitator, has largely proven its effectiveness with dozens of teams.

Preparing the Ground for the Expression of the Unspoken

Moreno's methodology basically comprises three phases: Warm-up, Action, and Sharing. In applying the Action Methods to work situations a further phase is added, the 'Putting into Perspective'. Together they form a complete cycle that maximizes encounters, discoveries and learning:

- *The Warm Up* "brings people to be present in the 'here and now'"[21] and "serves to produce an atmosphere of creative possibility"[22] towards the issues being addressed.
- *Action*, in which everybody, through showing rather than just by talking about, is brought to a deeper questioning and thereby a greater seeking of creative solutions to the chosen problem.[23]
- *Pooling*[24] (called Sharing by J.L. Moreno) ensures that the link is made between what has been experienced during the Action and the professional reality (past, present or anticipated of the future) of the members of the team. This "resonance phenomenon"[25] once expressed anchors the impact of the Action.
- The "*Putting into Perspective*" not only draws lessons (learning) from the process, both theoretically and practically, but also, and above all, elaborates their daily applications in future professional life.

The controversial nature of the expression of what is not openly acknowledged (whether unsaid, unspoken or unexpressed) requires, regardless of the team's LCT, several complete cycles of co-construction: from the least threatening cycle to the most high risk. Gradually, step-by-step, security is rebuilt, trust is reborn, certain obstacles to expression disappear — or at least become less of a problem. Belief in a real constructive dialogue returns — even on "hotly disputed matters." For a team of 8 to 12 professionals and based on two-day modules, this preparation will usually take at least one day (when the LCT is at a maximum of 4) or 3 to 5 days, (when the LCT is between 5 and 10).

---

21 Dayton, 1994, p.58
22 Karp, 1998, p. 3
23 Blatner & Blatner, 1988
24 Term used by companies
25 Leutz, 1985

The Action Methods are of course deployed using Sociometry[26] and Sociodrama,[27] both active promoters of collective progress. Since the simulations can sometimes give rise to stigmatization, they are practiced only on the basis of fictionalized but plausible roles — especially when the LCT is greater than 5.

In every situation, the Action Methods seek to go beyond the "simple" action, be it by JL Moreno's classic action techniques (the *double*, *role reversal*, the *aside*, the *mirror*, *etc.*) or by other means; throughout the preparatory stage, in the Warm-up phases (in which they can be set up relatively quickly) and in the Action phases (giving rise to a more elaborate and deeper exploration by combining various techniques).

Some classic examples of frequently used action techniques:

- **Locograms:** *e.g.* the virtual map of the world is placed on the floor; each member of the team is positioned at his place of birth (this is particularly suitable for intercultural teams, *e.g.* international organizations and companies)
- **Photolanguage:** provision of a stock of various images or photos; each member of the team chooses three, representing "when I joined the team," "now," "in 5 years time." These choices are then explored.
- **Who-like-me:** the team stands in a circle, each person comes to the centre asking a question that starts with "Who, like me, . . . ?" This gives the possibility to those who recognize themselves in the issues raised to associate themselves with the protagonist.
- **The interactive timeline:** *e.g.* a timeline is set on the ground, from the past to the future through the present, the team traces it's own history through actions and interactions (arrivals, departures, highlights . . .) including imagining future perspectives.
- **Enacted SWOT:** four labelled squares of the classic SWOT (Strengths, Weaknesses, Opportunities and Threats) are placed on the ground and used to draw out the diverse perceptions of the participants and their "contradictory" interactions. The dialogues from a square to the other deepens the understanding of each and everyone.
- **1,000 chairs:** representing the complexity of different points a view in a given situation with key phrases placed on chairs and creating, when appropriate, clusters. Each member of the team is positioned behind one of the chairs and becomes the advocate of a point of view that they can identify with, they then move on to another chair/argument that they feel less close to, then another and another . . . in so doing

---

26 Hale, 1942, 2009
27 Wiener, 1997

they become, by virtue of the interaction produced with the other participants, the advocate for defending a variety of diverse points of view. The observed effect is the enlargement of perspectives.

- **The cultural atom:** progressive role play based on the interaction of social and/or cultural identities.[28]

In this stage the Facilitator's transversal objective is to improve the operational and relational state of the team, *i.e.* bring about a decrease in the level of conflicting tensions(LCT). In this context more or less straightforward, more or less conflicting and more or less "controversial" issues can be addressed. Such as:

- The weekly team meeting (its structure, its function, its form, its duration..)
- Clarification of the roles played within the team
- The transmission of information, horizontal and/or vertical
- The simplification of certain procedures
- The division of labor
- Stress and / or heavy workload management
- Coherence of the team in client relationships
- Constructive communication within "a" team, and in "our" team

The prioritization of the issues to be addressed is made step by step, from the least threatening to the highest risk, as in the case of all warm-up procedures. Indeed, this preparatory stage is in a certain sense the warm-up to the Action that will be the Delayed Dialogue: in order to enable this specific and sensitive Dialogue it is necessary to ensure that:

- the "minor" achievements of Collective Intelligence in action succeed one another
- the "minor" successes thus produced accumulate
- the real effectiveness of the team in problem solving is highlighted.

For this reason, in each of the cycles, it is essential not to underestimate the importance of the phases of:

- Pooling of common experience, demonstrating the links that team members make in a similar or complementary ways, direct or indirect, between what they have just experienced and their professional reality.

28 See Stefanescu, 2016

- Putting into Perspective,[29] through 7 successive stages, thus completing the learning process by allowing (1) to identify the significant elements of the Action, (2) to analyze these elements, (3) to evaluate them, (4) to link theory and professional practice, (5) to broaden perspectives by proposing options, (6) to synthesize the lessons that have been learned and (7) to build bridges to the future by identifying concrete applications to be carried out in everyday working conditions.

From then on, motivation can be reborn and hope for a real renewal of perspectives can develop.

These preparatory cycles need to be continued until the Facilitator feels that the unspoken issues are ready to be expressed in safety.

Using Delayed Dialogue

During all the preparatory cycles, the Facilitator will have taken care to maintain peacefully and creatively their key role (facilitating). They will also have ensured that the active experiencing, the interactions produced and the creativity solicited make use of both the right brain and the left brain functions of each and everyone, and that the 6 dynamic integration lines are activated in such a way that awareness and change facilitated by Collective Intelligence become a meaningful and effective reality.

When to use the Delayed Dialogue?

The Delayed Dialogue is an option for 'practicing' reality, and perhaps for risking the Real Encounter. This means that the team needs to be prepared for this eventuality. It can be challenging to determine exactly when to use the Delayed Dialogue in the process of facilitating a team.

Nevertheless, the main indicator which the Facilitator must be sensitive to is whether the relational state of potential constructivity has been made easier, *i.e.* that (1) in their interactions, defensive-aggressive attitudes and behavior no longer seem necessary to team members for them to talk to each other and that (2) the team's LCT does not exceed 4.5.

---

29   N.B. the flipchart is an essential tool in the visualization and collective memorization of "acquired" learning

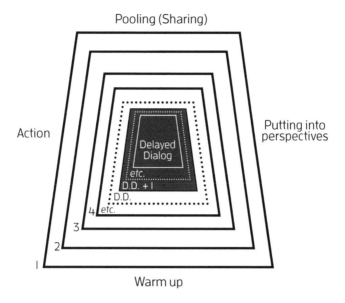

Figure 1 — The Delayed Dialogue, a technique within a process

Sometimes, sufficient positive progress in the general atmosphere and communication in the team is observable when it appears that the members:

- have experienced sufficient improvement in terms of security and trust
- feel that they are increasingly being paid attention to, that they are listened to and respected, even if hidden issues remain unspoken
- express themselves rather than reacting emotionally
- begin to notice the *person* beyond their respective attitudes and behavior
- become more precise, more factual in their description of the behavior of other people
- take more and more responsibility in the communication process
- seek—even inadequately—to respect themselves *and* to respect each other
- develop pro-active attitudes in problem solving
- appear ready and available to become involved in solving relational problems together

However, before introducing the Delayed Dialogue as such, it is very often necessary to address the issue of constructive feedback (since the Delayed Dialogue is constructed as a succession of feedbacks). Various warm-up exercises on this theme can be proposed after recalling the rules of Feedback.

There are a few basic rules to be observed in terms of attitude, and of the 'way of being':

- "Addressing the person opposite as a unique person
- Addressing the opposite person sincerely, from the 'self'
- Focusing on the opposite person's behavior, not on his / her being/self
- Describing, expressing practical observations without any judgment or interpretation
- Presenting a wide perspective, considering several elements, sometimes competing, sometimes differing
- Remaining realistic, avoiding all generalization and exaggerations; giving preference to precision (when? where? what?) and descriptive explanation;
- Acknowledging strong points and possible difficulties
- Using empathy while keeping an emotional distance; using our emotional intelligence[30] and paying attention to the other person's emotional intelligence as well;
- Offering sufficient space for retro-action"[31]

Initiating a feedback exercise on semi-fictional situations allows on the one hand to train for the roles of *Feedback Giver* and *Feedback Receiver*, and on the other hand to confirm (or not) the appropriateness of the moment to introduce the Delayed Dialogue.

Attention: if it turns out that the team is not ready, it is better to return to at least one or several complete cycles of preparation, *e.g.* on "Good Relational Practices."

How to Introduce the Delayed Dialogue?

> *"Everybody wants to talk. But there are many people who haven't met anybody capable of hearing what they have to say." —Tournebise*[32]

This technique has been conceived on this axiom.

In presenting the Delayed Dialogue to a team, the accent therefore needs to be placed on the fact that it is a technique for practicing expression and listening, *giving* feedback and *receiving* feedback . . . while at the same time taking a step back from emotions. To do this, it's important to systematically underline that everyone needs to respect themselves and others, to be aware of their feelings and to have the experience of being open towards others.

Sometimes it is worth adding: "This process is an opportunity for everyone:

- *to use everything we have learned together*

---

30 Goleman, 1995
31 Apter, 2012, pp 8–9
32 1995, p.147

- *to express to others those things that you have not been able to express so far or that have not yet been heard, or welcomed, whether they be positive or negative*
- *to experience congruence, by saying what you feel or think, what you have observed and what you would prefer. And this without judgment or reproach*
- *to practice empathy, the sensitive and sincere listening to the reality of the other in a safe setting where benevolence and a constructive attitude must prevail."*

After having set the frame, the technique can then be put into place in four stages:

I. Install the space.
The Facilitator suggests that chairs be placed in a semi-circle (without a table) and that the team should sit down. In front of the team, two chairs are placed face to face (not directly in front of each other, but slightly at an angle).

2. A brief explanation
Take a brief moment to give basic instructions; further indications will be given as the situation evolves:

> *This is an exercise where the group must remain in total silence, making no comments, no sounds, no mimicry of any sort. This attitude must be maintained throughout the duration of the exercise. This is very important!*
>
> *Sitting on one of the two chairs, one of you will invite another person to sit on the other chair and tell him just* one *thing, something pleasant, something nice, (e.g. "Thank you for . . .", "I enjoyed when . . .", etc.) or something less pleasant (e.g. "it was a shame when . . .", "I did not like when . . ." etc.). The other person expresses nothing, neither in words or non-verbally. They are silent and show nothing. When your interlocutor has understood what you have said, they say "thank you"; it's a "thank you for expressing yourself." They do not say anything else, and you will then sit on the seat that they occupied in the semicircle. They will then invite someone else from the team and the procedure is repeated. They cannot invite you (you just spoke to them), they will have to wait for another opportunity to invite you if they want to comment or respond to what you have expressed. And so on . . .*

3. Showing

Sit down on one of the two chairs and invite the leader (manager) of the team, in this example we'll call him Alan. Say something pleasant to him, something positive, such as:

> *Alan, I really appreciate the fact that you have made available to the team this time of collective reflexion, where everyone can learn from each other, with each other: the team has been able to address so many issues and we have built together renewed bases for collaboration. It's very exciting for me to be part of such a collective growth process. I'm moved.*

Wait for Alan's "thank you," then sit down on the seat Alan occupied in the semicircle and indicate the next step:

> *Now you have to invite someone to whom you want to say something.*

4. Accompanying

Alan invites *e.g.* Josy and tells her *one* thing. Josy says, "Thank you." Alan is then directed to Josy's seat in the semicircle and then Josy is asked to invite someone to the second seat.

This introduction to the Delayed Dialogue contains three positive inductions:

- The basic framework as presented underlines the notions of caring for oneself and others, fostering attitudes of openness, benevolence and constructiveness. This is a way — as far as is possible — of calming the fears of the team members on the one hand, and on the other hand of contractualising the state of mind in which the Delayed Dialogue is supposed to take place. This induced safety is of great importance in the use of such a technique given that people may feel quite exposed.
- Also, when the Facilitator demonstrates, they first refer to the manager. By openly showing this to everyone, the road is opened, thereby granting a form of permission for the team to play the game — even if this exercise may still seem surprising or frightening.
- the Facilitator voluntarily expresses something positive to the manager, inducing the group to begin — as always in the Action Methods — with the least threatening, in this case by the pleasant feedbacks.

How to Accompany the Delayed Dialogue?

Throughout the duration of the Delayed Dialogue, the role of the Facilitator is essential, even though, as a facilitator, they may also be asked to receive feedback (this often happens at the end of the process). The Facilitator needs to maintain a continuous and reassuring attention to everything that happens in order to give the team the means to experience this moment in trust and safety.

Taking the necessary and sufficient time

To ensure the effectiveness of this Action Technique, a substantial amount of time must be made available: at least 2h–2h30 for up to 7 participants; 3–4h for between 8 and 12 participants and at least one day between 12 and 15 participants (something I have experienced on only three occasions).

It seems to me that beyond 15 participants, which is already a huge number for such a process, it would be almost impossible to reach the end, and therefore the process would risk becoming prejudicial. In this way, when the participants are really given enough time, and they are aware of this and can feel it, then their reservations will gradually fade away, and then disappear, allowing them to progressively express their unspoken issues. The duration is all the more a key factor because the goal is and must remain the Dialogue. However, no response to a feedback can be given straight away: only a simple "Thank you" punctuates the reception of a feedback. The person receiving the feedback is in a controlled situation: they cannot answer "on the spur of the moment," they must take a step back from what has just been said and refocus on the colleague to whom they will then give their feedback. And this before sitting back in the group and witnessing the feedbacks that take place on stage (on the two chairs) . . . until . . . until they are in a position to invite their interlocutor back again and answer them. Sometimes several feedbacks and repeated actions will be essential, hence the necessity of enough time (which may seem initially to be rather long) that needs to be made available for the Dialogues to take place until a peaceful conclusion is reached.

Keeping within the frame

The security and potential of the Delayed Dialogue greatly depends on the creation of a framework. This is why the Facilitator throughout the process must remind participants, when necessary, in a gentle, peaceful but firm way, that only one feedback can be given at a time. This on the one hand encourages the feedback giver to stay focused and, on the other hand, protects the receiver from a possible 'flood' of feedback. Similarly, the Facilitator, when necessary, will remind the group, and/or the receiver of feedback, of the rule of verbal and non-verbal silence, thereby avoiding relational dispersal. Finally, if a particular intervention is not a feedback, but a judgment or a manipulation, the Facilitator respectfully reframes the remark, by re-phrasing it and/or re-emphasizing the importance of benevolence in this process.

Proposing variants

Having begun the Delayed Dialogue with a period of agreeable, positive feed-back, the Facilitator may find themselves in front of a group that continues in the same vein for a while. Although this has importance in strengthening the team, it may also represent an easy way of avoiding taking things further. After some time it will become necessary to suggest an alternative: *"You can also tell the other person, very respectfully, something less agreeable, something you may have disapproved of in their behavior."* Sometimes, 15–20 minutes later, using a different formula, it may be a good idea to reiterate this option, if no one has chosen to take the initiative. Once the process is well advanced, some feedback givers may stall and feel they "have nothing more to say." After giving them time to check if this is really the case, it can be suggested (if they have not already proposed it themselves) that they could talk to two or three people (by adding one or two chairs) or even to the whole group, (by turning their chair to face everybody). After this episode, the feedback giver chooses another person to continue the process. Then much later on, if a person really does not have anything to say to either another person, or to a sub-group, or to the group as a whole, they are given the opportunity to pass their turn and offer their place as a feedback giver to whomever they want to choose.

Being aware of when to conclude

This is the most difficult challenge. There often comes a time when everything seems to have been said. The first moment that feels like this is rarely the right moment to bring things to an end. It's better to wait before suggesting that the process ends, because the real value of the process is often hidden in seemingly unimportant details, which in fact may make it possible to reach a more advantageous conclusion. A succession of these moments can arise, until the Facilitator chooses to wind things up by suggesting to the whole team to return their chairs back to their original places.

The key role (facilitating) is and remains the principal asset in this con-trolled situation.

Follow Up

Even when, and most importantly if the Delayed Dialogue has been fruitful, it is absolutely essential to carry out a substantial follow-up to anchor the dynamics and dynamism of the team. This is achieved in two phases:

Immediate follow-up

Once the Delayed Dialogue Action has been completed, the Pooling period (sharing) follows. The Facilitator asks everyone present to express what the experience has been like for them, how they feel about the process, what it evokes for them, *etc.*

The facilitator gives the team the opportunity to hear what everyone has experienced, how everybody feels and the resonances that have emerged. *"It's difficult and unusual to feel so exposed in this way, in front of everyone else"*; *"At first I didn't believe in it . . ."*; *"Everyone got so involved!"*; *"Now we know we can talk to each other"*; *"It was moving and powerful"*; *"I would have liked to have been able to do this in other teams, I could have said such important things"* . . . some of the many comments coming from participants which illustrate the constructive aspect of the dynamics produced. The phase of "Putting into Perspective" which then follows generally allows the team to affirm not only its intention to continue this quality of dialogue and encounter, but also and above all to lay the groundwork for it's renewed empowerment. When this happens — and it happens frequently — there is a real collective sensation of success, of an enhanced efficiency full of promise for the future. They are eager to pursue direct constructive dialogue (not Delayed Dialogue).

Consolidation

It is now a question of capitalizing on this constructivity by engaging in one or more complete cycles of action to deal with operational problems that have not been dealt with up to this point and which may have appeared as perhaps "insoluble" or "important but not essential."

This consolidation work is crucial because it allows the team to appreciate the progress made in terms of quality and efficiency, leading to an awareness on the one hand of their greater capacity for dialogue, and on the other hand in their renewed ability to solve problems: two factors undoubtedly anchoring, reinforcing and energizing both for the team and for their manager.

Conclusion

Even though, despite the ambient stress, institutions, companies and organizations are not in the habit of providing significant periods of reflexion and hindsight for their teams, it has been demonstrated that they are essential, especially at times when conflicts arise and the team begins to suffer. This consolidation work can help to avoid relational disasters and avoid an increasing level of conflictual tension within the team. Each professional and the team as a whole in fact needs these moments to regain their trust, their security and their optimism . . . even if this means embarking on a process of bringing out the unspoken. In this sense and well beyond any action techniques deployed, the added value of humanistic Action Methods lies in securing and facilitating the awareness and change that are achieved by the combination of the constituent elements in JL Moreno's methods:

- a complete theory and a practical methodology

- the triggering of deeper, multi-dimensional awareness through action and interaction
- stimulating the creativity of the right brain and the left brain
- the 6 lines to dynamic integration
- active experiencing and "immersion plus hindsight"
- the promotion of Collective Intelligence
- precautionary co-construction

The Action Methods make it possible to produce complete cycles of action that can, step-by-step, prepare each and everyone to express unspoken issues. In this way, through the process of the Delayed Dialogue and with the precautionary and methodical support of the Facilitator, a space is created, as well as the time for each one to express themselves in safety, where their contribution is welcomed, recognized, legitimized, listened to and understood, and thus full communication is restored. The Action Methods also provide a framework, a structure and a means for everyone to be benevolently involved in the co-resolution of problems and for the team to move on and regain its dynamism.

Despite the undoubted added value of the Action Methods, this (sometimes long) process that the team goes through in order to diminish their tension and to dare speaking out the unspoken is far from being a panacea. In part results depend, of course, on the engagement of all concerned and on the extent of the skills and abilities of the Facilitator, their expertise, their charisma and their vision; they also depend on the follow up done by the manager and the team itself.

In general, the result of a successful consolidation process is the resurgence of an enhanced performance and a greater well being for the team. Given greater coherence and cohesion, each and everyone finally arrives at a place from where they can capitalize and build towards a future that is once again full of promise: the future remains, as always, something that must be constructed, but this regained constructive vitality opens new perspectives of meaning and optimism . . .

The consequent challenge for the team and its manager is to actively maintain this dynamism and momentum. A "new" paradigm of collaboration must be put into place, definitively based on a pro-active benevolent attitude and on the regulation of relational and/or operational problems, as and when they arise.

In fact, even without going through this whole process, just in a preventive sense, every manager should be aware of the intrinsic usefulness of this fundamental paradigm that fosters collective well-being and increased performance: take a step back regularly with the team and utilize their Collective Intelligence to address inherent strengths and difficulties, liberate their creativity and develop a collaborative efficiency which is greater than the sum of their individual capabilities.

Norbert Apter

Based in the francophone region of Switzerland, Norbert Apter is a leading pioneer in the deployment of Humanistic Action Methods, as defined by J.L. Moreno. He has worked in more than twenty countries worldwide as a qualified trainer and train the trainers.

His background in psychology has led him not only to have a private practice in psychodrama, but also to specialize in working with groups and teams in companies. Over the past thirty years, he has facilitated many (Executive) Coaching, TeamCaring, TeamBuilding and TeamMeditation programs. Since 2005, he has been supervising a monthly group of medical doctors. He has also trained hundreds of professionals in the development of relational and operational competences, published more than 35 articles and given approximately 25 lectures for different congresses and conventions, in companies and professional associations.

Thus, through his extensive work based on Action Methods, he promotes collective intelligence, creative problem solving and collaborative competences (mindset and behaviors) in the work place.

More details: *www.norbertapter.ch*

References

Apter, N. (2011). Using Action Methods for training in Institutions, Companies and Organizations. *Mercurius*.

Apter, N. (2012). Humanistic processing: the supervisor's role through reverse enactment. In H. Krall, J. Fürst, & P. Fontaine (Eds.), *Supervision in Psychodrama* (pp. 19–36): Springer Fachmedien Wiesbaden.

Apter, N. (2016). TeamCaring, TeamBuilding or Team Mediation? *The British Journal of Psychodrama and Sociodrama*, 31(1 & 2), 27–47.

ATS. (2018, jan.27). Travail: Un employé sur quatre épuisé. *Tribune de Genève*.

Bales, R. (1953). The equilibrium problem in small groups. . In T. Parsons, R. Bales, & E. A. Shils (Eds.), *Working Papers in the theory of action*. Glencoe: Free Press.

Blatner , A., & Blatner, A. (1988). *Foundations of Psychodrama: History, Theory and practice*. New York: Springer Publishing Company.

BPA (January 2018) *What are Action Methods ?* British Psychodrama Association *http://www.psychodrama.org.uk/what_are_action_methods.php*

Bohart, A. C., & Greenberg, L. S. (1997). *Empathy reconsidered. New directions in Psychotherapy*. Washington: American Psychological Society.

Bozarth, J. D., & Wilkins, P. (2001). *UPR Unconditional positive regard* (Vol. 3). Ross-on-Wye, UK: PCCS Books.

Buber, M. (1970). *I and Thou*. New York: Charles Scribner's Sons.

Dayton, T. (1994). *The Drama Within. Psychodrama and experiential therapy.* Deerfield Beach, Florida: Health Communication Inc.

Gardner, H. (1983). *Frames of mind. The theory of multiple intelligences.* New York: BasicBooks.

Gendlin, E. T. (1996). *Focusing-oriented Psychotherapy: A Manual of the Experiential Method,* . New York: Guilford Press.

Goleman, D. (1995). *Emotional Intelligence.* New York: Bantam Books.

Hale, A. E. (1942). *Conducting clinical sociometric explorations : a manual for psychodramatists and sociometrists.* Roanoke, Virginia (USA): Royal Publishing Company.

Hale, A. E. (2009). Moreno's sociometry: exploring interpersonal connection. *Group: the journal of the Eastern group Psychotherapy Society, 33*(4), 347–358.

Hudgins, M. K. (2007). Clinical foundations of the Therapeutic Spiral Model. Theoretical orientations and principle of change. In C. Baim, J. Burgermeister, & M. Maciel (Eds.), *Psychodrama. Advances in Theory and Practice.* London and New York: Routledge.

Karp, M. An introduction to psychodrama. In Karp M., Holmes, P., & Bradshaw Tauvon, K. (1998). *The Handbook Of Psychodrama.* London (England). New York, NY (USA): Routledge.

Kirschenbaum, H., & Land Henderson, V. (2001). *Carl Rogers: L'approche centrée sur la personne.* Lausanne (Suisse): Editions Randin SA.

Leutz, D. G.-A. (1985). *Mettre sa vie en scène. Le psychodrame.* Paris (France): Epi.

Maslow, A. (1972). *Vers une psychologie de l'être.* Paris: Edition Fayard.

Moreno, J. L. (1964). *Psychodrama* (Vol. 1). Beacon, N.Y.: Beacon House.

OIT (2016) *Workplace stress: A collective challenge.* Geneva : International Labour Organisation

Rogers, C. R. (1980). *A way of being.* Boston: Houghton-Mifflin Company.

Rogers, C. R. (1984). *On Becoming a Person. A Therapist's View of Psychotherapy.* London (England): Constable

Rogers, C. R. (1986). A client-centered/person-centered approach to therapy. In I. Kutash & A. Wolfe (Eds.), *Psychotherapist's casebook*: Jossey Bass.

Stefanescu, I. (2016, January 20). L'atome culturel. Retour sur un atelier international. *Relation et Action.* Retrieved from *https://www.odef.ch/relation-action/latome-culturel-retour-sur-un-atelier-international/*

Tournebise, T. (1995). *Se comprendre avec ou sans mots: Un concept original pour améliorer nos relations humaines.* St-Jean de Braye (France): Dangles.

Wiener, R. (1997). *Creative training: Sociodrama and team building.* London: Jessica Kingsley.

Wyatt, G. (2001). *Congruence* (Vol. 1). Ross-on-Wye: PCCS Books.

Using Action Methods to Facilitate Collective Intelligence

Chantal Nève Hanquet and Agathe Crespel

English translation by Kathleen Llanwarne

Because they provide a means of enabling groups to consider a single situation from a different angle, action methods can be a way of accessing new ideas, resources, and solutions. As such, they foster creativity, agility, and the development of collective intelligence within groups.

Over and above a description of the requisite techniques and tools, the general approach adopted by our book is steeped in a deep awareness of, and sensitivity to, human relations, thereby providing answers to the important question of just what it is that can enable a group to become more alive. This overall approach will enable a wide range of practitioners—trainers, consultants, supervisors, facilitators, coaches, academics, teachers, managers, coordinators, presenters, politicians, mediators, or facilitators—to gain, regardless of personal background and style, inspiration for their own particular form of professional practice.

Placing trust in the strength of the group

In the 1930s Jacob Levy Moreno revealed his genius by introducing into the world of psychology the notions of 'setting in movement', 'experiencing the here and now', and 'role-playing'. These innovations stemmed from the strength inherently present in groups and from the way in which individuals find themselves able, by taking on and playing roles, to develop new facets of themselves.

Today once again, a younger generation of visionaries such as the Belgian writer Frédéric Laloux,[1] are stressing the importance of the group which they designate using the term 'collective intelligence'. They are referring to a form of osmosis, to the emergence of a moment at which the group develops its own momentum, identity, and intelligence: something 'gels', and the whole thereby becomes something more than the sum of its parts. This is what happens in an orchestra, or within a sports team, when the group takes on a form of autonomy from which there emanates a new quality of harmony.

> Collective Intelligence refers to a context in which group interaction gives rise to something more than the sum of the individual persons constituting it. The group becomes, in and of itself, an entity endowed with its own intelligence.

Professionals in the workplace are constantly seeking answers to significant questions. How can we create a context for innovation? How can we welcome and adapt to change? How can we be clearer about who should do what? What ways can we find of improving communication? Or of becoming more efficient? Or more creative?

The action methods devised by Jacob Levy Moreno are a set of levers designed to stimulate creativity, co-construction, and the ability of teams of professionals to view a situation from different angles. It soon becomes apparent that it is through looking 'in new directions' and thinking 'out of the box' that such teams can tune into their collective intelligence, thereby gaining access to new resources, ideas, ways forward and action strategies.

It is a question of putting in place contexts in which collective intelligence can flourish, something which we set out to illustrate in this article by means of two examples taken 'from the field' in which facilitators instil momentum and action into professionals' efforts to carry forward their own tasks, responsibilities and ambitions. It is a question, in other words, of creating contexts that will enable professionals to find their own answers to their own questions and to carry their efforts forward in a spirit of collective intelligence.

The 'empty chair' technique

Here a facilitator is meeting, for the first time, two senior representatives of an organisation. For the first half hour the two professionals have been explaining that the reason they need help is that the level of motivation among their staff is dwindling. Colleagues are manifestly less committed to their work, and conflict

---

1   Laloux, F. (2014). *Reinventing Organisations—A guide to Creating Organisations Inspired by the Next Stage of Human Consciousness.* Nelson Parke.

is on the increase. After listening to the two leaders, the facilitator proposes the following course of action:

> **Facilitator:** would you agree that we take this chair standing here at the table and use it to represent your organization? I would propose, if you would agree, to come to stand behind this chair and to 'repeat back' to you what I have understood of the problem you are experiencing. I shall do this using a special approach that consists of speaking 'on behalf' of the organization.

The facilitator then gets up, comes to stand behind the empty chair representing the organization, and begins to speak 'on behalf' of the organization:

> **Facilitator:** (*standing behind the chair representing the organization*) I, the organization, have been in existence for more than 40 years and I was first set up by a group of very committed individuals. At the present time I am aware that my staff are running out of steam and am wondering what I can do to regain their motivation and commitment to my project. I'm very aware that the atmosphere is conflict-ridden and would so much like to see things running smoothly once more. So what I'm wondering is just what can be done to get people to work together in a more cooperative fashion.

The facilitator, returning now to her own seat, questions the two senior representatives:

> **Facilitator:** Does what you have just heard make any sense to you? Do you feel that these comments are in line with the questions you are asking? What do you have to say in response?

The two senior representatives are now able to express their position more clearly:

> **Jack (senior representative):** Yes, that's exactly how it is! What I would add is that our staff need guidance if they are to find more cooperative ways of working. So what we need from you is that you give them some space in which to express themselves and to practice co-construction, as well as offering us some advice in management terms.

The fact that the facilitator chose to play the role of the organization and that, to do this, she stood up and went to speak behind an empty chair, had created a surprise effect. What we see here is a form of meta-communication: by 'bringing into play' the organization, the facilitator 'brings to life' something that, until then, had been merely 'reported' by the senior representatives. The role-playing stance adopted by the facilitator was an enlivening experience for the two leaders. Their attention was sparked by what was going on. And it was in this live setting that the senior representatives of the organization were able to state more clearly exactly what it was that they wanted and needed.

The facilitator, for her part, in deciding to play a role in this way, was choosing to 'jump in at the deep end'. She was taking a risk in creatively 'repeating back' what she had understood.

When there is sufficient trust within a group or team of workers, the empty chair technique can be used, for example, in a meeting situation. The mere presence of this empty chair, because of what it is being used to represent, alters people's habitual modes of thinking, thereby creating new information.

> **Facilitator:** I would propose that anyone who so wishes should come to stand behind the empty chair that I am placing here and that represents our company. From this vantage point, you can say 'something' on behalf of the company.

An empty chair is brought in to represent, for example, a person, a group, an organization, and is invited to speak. This is a way of fostering spontaneity and creativity.

Frédéric Laloux,[2] in his highly successful book Reinventing organizations, illustrates in what way the empty chair technique can be used in a workplace meeting to represent a third party, in this case the company, in order to spark communication. This 'staging' procedure brings in a playful element that is devoid of judgment. Rather than representing the company, the empty chair can represent a project, a product, the client, the claimant, *etc*. When this type of technique is used in a meeting, it is essential to first request the group's consent, as a means of checking up on and ensuring participants' commitment to and involvement in the process. It is also important that there should be a person present to facilitate this action technique by encouraging role-playing and sometimes actually inviting people to get up and come to speak from behind the empty chair.

Participants will then get up and play the role of whatever the chair is representing, thereby opening up the field of communication by means of 'out of the box' enactment.

---

2   Laloux, F. (2014). *Reinventing Organisations — A guide to Creating Organisations Inspired by the Next Stage of Human Consciousness*. Nelson Parke.

The facilitator may also choose to accompany the role-taking by coming to stand next to the empty chair:

> **Facilitator (standing next to the empty chair):** What is the direction in which I, the company, wish to move? And at what speed?
>
> **Manager (standing behind the empty chair):** I would like to broaden my field of action and gain access to new clients, but I want to take the necessary time for a proper market analysis.
>
> **Facilitator (standing next to the empty chair):** What is my dream as a company?
>
> **Manager (standing behind the empty chair):** my dream is to travel to other countries.
>
> **Facilitator (standing next to the empty chair):** What do I, the company, think about what people are saying here around this table? What are my feelings about it all?
>
> **Manager (standing behind the empty chair):** I've noticed that there are some here who have remained silent; I'd be interested to hear what they have to say.
>
> **Facilitator (standing next to the empty chair):** Do I, the company, believe that we are being excessively bold? Or perhaps not bold enough?
>
> **Manager (standing behind the empty chair):** We could allow ourselves to be much bolder than we are. We're too afraid of catching cold! An injection of folly would do us no harm! (laughing)

The facilitator can launch other types of cue:

> **Facilitator (standing next to the empty chair):** Are there some other topics that I, the company, would like to discuss? Do I, the company, consider that the decisions taken are likely to prove beneficial? What is my stance now at the end of this meeting?

It is to be noted that the empty chair technique can be used in two different ways:

- 'Spontaneous' version: an empty chair represents, for example, the company and anyone who so wishes is at any time free to get up and come to speak from behind the empty chair, playing the role of the company.

- 'Sequential' version: a quarter of an hour is set aside during which participants who so wish can stand up and come to speak on behalf of the chair that represents, in this case, the company, after which a debriefing period is allowed to discuss what has been happening.

Representation

A facilitator is giving an aggressiveness management course in a local authority department. He proposes that, for the last part of the training, the director should also attend, to enable an exchange to take place on the work of the preceding two days. The director, before agreeing, has asked to speak alone with the facilitator to whom he explains his concern:

> **Director:** I'm prepared to attend the closing session of the training but I am adamant that this meeting must not turn into a trade union confrontation. I am quite ready to listen to feedback on the training, but not to institutional demands.

The facilitator has understood the director's point. He knows too that the staff have plenty to say, in particular about their dissatisfaction with the way the local authority operates.

This situation could well prove impossible, because to ask a person or group to abstain from 'making demands' will inevitably strengthen their inclination to do so.

As a means of working with the presence of the director together with his staff, the facilitator has chosen to use a 'representation': he positions two empty chairs in the work area and then addresses the group as a whole (staff plus director) as follows:

> **Facilitator:** I've placed two empty chairs here in our midst and I would like to tell you, if you agree, what I have understood about what matters most to you during this time for exchange while you are all together. To assist us, I have positioned one chair to represent the staff and one to represent the director. I am going to speak 'on behalf' of each of the two chairs, and you will tell me whether I have understood things correctly.

The facilitator goes to stand first of all behind the chair representing the staff and thus takes on the role of the local authority employees:

> **Facilitator (behind the staff chair):** we, the staff, have a strong need for dialogue with our hierarchical superiors and a large number of things to say. We appreciate the fact that our director has agreed to attend, and we would like to take this

opportunity to describe our experience and make a number of points concerning the way our offices are run.

The facilitator then moves on to speak from behind the chair representing the director:

> **Facilitator (behind the director's chair):** I, the director, am here for just one hour and I need to be absolutely sure that our time here together will be well spent. As such, I need each one of you to come up with some constructive proposals.

The facilitator, returning to his own seat, then addresses the group as a whole:

> **Facilitator:** would you say that the points I made while taking on your roles coincide with the way you feel? Is there something that struck you particularly? Do you have anything to add? Or to object to or comment upon?

> The 'representation' places both the staff and the director in the same situation of adopting a position in relation to what is taking place. And it is an experience that will serve to connect them rather than oppose them to each other.

Following the facilitator's intervention, participants comment as follows:

> **Director:** yes, that's exactly right.

> **Participant (to director):** It's true that it's important for you that we should have places where we are able to express ourselves.

> **Director (to staff):** yes, it is important for me too. That's why I came into your offices quite recently, to be close to you and gain a better understanding of the reality of your working conditions. But there are some among you who thought that I had come to exercise control, and so I stopped coming in the way I had previously.

> **Participant (to director):** personally, I appreciated the fact that you came into our offices because it showed that you were paying attention to our work.

> **Participant (to director):** in our department, everything is a mess. We can't cope with the work load and we fail to communicate well among ourselves. The claimants are becoming increasingly

aggressive and one reason for this is that they have to queue for too long before being seen.

Director: yes, I am very well aware that this department is not performing well. And arrangements are underway for a thorough reorganisation.

The staff and the director continue their exchange and develop their arguments. To conclude the proceedings, the facilitator takes the floor:

Facilitator: we've just spent nearly an hour talking to one another. And what I have been listening to is an exchange of a high standard. You have said what you had to say and you have listened to each other. I can only encourage this type of constructive exchange in your working environment.

After the training course, the director wrote an email to the facilitator as follows:

Dear Sir,

I would like to thank you for your facilitation which enabled me to experience some moments of constructive communication with my staff.

Continuation of this form of exchange is an excellent path to be developed and practised on a regular basis.

As a result of this experience, I am feeling much less discouraged.

Thank you for your inspiring work and commitment to training.

Kind regards,

A. J.

As we have seen, the facilitator spoke on behalf of both the director and the staff, each represented by a chair. This experience enabled all parties to gain some distance from their situation and to view it differently. What was said will open up new space because all parties expressed themselves non-judgmentally. Both staff and director were able to feel that their respective concerns had been understood, and so would be able to continue their exchange, supplying more details of their job-related concerns. In this way, a new level of communication was achieved.

Generally speaking, the 'representation' offers a means of reframing a tense situation, contributing a 'new gaze', a different way of considering each person's situation and role. People thus come to see one other in terms of their concerns and skills rather than seeking to place spokes in the wheels or engage in conflict.

The thinker and practitioner Ivan Böszörményi-Nagy[3] developed, along these lines, the notion of 'relational ethic', inviting each person to focus on issues of responsibility and sensitivity to give and take. Borrowing from this author's terms of reference, the facilitator is able to pay attention to ensuring that what is 'given' to individuals actually suits them and that they experience it as 'fair'. Should this not be the case, they will be offered the opportunity to express their needs.

In the above example, the 'representation' enabled the emotions experienced by both parties—director and staff—to be named. As the parties feel recognized, they no longer need to be in conflict and can take up a position in communication, giving and taking recognition to and from one another.

Some of the facilitator's interventions in the above case lend support to this notion of give and take, and of being attentive to the need for fairness and trust among persons to be restored and consolidated.

- What is the message you want to give to your director?
- How do you receive this message?
- How do you see things now that your staff have responded to your concerns?
- Do you feel that what you have been offered is suitable for you? Do you feel it be to fair?

This manner of stimulating give and take will help the group to become a fully-fledged entity, a collective intelligence representing more than the sum of its parts.

Some Hints for Using Action Methods

Work based on spontaneity, on offering contexts in which action methods can be used, entails the creation of a working space in which participants will sometimes reveal their true faces without recourse to a mask. Spontaneity frequently coincides with the expression of vulnerability. Hence the importance, as we have seen, of putting in place a safety frame that can enable participants to experience trust.

It is equally important for facilitators to develop inner attitudes that facilitate communication, to provide appropriate accompaniment for the group process, and to have already experienced on and for themselves the methodologies that are being put in place.

---

3 Böszörményi-Nagy, I & Krasner, BR; (2014) *Between Give and Take*, New York, Brunner Mazel, Routledge

In our book *Faciliter l'intelligence collective*,[4] published in 2018, we offer guidance for the use, in professional situations, of action methods that are designed to regulate group dynamics, project development, creativity, and so forth. (It will be published in English soon.) The focus of the book is precisely to support group facilitators and psychodrama directors with an existing practice, as well as team leaders, academics, trainers, and coaches who may have no prior knowledge of psychodrama.

The book is divided into 4 parts:

9 Inner Attitudes that will Facilitate Communication

Part 1 of the book presents Nine Inner Attitudes that will fuel and nourish open and flexible forms of communication within groups. It is important for facilitators—whether director, team leader, academic, trainer, or coach—to pay attention to and continue to work on their own inner attitudes. For a group to function fruitfully qua group requires an emotionally and physically inviting facilitator.

Seven Key Questions to Activate Collective Intelligence

Part 2 of the book offers Seven Key Questions to stimulate Collective Intelligence. Though it may be difficult to pinpoint precisely what it is that makes a group come alive, there are a number of key issues that it is essential to address:

1. How to work with the here and now?
2. How to create a safe frame and context?
3. How to stimulate cohesion?
4. How to strengthen a sense of personal competence?
5. How to take account of what remains unspoken?
6. How to see a single situation from different angles?
7. How to remain on a searching path?

Five Action Techniques for Broadening the Field of Possibilities

Part 3 of the book presents Five Action Techniques drawn from psychodrama. It begins with a brief presentation of Moreno's Methods, after which five techniques are described and illustrated in some detail and, in each case, according to a six-step process. This six-step process is particularly useful in working sessions that rely on intensive use of action techniques. As indicated in relation to the two examples described above, action methods can also be used in 'homeopathic' mode, *i.e.* in small doses by means of periodic or irregular insertion within a process (*e.g.* the empty chair). The initial setting up of a safety frame is, however, indispensable in all cases, as this is the prerequisite

---

4 Crespel, A., & Neve Hanquet, C (2018) C. *Faciliter l'intelligence collective: 35 fiches memo pour innover, co-construire, mettre en action, et accompagner le changement.* France: Eyrolles

for the creation of trust within the group. Each facilitator can develop his or her own style in creating a safety frame. The six guidelines given below, inspired by the work of Moreno and enriched by a Jungian approach, can provide a source of inspiration for facilitating the experience of 'holding', or the ability of the facilitator to 'carry a group' and ensure that its work is performed in a safe setting.

> In the absence of a safety framework, without connection having been established between group members, and where a sense of confidence and empowerment has not been instilled into the group, it may be difficult to use action methods in a constructive way.

1. In creating the *safety frame*, it will be helpful to refer to the rules of psychodrama which include attention to confidentiality, openness to spontaneity, the freedom to accept or reject a proposal, and respect for time as a 'container' for the action. Another rule used in psychodrama is that of 'restitution'. This refers to permission for comments or behaviour arising outside the official work procedures (*e.g.* during breaks, *etc.*) to be brought back into the meeting insofar as such elements are liable to contribute to the ongoing work.

2. *Warming-up* within the group refers to the process of preparing mind, heart and body by provision of a structure whereby people can connect up with themselves and each other. In some work sessions using action methods, empowerment experiments and movements are offered by way of preparation for the group to develop in various directions.

3. *Identification of the question* on which work will take place is a stage during which various significant questions can be formulated, after which the group selects the topic on which it wishes to work.

4. The *action* is the time during which action techniques will be used in a climate of experimentation. This step represents a kind of 'detour' insofar as it departs from the immediate search for solutions and strategies. Such a detour offers the opportunity to create new information and to think 'out of the box'.

5. The *sharing stage* is when participants communicate about what was important during the action and what has been learned.

6. A collective *search for solutions and strategies* follows on from the sharing stage, with a return to the initial question. This search is enriched by all the information created during the previous stages, and elements of solutions emerge from the whole process.

> In the knowledge that openness is connected to a process that
> is deeper and more complex than mere will, techniques from
> psychodrama are presented as a possible answer to the chal-
> lenging question: *how* can people be helped to see the same
> situation from different angles?

In this process, areas of both the left and right brain are stimulated, activated and interconnected because of the alternation between time for thought,
time for movement, time for feelings, and time for expression.

As approaches to achieving this holistic outcome, the book contains
detailed descriptions of the following five action techniques: Doubling, the
Empty Chair, the Empathy Circle, Revealing Chairs and Analogical Detours.

- The technique of 'Doubling' is described and illustrated as a means
  of giving sustenance to the presence, feeling or idea carried by one
  person in the group. The same technique can be used also to help a
  member of the group to specify a professional objective or strategy,
  assisting the colleague in the effort to achieve greater precision
  concerning the goal of a project.
- The 'Empty Chair' is presented as a technique which can be introduced, during a meeting, to represent a significant person or entity.
  For example, representing the founder of an organization, or the
  organization itself, by means of an empty chair, will alter the perspective. A facilitator can invite a group member to stand behind an empty
  chair and to speak from the standpoint of whatever that chair has
  been placed there to represent. Through this process, information is
  generated; and through the use of the empty chair, people can develop
  a new mode of involvement whereby implicit thoughts are able to be
  made explicit.
- The 'Empathy Circle', a technique created by Chantal Nève Hanquet,
  allows a group to help one person to enter into the role of another
  significant person who is not present in the room. This deep form of
  role-play can be valuable because, entailing very little movement, it
  puts in place a powerful 'circular container' that can generate sufficient empathy to explore a question stemming from a relationship
  that is experienced as in some way difficult or problematic.
- The 'Revealing Chairs' is a technique that enables participants to
  represent a specific context worthy of the group's interest. The
  facilitator first helps participants to identify the persons, groups,
  organizations and entities that are of significance in the context of
  its project or mission. Participants are then asked to represent these
  situational components using chairs. The chairs are positioned within

the working area to indicate how participants perceive the relationship between each named person/entity and the others. This action is 'informative', in that it invites people to make explicit the way in which they see things, thereby making subjective impressions more externally vivid. The facilitator invites participants to come to stand behind the chair of their choice, and to 'give voice' to whatever it is that this chair represents. More than one person can come forward at a time, allowing multiple and simultaneous role-playing in which role-players respond to one another.

- The 'Analogical Detours' are a set of creative techniques designed to represent a situation and its context by the use of metaphors, shapes and colors, use of symbolic objects, and metaphorical uses of textual composition.

35 Tools for use in group facilitation

In part 4 of the book, all the tools presented in this section link up with the Inner Attitudes, Keys to Stimulate Collective Intelligence and Action Techniques described and illustrated in the three earlier parts of the book. Here they are presented in alphabetical order, each on a separate page, and identified by specific titles such as Attitude, Empathy Circle, Cohesion, and so on. Each description contains similar sections covering 'goals', 'guidelines' and 'putting it into words', the latter offering suggestions as to how a facilitator might introduce a topic to a group. The index and the glossary provide additional navigational tools for readers, enabling individual facilitators to extend their practice in accordance with personal background and interests, style and signature.

Conclusion

Action methods offer a way of stimulating—simultaneously—word and action, body and mind, emotion and reason. Accordingly, they help us to experience and understand collective intelligence in an all-embracing, or holistic, manner.

The neurosciences have indeed shown that we generally make use of no more than a small portion of our potential capacities, and also that input from the body can be important for stimulating different areas of the brain. What is more, the relatively recent discovery of mirror neurons makes it clear that empathy is a skill that can be learned, insofar as there exist neurological processes that enable us to 'capture' sensory, emotional and conceptual information, thereby allowing us to enter into the intentions and emotions of another person. It is thus that the mirror neurons enable a person to put him- or herself in the place of another and, for this reason, they are known also as 'empathy neurons'. This quality of finely tuned cognitive and emotional awareness is vitally important in situations requiring cooperation within a team. Experiments such as the 'empty chair' and 'representation' are ways of practising and developing our ability to 'put ourselves in another person's shoes'.

The French psychodramatist, Anne Ancelin Schützenberger, who died in March 2018, referred—in one of her last books entitled *Le Plaisir de vivre*—to 'serendipity' as being the capacity to allow oneself to be surprised by something that one was not expecting, to regard seemingly chance events as welcome opportunities. In some cases, like those referred to in this article, action methods possess this capacity to reframe or overturn specific situations, to bring into being a novel point of view, to create an element of unexpected pleasure, play, or surprise. Groups frequently refer to the way in which movement can generate energy. Something is happening; attention is all of a sudden aroused and focused. Under such circumstances, fortunate coincidences are prone to arise, casting in a completely new light some of those tense or 'dead-end' situations that had previously seemed desperately inextricable.

Chantal Nève Hanquet

Chantal Nève Hanquet's career in psychology has encompassed psychodrama, Jungian analysis and family therapy. She is a founding member, as well as treasurer, of the Federation of European Psychodrama Training Organisations (FEPTO) and a member of the International Association for Group Psychotherapy (IAGP) and the European Family Therapy Association (EFTA). She developed with Jacques Pluymaekers (trainer in family therapy), a psychodramatic method called "landscape genogram," as transgenerational approach which integrates metaphor with the play of psychodrama. In the course of 50 years' spent working with groups, Chantal has contributed actively to the spread of psychodrama and is now keen to pass on the fruits of her experience in this and related areas as inspiration to younger practitioners, through Belgium, France, Bulgaria, Italy, Switzerland and Greece.

You can contact her at *hanquetchantal@gmail.com*

Agathe Crespel

Agathe Crespel, also a psychologist, has for the past fifteen years facilitated groups in professional settings in the fields of education, social services, business, culture and health care. She has made extensive use of the Moreno action methods as a tool for supervision, brainstorming and the enhancement of creativity.

You can contact her at *agathecrespel111@gmail.com*

The authors, both members of the Centre for psychosociological training and intervention (CFIP), Belgium, have, through numerous congresses and workshops, extended their practice to Italy, France, Bulgaria, Greece, Switzerland, Sweden and California. They are the authors of the book *Faciliter l'intelligence collective* (Eyrolles 2018), offering action methods for coaches, consultants, trainers and leaders, and which is going to be published soon in english. Website: *www.arc-facilitation.com*

References

Ancelin Schüzenberger, A. (2008), *Le Psychodrame* (nouvelle édition). Petite Bibliothèque Payot.

Ancelin Schützenberger, A. (2011) *le Plaisir de Vivre*. Payot

Blatner, A. *Acting-In. Practical application of psychodramatic methods*, Springer Publishing Company, New York. 1999.

Böszörményi-Nagy, I & Krasner, BR; (2014) *Between Give and Take*, New York, Brunner Mazel, Routledge

Crespel, A., & Neve Hanquet, C (2018). *Faciliter l'intelligence collective: 35 fiches memo pour innover, co-construire, mettre en action, et accompagner le changement.* France: Eyrolles

Dayton, T. (2004) *The Living Stage: a step-by-step guide to Psychodrama, Sociometry and Group Therapy*, HCI, 60281

Laloux, F. (2014). *Reinventing Organisations—A guide to Creating Organisations Inspired by the Next Stage of Human Consciousness*, Nelson Parke.

Rizzato, M. (2014) *I Am Your Mirror: Mirror Neurons and Empathy*. Blossoming Books

Catastrophe Years: Reinsuring for Resilience

Valerie Monti Holland

2017 was a 'catastrophe year' in the global insurance industry. It recorded the second highest (2011 was number one) losses in history due to natural disasters. But the insurers had a back-up plan: 'For all the gloom, the 2017 losses were also proof of the resilience of the reinsurance industry. Insurers have long spread catastrophe risk by taking out reinsurance policies.'[1]

The phrase *catastrophe year* was introduced to me during a coaching session with an insurance professional who explained how proud he was that his team's financial health had not suffered as a result of the catastrophe year that was 2017 due to careful and vigilant planning. It struck me as a useful metaphor for our personal resilience and I asked him how it might relate to his mental fitness. What sorts of 'reinsurance' do/might/can we take out to help us when things derail us as they inevitably will?

The insurance industry does not prepare for a crisis just prior to it; they foresee the possibility and contribute in small and significant ways to offset it. We do this with pensions and savings accounts for our personal finances, even with diets and exercise for our physical health. How can we also do it as a way of strengthening our mental fitness?

As a sociodramatist who works as a facilitator, trainer, coach, teacher and supervisor, I found the concept of reinsurance to guard against catastrophe years particularly helpful when thinking about people's ability to cope and even thrive under pressure.

My portfolio is very broad and currently spans a spectrum of contexts from working on leadership skills with senior managers in the insurance industry

---

1 *The Economist*, 2018: *https://www.economist.com/finance-and-economics/2018/01/11/natural-disasters-made-2017-a-year-of-record-insurance-losses*

to helping young people with disabilities choose the next step in their life's journey. Since qualifying as a sociodramatist from the MPV-SAM school in the UK, I've been fortunate enough to learn about a number of social systems from a variety of perspectives, *e.g.* for three years I delivered a bullying and victim awareness program in an adult male prison followed by seven years as part of a research center examining and evaluating criminal justice issues often commissioned by the Ministry of Justice. Moving from the role of Solo Practitioner to Research Team Member afforded me a richer understanding of the many roles in this part of the system that focuses on reducing re-offending.

Morenean methods have proven to be effective in helping people to better understand the system in which they are working, living and playing in order to gather and galvanize support, both internally and externally, for tougher times; in other words, people have become more resilient through using them in my experience.

Resilience is a word bandied about far and wide. The message that we all need it and should have it inspires an air of guilt when we don't demonstrate it. It's as if we haven't done our homework.

My introduction to resilience as a part of a framework necessary for taking responsibility for oneself began in 2013 when I was invited to be a part of an interdisciplinary research team (Probst, Boylan, Nelson and Martin) investigating the early careers of social workers, radiation therapists and mathematics teachers — three careers that experience a high percentage of departures from the field within the first 5 years. The university funding the research was questioning whether there was anything they could incorporate into the training that people received to help them become more robust in the field and sustain their careers for longer.

My role was to facilitate 3 focus groups: one for students, one for educators and finally an event that combined both groups. According to Probst, *et al* (2014):

> Emergent themes indicate resilience is dependent on a complex interplay between individual and organizational (or situated) characteristics. The key concepts were:
>
> a. Transitions: new identity demands
> b. Organizational and systemic issues: being treated unfairly, team culture, difficult cases, feedback and support, and professional demands
> c. Personal characteristics: personal actions and personal qualities (accepting, confidence, forms of reflection, interpersonal skills, and positive psychology)
> d. Professionality: agency, commitment, moral purpose, and value.

Equating these four themes to Morenean methods, I would reframe them as:

- Transitions: new identity demands can be explored through role training
- Organizational and systemic issues — an opportunity to deploy sociometry
- Personal characteristics & Professionality can be addressed through sociodrama and psychodrama

The conclusion stated:

> "By addressing issues of resilience, course credibility is enhanced as a preparation for professional life, with a subsequent corollary of reduced attrition. The data from this study can be used to inform a creative curriculum to enhance professional resilience in students and early career professionals."[2]

While a 'creative curriculum' may help, the forces encouraging people to leave these important and stressful occupations had their roots in socioeconomic reality.

The repercussions of the financial collapse on 2008 are still being felt worldwide and the forecast that it would take ten years to recover now seems conservative indeed. In the UK, austerity has been the selected approach for handling the crisis. Public services were stripped back and structural shifts such as the movement of Public Health from the National Health Service to local authorities and city councils meant that a focus on performance as measured by targets became the normative determination of success.

As an external practitioner working with the children and young people's public health team in a city in northern England since 2000, I watched support grow for programs that promoted the increase in health outcomes with the apex occurring in 2008, the year of the crash. By that year, with colleagues from the Children & Young People's Public Health (CYP) team, we had created a resource and an action methods-based training program for anyone working with children and young people. Hundreds of people learned how to deliver The Flower 125 Health Programme throughout our region. The program was thriving alongside Healthy Schools,[3] a nationwide initiative designed to improve health standards and raise achievement of children and young people, setting minimum standards as goals for schools. Eventually Flower 125

---

2 Probst H., Boylan M., Nelson P., Martin R.(2014). Early career resilience: interdisciplinary insights to support professional education of Radiation Therapists. *Journal of Medical Imaging and Radiation Sciences*, 45 (4), 390–398.

3 *https://en.wikipedia.org/wiki/National_Healthy_Schools_Programme*

was mainstreamed into Healthy Schools as a training resource that could be accessed by anyone in the city.

We realized as a result of the feedback we received from regular review events that it was not the resource pack and the activities that we advocated but the model of delivery, the 'how', that was the most powerful. The model is simple to articulate (but perhaps not so simple to implement):

- Creating a safe enough environment in which young people can learn through a group agreement and clear boundaries outlining consequences of stepping outside of them
- Praise and positive feedback (verbal or through physical touch)
- The use of Icons (small cards with a picture on one side and the behavior and impact of that behavior written on the other) and small, tangible rewards
- Modeling pro-social behavior
- Ignoring petty behavior that is not a threat to the health and safety of an individual or the group

We found that when all of the elements of the model are followed, groups take more ownership and the health promotion work can take place more effectively. The model emerged as the most important factor of the program's success: the two-day training is an action-based learning space where delegates experience the model and how it is effective by demonstrating the activities. In true Morenean spirit, we show and involve rather than tell.

Both the training and the program itself are built upon the use of action methods and creating the space for sharing and learning. Helping facilitators identify and develop the role of Positive Seeker is one of the principle aims of the training. It enables them to give out the icons, even to a young person who has been exhibiting less than desired participation for most of the session. It is the very act of looking for a reason to give an icon that nurtures the Positive Seeker role and helps the facilitator to reward—frequently, consistently and authentically. The young people, many of whom are rarely rewarded in home and school settings, eventually respond and want to earn more icons, possibly the tangible gifts and most predominantly and importantly, the praise of the facilitators.

While any young person can benefit from being a part of the program, it was those young people who are most deprived who inspired its start in 1998: 26% of 16-year olds smoked, 63% worried about their future and 59% about their health at that time. The housing estate where the first session took place offered nothing for the young people to do and nowhere to go.[4] Flower 125 gave them attention, more attention than some of them had ever had in their lives.

---

4 *Flower 125 Health Programme Resource Pack*, 2nd edition

Some comments from the young people (feedback gathered by facilitators delivering the program in their settings):

- "I've learned more doing this than doing 4 years at secondary school."
- "I have learned a lot about myself and others."
- "I feel like I have been treated like a person."
- "We have a laugh but learn things."
- "You get a chance to share all your thoughts and opinions."

Emotional health and wellbeing was a chapter in the first and second editions of the resource pack. With the third, we realized that the entire program fosters emotional health and wellbeing while addressing a variety of health topics and it became the underpinning aim.

However, as the economic situation worsens and the NHS fights for survival, we are finding that time has become as squeezed as money, if not more. We are nearing 1000 people who have been trained to use the Flower 125 Health Programme but so many would return to their setting and find they were unable to deliver.

Increasingly, alarmingly, we had been hearing from practitioners that they were not delivering the entire program. They did not have the space, the time, the resources to do anything but take pieces of the program and use them to augment their practice. Even more concerning was the clear understanding that while these educators were expected to deliver training that encouraged wellbeing, their own emotional health and wellbeing was suffering and that suffering is largely ignored.

This is more than an observation on our part. Teachers are leaving the profession at a much faster rate than ever before. The 2013 research may have been my awakening to the need to offer more to educators but the trend had been gathering force for some time. An article from Richard Adams in *The Guardian* in April 2018[5] describes a frightening scenario:

> More than 80% of respondents to a question circulated by the National Education Union (NEU) said that they were thinking about other careers because of the long hours now required of classroom teachers.

> About 40% of those polled said they spent more than 21 hours a week working at home during evenings and weekends, to keep pace with the demands of their schools.

---

5 *https://www.theguardian.com/education/2018/apr/01/*
vast-majority-of-teachers-considered-quitting-in-past-year-poll

The NEU survey's findings tallied with those of a similar poll by the country's other major teaching union, the NASUWT. It found 65% of respondents said they had seriously considered leaving the profession in the past 12 months.

Teachers said the heavy workload was putting a strain on their health as well as on their marriage or families.

"I don't know how I can change how I work, I don't know how long I can maintain it, and the impact that it's having on my family is horrific," one teacher said in answer to the survey.

Another responded: "We are not trusted to get on and do our job. We are accountable at every level, which creates more stress and paperwork. We are exhausted, and great teachers are being driven out of the profession."

Disheartened by this news and with it the demise of initiatives focused on health and wellbeing such as the Flower 125 Health Programme, we considered an approach that would address the needs of the educators themselves, using the principles, techniques and learning from Flower 125. After all, modeling was a critical part of the program. How could young people learn about health and wellbeing from people whose own health and wellbeing was in question? What messages were we sending?

The sociodramatic question emerged: "How can we help foster the resilience of educators to enable them to model health and wellbeing for their pupils?"

"They'll bite your hand off." This was the response from a manager in the multi-agency team that supports schools when I asked if one of the secondary schools with whom she worked might host the project and recruit participants for it.

Encouraged by her reaction, we wrote a bid to fund the project, knowing that it would make it more attractive and feasible if the school did not need to find the money themselves. When we were awarded the funding, we planned the program with a senior staff member who was perfectly situated to help make it all happen. She was very keen as the rise of self-harm is an issue for many secondary schools, not only this high-performing school. This particular school also had several students who had attempted suicide in the past year, a growing trend nationally. These factors were key to the senior leader being open to addressing health and wellbeing at the staff level.

Additionally, the senior leader was passionate about making the group of 12 a combination of pastoral (support), teaching and administrative staff. As in so many organizations, people tended to work in silos, often with little understanding of (and sometimes a lack of respect for) those working in other parts of the organizations. Our enthusiasm to work with staff in different roles was shared by the senior leader and her colleague with whom we planned the course. At that time, we saw this as a potential pilot for future work that might create spaces for stressed school staff—a form of reinsurance against the demands of an overburdened system.

I had asked a psychodrama psychotherapist, Sarah Morley, who had a background in teaching, if she would co-facilitate with me and together we planned to deliver six sessions over the autumn term (which is roughly 12 weeks in the UK mainstream school system). The hope was to introduce a framework for exploring the system, ideally to allow new perspectives and thinking with regard to it. "Using sociodrama in education is the core of what it is all about. When Moreno began his work in sociodrama, he hoped he would change the world into a more responsive, humane and compassionate society through the use of sociodrama techniques. Sociodrama gives us practice for exploring issues in any number of subject areas for every age, without fear of the consequences of a wrong answer . . . "[6]

We also planned 'homework'—techniques from Flower 125 as well as simple strategies from resources such as the Human Givens manual on Dealing with Anxiety[7]—and we felt that having time in between to implement some of the methods and learn from them would be helpful.

As part of the preparation, I returned to the learning from the 2013 research project and heeded its advice to design a creative curriculum for the participants as we sought ways to 're-insure' the educators against the often powerful forces of the school system.

Our private, working title for the project was 'Oil Tanker Sinks—Teacher Not Involved', a response to the overwhelming responsibility placed on the shoulders of school staff. In reality, the project was called 'Supporting Ourselves, Supporting Each Other'.

The six sessions would last 90 minutes each, take place after school with a mixture of 12 participants from administrative, pastoral and teaching roles and would include the senior staff member who had accepted our offer and approved the plan:

1. Mapping out the system: helping people to recognize the bigger picture through sociometric mapping
2. Identifying Fear-Based Thinking: exploring the messages that school staff receive that lead to anxiety and stress in the workplace.
3. Mistakes and Failures: redefining school as a place where staff can experiment, learn and reflect.

---

6 Sternberg and Garcia, 2000
7 Griffin and Tyrrell, 2007

4. Trusting Ourselves and Each Other: fostering a healthier environment for everyone
5. The Pressure Cooker: keeping yourself sane in a pressured environment
6. Sustainable Strategies to Move Forward: evaluating and consolidating our learning and next steps

That was the plan. It was ambitious . . . and immediately altered 15 minutes into the first session.

The teaching staff who had been invited to attend by the senior leader were told (by whom we were never certain) that they were not 'allowed' to attend. The senior leader was also not permitted to participate in the course. She delivered this news in person after which we did not see her again. (We heard a few weeks later that she was on sick leave and before the end of the course, she had left the school for a position elsewhere.) We did not know a great deal about the executive leadership of this school other than the fact that it is an academy, as nearly every secondary school in the city is, a legacy of the coalition followed by the Conservative government educational policy.

The six people who showed up at the first session—a mixture of pastoral and administrative staff—did not understand that this was a group for them rather than a training to be given to the students. "They've never offered anything that was just for us" was one response that seemed to summarize the sentiments of everyone else.

We quickly pointed out that while this was a forum for them to bolster their own health and wellbeing, a majority of the techniques were from the Flower 125 Health Programme, a resource for use with students. By learning and practicing these techniques in this environment, they could more effectively employ them with their students. This seemed to help people to justify their participation.

The miscommunication meant a slower, more gentle warm up for the group. Warming up to a focus on themselves rather than the students was the most difficult. One person was so startled by this news that he was not able to engage and did not return to future sessions. Our intention to map out the system had to be shelved on that first meeting and we concentrated on building the group to create as safe a space as possible in the awkward circumstances.

Each session was structured to begin with a check in, warm up prior to an enactment usually in the form of a game (that they could use with their young people!) and then a sharing and processing to end. We delivered using a mixture of action methods such as continua, timelines to explore the future, sociometry to map the system of the school and sociodrama including role reversal and doubling to encourage empathy and hear alternative voices. These were the creative techniques we had planned to use; we just needed to be flexible and spontaneous with the group and their warm up to these activities, ever mindful of the discomfort many still felt even into the third session.

The sculpture was particularly effective, as it entailed a gentle mode of movement and seemed different from traditional role play, the thought of which activated anxiety among most group members. Sculpting facilitates an embodied sharing of experience. It was powerful especially when the group demonstrated the conflict of home life and responsibilities versus work demands. 'Family Comes First' was one of the closing statements from the group. The implication was that this was not the culture of this school. There was a sense that they feel judged when they need to leave work for a problem at home and that they might be letting their colleagues down.

Another week, when we explored some continua related to our theme, Making Mistakes, the group seemed resistant and the progress in trust we felt we may have gained the week before was not immediately available. We were already aware that this group of people is harder on themselves than they are on others. There was still 'fear of the consequences of a wrong' (or too revealing?) point of view.

This was highlighted by the nervousness in the room when we asked how mistakes were tolerated by the school, asking them to stand on an imaginary line to indicate very tolerant or not at all. It emerged that according to this group of people, mistakes could mean serious harm, perhaps even death, for students who were suffering with their mental health. Tolerance of any mistake was equated with a lack of care and professionalism. Therefore, reframing mistakes, albeit less serious ones, was a necessary step in recognizing personal characteristics required to be a successful and resilient educator.

We mapped the system of the school putting 'Mary', a composite charac- ter we had invented with the group, at the center. The group was invited to place down objects or post-it notes to mark the different people in — as well as aspects of — Mary's environment. This also seemed to provoke resistance and perhaps trepidation that they might be seen to be criticizing or complaining. We finished with a brief vignette inspired by some of the pressures on Mary which became apparent from the mapping exercise.

People went on to talk about how fearful they were, especially if things erupted on a Friday and they were left to worry over the weekend. As there is no formal supervision (space for reflection as opposed to line management) for school staff, this made it alarmingly clear just what level of stress they could be under when they were meant to be decompressing from a week of work. This is in turn had an impact on their loved ones with whom they might be spending leisure time instead of fretting about a troubled student.

Taking advantage of the time to play and think more creatively outside of the rigidity of the system was the most challenging for them. It was frivolous to think of oneself; being tough and handling the most difficult cases was a badge of honor.

Additionally, this group seemed to expect to have less agency. Their positions in the school, while discrete and important, were nonetheless low in the hierarchy. Things were done to them rather than having the freedom of choosing one's own actions and taking responsibility for them. While they could control their interactions with the students on their case load, the rest of the system may have seemed beyond their control and outside of their remit.

They managed to get from one school holiday to the next with very little in between to lighten the load, offer relief or alleviate stress. Therefore, this course was completely outside of the culture and by the end of it, there was a sense that it was like a secret club—outside of hours, in a quiet part of the building, discovered by a select few.

Little wonder that so many people leave schools as indicated by The Guardian article (and other research). With no reserves in the 'bank', any catastrophe—even a minor one—would completely drain a person of any capital.

On the final session we created the Ideal School, an invented reality where anything was possible: school began at 10:00 after a coffee at their own café. They could select the first place they went each day whether it be a meditation room, small classes in academic subjects, a place to speak with someone if they had questions or just needed to unload. Half the group played the students and the other half were staff. We all revelled in this imaginary place that no one would dread on a Monday morning.

Sarah and I had envisioned that the handout with strategies for stress management which we gave out at the first session would be deployed in between the sessions. It was received rather tepidly, perhaps because the notion that they needed help of any sort was an embarrassment or a sign of weakness. We do know that people used the techniques:

> "Thank you for your time and energy that you gave myself and my colleagues in last term's evening sessions. I was wondering if you had the 'script' for the relaxation practice that I could have please so that I can introduce it within the sessions with the children within the Intervention groups I run? We are spending 1hr on Relaxation next week; I have introduced them to the idea already and they have all asked if we could spend more time on it. The children are Y7 (12 year olds) and really enjoyed the quiet time within a busy day . . . one student even fell asleep the first time he tried it!"

One participant also shared that she used the breathing techniques for herself when things felt overwhelming. She would retreat into the staff toilet to get some private space in order to breathe and found that just knowing she could do that made things more manageable.

At the end of the first session we gave out reflection sheets to gather feedback. When we asked for them back at the beginning of the next session, the group seemed confused. They thought it was just for the end of the course. This was a clash of cultures indeed. Taking time to integrate any learning as we proceeded was a tenet of the Flower 125 team and each session is evaluated by both students and facilitators, both in the training and on the courses with young people. Time to think, for just a moment, is critical to stepping off the treadmill. No one says it better than Nancy Kline: "To take time to think is to gain time to live."[8] We claimed that time at the end of the sessions with short meditations. It is evaluative and reflective mechanisms that are much more likely to be squeezed out of a school timetable where time is even more rare than cash.

But it is those short, regular things that make the difference over time. The research on the effects of meditation practiced over a consistent period of time strongly point to the need to find even a little bit of space — in the staff loo if necessary! — and be with yourself. After this, you can be capable of going out there to be with everyone else in a role that you've made your own, even if it was assigned to you in the beginning. Introducing this concept as not being selfish but one that better prepares you for the task ahead and gives you the wherewithal to help others is the essence of Supporting Ourselves, Supporting Each Other. I'm not certain we articulated that as clearly, thus the need for reflection!

We cannot be sure what impact the program had, if any. In the end, we received two forms back from the 11 people who had participated, despite repeated requests. We expected about 6 given the level of energy and consistent attendance of the core group. We do know that by that last session in December, people were limping home to the finishing line of the term. They had expressed appreciation for the course repeatedly and described how they felt more relaxed upon leaving than they had entering the room. A more in-depth evaluation was not part of this culture.

It is one example, one short and contained piece of work in a complex and often chaotic system and I cannot draw any conclusions from it. For me, it asked far more questions than supplied answers: Where is the educational system headed? How much more can staff in schools handle? What impact will this have on the young people? What are we doing to reverse the trend of self-harm and suicide among young people?[9]

---

8 Kline, 1999

9 *https://www.mentalhealth.org.uk/statistics/mental-health-statistics-suicide*

We met incredibly dedicated and competent professionals who stepped far outside of their comfort zones to play and think for a short time. As the beginning of an intentional journey to foster resilience, it might have been a springboard. But the usefulness of one intervention that is not an accepted and encouraged part of a wider system may be a minor amusement or even a disruptive force. Having the inadequacies of a system on which people are dependent and are still a part of laid bare might exacerbate feelings of hopelessness or even lead people to despair. We know the methods are powerful and we must use them wisely and well.

Moreno's vision that sociodrama and its techniques can nurture compassion and creativity is one that I share. The gift of sociometry, seeing the bigger picture of an organization in which one is involved, allows the helicopter view that is so valuable in times of stress or busyness. It can offer insight and inspire or affirm action. And after looking at the situation from a meta-view, flying back into it, taking one's role up with renewed vigor can be the difference between loving one's path and barely participating as a protagonist in one's own life.

Through a career of more than two decades, I have found ways of caring for myself that have enabled me to weather the catastrophes of political upheaval and economic downturn. These are not event-based nor particularly time-consuming. They are short, regular practices that work for me: yoga, meditation, walking in nature, connecting to people. Sleeping and eating well are a conscious part of this and gratitude on a daily basis is *de rigueur*. Supervision is an absolute necessity for me — an advantage that those working in schools do not have.

I have been blessed. The work developing the Flower 125 Health Programme over the last 18 years has heightened the awareness of all aspects of health for me and this work has impacted on me in a such a way that often I can embody these principles and model them in my world. It is in these encounters with other worlds that I am able to learn about the trends, the movements and the pain that others suffer. It is understanding these that helps me to hold an appropriate, safe enough space for the work of others to start.

Valerie Monti Holland

Valerie Monti Holland is a facilitator, trainer, mentor and coach. Following her M.A. in Applied Theatre (University of Manchester) and a diploma in Sociodrama and Action Methods, Valerie has developed a portfolio working in the UK, the US and across Europe using these creative and dynamic methods to enable greater team cohesion, candid communication and embodied leadership development in the public, private and voluntary sectors.

As a co-founder of the Flower 125 Health Programme, she and the team have trained thousands of professionals who work with young people to nurture their emotional and physical well being. Training is available more widely—please see the website for information on how to bring this award-winning programme to your setting. (*www.flower125.co.uk*)

Valerie lives on the edge of the Peak District in England where she cycles, runs and walks balanced by a lifetime passion for yoga. She is the proud and grateful mother of a son and a daughter. Contact her at *val@leftluggagetraining.co.uk*

References

Probst H., Boylan M., Nelson P., Martin R.(2014). Early career resilience: interdisciplinary insights to support professional education of Radiation Therapists. *Journal of Medical Imaging and Radiation Sciences*, 45 (4), 390–398.

The Flower 125 Health Programme: *www.flower125.co.uk*

Roberts, J. and Holland, V.M. *The Flower 125 Health Programme Resource Pack, 2nd edition*, p.16 (unpublished)

Morgan, C., Webb, R.T., Carr M.J., Kontopantelis, E., Green J., Chew-Graham, C.A., Kapur, N., Ashcroft D.M. Incidence, clinical management, and mortality risk following self harm among children and adolescents: cohort study in primary care *BMJ* 2017; 359 doi: *https://doi.org/10.1136/bmj.j4351* (Published 18 October 2017)

Sternberg P. and Garcia A. (2000) *Who's in Your Shoes?* (2nd ed.) Westport, Connecticut & London: Praeger.

Griffin J. and Tyrrell I. with Winn D. (2007) *How to Master Anxiety* (Essential Help in Troubled Times—The Human Givens Approach) Chalvington, East Sussex: HG Publishing.

Kline N. (1999) *Time to Think: Listening to Ignite the Human Mind* London: Ward Lock.

Where The Rubber Hits The Road

Vignettes From The Application of Morenian Methods When Coaching In Organizations

Jenny Postlethwaite

My education in the use of JL Moreno's psychodramatic methods has been anchored in the production of "classic" psychodrama. There's a group, a group leader/producer, a stage. From a period of warm up a protagonist emerges. An enactment of some sort begins, auxiliaries and audience engage. The action is followed by integrative sharing. The work is often deeply personal and, given the nature of the method, involves at least some degree of feeling and emotional expression.

As a scholar of the method I have found much of the focus in the literature relates to its application in the therapeutic sphere. Similarly, many of my psychodrama professional association colleagues practice in the therapeutic field, where free ranging group work is a well recognized and commonly utilized modality.

By contrast, the world in which I professionally practice—individual, team and group coaching in organizations—is far less familiar or comfortable with such relational approaches. It is a world generally characterized by a valuing of cognition and logic over feeling, and impersonal professional interaction over relational expression.

So, when initially considering for myself how to apply Morenian methods in my work, I had two hurdles to clear. The first was to get myself comfortable with transposing the method into a non-therapeutic environment and context. The second, to do so in a way that would be adequately received by an unfamiliar and potentially unwelcoming audience.

For the first hurdle, Moreno himself provided my inspiration, in the opening words of his opus *Who Shall Survive*. '*A truly therapeutic procedure cannot have less an object than the whole of mankind.*'[1] Within the context of 'the whole of mankind' I found a freedom, a license and indeed an encouragement, to apply the method in my non-therapeutic context.

In practice, my organizational client base is broad. I work with people at all organizational levels, from naive workplace ingénue to seasoned CEO; with individuals and with groups; with front line teams and with corporate executives; with those transitioning through management and leadership; with people eager for more influence and with those for whom 'bosses' are the 'enemy'; with under-performers and with high achievers.

When it came to seeking adequacy in practical application of Morenian methods across such a diverse population, the rubber hit the road for me through bold experimentation.

The anecdotes which follow provide some snapshots, vignettes of my experience with this endeavor. I offer them not as a lesson in "how to," but rather in the spirit of "what can be," warming us all up to our spontaneity and creativity as practitioners.

Starting with two anecdotes in which I am the protagonist, I then move on to my work with groups and with individuals. Names and details have been changed to protect the confidentiality of those involved.

Spontaneity Starts At Home

A professional coach is expected, in partnership with their client, to focus on defining and achieving goals, to deliver results, to 'maximize the client's potential'.

Pursuit of the client's desired outcome—skill development, behavior change, role transition, workplace conflict or other problem resolution, confidence building or whatever other performance enhancement focus it may have—is the anchoring purpose, particularly so when working in an organizational context.

To be effective in this pursuit the coach is expected and required to access a range of core competencies—to set a foundation and build relationship with their client, and to communicate effectively in order to facilitate learning and results.[2]

In practice, the coaching dynamic is typically verbal and cognitive, characterized by a cycle of question and answer between the coach and their client. Indeed, I was taught from very early in my professional training as a coach,

---

1 Moreno, 1993:3
2 International Coach Federation Core Competencies: *https://www.coachfederation.org/credential/landing.cfm?ItemNumber=2206*

that the basic skill of a master coach is their ability to ask questions. Powerful questions.

Discovering and then incorporating Moreno's philosophies and action methods into my coaching practice put an impactful new slant on this picture for me.

You Don't Ask Many Questions Do You?

I am here with Barney, telling him how excited I am to have just signed up for psychodrama training. I am almost completely naive in the field, having attended only a single workshop before deciding to take the plunge as a trainee. Barney, on the other hand, is an experienced psychodrama practitioner, but we also have something in common—like me he is an organizational coach. He is to be my supervisor, and this is our first one on one session together.

We talk about how our supervision will work, my existing coaching practice, what my interest is in psychodrama and what I am hoping for in my development as a practitioner. There is a fruit bowl on the table, full of passionfruit, which somehow or other make their way out of the bowl and onto the table as auxiliaries to our conversation. My emotions are more to the fore than usual. I am enthused, excited, worried about my naivety and lack of knowledge, yet happy and hopeful.

In the midst of the session I suddenly wake up to the dynamic between Barney and I, and to how he has been proceeding. I look at him, puzzled, head tilted to one side, eyes narrowed.

> **Jenny:** Gee, you don't ask many questions, do you?
>
> **Barney:** No.
>
> **Jenny:** You make lots of statements.
>
> **Barney:** Yes.

Without even realizing it I've just received my first lesson in the use of doubling and mirroring. It is a powerful personal experience which immediately heightens my appreciation of a different way—a less question and answer centric way—in which I might approach a coaching conversation.

In this first session with Barney my spontaneity is flowing and I have experienced and taken into my being the powerful difference between being doubled for affect . . .

> **Barney:** It's exciting and enlivening to be a trainee.
>
> **Jenny:** Yes!!!!!!

and being questioned . . . *How is it, being a trainee?* . . . pause for thinking . . . *Well, it's exciting.*

My Purpose?

It's supervision time, and I am here again with Barney. We are discussing two coaching clients, Alan and Karl, that I am experiencing some difficulty with.

> **Jenny:** They have both been sent to me by their boss to be "fixed." He's been unable to clearly articulate to them what he is dissatisfied with, so he's sent them to me instead! He wants me to "assess" them and come up with goals for their coaching. (Barney raises one eyebrow.)

> **Jenny:** Alan and Karl aren't committed to doing what it takes. I'm the one stuck holding the baby!

> **Barney:** What is your purpose with them?

> **Jenny:** My purpose?

> **Barney:** Yes, your purpose. The purpose that anchors your warm up.

> **Jenny:** Oh.

His question challenges me to separate myself from the goals of the coaching and to focus on my own warm up. After some discussion I arrive at a purpose for myself. Stepping back from coaching's goal centric focus, I instead take inspiration from Moreno's Canon of Creativity.[3]

> **Jenny:** My purpose is to warm my clients up to spontaneity, to enable their adequate functioning in their world.

This purpose warms me up to my own being, as well as to that of my client. I like that it inherently mirrors the relational nature of our coaching — I must first be able to access my own spontaneity, in order to support my client to access theirs. It is a crucial prerequisite and a vitalizing complement to our goal oriented work.

Working with Groups

My application of action methods with groups in organizations has a sociodramatic focus.

"Moreno's methodologies inherently engage the group as the vehicle for change. In psychodramatic work the group is engaged in service of an individual protagonist; other group members in turn benefit from their involvement and experience. However, Moreno identified the limitations of psychodrama in dealing with collective issues, and in response created sociodrama as a vehicle

---

3 Moreno, 1993:11–20

to 'focus its dramatic eye upon the collective factors.' In an organizational context it is the interests and issues of the group, the team as a whole, which is paramount. As such, a sociodramatic approach is advantageous as 'the true subject of a sociodrama is the group. . . . it is the group as a whole that has to be put on the stage to work out its problem.'"[4]

The Stage As An Enabling Structure

It is my first session working with this executive management group of twelve men. For a long period they have been operating as independents, disconnected from one another. Their lack of collaboration has diminished the effectiveness of their organization. My brief is to develop their cohesiveness as a leadership team. They are used to engaging across a meeting table, or in some other formal environment, where the space is dominated by furniture. Power and status is important to them. Their culture is highly competitive and authority focused.

I have set our work room with no furniture in it other than an arc of chairs. My intention is to create an open space between individuals, a stage on which we can interact and create without physical obstacles.

As each participant arrives and enters the room, I observe his reaction. Most do a very visible double take, pausing mid step, unsure of the open space and where to place themselves in the absence of a table.

The signal is clear for everyone that this gathering will be a different experience for them. Holding my nerve and leadership in the face of their initial discomfort, we go on to have a productive day of discussion and sociodramatic exploration.

During one session we are exploring how the various departments managed by each executive are interacting with each other. There are objects scattered about the stage, representing the departments, and several of the executives are actively engaged in tweaking their position in relation to one another. One man is on his knees on the floor, fine tuning the way each object is facing. Others are giving helpful directions from their seats—*"a little more to the left, yes that's it."*

Their mood is light and playful—a few of the objects they are working with are children's toys and this is generating a little amusement—but at the same time the group members are focused intently on their task, interested and intrigued by what they are producing on the stage.

I am struck, as I observe from the edge of the space, how very different the quality of this interaction is from their typical meetings. They are relaxed with each other and there is no sign in this moment of their usual power and authority centric behaviors. Setting the stage has provided an enabling structure for a different quality of engagement, warming them up to spontaneity.

---

4 Postlethwaite, 2015:6. The source text contains references for the Moreno quotes.

Another moment from the day stands out for me in relation to the simplicity and elegance of utilizing action methods in practice. We are all seated and I am encouraging the men to express themselves to each other across the group, as to how they perceive they have been functioning as a team. I sense that one man in particular, although participating in the discussion, seems to be holding back, so I rise from my seat and move behind his right shoulder.

> **Jenny:** I am going to say something that might fit here for you. If it's not right just ignore me. If it does feel right for you then you can pick it up.

I make a couple of doubling statements and his demeanor lifts noticeably. He proceeds to express himself in a more forthright manner. The man to whom he is speaking listens closely, then sits very still, not speaking. I move around behind the listener and double again.

> **Jenny:** I'm surprised by what you've said. I don't know what to say in response.

It is enough to get him started and the conversation deepens to a new level. This small amount of judicious doubling, to bring out what is not being said, provides a springboard to more open expression, and has a significant impact on the quality of the ensuing discussion.

Cue Action!

In my experience, work groups in organizations often default to discussion and story telling. Their communication norm is language dependent and heavily cognitive. By contrast, a psychodramatic approach values action, concretisation, kinesthetic and spatial intelligence and an integrative experience of thinking, feeling and acting.

So, when working with organization groups I am listening for, within the context of my brief and purpose, produce-able action cues.

Sacred Cows

I am working with a senior management team as they discuss a vexed issue of resource allocation. They want to branch out with some new products but feel constrained and frustrated by "the system." The discussion has become bogged down in detail. The group's spontaneity is low.

> **Hilary:** (Shoulders slumped forward) It's all too hard.

> **David:** There are so many sacred cows.

> (*Others nod their heads in agreement.*)

Jenny: Sacred cows, eh? Where are they? (Looking around)
Let's have a look at them.

I invite David to join me on the stage and we proceed to concretise the sacred cows. One by one, group members are enlisted as auxiliary cows. Each auxiliary becomes more animated and playful as they enact their particular "sacredness." We end up with ten cows in all. They make for a noisy herd, physically imposing, each looking confident of their sacred standing in the system. David stands looking at the herd, shakes his head and then moves to sit down. His initial spontaneity has ebbed in the face of the herd.

Jenny: Hang on there David. The herd seems a bit restless.
Maybe we need a vet to check them out. How about you be
the vet?

David accepts the invitation and tentatively proceeds to inspect each of the cows. The cows are playful, some resisting the vet's examination, others happily raising their feet for a hoof inspection. The vet interacts with each cow and, with a little direction from me, interviews each cow to explore its relative health in organizational terms. How fat is it? That is, how big an obstacle is it in actuality. Can it be put out to pasture? That is, can we afford to ignore it. And so forth.

By the end of the veterinary inspection the cows have been divided into different paddocks, according to the nature and extent of their constraining impact on new product development. The energy level in the group is high. They return to their discussion with rekindled spontaneity and a purposeful focus on how to move ahead with their product development objectives.

The Chasm

Two dozen senior and middle managers are gathered for a team development workshop. I am aware, through previous work in their organization, that there is a disjoint between the most senior management group and the next layer of managers. This disjoint is an open secret in the organization, oft whispered of in the corridors and behind closed doors. There is some individual variation of perspectives within the two sub-groups, but in general the senior managers are puzzled and perturbed by the dynamic, and the second layer are frustrated and angry, feeling they have been let down by the senior leaders.

My brief for the day is to create an environment in which this issue is publicly and jointly discussable.

We are in a large room, some ten meters square, with the group sitting in a wide arc of chairs. The discussion has been progressing in fits and starts. Only a handful of people have expressed themselves, mainly those individuals with the most forceful views, who typically are also the dominant influencers in the sub-groups. The mood in the group in this moment is one of awkwardness and simmering agitation. Peter, one of the senior managers, speaks up.

> **Peter:** It feels like there is a chasm between us. I don't understand it, we've come here today and people aren't saying what they really think and . . .

Rather than let him launch into a potentially long winded exposition I interrupt and move to produce the immediacy of what he is expressing.

> **Jenny:** Peter how about you show us rather than tell us. Use this space (pointing to the stage). Show us how big or small the chasm feels for you.

The group laughs nervously, teasing Peter—*"That'll teach you to speak up"* and *"Now you're on the spot, ha, ha"*—but Peter, nothing if not courageous, steps onto the stage, accepting the invitation to concretise the chasm. He does this by placing two objects, one on either side of the room, some ten meters distant, just about as far apart as they can physically be. One object is for the senior managers and the other represents the second layer of managers. Group members are watching Peter closely as he moves about on the stage.

> **Jenny:** That feels right for you?
>
> **Peter:** Yes.
>
> **Jenny:** It's a *big* chasm.
>
> **Peter:** Yes

We both sigh audibly. The emotional mood has shifted.

> **Jenny:** I wonder how it is for others.
>
> **Peter:** Me too.
>
> **Jenny:** Okay, let's find out.

All group members are invited to place themselves somewhere along the continuum of the chasm, according to how big or small they personally experience it. The spread of bodies is surprisingly large, from those in full agreement with Peter, to those who barely experience a gap. I invite the individuals to share, first with their neighbors and subsequently with the full group, what led them to stand where they are and what is their actual experience of the dynamic between the two sub-groups.

Producing Peter's chasm has unlocked the door to public discussion of the group's dynamics. And requiring each person to take a stand on the chasm continuum has set an expectation and norm of active individual involvement. There are no whispering spectators in this production, only participants.

During the course of the day much ends up being expressed within and between the subgroups and across a broad emotional spectrum. There are moments of conflict, appreciation, surprise, panic, anger, sadness, helplessness, dissatisfaction and delight.

This day was the first step in a developmental journey for the group, which still continues, years later. It was an impactful kick start which has subsequently entered the folklore of the organization. "*Hey, remember the day we did the chasm?*"

Reverse Roles with the Child

The enactment, a scene from the everyday work life of group members, is in full swing.

They are nurses and practice managers from a private health organization and we are gathered for a training day in emotional intelligence (EI). As part of teaching them about the EI skill of Understanding (of the blends, causes and transitions of emotion over time), I have asked them to set a scene of an everyday situation which they struggle with. They nominate "working with difficult doctors."

So here we are. There is a young child, laying on a gurney in a doctor's surgery. The child is here to have a minor surgical procedure. On one side of the gurney is the doctor and on the other side is the assisting nurse. The child's mother is sitting off to one side.

In the surplus reality of this enactment, the participants are expressing more fully the tension which is felt but not voiced in their real life situation. The nurse is annoyed and frustrated with the doctor, who isn't following what she believes is the correct procedure. They are arguing with each other. The mother gets increasingly alarmed, but is unsure about how to intervene to comfort and protect her child in the midst of the tension. The child lays, body tense and stiff, looking anxiously from one to the other of the adults.

It is a scene all the group members claim familiarity with and this is visible in the fullness with which they take up their roles. I role reverse the various auxiliaries at different points, as the tension between the doctor and nurse continues to escalate.

The experience of taking up and extending the roles of the mother and child is significant, both for the auxiliaries directly involved and for the rest of the group watching from the edge of their seats in the audience. In the sharing following the enactment, it is the mother and child that are most referred to.

> **Group Member A:** I was thinking about it only in terms of the doctor being the problem. I hadn't thought about how stressful it was for the child and mother. She looked so helpless, so

caught in the headlights, worried but not knowing how to stop it.

Group Member B: The poor child was so scared. The doctor and nurse didn't even notice!!

Group Member C: We were so caught up in our own frustration we forgot about the child.

They are deeply impacted by the enactment and reflective as to what they have been contributing to the dynamic and how they want things to be different in the future. The enactment, and particularly the role reversing, has awakened a new system awareness for them and rekindled their natural empathy in relation to all characters in the scene.

I Had No Idea You Felt Like That

The group of eight men in front of me has only recently been formed. They are an amalgamation of two separate executive groups, originally from different arms of their corporation. This new group has been charged with responsibility for the entire organization and our purpose here today is to begin the work of knitting them into an effective leadership team.

All the individuals know each other to some extent, but they are not practiced in working collaboratively together toward a common purpose. There is a history of competition and friction between some of them, and so my initial focus has been on exploring the degree of trust present and their preparedness to be vulnerable with one another.

The conversation in the group is feeling somehow peculiar to me in the moment, as if the individuals are speaking different languages at one another and yet assuming a shared understanding of what they are expressing and hearing. I decide to move to action, producing aspects of the group's sociometry.

We have plenty of space in the room to work with and I set out a continuum—*to what extent am I confident that the group will not use or hold my weaknesses and mistakes against me.* In other words, *how comfortable am I showing my vulnerabilities in this group?* The group readily responds to my invitation, taking up positions along the continuum.

Brett stands alone toward the 'very uncomfortable' end, some three metres distant from the next closest person. Michael is also standing alone, at the other pole, 'completely comfortable'. The rest of the group is clustered together on the 'comfortable' side of the midway point.

I invite people to express themselves. Michael speaks first, talking about his confidence in dealing with the others and praising them as an open and trustworthy group. He doesn't understand why the others aren't standing with him. James, from the middle of the cluster, responds to Michael, reminding him of some instances of past conflict. Michael counters with stories of their past successes.

So far, the pattern of not quite hearing one another is still in play. And the attention has all been toward the top end of the continuum—no one has addressed Brett and neither has he spoken. It seems that they are playing it safe, a restrictive response to the provocation of the continuum. I invite Brett, who is standing stiffly, arms folded tightly across his chest, to speak.

> **Brett :** I don't feel confident at all. I see what happens. We aren't straight with each other, we complain about each other behind backs, not face to face. I don't speak my mind because I don't trust that you won't give me a hard time.

He stops abruptly, head slightly bowed but eyes fixed firmly on the rest of the group. They appear shocked, momentarily dumbstruck. Brett's openness and preparedness to be vulnerable in this moment, despite the relational risk, has cut through the fog of safety, inviting others to a more frank exchange of views. Alan, the recently appointed leader of the team, finally breaks the silence, speaking quietly but surely across the gap to Brett.

> **Alan :** I had no idea you felt that way. (*He appears genuinely puzzled and perturbed by what Brett has said.*) We need to talk more about this. (*Taking a couple of small steps toward Brett as he speaks.*)

In this crucial moment Brett has not been rejected. Alan has accepted and moved toward him. They continue talking and others progressively join their conversation. The tone is now significantly changed, as group members work at understanding Brett's perspective and at being more frank in their own expression. "*Well now that you mention it . . . ..*" The continuum is also progressively reforming itself, its center of gravity shifting down to below the midpoint. Group members reflect openly that this now feels a 'truer' picture for them of their existing relations.

Concretising group members' perspectives on trust and vulnerability—a symbol of the quality of their relationships—has surfaced a lot of unstated assumptions of common thinking. It has made the friction that was unspoken and invisible suddenly visible and discussable. This is the beginning of a new path for this team. From the seed of this simple sociometric production they have subsequently gone on to become a tight knit, highly effective leadership team.

Working with Individuals

When coaching an individual there is obviously no group present to draw on as a resource in applying action methods in the classic style. However, the absence of a group certainly doesn't preclude utilizing Moreno's philosophies and methods in one on one coaching practice.

No, You Can't Take That Spoon!

Helena and I are well into our coaching session. We are sitting in a café, discussing a difficult conflict she is wrestling with at work. The conflict is complex and fraught and Helena is emotionally agitated as she shares her story with me.

"How about you set this out on the table here," I suggest. *"Choose something to be you."* "Ok," she replies, choosing a salt shaker and placing it in the middle of the table. Other objects are progressively added to the scene — the pepper, a coffee cup, sugar dispenser, her purse, a pen — representing various characters and aspects of the situation.

Setting out her story is providing Helena with a fresh perspective. We have effectively stepped up into the mirror position of Moreno's balcony. Whilst she is still full of feeling, her thinking has engaged, providing her with a more integrated sense of her situation.

Key to the issue is the relationship between Helena and her boss. He is concretised in the scene as a teaspoon. Although we are working only with the basic objects available to hand on the café table, concretising the situation has been effective in deepening Helena's warm up and fueling her spontaneity. She is moving the teaspoon and salt shaker around the table exploring different options for what she might do to resolve the issue.

We are both leaning forward, fully involved with the concretised scene, when a waitress appears and reaches out to begin clearing the table. She sees only our dirty cups and plates, not the living scene in which Helena is immersed.

"No!!" exclaims Helena. "You can't take that spoon. That's my boss!!"

Name That Role

It is our first coaching session together and Yvette is looking for new ways of responding to work colleagues she is clashing with.

> **Yvette:** I get so frustrated with them. I've been made responsible for this project but I haven't been given any authority over them. We have completely different ideas about the right things to do and we just keep butting heads. I turn into a goat!

We talk further and it becomes evident that part of her difficulty lays in an ethical clash with her colleagues. She is disturbed by what she sees as their unethical decision making, but feels helpless.

> **Yvette:** The only thing I could do is go to the boss and dob them in, like a snitching do-gooder.

Using the objects we have to hand, Yvette sets out the situation on the table in front of us and as she does so her frustration with the questionable ethics of her colleagues continues to be expressed.

> **Yvette:** I become a demented crusader. (Waving her arm above her head, as if wielding a mighty sword.) I want a public hanging!! Nothing else will suffice!!

Yvette's stuckness and lack of spontaneity is clearly evident. She is caught in a series of coping roles, moving against her colleagues. These roles are evident in her language and her physical movement and I move to mirror them for her by highlighting some of her expressions.

I continue on, providing a simple overview of the concept of a role and how roles can be categorized as coping or progressive.[5] She is attentive and interested in what I am describing, quickly catching on, and is now re-hearing the story she has just shared with new ears. We explore this together, beginning with Yvette naming some of her roles for herself.

She settles on Block-Headed Goat, Powerless Goody Two Shoes, Righteous Judge and, her favourite, Demented Crusader. She is visibly pleased with the names she has chosen. Amused and softer in her being, her spontaneity has lifted. Having her experience synthesized through these simple metaphors, which she readily identifies with, opens the door to a deeper exploration of Yvette's actual experience—the quality of her thinking and feeling—in the moments when she engages with her colleagues.

Seizing on her elevated spontaneity, our focus returns to Yvette's original goal—developing new responses, new roles from which to interact with her colleagues.

> **Jenny:** If you weren't a block headed goat, who would you be?

> **Yvette:** Hmmmm. I'd be a lyrebird.

She goes on, warming up to the role qualities of a lyrebird which appeal to her, but then she has a new idea.

> **Yvette:** I want to be Galadriel!! (the Elven leader from JRR Tolkien's Lord of the Rings)

> **Jenny:** Wow! What qualities of Galadriel's would help you here?

> **Yvette:** She is calm . . . Wise . . . Strong and steady . . . Very fair and just . . . Full of grace . . . She sheds light on things.

---

5   Clayton, L (1982) The Use Of The Cultural Atom To Record Personality Change In Individual Psychotherapy. In *Journal of Group Psychotherapy, Psychodrama and Sociometry*, 35. Heldref Publications New York

Yvette continues, warming up further to developing aspects of this role for herself. Our session concludes with a clean statement of her new intent.

Yvette: It's time for my demented crusader to take a back seat.

Our shared adoption of a role development mindset has been effective in this coaching session and provides a reliable platform for fostering Yvette's spontaneity in all our subsequent work.

I Can See Straight Through It

Working in action demands a practitioner's attention to the phenomenology of the here and now moment. Working with *what is*, in the real time here and now, provides a rich complement to working with a client's story.

Vi, a supervision client, is telling me about a group she has recently experienced a difficulty with in her workplace. As it is a supervision session, our focus is primarily on her functioning, rather than on her client group. Using a tray of figurines and other small objects, Vi has set out the group on the table in front of us. As she does so she is speaking rapidly, describing how each group member behaved, how she experienced them and how difficult she found it to work with them.

Jenny: Where are you in this scene?

Vi: Oh yes (laughing) I had better be there.

Vi quickly chooses a large standing figurine, taller than all the others, with its arms outstretched, placing it well out and offset from the group. And she speeds on with her story. I focus on slowing her down, working moment by moment with the scene, rather than rushing on.

Jenny: Slow down, slow down, back up a bit. The group is here, but you haven't started yet. What are you aware of?

Vi: (Pauses and takes a deep breath) Everyone is waiting. Waiting for me to do something. I have to fill the silence. I have to take care of everyone. I am responsible for everything. It is my job to perform as the leader.

Jenny: Choose something to be you the Carer.

She chooses a bright yellow tab and places it close to the group.

Vi: I like this role. I feel playful and warm. I really do care about these people.

Her body has softened and her breathing steadies as she warms up to her Carer role. We sit in silence for a little time.

Jenny: This is deeply important to you.

Vi: Yes

Jenny: Here is the group . . . (gesturing to the figurines)

Vi shakes off her calm and warm hearted self-appreciation, her body stiffens as she speaks.

Vi: They are waiting for me to start. I have to put on a performance for them.

Jenny: Choose something to be Vi the Performer.

She looks at the objects available and chooses a sparkly, lightly tinted, transparent glass bead, placing it on the table in the middle of the group. I notice the placement—its as if she is 'center stage'—but my attention is more immediately taken by the bead itself.

Jenny: Wow, it is so sparkly.

I smile at her and then return my gaze to the bead and make a simple descriptive statement.

Jenny: I can see straight through it.

Vi breathes in sharply. Goes still. Her eyes tear up. After a moment or two she speaks.

Vi: Oh my goodness. That's it. I'm worried they'll see right through me. I want everyone to like me. I feel this pressure to perform, to put on a show . . . .

Jenny: The surface is quite reflective.

Vi: Yes!! It reflects everyone else, but you can't see inside it. I can't be seen for myself.

She continues on, to further tearfully express what this is about for her, the genesis of this Performer role, where it sits in her system and how it impacts her moment to moment experience and spontaneity with the group. It is a deeply cathartic experience for Vi to become fully aware of and reflect on this aspect of her functioning.

After a time, she lifts her head from her pose of tearful reflection, straightens in her seat and becomes quite spontaneous, deciding upon a new role she would like to develop and access for moments when the group has gathered, waiting expectantly for her. She is now excited and bubbly in expressing herself and contemplating future encounters with the group.

Vi's spontaneity and creativity have been rekindled through slowing down into the here and now immediacy of what is present in front of her and within her in the moment.

Conclusion

In writing these vignettes to share with you I warm up to my own spontaneity and creativity as a practitioner. These stories provide a deeply satisfying mirror for me of how my professional practice, and my being, has been enriched through the integration of Morenian philosophies and methods. And of how this benefit ripples out into my clients' worlds and beyond.

Jenny Postlethwaite

Jenny Postlethwaite is an accredited Sociodramatist (Australia Aotearoa New Zealand Psychodrama Association) and a Professional Certified Coach (International Coach Federation). She has her own organisational coaching and consulting business, Reach Coaching. Since first encountering psychodrama in 2010, Jenny has enthusiastically integrated and applied Morenian philosophies and methods into her practice and actively promoted the method in her professional coaching community, through delivery of professional development sessions and Action Methods In Coaching training workshops.

Contact her at *jenny@reachcoaching.com.au* or *reachcoaching.com.au*

References

Clayton, L (1982) The Use Of The Cultural Atom To Record Personality Change In Individual Psychotherapy. In *Journal of Group Psychotherapy, Psychodrama and Sociometry*, 35 Heldref Publications New York

Moreno, J.L. (1953/1993) *Who Shall Survive? Foundations of Sociometry, Group Psychotherapy and Sociodrama.* (Student Ed.), Beacon House: New York.

Postlethwaite, J.L. (2015) *The Naked Sociodramatist — Critical Moments In A Team Building Workshop,* Australian and Aotearoa New Zealand Psychodrama Association Thesis

Section 2

Action Explorations
in Education

Action Methods in Education

Linda Ciotola

I was educated as a teacher before I learned about psychodrama, and many of the things I've learned can be taught—and indeed, taught better—using action methods. Indeed, these methods may be adjusted to the level of the students, from early elementary school to graduate and post-graduate professionals getting continuing education. This chapter illustrates some examples:

Concretization

Concretization is the conversion of something abstract into something more concrete, thus making it more accessible to be used or worked with. For example, scarves or "furry auxiliaries" (stuffed toys or hand puppets) may be used to concretize strengths. Metaphors may become concrete and actualized. With children that is achieved by using puppets or stuffed animals. Even more contemporary findings in neuro-psychology can be taught this way: For example, "mindful witness" can be taught in tandem with the "triune brain."

Indeed, there are schools today that now give kids "brain breaks," *i.e.*, teach mindfulness, yoga, and meditation in order to help children relax and improve their ability to focus. The role of the "Mindful Witness" is held by the eagle who holds an "eagle eye view," witnessing internal states and responses. The reptilian brain is represented by the dinosaur who can plod along noticing the heart beating, the breath coming down to the throat, moving the ribs and so on. Everything remains in homeostasis unless danger is perceived. When that happens, the heart races, breathing patterns change and the body prepares to fight or flee. This shift in the reptilian brain is held by the snake puppet who can hiss and strike or slither quickly away.

The mammalian brain—the limbic system—is represented by two dogs—one the border collie who "barks" "danger danger," and the other a golden retriever who signals when everything is OK, and sends the message, "safe to play" and "safe to connect." Two owls hold the role of frontal cortex, left side and right side. The brown owl puppet becomes the left side of the brain, the "thinker." Balancing this, the white owl puppet represents the right side of the brain, the "big picture taker." The owls are able to rotate their heads in a full circle, representing the abilities to see the big picture. When the dinosaur is plodding along and the golden retriever is in charge of the limbic system, the frontal cortex can view things clearly, currently, and accurately making reasoned decisions. However, when the snake "hisses" then the owls are unable to move, "think," or make good decisions. The teacher shows by picking up each hand puppet, each "furry auxiliary" one at a time and "becoming" that part of the brain and saying "I am the reptilian brain and it's my job to . . ." and so on.

Once the teacher has gone through all the parts, the students take turns in the various roles using the hand puppets. The teacher observes and watches to see if the children have accurately perceived the various roles and brain parts. The teacher facilitates the action and then follows with questions for the children about what they noticed happening in their bodies in various roles (*e.g.* heart pounding, or fast breathing or an impulse to run, *etc.*). Then the teacher assigns children the role of the eagle to observe while s/he takes each role, one at a time, and afterwards asks each "eagle" to say what s/he noticed (mindfulness training).

S/he then teaches the class how to self-soothe when they observe "the barking dog"—helping students to observe their breath, then slow down their breathing, practice gentle swaying, rocking, humming, yoga poses, *etc.*

This action structure teaches young children the basics of brain science and body awareness while introducing the concept and practice of mindfulness.

Circle Sociometry

Circle Sociometry is an action structure that shows similarities in a group. A group member stands in the center of a circle, names a criterion that is true for himself or herself and asks that others who meet the criteria step into the circle. This builds group cohesion.

My colleague, Cathy Nugent, calls circle sociometry "circle similarities" which is a very user-friendly way to label this action intervention. Students stand in a circle and the teacher explains that this is a way to discover things we have in common with others ~ other students or with characters in a book they are reading or in a play they are studying. The teacher states a criteria and asks that if that criteria applies to them to "step into the circle."

If the space does not accommodate a circle, "step to the line" can be used instead. This is an activity similar to circle sociometry, but instead using a line drawn down the center of the floor (perhaps using masking tape) in which a given criteria is stated and all those who meet that criteria step to the line.

These action structures can help students see how material they may be groaning about having to study may actually have some relevance to their lives—*e.g.* Shakespeare.

For "step to the line" the teacher draws a line using masking tape down the center of the room. Students are divided into two groups, randomly, on either side of the line. Let's say the students have been studying *Hamlet* in their junior or senior year in high school. The teacher might ask, "Anyone who ever had a boyfriend/girlfriend behave strangely and in troubling ways, step to the line." As students step in, the teacher can then ask which characters in *Hamlet* were in a boyfriend/girlfriend relationship and exhibited strange and troubling behavior. (Hamlet and Ophelia). The teacher can then ask, "Anyone who ever felt angry at a parent, step to the line" (Hamlet/his mother).

Helping the students identify how their current lives have some emotional relevance to that of the characters they are studying occurs more easily in action and also has the additional benefit of engaging students while allowing them to see that they are not alone amongst peers in their feelings. If the room is more conducive to creating a circle rather than a line, the teacher can ask the students to stand in a circle and when they can relate to the criteria being stated, they are asked to take a step into the circle. (To view a dramatization of how a teacher used "step to the line" to bring her students from warring gangs together, view the film, *The Freedom Writers*, starring Hilary Swank.)

Timelines

Timelines are a linear representation of a series of important events that are concretized in some way. They have multiple applications to express the history of anything in a multi-sensory way. Historical events, figures, literary figures; art history, music history and more can all be viewed using an action timeline. I will use the example of how I implement the timeline to teach *Romeo and Juliet* by Shakespeare. I use the device of sheets of yellow paper, a "yellow-brick road" on the floor—drawing from the song from the *Wizard of Oz*, "Follow the Yellow Brick Road." There are events and dates, one on each of the yellow papers. For example, William Shakespeare and his date of birth and the date he wrote *Romeo and Juliet*. The yellow papers have the various scenes and characters named on them and are placed in order on the floor.

> Prologue ~ The Chorus
> Act 1, Scene 1 ~ Verona
> > Sampson, Gregory, Abram, Balthasar, Benvolio, Tybalt, Capulet, his wife, old Montague, his wife, Prince Romeo
> Act 1, Scene 2 ~ A Street
> > Capulet, Paris, Servant/Clown, Benvolio, Romeo
> Act 1, Scene 3 ~ Capulet's House
> > Capulet's wife, Nurse, Juliet
> Act 1, Scene 4 ~ A Street
> > Romeo, Mercutio, Benvolio, Maskers, Torch Bearers

Act 1, Scene 5 ~ Capulet's House
Serving men with napkins, Capulet, Romeo, Tybolt,
Juliet, Nurse

The remainder of the play is laid out similarly. I have found that one Act per class period works well, but more time per Act may be needed, depending upon students' abilities, previous preparation and class length and size.

The teacher has prepared index cards each with a character's name and a brief description of the character and his/her importance in the play.

For example, Romeo: "I am Romeo, member of the Montague family and a teenager. My best friend is Mercutio and my family is in a long-standing feud with the Capulets. When I meet Juliet Capulet, I fall for her immediately, but tragedy follows."

Juliet: "I am Juliet, member of the Capulet family. Although I am a teenager, I have a Nurse who is rather like a baby-sitter who watches over me. My family has a long time feud with the Montagues and when Romeo and I fall in love, tragedy follows."

Depending upon class size, there may be enough cards (characters) for each student in class to have one, but it might be necessary in smaller classes for students to play more than one character. The teacher can decide if s/he assigns roles or uses a lottery system or other method of making role assignments.

Students are asked to stand by the yellow paper that indicates the first scene in which his/her character appears. Then the teacher calls upon the student-characters in order of appearance to say what is written on their index card. In other words, each student steps into the role of the character.

The process continues with students in character, moving through the timeline. The teacher can ask questions of the students "in character" to help them discern the characters' emotions, motivations, *etc.* For example, following Tybolt's slaying of Mercutio the teacher might role reverse Tybolt and Romeo to help students see both perspectives.

When using the timeline, role reversal and enactment in teaching historical or literary events and figures, the students are able to go beyond merely learning facts into exploring the multi-dimensional facets of characters and the issues and times that shaped them.

Locograms

A locogram is an activity that designates locations on the floor that represent certain roles or preferences about specific questions in a given moment.

My examples here are applying locograms specifically in classes on civics and social studies. However, locograms can be used in a variety of classroom settings to explore numerous topics.

Here, we are focusing on various forms of government: democracy, republic, parliamentary, monarchy, communist, socialist, dictatorship, and others. Students will have previously studied these in class and assigned a type of government to represent. One student per each type on the corresponding locogram.

Remaining students are "citizens." One at a time, each student representative of a type of government states the advantages of that type of government. The teacher facilitates and opens the floor for questions from the "citizens." This is given a time limit by the teacher for each one and also a time limit for questions. The teacher can ask questions too.

Then the teacher has the" citizens" go to the locogram that indicates the type of government under which they would like to live. The students who held roles do not have to stay on that particular one — they can also choose.

Next, students say why they chose that particular one. There can be a follow up to this where students stand on the locogram showing the form under which they'd least like to live, and make a soliloquy about what it is like to live under that form of government.

This activity requires that the students prepare ahead to become familiar with the various types of government and so will reveal in the activity which students are prepared and which ones are not.

It also elicits careful consideration by the students about the advantages and/or disadvantages of the various types of government and invites speculation about what it might be like to live under the various forms.

I have found this activity works well in secondary and higher education. It can also be adapted for middle school students.

Conclusion

These examples are just a few of the many action method techniques that can be easily and creatively applied in educational settings.

Linda Ciotola

Linda Ciotola, M.Ed., TEP is a certified trainer-educator-practitioner of sociometry, group psychotherapy, and psychodrama with 45 plus years of experience in teaching and group facilitation: elementary, secondary and higher levels of education in English, Drama, Communication, and Health.

She has led or co-led a number of training workshops in action methods. As a certified trainer in The Therapeutic Spiral Model™ of psychodrama (specifically designed for work with trauma survivors) she has worked both as clinician and trainer in private and group settings. With psychotherapist, Nancy Alexander, LCSW-C and team she co-created the first on-line educational program, entitled ACTS, to show how action methods can be used to heal trauma. She hold multiple certifications in fitness, health, yoga, nutrition, Reiki and is an interfaith minister. Her writing includes a number of journal articles and co-authorship with Karen Carnabucci: *Healing Eating Disorders with Psychodrama and Other Action Methods-Beyond the Silence and the Fury* (Jessica Kingsley, London, 2013).

Linda received the ASGPP Zerka Moreno Award in 2008 for outstanding contributions in the field of psychodrama and, with Nancy Alexander, the 2019 ASGPP Collaborator's Award. She is a Fellow of the ASGPP and presents widely at national and international conferences. Linda resides in Maryland with her husband, Joseph, and their pet therapy collie dog, Lassie. She is the proud mother of two children and three grandchildren. For more information visit her website at: *healing-bridges.com* and ACTS: *ac-ts.com*

Simulation: Gateway from Information to Knowledge

Interactive Learning (Role-Playing) in the Classroom

James H. Henry

"Do away with lectures all together." Some who use role-playing in their classrooms would advocate this. I do not. There is still a place in education for the sage on the stage. After all, information must be disseminated to your students. However, there is great value in role-playing in the classroom as well.

Today's youth are easily distracted and become bored if they are not involved on a personal level. Remember, these youth grew up with computers and the internet. The age of instantaneous gratification. While this is a good thing in certain ways it also has shown us youth that are easily distracted and lack the patience or desire to sit for an entire class just listening and taking notes. In his book, *Generation iY*, Tim Elmore states it this way, "Teachers must remember that a lecture is not enough anymore."[1] He goes on to write, "If we want to be heard, we must engage students' interest with an experience that captures their imagination. They want action and interaction."[2] Notice the interaction part of that statement. This chapter is about interactive learning. This is why role-playing in the classroom has become such a valuable tool for teachers at all levels of education.

So, what is role-playing, let's define it.

> **Role-Play:** "Is a technique that allows students to explore realistic situations by interacting with other people in a managed

---

1 Elmore, 2010, p. 49
2 Ibid.

way in order to develop experience and trial different strategies in a supported environment."[3]

Simply put, in order for this generations' learning goals to be met, we as teachers must find a way to capture their attention and keep it. Role-playing is one such way of accomplishing this. In this chapter, I will attempt to allow you to see the benefits and detriments of role-playing, how to implement role-playing in your class, and when to use it and when to not use it.

Benefits of Interactive Learning (Role-Playing)

If you ask any teacher of any subject, they will tell you that the most difficult part of their job is to capture their students' attention and keep it. Now this is not a new struggle; however, in recent years it has become next to impossible to keep and maintain students' attention. As an instructor of speech and communication at a university, I can tell you that if I do not achieve the goal of getting my audience's attention, then most or all of what I teach will be lost on most of the students in my class. The internet and social media apps beckon, and to this generation of students it is easier to google a subject than listen to someone speak on the subject.

The issue with just searching the internet for answers on any given subject is that you can gain information, but you do not gain knowledge or wisdom.[4] This is the difference between surfing the internet for answers and having a live human being teach you about a subject. Yeats said this about education: "Education is not about filling a pail, but the lighting of a fire." Like Yeats, I do not believe in merely filling the pail with information. I want to light the fire of learning. Students, especially in this age of information need teachers that are a conduit between information, knowledge, and wisdom. Surfing the internet for information is merely filling the pail. Shoving facts into the brain does not indicate understanding of that information, nor does it prepare today's youth for how or why to use the information. Knowledge is being able to apply information. Wisdom is knowing when to use knowledge and when not to use it.

You see, when teachers use role-playing, they increase their students interest in their subject. There is increased involvement by the students to the subject, as they are not just passive recipients of a teacher's lecture. Students also learn empathy and understanding for different perspectives during role-playing.[5]

When students are involved and not passive learners; they begin to comprehend the implications and subtleties of the information that the teacher

---

3 Patil, 2016

4 Henry, 2014

5 Poorman, 2002

gives in lecture. This allows them to apply this information, or as previously stated, this becomes knowledge. Notice, that this is not merely information anymore. Why? Because, the student has taken the next step. They begin to understand how to use the information in their lives, their jobs, and use that knowledge to make their lives better. Below are some of the benefits that the Science Education Resource Center at Carlton College (SERC) have noted about role-playing.

- Students immediately apply content in a relevant, real world context.
- Students take on a decision making persona that might let them diverge from the confines of their normal self-imposed limitations or boundaries.
- Students can transcend and think beyond the confines of the classroom setting.
- Students see the relevance of the content for handling real world situations.
- The instructor and students receive immediate feedback with regard to student understanding of the content.
- Students engage in higher order thinking and learn content in a deeper way.
- Instructors can create useful scenarios when setting the parameters of the role play when real scenarios or contexts might not be readily available.
- Typically students claim to remember their role in these scenarios and the ensuing discussion long after the semester ends.
- But, most importantly, students apply the information you, as their teacher, have been giving them. When this happens they start to use their own thought processes on the information, their own imagination. They start the transformation of that information into knowledge, they make it their own.[6]

In addition to those benefits listed above, here are some other benefits that I have noticed in my classroom.

- They learn about communicating in a group.
- They learn to work together in a team.
- They learn about problem solving.
- They get to know their fellow students and develop relationships.
- Most importantly, students begin to apply the information that they have been given. This begins the journey between just information to knowledge.

---

6 The Science Education Resource Center at Carleton College, 2017

Disadvantages of Role-Playing

As you probably understand already no system of teaching is perfect. So, in this section we will discuss some of the disadvantages to role-playing. While role playing is a powerful instructional technique, often it is misused by trainers or trainers use it without considering that it also may have drawbacks or disadvantages. Here are some things trainers should know about the use of role plays. Below is a list of disadvantages of role-playing.

- The power of role playing is only harnessed when the role player receives expert feedback. Inexpert feedback or feedback from group members who are at the same level of competence as the role player is often useless, and does not further learning. Unfortunately, most role plays in training sessions are done in small groups, and most feedback given by other, less than competent group members.
- While trainers may like role plays, many people who attend training actually hate them and feel exceedingly uncomfortable in roleplay situations. This does not necessarily mean that people who hate them cannot benefit by them, but trainers need to consider the tradeoffs between the use of role plays and the discomfort and anxiety they create.
- The role playing of highly emotionally charged situations tends to be less effective in large groups, since the role playing tends to take on the characteristic of acting performances, or, the performance becomes too artificial and sounds funny. It's hard, for example, for learners to pretend to be very angry without going over the top or starting to giggle. This is less of a concern in therapeutic settings, but is a factor in training.
- Almost every use of role-playing in large group training sessions involves extreme compromise, often to the extent that learning does not occur, or is interfered with. That's because role playing works best when there is sufficient time to prepare people for the role play, do the actual role play, provide expert feedback, and do any debriefs. Larger group sessions involve role-playing that goes basically "out of control" of the trainer, since the trainer cannot monitoring constantly, or be the source of expert feedback (The Training World, 2017).

In addition to the above disadvantages, here are some that I have noticed in my classrooms.

- Students don't always take the scenarios that the instructor lays out for them seriously. If this happens then the session becomes playtime for them not learning time. It is a good idea for the instructor to canvas the room and keep the students on task and assure that they take the interactive learning seriously. It is important that the students have fun with the role-playing, but it must be productive to the learning objectives.

- Some students are introverted or just embarrassed that they must participate in a group or one on one. If you identify a student like this try to make sure that they are paired with someone they know, this will lessen the impact of their embarrassment.
- If the instructor is not prepared for the role-playing session then the session will not achieve what the instructor intends it to achieve. As the instructor you must be prepared to cover material that is pertinent to the role-playing session before you begin it. You must also make sure that you have a pertinent and believable scenario for your students.

Theory is Fine but How

So let's take a look at how these things happen in the classroom. As I mentioned earlier, role-playing is not meant to and cannot replace lecture. Lecture is how professors impart information to their students. Whether you are teaching speech, media communication, chemistry, nursing, or engineering, your students need this initial influx of information so they can start the journey to knowledge. The next step is to use role-playing, this allows the students to apply information. This is how information becomes knowledge.

How can role-playing allow students to become more empathic and understand different perspectives? How can it begin to allow them to accumulate knowledge and not just information? I can best explain these by giving you an examples of the role-playing that I do in my classrooms. During my communication class I pair the students off. They are instructed to interview each other (as for a job). One is the interviewer and the other the interviewee. After they finish the interview, they must switch roles. Each one is given difficult questions to ask the other. In this way both students understand the pressures on the one asking the questions and the one answering the questions.

Another role-playing scenario is the students are put into groups of four or five. They are told that they are a team in a company. I then give them a problem that is common to most companies these days and they are asked to come up with solutions. They are then asked to elect a spokesperson for their group and they must present their solutions.

By putting students in real-world scenarios, the information becomes real to them. They see how it can be used to benefit them, thus it becomes important enough to them to learn it and apply it. The Science Education Resource Center (SERC) offers these tips for implementing role-playing in the classroom.

1. **Offer a relevant scenario to students.** This scenario should include the role the student must play, the informational details relevant for decision making in this role, and a task to complete based on the information. This information might be provided on the screen through power point or by using a handout. It is highly recommended that the instructions be provided in writing so it is clear to students what they must do and how?

2. **Give students five to ten minutes to complete the task.** The instructor might have students do this alone or in small groups or follow the think-pair-share format in which students work individual and then discuss their results with their partner.

3. **Find a way to process student deliberations.** The instructor might ask students to write their replies to submit or this might be a very good lead in to a larger class discussion where students can justify their differing outcomes or opposing views.

Implementing role-playing into your classroom takes more time and effort, but if you want your lectures to come alive for your students then this is a great way to accomplish it. Take your time, come up with as realistic scenarios as you can, allow your students to explore their own thoughts and imaginations when conducting their run through of the scenario you have presented them with, and make sure that you come with a way to analyze their performance and give them feedback. These steps are key to experiencing interactive learning, and expanding your students' minds from just information to knowledge.

Role-Playing in Engineering Classes

At several engineering universities; including the one I work at, the students do a Senior Design Project or Capstone during their senior year. In this project they are expected to perform every aspect of an engineering team. They are expected to vet and purchase parts, attend weekly meetings with their customers to give project updates, and create, manage, and maintain a budget for the project. This is in addition to the design, build, and testing part of their project. This project allows our students to get a taste of what being a real engineer in the real world is like. It prepares them for their first job.

This senior design project is the ultimate role-playing scenario. It is as real as it gets before they take their place in their first job. So, one of the goals of previous classes, is to get them ready to be successful at this project and by extension successful in their job / career, then we; as educators need to prepare them for their project. How? We can put them into more role-playing scenarios; during their freshman, sophomore, and junior years, and prepare them more adequately for when they must step up and do this role-playing for real. Because role-playing is beneficial to learning engineering or the sciences.

In addition to learning the intended concepts and principles, role playing enactment of real life situations promotes the development of critical thinking skills, and humanizes science by discerning its importance to everyday life. It can also develop importance skills needed in the "Real World"; Such as, teamwork, collaborative learning and effective communication.[7]

In addition, what has been discovered about role playing in engineering is that students find that it helps them learn and they enjoy it. At Wuhan University Dr. Peng Liang and Dr. Onno de Graaf used role-playing in their Requirements Engineering class. Here is what they discovered about the experience.

"Role Playing method is useful: 24 out of 26 students (92.3%) believed that role playing method was useful for them to practice RE skills and understand the real problems during the communications for requirements."[8]

In the following sections of this chapter implementing role-playing into an engineering curriculum will be discussed.

Engineering Use Role-Playing?!

I am sure that most of you had this reaction to this subject. Role-playing in engineering? There is no place for it right? Wrong, role-playing is used to transform information to knowledge, by allowing students to apply that information in a safe and controllable environment. Engineers are some of the smartest people on the planet; however, too many times in the past, engineering education has focused solely on teaching the math and theory of engineering. While I agree that these are of vital importance, long past are the days when engineers can just sit in their cubicles and watch the rest of the world drift by. Today's engineers must learn cooperation, critical thinking, and communication skills that they sorely need in today's competitive markets.

Instead of having your students' fill out a lab report, allow them to write a project summary. This would include, but not limited to, budget, efficiency reports (allocation of time), design parameters, testing methodology, and test results. This type of role-playing has been successfully implemented in other engineering courses as far back as 1996, as noted by Bartz and Deaton in their paper presented to The American Society of Engineering Education (ASEE).

"At The University of Memphis, an inter-course project used role playing to introduce students to these "soft" engineering skills. The inter-course project

---

7 Fadali, McNichols, & Robinson, 2000, p. 2
8 Liang & Graaf, 2010, p. 4

involved a senior elective in Discrete-Time Signal Processing (DSP), and junior electronics courser.[9]

Below, Bartz and Deaton show us some of the areas that study that benefit from role-playing, as the authors note in their paper to ASEE.

"Role playing allows engineering students to participate in many activities in which professional engineers engage. Examples include product research and development, job hunting, identification and evaluation of vendors, business present at ions and meetings, team projects, reports, and management."[10]

How do I go About Doing Role Playing in an Engineering Class or Lab

If you have never done any role playing, it can be intimidating. However, if approached properly, then it is quite easy to set the scenario for your students. In this section we will discuss, setting up the teams, setting up the lab / project, the role of the professor in the role playing, and the different possible outcomes of the scenario presented to the students. Below you will find the four basic steps to interactive learning (role playing).

1. Preparation and explanation of the activity by the teacher
2. Student preparation of the activity
3. The role-playing
4. The discussion or debriefing after the role-play activity.[11]

Forming the teams and team roles

So, let's say that you have labs in your engineering program. Some schools have labs, other schools have eliminated labs from their curriculum. If you do have labs then you can use role-playing in these labs to simulate delivering a product to a customer; if not, then use the scenario in the classroom. You, as the lab instructor will play the part of the customer. If you can identify or know which student will work well together while also challenging one another then assign them to be team mates. Make the teams 4 students, if possible.

Assign each student on the lab team different roles within the organization or have them share the different responsibilities equally. For example, if there are 4 students in the lab group, assign each a significant role. One will be budget officer, one will be lead designer, one will be lead tester, one will be quality control *etc*.

The role titles do not matter. What does matter is that each member of the lab team has a different realm of responsibility. This allows the students

---

9 Bartz & Deaton, 1996, p. 1
10 Ibid.
11 Jarvis, Odell, & Troiano, 2002

to approach their mutual goals and issues from different perspectives. This promotes critical thinking, communication, and allows specific application of the information they have been exposed to in class.

Here is how the professors at the University of Memphis formed their students' teams.

The engineering teams were allowed latitude in their formal composition, but all teams were required to have one project manager. Other identified functional areas included the following:

1. Design engineer: designs and constructs the laboratory prototype.
2. Quality control engineer: specifies the manufacturing quality plan
3. Manufacturing engineer: specifies the manufacturing process including costs
4. Sales engineer: develops technical sales literature and price information

Some teams assigned one individual to each functioned area, whereas other teams used a shared responsibility approach. Exact configurations of the teams was the purview of the project manager, who was directly responsible to the instructor.[12]

The Professor's Responsibilities

You are going to have to change your paradigm about how you go about teaching your class / labs. In the past, you would present the theory and components that are being taught. You would give lecture on those theories and components and then hand a lab assignment to your students that gave them practical experience with what you taught them in the classroom. Practical experience or hands on, as it is also referred to, is great. However, you can go to the next level.

Maybe each lab, right now, is a standalone version if you taught capacitors and filters in your class, then the lab is over capacitors and filters. When you do role-playing you need to broaden the scope of your labs. For example, instead of just teaching amplifiers, filters, and modulators circuits. Your goal is to introduce your students to how to build an FM radio. So, their customer (you) expects a working FM radio by the end of the semester. In order to deliver the product they as students must build and test each section of that radio. You as their customer expects weekly reports on the progress of the end product. This means that the students have to write a report for each lab that they complete.

You see why this type of learning is called interactive learning. The students must interact with you, their fellow students, and you with them in order to compete the task at hand.

---

12 Bartz & Deaton, 1996, p. 2

The Labs

Of course just as how you form your lab groups and students' roles within those lab groups' changes, so does the lab itself. This is not just about taking whatever theory or component was learned in class and building it. It is about having your students act like real engineers that are delivering a product to their boss or customer which is you as their professor. Just as their roles have changed, so too must yours. Your students are not going to be handing in a lab report; that you have given them, after they finish building and testing a circuit. Instead they will be handing in a written report that addresses all of the issues and successes. Yes, this will include information that is normally on a lab report, but it also needs to be written by the students, and address all of their roles within the team and project. This report can be seen as a weekly progress report. At the end of the semester, your students need to present an overall report that includes a summarization of their work on the overall project. Remember, you have restructured your labs to be project based not individual circuits based. Below you will find some examples and results of implementing role-playing into classes and labs. If you are like me then you will find there is more work involved on the part of the professor; however, the learning experience for the students make the extra work well worth it.

For example, at the University of Cantabria in Spain, the following scenario is presented to the students. This scenario is used in their Optical Communications class and lab.

> The activity begins, as in most network maintenance companies, when the technician (our student) receives a "trouble ticket" by email from the network operation center (NOC). This document contains only a brief description of the symptoms of the problem. Fig. 1 shows an example of the instructions given to the students to start the activity. In a real-life situation, the technician would collect all the required information, and based on his/her training, perform on-site measurements or remote monitoring procedures to locate the cause of the problem and the failure point in the network. Finally, a corrective action to fix the problem is then performed. (Normally this consists of replacing equipment—be it a piece or the entire machine or mechanism).

> In our simulation, we consider a fictitious situation where the technician is unable to perform the measurements by her/himself, but is able to contact NOC staff by email to request onsite measurements, verifications, or all available information at the company. While NOC staff supposedly lack technical knowledge in optical communications, they have experience

with past failures and are able to provide information about the network, and request onsite measurements from other technicians. In this activity, the instructor plays the role of the NOC staff, and in this way is able to interact with the student by email. One advantage of communicating via email is that both teacher and student can choose when to reply.

The evaluation of the activity is not only based on the ability of the student to locate the problem and to propose a proper solution in a short time, but also on the relevance of the questions posed and the information requested. The student's questions are used to reveal conceptual flaws and to select the learning material (concepts, procedures, *etc.*) that should be provided to the student so that he or she may continue with the activity. The replies from the instructor are crafted to take into account both learning objectives and real-life issues, such as missing information or the need for complicated, expensive, and or time consuming measurements).

At the end of the activity, the instructor sends students his feedback and comments. The instructor should focus on students´ conceptual flaws and the reading material available to correct them. The instructor performs a final evaluation by using a rubric that considers the following aspects: Completion of the task; information and interaction needed; relevance of student's questions; knowledge of theoretical aspects; choice and use of instrumentation.[13]

The professors that implemented this role-playing in their classes and labs received the following feedback from their students. "According to student evaluations of their experience, students consider the activity of working in a "real-life situation" to be very valuable and relevant to their professional future."[14] Their students also reported, "Students also feel they have gained valuable knowledge about instrumentation, available information and/or measurements in real situations."[15]

Let us be clear though, while there are potentially great benefits for the students when role-playing is used in classrooms and labs, it is by all accounts more work for the professors involved. At the University of Southern Florida,

---

13 Cobo, Conde, & Merapeix, 2011, pp. 50–51

14 Ibid. p. 57

15 Ibid.

Professors Elaine V. Howes and Barbara C. Cruz had the following to say in their article which appeared in the *Journal of Elementary Science Education*.

> As with any active learning strategy or project, thoughtful planning on the part of the professor is essential. Resources, time allocation, and the integration of content and skills all must be considered ahead of time. This type of exercise requires up-front preparation to ensure that students have the time and the support in searching out scientists.[16]

So, it is clear that the role-playing method of teaching involves a change in the professor's paradigm and also requires more prep work than most professors are accustomed. However, when the benefits to the students are measured against the extra time and effort put forth by the professor, isn't it worth that time and effort. After all, none of us get into teaching to get rich. We get into teaching so that we may pass on knowledge to the next generation. How we do that impacts our students just as much as what we are teaching them.

Conclusion

Today's generation of computer literate, internet information, instant gratification students require more than just lecture from their classrooms and their professors. They require a more interactive and proactive approach to learning. Role-playing is a vital tool in the modern day professor's belt to engage his or her students on a different level. Proper use of role-playing not only teaches the subject at hand, but it also teaches life lessons to your students. As professors when we are able to connect with our students; we don't just impart information, we start their journey from information to knowledge to wisdom. As Yeats put it, "We light the fire of learning."

As we have seen in this chapter role-playing requires more preparation and work up front from their professor. In addition let us take another look at some of the pitfalls of role-playing. Students don't always take the scenarios that the instructor lays out for them seriously. Some students are introverted or just embarrassed that they must participate in a group or one on one. If the instructor is not prepared for the role-playing session then the session will not achieve what the instructor intends it to achieve. While these are a concern; they are also very manageable, especially if the professor is willing to devote some extra time and effort for his or her student's sake.

Now speaking for the students let's take another look at the advantages of role-playing that were discussed earlier in this chapter.

- Students immediately apply content in a relevant, real world context.

---

16 Howes & Cruz, 2009

- Students take on a decision making persona that might let them diverge from the confines of their normal self-imposed limitations or boundaries.
- Students can transcend and think beyond the confines of the class-room setting.
- Students see the relevance of the content for handling real world situations.
- The instructor and students receive immediate feedback with regard to student understanding of the content.
- Students engage in higher order thinking and learn content in a deeper way.
- Instructors can create useful scenarios when setting the parameters of the role play when real scenarios or contexts might not be readily available.
- Typically students claim to remember their role in these scenarios and the ensuing discussion long after the semester ends.
- But, most importantly, students apply the information you, as their teacher, have been giving them. When this happens they start to use their own thought processes on the information, their own imagination. They start the transformation of that information into knowledge, they make it their own.

In addition to those benefits listed above, here are some other benefits that I have noticed in my classroom.

- They learn about communicating in a group.
- They learn to work together in a team.
- They learn about problem solving.
- They get to know their fellow students and develop relationships.
- Most importantly, students begin to apply the information that they have been given. This begins the journey between just information to knowledge.

Finally, there is no denying that it is more work to implement role-playing in your classes. There is no denying that role-playing may or may not be for your particular class. However, it is a viable teaching tool and one that you cannot just dismiss as being for business or communication classes any longer. It can be utilized in science and engineering classes. It is vital for engaging the computer age students that are in our colleges and universities. Also, you owe it to yourself as a professor to explore the subject that you teach well enough, so that, you can apply your own imagination to the subject and get your students to love it as much as you do.

James (Howard) Henry

James (Howard) Henry's field of interest and research is pedagogic communication; in other words, how to communicate with students so that they learn. This involves several aspects of communication. Computer Mediated Communication (CMC) as social media and texting have become such a large part of our youth's communication medium. It involves psychodrama as an improved method for communicating and thereby teaching. It of course involves face to face communication. It involves verbal and non-verbal communication to receive the feedback necessary to indicate whether different methods are being effective.

Howard is employed by LeTourneau University as a Speech Instructor and Engineering Technician, and his duties include teaching and mentoring students in public speaking, technical writing, research, and engineering principles. He has a Bachelor degree in Communication (Technical Communication) from Kaplan University, and a Master of Arts in Communication and Leadership from Gonzaga University.

His thesis work while at Gonzaga was about the current generation of college students; it is entitled, *The Influence of Social Media Technology on Generation iY's Ability to Communicate Face to Face in Their Academic Careers.*

Henry notes, "I want to light the fire of learning. Students, especially in this age of information need teachers that are a conduit between information, knowledge, and wisdom. Surfing the internet for information is merely filling the pail. Shoving facts into the brain does not indicate understanding of that information, nor does it prepare today's youth for how or why to use the information."

References

Bartz, M., & Deaton, R. J. (1996). Role Playing in Eingineering Educaiton. *American Society for Engineering Education* (p. 5). Washington DC: American Society for Engineering Education.

Cobo, A., Conde, O. M., & Merapeix, J. (2011). On-Line Role-Play as a Teaching Method In Engineering Studies. *Journal of Technology and Science Education*, 49–58.

Elmore, T. (2010). *Generation iY: Our last chance to save their futures.* Atlanta: Growing Leaders, Inc.

Fadali, M. S., McNichols, K., & Robinson, M. (2000). *Teaching Engineering To K 12 Students Using Role Playing Games.* Berlin: Research Gate.

charityfocus.org (2013, September 12). *DailyGood: News that inspires.* Retrieved from: *http://www.dailygood.org/search/quote/education/*

Henry, J. H. (2014). *Thesis on IY Generation.* Longview: Oxford Univeristy Press.

Howes, E. V., & Cruz, B. C. (2009). Role-Playing in Science Education: An Effective Strategy for Developing Multiple Perspectives. *Journal of Elementary Science Education*, 33–46.

Jarvis, L., Odell, K., & Troiano, M. (2002). *Role-Playing as a Teaching Strategy.*

Liang, P., & Graaf, O. d. (2010). Experiences of Using Role Playing and Wiki in Requirements Engineering Course Projects. *Wuhan University* (p. 7). Hubei, China: Wuhan University.

Patil, D. Y. (2016). *Role Play Model of Teaching.* Navi: School of Education.

Poorman, P. B. (2002). Biography and role-playing: fostering empathy in abnormal. *Teaching of Psychology*, 32–36.

The Science Education Resource Center at Carleton College. (2017, October 27). *Role Playing.* Retrieved from SERC: *https://serc.carleton.edu/introgeo/interactive/roleplay.html*

The Training World. (2017, November 9). *The Training and Development World.* Retrieved from The Training World: *http://thetrainingworld.com/faq/roledisad.htm*

Science Communication in Action

Justine Jones

Around and around they went, weaving in, breaking out, pulsing up and down. It was beautiful, like no machine game machine I had ever seen before. Stopping, they turned and said in unison: "The Differential Equations Machine." Then a bow. Everyone laughed and clapped. It was post modern dance, uniting these Maths PhD's in this moment. The last group had portrayed a confused group of students mechanically responding to a pedantic professor. The one before that showed aspects of arriving to this PhD kick off camp. Just the basic Machine Game . . . with a twist. Science Communication had begun.

A few years ago a group of high school students at a science conference were asked to describe the image of a typical scientist. Working in small groups a picture soon emerged. A typical scientist, they said, was male, wore a stained and rumpled lab coat, had unruly hair and peered through thick lensed glasses. Most agreed that this was accurate. This image might have come from *The Simpsons* or some science fiction film, but nonetheless these British teenagers attending a science conference still clung to this stereotype.

In the twenty-first century science has taken a hit, a big hit. Once scientists were imagined as heroes who could save the world through new discoveries in medicine, space exploration, and the invention of computers. Science was cutting edge and would carry the world onto a safer more prosperous future. Young people thought seriously about joining these pioneers and contributing to the growing pool of knowledge that was emerging as a force.

Then science became politicized. Politicians serving their own political and financial agendas spent time and money trying to foment doubt as to the intentions of the scientists who, they said, were unaware of the needs of the average person. Instead of partaking of meaningful dialogue on important subjects such as climate change and stem cell research scientists were being portrayed as out of touch or deliberately deceptive.

And what did we hear from these defamed scientists? Al Gore, arguably not a scientist but a keen amateur, made a valiant attempt to communicate the basics of climate change with his film *An Inconvenient Truth*. Using animation and very basic scientific concepts, Gore explained the phenomenon of global warming even a teenager could understand.

The film was very well received among the general public, its detractors being advocates of the coal and oil industries who might lose their grip on the economy if the film's message were to be heeded. Still, though , science and scientific research needed more communicators. Why not the scientists themselves? Business and industry leaders bemoaned the seeming inability of science graduates to communicate, both verbally and in written language. They also complained that science graduates could not work effectively in groups. Why? And, most importantly, what was to be done?

Enter the academic establishment. Seeing clearly that these business leaders were correct, courses on how to give an effective speech were implemented. Information on designing effective slides proliferated. Still the problem persisted. What was it about science education that was not meeting these needs? Time for action methods!

I was in the middle of a very classical program on psychodrama, one so traditional that each session took three to four hours. That particular program and I were not a good match, but much of what I learned in my 3.5 years there was easily adapted to my work with undergraduates in Imperial College's Mathematics department. Action methods, as they were called, had many broad applications. Under the guise of training students to give presentations in secondary schools my *Math Matters* students explored their own ways of working in small groups and communication styles.

We started with very basic sociometry.[1] Since most did not know each other we introduced ourselves in Action. Standing in a circle I called out categories such as hobbies, favorite books, travel destinations, *etc*. As a warm-up, it was very effective in injecting not only trivia bits but humor. We then moved on to classical time lines: who was born farthest/closest to London, who felt comfortable/uncomfortable speaking in groups, who was feeling excited/worried about this course.

Of course the information and inevitable comparisons were important, but the fact of obtaining this information in Action was equally as important. It was a totally new experience for all of them. Not only were they not used to

---

1 Hale, 1981

speaking about increasingly more personal information but they were definitely not used to a course where they could be on their feet. An entirely new energy entered the group. Sitting back down in their seats was almost a disappointment! But not for long!

Over the course of six Saturdays we experimented with various role play situations. In one each participant had to adopt the posture of a supposed secondary school student and then be interviewed in role. In another they presented themselves as their favorite high school teacher and explained to us their philosophy of teaching. In a fishbowl structure half the group took on roles of various types of students listening and responding to a presentation by the other half. After all these simulations we processed our personal feelings and thoughts on the experiences. Of course this was not therapy but training to ready themselves for presenting in schools. But it became clear soon enough that these participants were not only being trained to speak to and with high school audiences; they were learning to communicate themselves, who they were and why they were passionate about their subject. And in this shared experience they were learning to interact as a cohort.

Math Matters continued as a Saturday course for eight years reaching thousands of London's secondary school students with these group presentations, master classes and even plays and musicals. The participants were extremely receptive to the experience, and, at one time, a third of them decided to go into teaching, a very unexpected and unanticipated outcome. Although the stated goal of the program was community outreach it was clear that the students gained immeasurably from their experience.

But the program only reached a small group of volunteers. And the problem of inspiring better science communication only intensified. I was asked to offer two hour sessions to the entire first year class, all 300 of them, on how to communicate effectively giving a poster session. Obviously lecture would not be as effective as small group enactments! Divided into groups of 24, the class was structured where, during the first hour, the students, in groups of four, designed an off beat tour of London to be "sold" to the rest of the class. The object was to be as creative and persuasive as they could in order to convince the others that they wanted to go on this imaginary tour. Some of these tours were so creative that I wished they were offered in reality! Who wouldn't want to go on the secret shopping tour of London's hidden markets or the tour of Soho alleyways and their seedy history?

Our second small group activity was called The Archeology Game.[2] In this game all students were told that they were descendants of survivors of a terrible disaster that had leveled London and most of the world five hundred

---

2 Jones and Kelley, 2014

years previously. The survivors of 21st century London had to remake civilization as best they could, underground. Their descendants, all scientists, had somehow made their way to what was left of London above ground. There, each group had found an ancient artifact which they had to try to explain to the other groups. Then they had to make an impassioned plea for its relevance for inclusion in the new British Museum. Everyday objects I gathered included staplers, key rings, toys, eye shades, highlighting pens, sunglasses, scotch tape, flashlights, *etc.* Really, anything found lying around the house could be imagined as a strange and perplexing item to people from five hundred years in the future. The creativity that went into these spontaneous explanations of the items' importance to our "ancient" civilization was astonishing, not to mention hilarious. But they had to present these explanations seriously, "as if" these insights were hugely significant!

The second hour of the class consisted of poster design in small groups, presentations of these posters and the fielding questions about them. The structure was a bit more traditional, no role play or amazing flights of fantasy. But the energy created in the first hour carried over, and answering questions with which they might not really feel comfortable became significantly easier. Since the implementation of the program six years ago the professors have expressed great satisfaction with both the posters and their presentation.

How to design a poster and defend it could be taught traditionally, of course. In fact, I think my supervisors were surprised when I entered the classroom carrying bags of strange objects. I think a strong argument can be made, though, that experiential learning can accelerate and enhance the traditional lecture format, even if the stated goal has very little to do with presentation training.

At the same time I was experimenting with Action Methods in science education the American actor Alan Alda was, too.[3] He was hosting a science program, Scientific American Frontiers, on television and discovered that he just didn't completely understand what was being said. He found he could not effectively even interview these scientists and wondered why. Was it his lack of scientific knowledge? Granted he was not a scientist. But then he reasoned that most listening to his show weren't either. How could he encourage scientists to communicate with his listeners, educated people but without an extensive science background? And why would they even want to?

It could be argued that there may never have been a time when communicating science to non scientists was more urgent than in the late twentieth/ early twenty first century. Sensing this critical need Alda sought ways to train scientists how to present their research in more accessible form. After receiving funding from The State University of New York at StonyBrook he founded the

---

3 Alda, 2017

Alan Alda Center for Communicating Science in 2009. And a cornerstone of his training for scientists was Action methods based on the teachings of Viola Spolin, often called acting improvisation or drama games.

Viola Spolin (1906–1994) was a theatre educator who designed theatre games based on playful activities inspired by the recreational games work of Neva Boyd, a Chicago settlement worker in the 1920's and the work of JL Moreno.[4] She borrowed many of Moreno's ideas eventually culminating in the founding of America's first improvisational theatre, The Second City, in the 1950's. A cornerstone of her philosophy was the Approval/ Disapproval Syndrome which encourages actors to explore their natural creativity without trying to just perform to please audience expectations. Encouraging spontaneity often based on audience suggestions, improvisation soon was being incorporated into acting programs all over the world.[5]

Alda saw that spontaneity and a comfortable give and take was a prime component for the success of an interview. His center "empowers scientists and health professionals to communicate complex topics in clear, vivid and engaging ways leading to an improved understanding by the public, media, patients, elected officials, and others outside of their own discipline." Note the "outside of their own discipline." Until very recently it was not a priority to communicate research outside of the immediate discipline. Now it was. And the core of this training is improvisation aka action methods!

In 2015 Imperial College's mathematics department received an EPSRC (Engineering and Physical Sciences Research Council) grant for the establishment of a nine year Centre for Doctoral Training in the Mathematics of Planet Earth (MPE CDT). Following business and industrial leaders' recommendations, one of the council's recommendations was an emphasis on Cohort building and presentation skills. I was invited to design a program for the first year of the four year PhD that would address these needs.

I doubt that anyone in the Graduate School anticipated a year long course using action methods and what is now called Applied Improvisation. Although AI was gaining ground in Organizational Development and business circles it certainly was not well known as a way of training scientists. But I strongly felt that presentation skills could not be taught in lecture format. And why not combine Cohort building with presentation skills? Anyone who has ever led a session using any kind of action methods knows that a rapport quickly develops between the participants. Since establishing a safe place to try new ideas is essential to any new presenter I reasoned that two hour sessions once a month would establish just that. Of course it would have been ideal to hold

---

4 Spolin,1953
5 Moreno, JD,2014

these weekly but there was no time for that, unfortunately. Stay in the now and deal with what is!

Expectations play a big part in whatever you teach, especially if it is out of the norm. Of course I was concerned about what these very serious PhD students would make of a class in Improv. Indeed, on the first day of the Kick-Off camp in the first session one student told the group about how he had been humiliated by his high school drama teacher and forced to perform in front of the group when he was not comfortable to do so. I hate hearing these stories because they are so unnecessary. My philosophy has always been to ease participants in to a group session and never force anyone to participate if they are not comfortable. As a result almost all activities start with inclusive entire group exercises designed to be fun and to make everyone feel safe.

Keith Johnstone is a big fan of clapping so I have him to thank for the use of this energy raising experience. After and sometimes during every exercise I encourage the group to clap loudly and enthusiastically. This is not just to show appreciation but to keep the energy of the group going. A seemingly simple and nonspecific exercise is to stand in a circle. One at a time participants run into the center, do a movement of some sort to wild clapping. These movements do not have to be anything specific; they could be as simple as walking in, turning around, and walking back out. The point is to continue clapping as a way of keeping the energy going. Everyone is contributing in a performance of sorts yet not having to worry about doing anything specific. No skill is involved yet appreciation is shown. A feeling of safety is assured. The students are amazed at how some activity thought of as so trivial can give them and the group a feeling of satisfaction on a job well done.[6]

Once safety is assured through simple group experiences such as the step in and line up sociometry games I used with my undergraduates in *Math Matters* the students begin to loosen up a bit. Performance anxiety usually disappears, but I stress that they always have the option to pass. Sitting in a circle I usually use a Koosh ball to toss around in order to get into a rhythm for a game of categories leading to Word Tennis. This gets them into a spontaneous mindset. If the category is, say, names of cities, the first person might say Chicago as they throw the Koosh to someone who will catch it and throw it on to the next person saying New York or some other city name. And on it goes until someone pauses too long or repeats a name.

Now comes the fun part. Usually, when someone misses we just change categories. But sometimes, to add to the fun,I ask the person who missed to "die." Then they either fall to the ground in convulsions, act as if shot or perform some other silly action to show that they have died. This can be a lot

---

6 Johnstone, K., 1960

of fun, but you really need to know your group. If they are still self conscious it might be better left for later sessions. Interestingly enough I find that the younger the participants the more eager they are to die. Somehow dying is not seen as dignified to PhD's until they feel really safe.

Following after Koosh can be Word Tennis which actually begins work in pairs. Two people stand across from each other and throw words in a set category back and forth until one misses. Obviously the intention is to encourage quick thinking on their feet, also known as spontaneity. But it can be a true ice breaker if played at a fun breakneck pace always stressing that there are no winners or losers; it's all just for fun.

I cannot stress enough the "just for fun" aspect of these sessions. In fact, many past participants still think that these were included in the curriculum as stress busters or, as one student put it, "cohorting." Working on PhD research is stressful and often solitary work, so coming to these sessions is, at the very least, a change of pace.

Another Keith Johnstone idea is the idea of Yes And, often referred to as the first rule of Improv. I don't like to think of rules in improv, but it is certainly true that participants need to know about accepting and adding on to offers. And not blocking. For this reason I include it in the first session. Sitting in a circle I ask someone to make an "offer" to the person sitting next to them. For example, that first person might say: "Let's go to the Zoo!" If the second person answers something like: "But, I would rather watch TV," that is considered blocking the offer. But if the person says: "Yes, and maybe we can see the lions feeding!" then the offer has been received and built upon. Play continues as the second person makes an offer to the third and so on. No scenes need to be acted, or stories told. Interestingly enough not every group can easily do thus exercise. There seems to be a great temptation to do a "yes, but" which is a common way of blocking an offer. Discussion often ensues as to whether it is easier to do a "yes, and" or a "yes, but." It is worth considering,

The group should now be relaxed and feeling relatively safe. Remember that we are still in the first session. So far the focus has been on safety, spontaneity and introducing a few concepts. Now we move into creativity. Still sitting in a circle I pass a small stick or pencil to the person next to me asking them to use it as something it isn't. It could be a knife or an arrow or a shoe horn. Going even farther it could be the leash on a dog, a snake or a bomb. And if we use it as a different shape it could be a baby or a jacket or a book. Remember that the student can always pass. And some do. No blame. This is in no way a competition. This should be stressed to help alleviate performance anxiety.

Followup games might include stories one word or sentence at a time or free association where the group starts with one word and each person free associates on the word they were just given. For example if we start with the word night the next word could be dark. After that we can get tunnel, coal, energy, sports, football, head injury, *etc*. After a couple of rounds there are two words, the first and last. I then ask for volunteers to tell a very short story based on these two words.

I usually end the session with a focus game of You! Where I pint at one student, arm extended, and say You! While walking towards him to take his place. He then quickly points to someone else and starts walking towards them. And the game continues. After the pace is established I start another word in a category such as girl's names going concurrently with the You. If the group is sufficiently warmed up and focused then yet another category can be added. Remember: it really doesn't matter how well they do, just that they try to stay focused while having fun! The first session usually ends in lots of laughter although if we have more time we process what we have learned. I always ask them, and I am always amazed at their insightful answers, many of which I never anticipated!

There are usually three or four more sessions before we have to focus on actual solo presentations for the end of the year Jamboree speaking in front of the centre's industrial partners. As I said before, sessions are on once a month, so skill building is slow, and the emphasis must always be kept on the comfort level of the group.

In the second session I usually start with an all group activity I learned from Tom Salinsky[7] of The Spontaneity Shop, an improv training organisation in London. It is important to remember that these activities are more or less floating in the Zeitgeist; few know for certain if they came from Moreno, Spolin, Johnstone, or some other improvisation guru or group. Some I might have made up on the spot. Nonetheless I think it is important to try to source and cite sources if at all possible. Participants walk around the room on their own touching objects and calling out their names: chair, wall, carpet, pencil, *etc*. After a few minutes of this warmup, they are asked to continue but to call these objects what they are not: a chair might be a gorilla or a pencil could be a television. Coming back to the circle, processing includes a discussion on which of these activities is easiest for the participants. Interestingly enough some groups prefer reality while others prefer fantasy.

After the warm up we stand in a group and play What Are You Doing? . Similar to Johnstone's Performance Game participants go into the center and perform a random movement. I call out: "What are you doing?" and they have to answer something clearly not what they were enacting. Like the first activity of the session, cognitive dissonance contributes to creativity or thinking quickly outside the box!

They are now sufficiently warmed up for beginning scene work, again played in a circle. Change IT! is a stock improv game in which someone goes

---

7 Salinsky, T, 2008

in the middle and starts moving around until I call freeze. Someone else then enters, looks at the frozen image and starts a short scene with the now unfrozen person. For example, if the first person is frozen, staring at the floor, the second person might start a scene about helping them look for a list contact lens or a button. The first person then needs to find a reason (motivation) to leave the scene, something like remembering where they dropped it and rushing off. Then the leader calls freeze, and the second person freezes. And the play continues. At the end of the game everyone gives the entire group a big round of applause. The focus here has to be on pacing so that the energy level stays high and, most importantly, that the participants do not get much time to think. Spontaneity is the name of the game!

Students are now ready for more small group work. Important concepts to introduce at this time are endowments (Johnstone) and accepting offers in scenes. I like to play a game of Experts at this point, an old favorite from Whose Line Is It Anyway. A panel of experts is chosen to be interviewed by a host, all volunteers from the class. The experts are endowed with their areas of expertise by the rest of the group, things like flea circus trainer, international spy, medieval belly dancer, or time traveler. The host and eventually the rest of the group as audience members then ask the experts questions on their areas of expertise. The focus is on the experts trying to pretend to know what they are talking about! A variation on this has the experts in the hall while the group members decide on w their areas of expertise. Only the host and the audience knows what they are, so the game is for the experts to answer interview questions while trying to guess their occupations. Taking what is offered and just going with it is a basic improvisational skill. A case could be made that this is the beginning of role play.

I will not detail every activity/game we play after this, but I do want to mention The Machine Game simply because it is a typical game played in Improv classes that really emphasizes team work. A machine works in synchrony, each wheel and cog doing its part in order to function. So, too, a small group if all goes well. The game starts by one person going into the Center and starting a mechanical movement. Then another joins him, adding a complimentary movement. After the second person the temptation is always strong for the group to form an assembly line, but that is too easy and, in a sense, too loosely connected. Because of this I try to encourage the machines to work together in a tight space, much like a watch. After the first machine I ask each part to add a sound to their movement, adding yet another dimension to the machine but always emphasizing the mechanical movements and sounds.

A very successful variation on this game is what I call The Metaphor Machine. Participants still keep the mechanical functioning aspect of the machine, but instead of a mechanical machine they choose a topic to illustrate in mechanical movement. It could be as simple as a television machine perhaps anchored by a newscaster saying " And now the news," in a repetitive fashion while others work around him portraying different aspects of television programming. These might include weather forecasters, on the scene reporters, previews of upcoming shows, or even viewers reacting. The object is to create a functioning machine in sound and movement but still illustrate aspects of the topic. As mentioned before, one group even performed a differential equations machine, and I have seen amazing addition and multiplication ones as well. As a leader you can also slow down the pace or speed it up, the object being to still work in synchrony.

After about four weeks of improvisation the students are usually warmed up enough to work in pairs, and this usually is the beginning of their work on presentation skills. In the CDT there is a time constraint which is dependent on a product, a short three minute presentation on each student's research. The catch here is that they will not be communicating their research to other mathematicians or meteorologists but to business and industrial partners, most of whom are interested in the bottom line of the research, not the details. Preparing for the presentations can also start in action!

It is important to remember both content and style when planning a speech. Addressing content we focus on narrative. What is a presentation if not a story? And how do we tell a story? Gibberish is a very important component. Sometimes trying to think of a story structure is easier if you do not need to use words. So, we often start by telling a simple story like The Three Little Pigs in gibberish. Believe it or not but it is not easy to tell this story in a monotone. Magically, students start to use voices, pause, inflections and stress in order to communicate meaning. And it really helps that the class is usually laughing uncontrollably as they tell it! They instantly become stars.

But before telling stories we sometimes use gibberish to introduce our partners or try to sell a product. Movement just seems to flow when they do this, and students who are not usually very animated easily become so. Moving on to words we then play Yes and No where one person can only say yes while the other can only say no. Of course it is tempting to have an argument, but I ask them to work against that. After all, we all have heard how yes can sometimes mean no, and no often means yes. It is all in the intonation, so students are encouraged to use their single words for sound, not just content.

Another animating activity is for students to play Buy and Sell or the Real Estate Agent Game. Again, I have no idea where these games originated. In pairs, one student is the buyer and one is the seller. Ordinarily, the seller would try to persuade the buyer to buy a property or some other object of your choosing. Indeed, we start the game with the entire class playing simultaneously in pairs. The seller is eager to sell and the buyer is eager to be persuaded to buy. The energy level is high. Then we switch intentions: the seller is indifferent about selling, and the buyer is eager to buy. This creates an entirely different energy.

Other variations include a seller who is eager not to sell and an uninterested buyer. The energy is totally lowered! After these exercises we discuss how we felt differently in each scenario, how we had different energy levels. Then we discuss how we used our bodies and our voices differently.

We are now ready to focus on the content level of the presentation. In an activity from the Alda Center we use role play to simulate explaining their research to different types of people. In one scene they might have to explain it to a parent, and in another to a complete stranger on the bus. Or perhaps they might explain it to your five year old cousin or a friend studying business. Or a politician. Perhaps they are being interviewed for a magazine article about climate research or a technical journal. The possibilities are endless, and the way the research is explained will be very different depending on the audience. This is usually a revelation to the students who, until this point, only needed to explain it to their peers in the CDT or their advisers. At this time I point out that I am a lay person with limited scientific background. Then I ask them to not only explain their research so I can understand it but to try to express their enthusiasm for their subject. Why did they choose this area to explore? Hopefully there might even be a story behind it!

The structuring of the presentation then follows more traditional lines. But an important aspect is choosing the one slide to which they are limited and a title to try to capture the essence of the speech. A good exercise for doing this might be to try to explain the research to a partner in one minute, thirty seconds, fifteen seconds and then one sentence, one phrase, and one word. It can be fine despite the loud protestations of the students!

Basically almost everything can be done in action. But what is the point? Isn't it simply easier to present information in a series of power point slides? It certainly is less time consuming! Remember the old adage about teaching a man to fish? As long as teaching remains in a top down lecture format students become isolated and confined in the traditional solitary learner mode. Science today is being done in cohorts, small groups in which learners can collaborate. Far from holing up in small rooms hunched over a computer and occasionally touching bases with an adviser the new way of learning encourages students to interact, to collaborate, and to communicate to larger and more diverse audiences. Action methods take scientists into new realms where they can test their passion for their subject with like minded peers as well as possible skeptics. Refining ideas must take into account other possibly contradictory ideas in order to form a whole. Breaking research down to its basics reveals underlying truths that might have been overlooked. A holistic action oriented component in science education addresses the new necessities of twenty first century science and welcomes it into the conversation.

One hundred years ago Moreno played with children in the gardens of Vienna. Through observation and interaction he formed his ideas of groups and how they form and reform. He noticed how a group can act as an agent for change and how, within that group, children can try on and experiment with roles. One hundred years later, using some of his observations about groups, scientists experiment with their own selves, discover safety and comfort zones, and grow as communicators not only of science but of themselves. They learn to tell their stories. They are listened to. It is a small step, based in playful experimentation, but truly the beginning of a great adventure.

Justine Jones

Justine Jones is an American expat living in London. Formerly a secondary school drama teacher she studied psychodrama in both the US and UK eventually ending up practicing psychotherapy as a Jungian sandplay therapist with children and adolescents. Currently she is specialising in Science Communication and is associated with three Centres for Doctoral Training at Imperial College London where she teaches year long Applied Improvisation (Action Methods) courses and coaches students there in group and individual presentations. She also works using Applied Improvisation in teacher training at Queen Mary University for students interested in teaching mathematics incorporating Action Methods. She is the author of four books on using Improvisation in the classroom. Contact her at *justinewjones@gmail.com*.

References

Alda, A. (2017) *If I Understood You, Would I Have This Look on My Face?* Random House, New York.

Hale, AE. (1981) *Conducting Clinical Sociometric Explorations*. Royal Publishing.

Johnstone, K. (1981) *Impro: Improvisation and the Theatre*, Methuen Ltd, London.

Jones, J.and MA Kelley (2006) *Improv Ideas*, Meriwether Publishing, Colorado Springs, CO.

Jones, J and MA Kelley (2014) *More Improv Ideas*, Meriwether Publishing, Colorado Springs, CO.

Karp, M. and P. Holmes,ed. (1998) *The Handbook of Psychodrama*, Routledge,, London.

Moreno, JD (2014) *Impromtu Man*, Literary Press, New York.

Salinsky, T and D. White (2008) *The Improv Handbook: The Ultimate Guide to Improvisation in Comedy*, Bloomsbury Publishing, Inc, London.

Spolin, V.(1963) *Improvisation for the Theatre*, Northwestern University Press, Evanston, IL.

Spontaneity Training with Children: Action-Based Learning

Merav Berger

Creativity has been a significant force behind the development of human civilization and the capacity for imagination is one quality that has allowed humans to survive and thrive in the world. It would seem logical, then, that cultivating creativity in next generations would be a top priority for society.

Decades of research on creativity shows a clear necessity for it in human development[1] and its effectiveness in teaching and learning.[2] It also indicates a decrement between creativity and learning in K–12 classrooms around the United States that has transpired over the past twenty years.[3] For this paper, creativity is defined as the process leading up to and including an original thought and/or object that is adaptive to reality and accepted as useful by some group at some time[4] and examines the necessity and effectiveness of adapting principles of expressive arts therapies in general and psychodrama in particular, to classroom teaching in the United States. Creativity in U.S. classrooms is encountering curricular standards that are based on rigid, standardized testing criteria that become a barrier for creativity.[5] According to Ken Robinson (2006) in a TED Talk, "we're running the national school system where mistakes are the worst thing you can make and the result is that we are educating people out of their creative capacities." Certain conditions in the U.S. education system

---

1 *e.g.*, Gardner, 1973; Kaufman & Sternberg, 2010; Moreno & Moreno, 1955
2 *e.g.*, Beghetto, 2010; Dewey, 1917/1970; Kipper & Giladi, 1978; Runco, 2010
3 Kim, 2012; Runco, Selcuk, & Cayirdag, 2017
4 Runco & Jaeger, 2012
5 Beghetto, 2010; Niu & Sternberg, 2003

make it more challenging to learn and teach creatively[6] and this article explores the advantages and challenges of integrating expressive arts, and specifically psychodrama (also referred to as action exploration outside the clinical setting), into everyday classroom curriculum to strengthen creative thinking and action and to foster social connection, innovation and adaptability for both student and teacher. As an early child and primary school educator, and in my work as a mentor for teenagers, I continuously come across examples of what I call "the catastrophe of creative atrophy" and believe me, it is not pretty. This written discourse first considers the impact of creativity on human development, then examines the significance of and necessity for creative teaching and learning in general, and finally, explores examples of how the philosophies and applications of psychodrama have been used as pedagogical practices in working with kids in pre-K through high school.

To begin with, creativity is a function of survival. The earliest evidence of creativity are simple but functional tools from approximately 2.4 million years ago[7] and "everyday creativity . . . is not only universal, but necessary to our very survival as individuals and as a species."[8] Around 30,000 to 60,000 years ago the human brain developed the mimetic mode of cognitive functioning, that is, the possession of self-triggered recall and rehearsal loop (SRRL) which voluntarily accesses memories independent of cues[9] and allows thinking about the past, present, and future. This emergence of "an ability to internally represent complex, abstract, internally coherent systems of meaning, including symbols and the causal relationships amongst them" (p. 284) opened the path for human development as is observed today. As humans became more adept at thinking about thinking, the tools took on more aesthetically pleasing shapes, and creation no longer served as a lone purpose for survival, its innovation transformed to telling a story about the *experience* of survival. These stories of experience, in turn, became the lessons that were passed down, refined and re-defined, from generation to generation, most often through creative-based expression. With the SRRL in full effect, humans' neural capacity to remember their own past experiences as well as the experiences of others', along with the brain's ability to combine, synthesize, and apply these experiences, became the *locus nascendi* for cognition and for imagination, a "lifelong cognitive and affective endeavor that acts as the catalyst for all creative actions."[10] With the goal of depicting the human condition through language, vision, sound, movement, story, and enactment, creative expression attempts to communicate the

---

6 Beghetto & Kaufman, 2014
7 Gabora & Kaufman, 2010
8 Kaufman & Sternberg, 2010, p. 190
9 Gabora & Kaufman, 2010
10 Eckhoff & Urbach, 2008, p. 180

subjective aspects of life by creating something that captures these subjective factors[11] and even though it is an integral element to the human experience, it is not an in-born quality and is something which must be developed and exercised so that it may flourish.

Creative expression "makes use of a creative intelligence [that] when used in contemplative ways can produce understanding, truth and wisdom that involves our whole being, mind, body and spirit" (Kossak, 2015, p. 26) and, like any other form of intelligence, creative acumen must be strengthened through a process of meaning-making, internalization, and application of that knowledge in a novel or useful manner. Knowledge, according to John Dewey (1917/1970), is a transformative process that transcends language and even though Piaget (1951) asserted that peers play an important role in creative problem solving, Mezirow and Taylor (2009) described transformative learning in adults as a process of developing autonomous thinking through learning to "negotiate [one's] own values, meanings, and purposes rather than to uncriti-cally act on those of others" (p. 11). Gergen (2009) suggested that "virtually all intelligible action is born, sustained, and/or extinguished within the ongoing process of relationship" (p. xv). What is apparent and inherent in both social and autonomous development is the implication of 'another'.

Humans are social by nature and although western culture has engendered concepts of knowledge and education as occurring separately, it is "through a relational re-orientation of these concepts and the practices in which they are embedded, [that] we can realize more fully the potentials for human and environmental well-being."[12] Knowledge, according to Gergen, is an outcome of relational processes, where the world is generated through co-action and communal agreements, and that "knowing comes into existence only through social participation" (p. 229). If knowledge is a communal creation, then education is a process for enhancing participation in relational processes, aka knowledge building. Psychodrama is certainly a fitting form for understanding existence through action and what better vehicle for celebrating communal creation than action exploration! The classroom is a setting rife with psycho-social opportunities to exercise, learn, and practice knowledge building through spontaneous social creative action. Adaptability of thought and the ability to recognize other ideas are crucial to cognitive and creative processes, and necessary to solving problems and communicating with others, even in nonlinear ways, so when social encounters are facilitated and driven with an intention for connection and creative learning, as one might see in a classroom, then learning can happen on both an autonomous level and a socially contributory one, simultaneously.

---

11 Gardner, 1973
12 Gergen, 2009, p. 202

The structure of the U.S. public school system today is one that does not wholeheartedly support creativity and creative teaching or learning,[13] nor does it truly support autonomous thinking. Although early child education best practices incorporate experiential, child-centered, and play-based standards to both teaching and learning, primary and secondary schools' focus are singular-minded in that their objective is to meet standardized quotas that bear little relevance to nurturing and growing competent, compassionate, and contributing members of society.[14] One caveat of creativity, and perhaps one reason for its decline, is that it is an elusive force that "presupposes a radical change to all the old kinds of form [and] brings totally unknown and fresh sensations."[15] Creativity, in this case, implies change, which connotes chaos and most people don't like chaos, so they avoid it — particularly teachers who have a very strict agenda to which they must adhere. In fact, researchers have found that teachers have an aversion to creative thinkers or "unexpected student ideas,"[16] and "when teachers view unexpected ideas as disruptive and habitually dismiss them, they are seriously undermining opportunities for students to share and develop potentially creative ideas" (p. 451). This is a most unfortunate, albeit blameless, event, since, ultimately, unexpected ideas and original thought are adaptive qualities that markedly improve chances of thriving in life. Vygotzky (1967/2004) passionately emphasized cultivating creativity in school-age children, explaining that "the entire future of humanity will be attained through the creative imagination" (p. 88).

Alas, there's the rub. We come back to the catastrophe of creative atrophy. I use the word atrophy knowing full well it is a term most often used to reference muscle density. Creativity, as noted by developmental theorists, is not an innate system, rather, it is a complex structure whose navigation thereof must be learned and reinforced. It's a muscle that must be flexed and strengthened to support healthy biological, psychological, social, and emotional development. An essential task of education is to provide a stimulating environment in which creative thought is encouraged[17] so that young children have opportunities to "experience new things, draw upon experiences of others, and to be allowed many opportunities to create materials that embody their imaginative thoughts" (p. 185). Vygotzky (1967/2016) recognized that "imagination is a new formation that is not present in the consciousness of the very young child, is totally absent in animals, and represents a specifically human form of conscious activity. Like all functions of consciousness, it originally arises from action" (p. 7). He further

---

13 Smith & Smith, 2010
14 Beghetto, 2010
15 Garcia-Lorca, 2007, middle of page
16 Beghetto, 2010, p. 450
17 Eckhoff & Urbach, 2008

described the phenomenon of a child letting the basic categories of reality—not symbolism—pass through its experience in play, so that "the child, in wishing, carries out his wishes; and in thinking, he acts. Internal and external action are inseparable: imagination, interpretation, and will are internal processes in external action" (p. 16). In this instance, the child is simultaneously experiencing act hunger *and* act completion.[18] In addition, the child is both acting-in *and* acting-out,[19] creating a third, albeit slightly more pedagogical branch, of what I call *acting-through*. Vygotzky (1967/2016) contended that "play with an imaginary situation is something essentially new, impossible for a child under three; it is a novel form of behavior in which the child's activity in an imaginary situation liberates him from situational constraints" (p. 11). In acting-through "as-if" moments as "as-is-and-can-be" moments, the child fully embodies the here-and-now, and in that time spent in liminal space and surplus reality, there is inherent movement through unchartered space, and already we are looking at four major components of psychodrama as they relate to creative learning: time, space, action, and spontaneity.

Spontaneity, defined by Moreno (1946) as a force that leads a person to respond adequately to a new situation or give a new response to an old situation, is a key concept of creativity. Mezirow (2000) described a disorienting dilemma, which occurs when someone encounters an experiences that does not fit their expectations and they cannot resolve the situation without some change in their thoughts and action. In expressive arts therapies, the concept of decentering[20] describes "the move away from the narrow logic of thinking and acting that marks the helplessness around the 'dead-end' situation in question. This is a move into the opening of surprising unpredictable unexpectedness, the experience within the logic of imagination" (p. 83). In theatre, being spontaneous means *being in the moment*. What these all have in common is the idea that to move forward in any situation, we must first encounter an event that may or may not deviate from our normal perceptions and expectations and to which we may or may not respond accordingly. In those moments of chaos our brains burst into activity as "cells across the cortex reform into a new network, which is able to enter consciousness"[21] and this clash of titanic and tumultuous neurons propels us to a new state of being with newly formed connections, that is, we are now older and wiser! The act of moving forward connotes movement, aka action, and the encounter triggers spontaneity. Vygotzky's references to the imaginary activity as a release from situational constraints lay along the lines of spontaneity as a catalyst for insight and catharsis, only

---

18 Blatner, 1996
19 Ibid.
20 Knill, Levine, & Levine, 2005
21 Richards, 2010, p. 203

instead of psychological gain, the proprietor of released constraints gains critical knowledge and understanding of the workings of the world around them. This construction of meaning is crucial to cognitive development in the early years and research indicates an association between intelligence and creativity. A recent study probed the prominent notion of the threshold hypothesis, which holds that the relationship between creativity and intelligence assumes that "above-average intelligence represents a necessary condition for high-level creativity."[22] Findings showed evidence for a segmented linear relationship between intelligence and creative potential, and that intelligence significantly predicted creative potential in a lower IQ range, but not in the upper IQ range. In other words, intelligence helps you be creative up to a certain point; after that it's all about an openness to experience that dictates the level of creative ideation and output. Spontaneity training from a very early age can contribute to a students' ability to practice openness and adaptability, ultimately leading them to a more productive and healthy adulthood.

We know that creativity is a function of survival and a function of a thriving society; we know that creative action promotes cognitive growth and neural connections; and we understand that intelligence is important but that a sense of openness far outweighs our mental capacities. We know these things and yet we still insist on archaic methods and irrelevant government mandates to determine the standard of how our society attains knowledge. As of the writing of this chapter, many U.S. school districts, particularly those in urban communities, have adopted scripted curricula wherein teachers read *verbatim* from instructional scripts rather than tapping into their own creative potential or subject matter expertise.[23] As rote and robotic learning slowly pervade classrooms around the United States, children and adults lose their power for spontaneity and thereby their power for creative thought and action, ultimately constricting the ever-continuing development of humanity. Instead of raising a generation of innovative and open-minded problem-solvers, we are rearing a nascence of impotence that may end up causing great harm. With that, "creativity is part of the general human potential, something that we can cultivate in ourselves . . . [and] something that can be nurtured in others"[24] so not all is lost!

Contrary to some early developmentalists' beliefs, children as young as three are exhibiting creative thinking and yet there seems to be little room to further develop those skills under current curricular standards in the United States. One area that could inform creative teaching practices as processes for meaning-making and is easily adaptable as a pedagogical tool, is expressive

---

22 Jauk, Benedek, Dunst, & Neubauer, 2013, p. 212
23 Beghetto, 2010
24 Barron, Montuori, & Barron, 1997, p. 5

arts in general, and psychodrama in particular. Used as a supplement to or an integration of the current curriculum, arts-based action explorations and experiential inquiry can enhance the classroom learning experience for both teacher and student. The psychodramatic relations between spontaneity, creativity, and learning are conducive to both spontaneity training in educators and in creating immersive and experiential learning environments for children. According to Miekle (2014), "experiential learning is the process of learning from direct experience . . . Students are not treated as passive receptacles to be filled with information; instead, they are active participants who shape the classroom experience" (pp. 67–68). It is more important than ever to integrate creative learning in the classroom, and more specifically, spontaneity training. Kids nowadays practice simulations in school all the time, whether it be earthquake or fire drills, active shooter exercises, or skills practice-tests; it shouldn't be too far-fetched to fathom classrooms engaging in action explorations of concepts being studied. As daunting of a case as it may be, it can be done. Following are some examples from the field that demonstrate the significance and success of creative teaching and learning, particularly through psychodramatic practices to promote spontaneity and, ultimately, richer, deeper, and more meaningful understanding of and connection to the world.

Softening Rigidity and Literal Thinking: A Preschooler's Experience with Spontaneity

Artie (not his real name), a precocious and extremely intelligent three-and-a-half-year-old boy, loved trains. He spent most of his days at preschool building train tracks and train stations and, his favorite, creating train schedules. He created large and intricate landscapes using the classroom's wooden tracks and train set materials, often playing alone, and he did not like it when other children touched or wanted to play with or add to his creations, especially if they altered his work or added an object that was not an actual part of the train set. This was something I'd observed in his experience of the rest of the material in the classroom, too, a sense that each toy/object served its own purpose *as is* and therefore could not be anything else—blocks were for building structures, train sets were for playing with trains, gems were for pattern making, and a hat was for wearing on one's head. I introduced the class to a game I call "Anything But" where one object becomes anything in the world except for what it really is. Our first practice of the game involved a simple wooden block. Artie, who always loved being first, immediately volunteered to be the first to try it. He came up to the front of the class ("on stage"), took hold of the block, stared at it, looked up, and said "it's a block to build with."

> **Merav:** Yes, that's what it really is. Let's pretend it's something else.

Artie: But it's a block.

Merav: Look at its shape. What things have a similar shape?

Artie: I don't know. A brick.

Merav: Ok, great! Now, what color is your brick?

Artie: I don't have a brick.

Merav: What color is your pretend brick?

Artie: This color (*holding up the block*). But it's a block.

(*a child interrupts, calls out "it looks like a phone!"*)

Merav: That's true! Artie, maybe you could pretend it's a phone?

Artie: But it doesn't have a screen. How would I push the buttons?

Merav: What happens if you hold it up to your ear like you would hold up a phone?

(*Artie tries it*)

Artie: There's nothing. It's nothing. It's a block.

The "Anything But" game (ABG) became a staple in our daily routine and Artie's inability to imagine an object as anything else but that object continued with one observable shift: whereas Artie had previously been far more intent on being first, taking up all the time, and being disruptive when he wasn't on stage, he was now raptly attentive to his classmates during ABG. During this period, I also began introducing elements of ABG into his train play, offering a block as a mountain, or a blue piece of fabric from the drama corner as a lake ("but it's a napkin!"). Several weeks into our ABG series, the class came back to using the block as the object. Artie's hand shot up and with confident strides in place of his usual small toe-steps, he faced the class and presented his "train with no wheels because it's in the rail yard because it's had its wheels removed to be fixed so that's why there's no wheels, but it's a train." Playing ABG as a daily exercise in spontaneity provided Artie with contextual and physical practice of pretend play where he could supplement, if not integrate, his logical and rigid thinking with imaginative and creative cognation. In practicing spontaneity, Artie was able to widen his range of conceived reality and recognize that patterns could be rearranged and that some concepts could be malleable and manipulated.

Role Diagrams and Psychodrama Vignettes:
A Third Grader's Experience as an Auxiliary

In teaching Jewish heroes to a class of third graders, my intention was for the children to resonate with these figures as people who were just like them, so that by connecting themselves to these famous figures, the seemingly unreachable qualities of a hero could feel more accessible. I asked the children to create a collage from magazine clippings of their own heroic qualities, very much like a role diagram, then invited one of them to come up as protagonist in an enactment of his composition. He had several images of glass objects, including ornately decorated blown glass vases and bottles, in his art piece and when I asked him what he felt was heroic about them, he shrugged his shoulders and replied that they "make me feel calm, they're quiet but really beautiful." Using tele, he selected a slightly reluctant classmate to play the glass bottles auxiliary. The reluctant boy was a physically exuberant child whose high spirits could often be disruptive in class as well as in the play yard, and I'd observed that he often played or worked alone.

I was curious to note that he'd been selected to play a role that demonstrated quiet calmness and beauty. I asked the two boys to switch roles so that the protagonist could show his auxiliary how he wanted him to move and speak. The auxiliary, in taking on the role, completely transformed; he became still, only moving in the distinct manner with which he was asked to move. The role made no sound and neither did he for the rest of the exercise . . . and for the rest of class. Later, as we were coming back to the classroom from a break, I heard a commotion and a bunch of boys exclaiming "Woa!", "Epic!", "Dude, that was *awesome!*" And then I heard: "It's because of his legendary glass bottle powers." I saw a group of children surrounding the auxiliary boy who was all smiles and I was stunned. And *verklempt*. It was a powerful reminder that the creative process knows no bounds and that time, space, and trust in the unknown, lets social spontaneous creative action venture forth to new, unchartered territories ready to be discovered by those heroic enough to take on the challenge.

Even though the boy continued to demonstrate high energy throughout the rest of the year, there was a distinct difference in his attitude towards his peers and theirs' to him. They invited him more often to play games, especially when they needed someone to help them solve a problem and the glass bottle reference continued to come up in class (*e.g.*, "dude, we need your glass bottle powers, be in our group") and were less inclined to get angry at him during his disruptions. In providing the class with time, space, action, and spontaneity to explore the subject of Jewish heroes, the students were able to embody and connect with the heroic parts of themselves and each other in a concrete manner that applied itself to real life as in their acceptance and inclusion of their classmate. The boy was better connected with his calm and quiet sides, able to draw on them in times of need without adult prompting. In other words, the glass bottle embodiment in the re-enactment granted him self-regulation tactics that he was able to use during the year to further himself socially and academically.

The Empty Chair: Giving Voice to Kindergarteners

In one of my enrichment programs for preschool and primary school-aged children, *Improv with Merav*, I read a Jewish folktale about a woman who constantly complains in an exaggerated manner and one day everything she complains about becomes real. For example, she complains that her feet are swollen like melons and so her feet turn into actual melons. The story embodies the lesson that words matter and that we can control our perception of our surroundings by seeking the good in the world rather than the bad. Upon finishing the story, I placed two empty chairs: one representing "a complaint" and the other symbolizing "the good side of it" and invited the kids to take turns coming up to the chairs and making their own statements.

Many of the children copied one another, as is typical in a preschool classroom, but some of them came up with original complaints and relevant flip sides. In one instance, a six-year old girl from a religious family sat on the complaint chair and cried out dramatically "why do I always have to help with my baby brother?" When she moved into the other chair, she sat for a moment thinking and swinging her legs. Suddenly, she froze and said, "this is a mommy moment, I have to think different." I invited her to pretend to be her mommy and to speak to "herself" sitting in the complaint chair. In this spontaneous role reversal play, the young girl told herself, "you're six years old and you know how to do a lot of things by yourself, like use the stove and the microwave and put on a diaper on a real baby not a doll baby." I had her switch chairs and respond to "mommy" to whom she very quietly responded, "I'm also the only one who knows how to make him laugh," and then she broke character and turned to the kids and myself and eagerly explained, "everyone always tries to make him laugh but only I can do it. I like to make him laugh because it makes everyone happy and so I like to do it. I don't want to complain about it anymore, can I pick something else?" In these precious moments, the child encountered external relationships within herself and through spontaneous and creative actions, she practiced empathy, logical thinking, ideation, and implementation, and in so doing she grew in mind, body, and spirit. The other children, who had sat enraptured during her personal dialogue, spent the rest of the day playing house and with dolls, with everyone trying to make the other laugh. The strength of undergoing and witnessing the authentic creation of new knowledge is well attested to in psychodramatic practices, and its philosophical foundation as it relates to effective education was evident in this classroom exercise.

Feeding Act-Hunger: Sociodrama and Teenagers

A group of teen girls from a Jewish youth movement with whom I work encountered an issue within their cohort where older girls where leaving the group and newer girls weren't making strong connections to current members. They held brainstorming sessions, created lists, established protocols but no concrete and sustainable solutions came up. I invited them to (re)create one of their social gatherings here-and-now, that is, I encouraged them to enact a scenario as if it were happening. At first, they appeared confused and then slowly some of the girls began to take on roles ("I'll be a new girl", "I'll be a board member") and eventually there emerged a setting, a time, and an entire world existing in the liminal space created by the force of imagination. The young ladies transformed into and fully embodied their self-selected roles and immersed themselves completely in the simulation. When the action-based experiment came to its end, the girls were eager to share their experiences, particularly their insights and revelations to their conflict. In exploring their problem through active and engaged embodiment, they were able to let feelings and ideas rise spontaneously so that they could then see and confront the issues at hand in the moment in real time. The improvisational work concluded with a finite idea and a concrete plan which the girls successfully placed into effect at their next social gathering.

Just as "a true therapeutic procedure cannot have less an objective than the whole of mankind,"[25] so, too, a true educational methodology cannot have less than the whole of humanity as its objective. John Dewey (1897) opened his creed for pedagogy with the statement that "all education proceeds by the participation of the individual in the social consciousness" (p. 3) and psychodrama, when adapted as an action-based learning practice, taps into the collective and individual consciousness while balancing a bonded and relational being with the world. Using spontaneous action in the classroom need not come at the price of a more traditional approach, rather it can very easily be integrated or supplemented into an existing method of teaching. Learning creatively takes us back to our developmental roots that rely so much on our abilities to adapt to change and creating a culture of creativity in the classroom can enhance our abilities to teach and learn effectively and in a way that advances humanity to become all that it can be.

---

25 Moreno, 1953/1993

Merav Berger

Merav Berger, MA, is an educational consultant focused on providing new and veteran teachers support in cultivating a creative and person-sensitive classroom environment. With her extensive background in theater, management, expressive arts therapy, and education, she has developed a series of experiential workshops for teacher professional development, preservice teacher training, and socio-educational supervision.

In addition to her work with educators, Merav offers leadership training for Jewish youth and teens, and facilitates enrichment programs for youth in synagogues and Jewish day schools. One of her favorite projects is "Improv with Merav," a spontaneity training program for pre-K–3rd graders. As a Jewish educator, she works with a wide range of ages, including grade level, mixed-aged, and families, and works hard to foster innovative leadership, life-long Jewish learning, and community service through creative and artistic expression.

At the time of this publication, Merav is undergoing her doctoral studies where she is researching psychodrama outside the clinical setting as it pertains to education and teacher training and development. For more information on her workshops, please contact her at *merav.berger@gmail.com*

References

Barron, F., Montuori, A., & Barron, A. (1997). *Creators on creating: Awakening and cultivating the imaginative mind.* New York, NY: G. P. Putnam's Sons.

Beghetto, R. A. (2010). Creativity in the classroom. In J. C. Kaufman & R. J. Sternberg (Eds.), *The Cambridge handbook of creativity.* New York, NY: Cambridge University Press.

Beghetto, R. A., & Kaufman, J. C. (2014). Classroom contexts for creativity. *High Ability Studies, 25*(1), 53–69.

Blatner, A. (1996). *Acting-in: Practical applications of psychodramatic methods* (3rd ed.). New York, NY: Springer Publishing Company.

Dewey, J. (1897). *My pedagogic creed.* New York, NY: E. L. Kellogg & Co.

Dewey, J. (Ed.). (1917/1970). *Creative intelligence: Essays in the pragmatic attitude.* New York, NY: Octagon Books.

Eckhoff, A., & Urbach, J. (2008). Understanding imaginative thinking during childhood: Sociocultural conceptions of creativity and imaginative thought. *Early Childhood Education Journal, 2008*(36), 179–185.

Gabora, L., & Kaufman, S. B. (2010). Evolutionary approaches to creativity. In J. C. Kaufman & R. J. Sternberg (Eds.), *The Cambridge Handbook of Creativity.* New York, NY: Cambridge University Press.

Garcia-Lorca, F. (2007). Theory and play of the duende. from *http://www. poetryintranslation.com/PITBR/Spanish/LorcaDuende.htm*

Gardner, H. (1973). *The arts and human development: A psychological study of the artistic process.* New York: Wiley-Interscience Publication.

Gergen, K. J. (2009). *Relational being: Beyond self and community.* New York, NY: Oxford University Press.

Jauk, E., Benedek, M., Dunst, B., & Neubauer, A. C. (2013). The relationship between intelligence and creativity: New support for the threshold hypothesis by means of empirical breakpoint detection. *Intelligence, 41*(4), 212–221.

Kaufman, J. C., & Sternberg, R., J. (Eds.). (2010). *The Cambridge handbook of creativity.* New York, NY: Cambridge University Press.

Kim, K. H. (2012). The creativity crisis: The decrease in creative thinking scores on the Torrance Tests of Creative Thinking. *Creativity Research Journal, 23*(4), 285–295.

Kipper, D. A., & Giladi, D. (1978). Effectiveness of structured psychodrama and systemic desensitization in reducing test anxiety. *Journal of Counseling Psychology, 25*(6), 499–505.

Knill, P. J., Levine, E. G., & Levine, S. K. (2005). *Principles and practice of expressive arts therapy: Toward a therapeutic aesthetics.* Philadelphia, PA: Jessica Kingsley Publishing.

Kossak, M. (2015). *Attunement in expressive arts therapy: Toward an understanding of embodied empathy.* Springfield, IL: Charles C. Thomas Publisher.

May, R. (1994). *The courage to create.* New York, NY: W. W. Norton.

Mezirow, J. (2000). *Learning as transformation: Critical perspectives on a theory in progress.* San Francisco, CA: Jossey-Bass.

Mezirow, J., & Taylor, E. W. (2009). *Transformative learning in practice: Insights from community, workplace, and higher education.* San Francisco, CA: John Wiley & Sons, Inc.

Miekle, S. (2014). Embracing our creativity. *Independent School, 73,* 64–69.

Moreno, J. L. (1946). *Psychodrama* (Vol. First). New York, NY: Beacon House.

Moreno, J. L. (1953/1993). *Who shall survive? Foundations of sociometry, group psychotherapy and sociodrama* (Student ed.). Roanoke, VA: Royal.

Moreno, J. L., & Moreno, F. B. (1955). Spontaneity theory of child development. *Sociometry*(4), 137. doi: 10.2307/2785851

Niu, W., & Sternberg, R. J. (2003). Societal and school influences on student creativity: The case of China. *Psychology in the Schools, 40*(1).

Piaget, J. (1951). *Principal factors determining intellectual evolution from childhood to adult life.* New York, NY: Columbia University Press.

Richards, R. (2010). Everyday creativity: Process and way of life—four key issues. In J. C. Kaufman & R. J. Sternberg (Eds.), *The Cambridge handbook of creativity*. New York, NY: Cambridge Press, Inc.

Robinson, K. (2006). Do schools kill creativity? *TED2006. https://www.ted.com/talks/ken_robinson_says_schools_kill_creativity.*

Runco, M. A. (2010). Divergent thinking, creativity, and ideation. In J. C. Kaufman & R. J. Sternberg (Eds.), *The Cambridge handbook of creativity*. New York, NY: Cambridge University Press.

Runco, M. A., & Jaeger, G. J. (2012). The standard definition of creativity. *Creativity Research Journal, 24*(1), 92–96. doi: 10.1080/10400419.2012.650092

Runco, M. A., Selcuk, A., & Cayirdag, N. (2017). A closer look at the creativity gap and why students are less creative at school than outside of school. *Thinking Skills and Creativity, 24*(2017), 242–249.

Smith, J. K., & Smith, L. F. (2010). Educational Creativity. In J. C. Kaufman & R. J. Sternberg (Eds.), *The Cambridge handbook of creativity*. New York, NY: Cambridge University Press.

Vygotzky, L. S. (1967/2004). Imagination and creativity in childhood (M. E. Sharpe, Trans.). *Journal of Russian and East European Psychology, 42*(1).

Vygotzky, L. S. (1967/2016). Play and its role in the mental development of the child (Veresov, N. & Barrs, M., Trans.). *International Research in Early Childhood Education, 7*(2).

Section 3

Action Explorations in Social and Community Contexts

Forum Theatre as Restorative Practice

Applying Boal's Methods to Justice Systems

Mecca Antonia Burns

They say "revenge is sweet." Could remorse feel sweet? Indeed it can mobilize deep change— if it is bearable, if it is authentic, and if it is action-oriented. Experimenting with mercy as an antidote to cruelty opens us to new choices in life. Theatre offers the aesthetic distance to slow down, breathe, and try out unfamiliar roles and behaviors.

· · ·

Since 1992, I have been a practitioner of Forum Theatre, a theatrical form invented in Brazil by Augusto Boal and others. In this model, spectators influence the outcome of a dramatic scene. Across the globe, participatory theatre emerges as an ongoing dialogic game where audience members enact leadership roles in an atmosphere of creative experimentation, without the risks of real life.

"Restorative Justice" is an approach to criminal justice focusing on reconciliation with offenders, victims, and the community.

What is Forum Theatre?

Forum theatre was invented by Brazilian theatre-activist Augusto Boal during the 20th century. Specially-devised theatre games illustrate models of shared power, and a skit depicts an unresolved conflict. But instead of the actors, the spectators — "spect-actors"—step into the action and pose solutions.

How can Forum Theatre support Restorative Justice

Theatre can be applied as a community crime-prevention strategy, with offenders serving as the actors and script-writers. Forum Theatre lets us dream up images of restoration. What might heal the situation? In a related technique, Three Wishes, someone who has been harmed can witness three levels of wish fulfillment, each of which is enacted on the spot. The first wish might be a revenge fantasy, and once this is gratified, deeper and more compassionate desires may emerge.

Boxing Match is an alternative strategy for participants who have good suggestions but are too shy to step in as a character. People often have good ideas while watching. Here's how it works:

After calling out "Round One!" we see a two-minute improvised scene of a conflict between two people. When the leader makes a bell sound, the actors each step to their "corner." Now audience members have an opportunity to assist in the role of "Coach"—for one minute. (People seem to feel quite comfortable giving advice for other people to act on!)

When the bell rings for Round Two, the two actors re-enter their conflict situation, now armed with new strategies to try. There can be as many rounds as needed for the conflict to transform. In each round, the strategies are refined through careful listening and earnest advice from a range of spect-actors.

Durham, NC: What is Restorative Justice?

Restorative Justice (RJ) is a philosophy about healing the psychological and emotional effects, impact, and causes of crimes and wrong-doing. RJ is a group of facilitated dialogue and listening practices that engage the person who was harmed, the person responsible for the harm, plus supporters and community.

The purpose of RJ is to provide safe dialogue processes that are flexible enough for participants to communicate, usually face-to-face, about what happened, what they think and feel, how they are impacted, and what needs to happen to put things right and move on from a harmful incident.

Circles are used to deepen participants' understanding of values, and to create collective knowledge among participants about what others experience and understand. It is imperative that RJ facilitators reflect on the values that guide the practice, including honesty, integrity, compassion and responsibility.

The values support us in being our best self; they tune us into that frequency and establish the rhythm of listening and talking. Values provide a compass that guides the performative aspects of RJ. It is challenging for people to talk directly about crime or harmful incidents. Circle Process grows us and calls us into being able to sit with the emotions that are stirred up in us and others.

According to Amy Elliot, PhD, RDT, drama therapist and licensed psychotherapist in Durham, NC, several elements of RJ echo theatrical processes. Here are three parallels with performance:

- Ritual, which provides a framework for Circles.
- Scripts and role-plays for RJ conferencing and pre-conferencing.

- Performatives: chosen actions that are sincere and serious, voluntary and intentional; they enact or clarify an agreement, changing status, or role.

I. Circles as a form of Ritual

The Circle process is associated with Rituals via forms, practices and guidelines that are predictable and grounding, with room for creativity. For example, Circles may begin with music, movement, a poem, a story, or a group task.

Everyone begins by sitting in a Circle facing the center. There is often a centerpiece of objects that set a tone or theme for the Circle. A Talking Piece is used to clarify who is talking and listening and ensures that everyone gets an equal opportunity to be heard. It slows the rhythm between speaking and listening; it creates little pauses of silence as the piece is passed. People can always pass and be returned to later, or just hold the piece in silence.

2. Use of Scripts and Role-playing in training

RJ conferences and pre-conferences typically do have a script that is used for training purposes, and to stay on track. The scripts can simply be a list of bullet points, freeing up the facilitator to improvise and follow the natural flow of the unfolding dialogue.

Amy Elliot observes that trainees often complain about role-playing, though afterwards they recognize its value. She speculates on why this is and offers tips on how to improve role-playing in training contexts

"Participants misconceive that role-playing is about acting. Talk with a group about why we are role-playing before introducing it. This is not acting, except in the sense that we are all social actors in everyday life.

"Give time for people to stand up if they have been sitting. Let them move about, say a sentence about what they do, to get to know each other."

Role-playing supports trying out the various roles that are fundamental to the RJ Conference: two facilitators, the person(s) harmed and their supporters, the person(s) who did the harm and their supporters, and any community members who were affected by what happened.

"Give time for the person playing a role to reflect on the role and the questions that may be asked of them during the conference. Consider putting them together with related roles: *e.g.* the harmer spends a few minutes with the person they harmed. They talk over what they feel and think about what happened, who has been affected and how, what they have thought about since and what needs to happen to make things right."

Other benefits of role-playing include:

- Experiencing the dialogue process through embodied learning.
- Assessing people's readiness to do this work in the community.

- Having a felt sense of what it's like before you launch.
- Working with the people with whom you will be co-facilitating to get a sense of their style, their strengths and their challenges.
- Processing afterwards to ascertain if participants felt that these marks were met.

3. Performatives

A performative has been defined as a statement that can function as an action. In family therapy, enactments are prescribed to move relationships closer. It's like an agreement or commitment, acknowledging a desire to repair harm. In RJ, for example, a child might fix a window s/he has broken.

Budondo Village, Uganda

When a crime is committed in America it is customary to call the police and swiftly remove the wrong-doer, who then doesn't need to directly face those harmed. Police and jails are prominent in Western societies but not ubiquitous elsewhere. Out of necessity, restorative justice (RJ) has been re-invented throughout the world. Perhaps this author's own encounter, on a rainy night in rural Uganda, will serve as an example.

Three of us shambled along a muddy path, guided only by our cell phone lights. Eventually we reached the home of the woman who had summoned us after being beaten by her husband. Neighbors and relatives sat in a circle near her hut, animatedly discussing how to respond to the violence. The harm-doer sat outside the circle listening to everything that was said. He appeared interested in how he might restore his family's and neighbors' faith in him.

As I joined the circle, I recognized this as a homegrown version of restorative justice—something their ancestors had likely done, which is being taught and practiced anew in the 21st century.

In cultures with an ethos of interdependence, restorative justice is especially vital. We humans are social animals, with an archaic horror of exile. Western societies have an individualistic ethos and may not naturally embrace RJ habits. Retribution is deep-seated, and we place less emphasis on rehabilitation.

In this essay, we will note American cities where RJ efforts are currently being made, and innovations in the Kenyan justice system.

Charlottesville, Virginia

In October 2018, a group of people gathered at a community college in Charlottesville, Virginia to explore the interface of RJ and Forum Theatre.
To stimulate story recall, we formed a Memory Circle on the floor, lying with our heads toward the center.

Someone begins sharing a memory—an instance of injustice or unfairness that remains unresolved. It is told in the first person, present tense so we are all in it. It ends with " . . . and I'm feeling . . . ," to indicate the teller is finished and someone else can begin. These stories may build on each other, or may not.

The main story we enacted featured a high school football team. The teller, Bart, had been bullied and ridiculed all summer by Cliff, a member of his own team. During tackling drills, the coach urged the boys to "hit harder"! Our protagonist's suppressed anger took over, and he suddenly slammed Cliff down, breaking his leg.

We realized that the roles had switched, and the antagonist had become the victim. Cliff was harmed, and needed restoration. When the protagonist had tried to explain how terrible he felt, Cliff snarled back: "I don't care how you feel! You get to play and I have to sit on the bench all season."

Together the group proposed solutions and played them out. For our enactment, Bart cast actors as himself and the teammate. We used the *"three wishes"* technique. His first wish was to see his character apologize to Cliff. His second wish was for the teammates to encourage and witness the apology.

· · · ·

What's the difference between regret and remorse? According to youth mentor Alethea Leventhal, remorse implies heartfelt shame or guilt. Remorse can mobilize transformation—if we can let ourselves feel it enough to face it.

Members of the group were next drawn to a story Alethea had lived, in August 2017 when armed white supremacists marched on our city.

For this we used *Real to Ideal*.

Arranging their bodies in a tableau, members sculpted a living image of the "real" atmosphere in Charlottesville. Those in the sculpture had a chance to rotate out, to see the whole picture and fine-tune it.

Next we began to dynamize the *real image*, first through interior monologue (all characters simultaneously murmur their own feelings and wishes). Then we added sound and movement: On a cue, each figure takes one step toward what they desire.

On the opposite side of the stage, we sculpted the *ideal image*. We finished by moving on ten counts from the real image to the ideal image, through transitional images, which portray the hard work of organizing—finding consensus when moving step-by-step toward change. When approaching one's own desire, one may find someone else on that same path. Flexibility and creativity are needed to surmount obstacles.

To summarize, we value physicalizing the experience, putting things into motion and witnessing the repercussions. Restorative justice asks us to imagine reparations, and theatre offers a cornucopia of games and techniques to envision wrongs being made right. We are offered enough aesthetic distance to feel remorse, and hope for mending and healing.

New York City

You Are the Shift, LLC is an empowerment and creative arts-based consulting company founded by Lindsey Sherwin in New York City, with a workshop and training curriculum dedicated to supporting the behavioral and emotional wellbeing of young people ages 13–18, and gender-specific sessions for young men in schools, in residential facilities, and in the criminal and juvenile justice system. YATS specializes in developing trauma-informed restorative justice response practices through a structured framework applying therapeutic drama techniques and the creative arts therapies for socio-emotional development and life skills practice. Young people learn how to shape and shift internal needs in order to apply these skills to their relationships in daily life.

In what Sherwin has coined a "restorative regulation model," You Are The Shift's first workshop series is called "De:Coding the Mask and Claiming Our Power." It looks at how to effectively regulate or "shift" the perspectives, emotions, and behaviors of youth who have been affected by conflict, trauma, violence, neglect, bullying, grief, and loss.

The objective is to transform these experiences via therapeutic drama, using the principles of restorative practice.

"As follows in the RJ process, one of our values is to respect the other person's story as part of the circle process. In drama therapy we show respect to ourselves and others through creating a narrative that shares the inner parts of ourselves openly and publicly via the stage."

"The language code we use in order to measure the shift or changes in regulation levels in mood and behavior is what we refer to as *upshifting* and *downshifting*, interwoven as part of the model's framework for 'restoring, regulating, and repairing'."

Through its diverse methodologies (drama therapy, and the creative arts therapies within a restorative justice frame), the program model assists young people to form healthy attachment styles — communication, socialization, strengthening cognitive behaviors and emotional intelligence, spontaneity, flexibility, and building solidarity with others.

How we Shift incorporates the ways in which we learn to live. Through practicing and rehearsing new behaviors in the presence of our own will we help build our confidence and learn how to rebuild the conditions to solve social problems experienced daily.

You Are The Shift's programs are designed to build a group's identity, to name and express feelings more truthfully and openly, and to solidify language/ emotional beliefs in order to shift physical, emotional, and mental states. Through providing and modeling these new skill sets using intentional theatre games, YATS' programming adopts and proactively utilizes real life situations through role playing specific scenarios important to our young people. Methods include improvisation, masks and embodiment, intentional movement, scripting, video and playback theatre, poetry, collage-making, sociodrama, and ethnodrama performances.

> We consciously help connect our participants to the internal resources they need in order to shift beliefs and behaviors and improve their lives: through fostering more awareness, encouraging emotional growth and resilience, and most importantly by enhancing relationships.

> We are committed to ensuring that our young people leave a completed YATS cycle with a diverse set of acculturated values, new perspectives, and insights into their own lives and into the lives of others.

For more on YATS, see *lindseysherwin.wordpress.com*

Peacebuilding and Conflict Transformation

Colleague and co-author Bonface Beti shares his experiences in Kenya and Canada:

"In 2012, I was lucky to be one of two storytellers from Amani Peoples' Theatre (APT) in Kenya, invited to help lead the Winnipeg International Storytelling workshops. This annual event is organized by the University of Manitoba's graduate centre for Peace and Conflict Studies. Before this momentous experience, I had been a member of APT for years, an indigenous theatre organization applying the arts to conflict transformation. APT utilizes the power of storytelling with indigenous African meditative and restorative elements to create a culture of peace with grassroots communities.

"Previously I had spent part of my childhood years with Shangilia Mtoto Wa Afrika, a street children theatre organization, founded by celebrated Kenyan film-maker Anne Mungai. The organization utilizes theatre arts to rescue children from the streets of Nairobi and offers them alternative livelihoods.

"It was with Amani Peoples Theatre that I learned a wide range of theatre-based techniques including Forum Theatre and its application to restorative justice, with youth at Kabete Remand Centre in Nairobi. As a key facilitator on this project, I used Boalian theatre games as warm-up activities before exploring deeper issues with youth aged 5–17 years. In our collective quest for alternatives to youth incarceration and police round-ups, and to break the cycle of offending and re-offending. Forum Theatre was a natural ally. Some of the youth had been arrested for petty crimes such as loitering, or stealing someone's gold chain on Nairobi streets; others for serious offenses like pushing another child over a cliff to their death.

"Kids shared freely and laughed over these crimes as if they meant absolutely nothing to them. I utilized image theatre as a playful tool for reflecting on self and others, and to work on emotions and regulation. We saw youth embody contrasting emotions, for example, sadness turning to happiness and vice versa. The project combined Forum theatre with drawing activities. Children got an opportunity to watch complete Forum Theatre plays on complex social issues such as family violence, poverty and child abuse—displaying transformative solutions proposed through replacing of roles by the youth themselves.

"Back to 2012: I visited Winnipeg Manitoba in a team of about 20 storytellers from different countries. We visited schools and community centres and conducted dozens of story-shops. I was lucky to be assigned Manitoba Youth Remand Centre to conduct a Forum Theatre workshop with my colleague Maxwell Okuto. We were led into a highly-guarded facility on the outskirts of Winnipeg town. After a series of security checks we were led into a heavily guarded waiting room, and then a medium-sized workshop hall. We found almost a dozen youth age 10–16 waiting for us, seated in random ways. The room felt lifeless and quiet. We started to sing a rhythmic tune (Tuufboom . . . Tuff . . . Boom) going around the space.

"We asked each participant to add a sound of an instrument or animal as they deemed fit to build this piece of improvised ensemble. This was our warm-up. Before long, the youth began to clap, sing and some were dancing with the rhythm. We ended the rhythmic movements with an intro- game. Arranging the room in a Circle, we began playing ice-breaker games together, and ventured into exploring emotions through Boalian games. We were now at that point for employing theatrical reflections on issues related to crime and violence. Participants created an emotional machine, a crime machine and activated both. Eventually, participants experimented with replacing parts of the machine and discussed solutions in a Forum session. In 2017, University of Manitoba and Manitoba Storytelling Guild founder Sandra Krah had this to say: 'I saw these youths were stone-faced when you entered the room but soon the room was electrified as you began working with them'."

Kakamega, Western Kenya

While working in Africa, I heard about The Center for Justice and Peacebuilding in Harrisonburg, Virginia. Various people I met had studied there, in a program combining restorative justice, art and spirituality. I was amazed because I live only one hour away across the Blue Ridge Mountains, in Charlottesville.

One year a team of women peacebuilders came from Kenya. I sat with senior probation official Judith Mandillah at lunch and heard about advances in the Kenyan justice system since the 2010 constitution. I told Judith about America's "school to prison pipeline" and was amazed by the "community-based sentencing" that she implements. Women convicted of violent crimes turn their lives around with Judith's help.

A few months later I tried to cross into Kenya with the Suubi Health Team (ten Ugandan village women trained in health care and forum theatre). For years we had done Village Outreach, but had not left the country. This proved even harder than anticipated. We were proud to move as a group, until we were held at the border for five hours, interrogated and threatened.[1] Ultimately the Ugandans were sent home. As a border guard mused, "What would their husbands say if we let them slip across?"

When the crooked officials first accused us of trafficking, I bristled with outrage in my righteous innocence. But I realized this sassiness could make things worse. I redirected myself to respond with friendliness and forbearance.

I was heartbroken to enter Kenya that evening without my friends, but the next day brought relief via theatre. My hosts gallantly reenacted our border trauma. The Kenyan women became the Ugandan team and I became one of the guards, upon whom I had projected evil.

Can theatre help us reclaim projections? In real life, when someone says "Why are you so controlling?" the one so accused may disagree — after all, our defense mechanisms are (by definition) unconscious.

In the Projection Game, the receiver of the projection accepts it as an improvisational offer and playfully exaggerates: "How dare you speak to me that way! Guards, seize him!"

The Kakamega women participated in theatre games and enactments, along with their probation officers.[2] Judith says, "in Kakamega I am using theatre to sensitize the community on the dangers of crime and the need to cultivate youthful talent for community peace."

Nairobi, Kenya

After leaving Kakamega, I returned to Kerith Brook Secondary school in the Nairobi slums. We sustained our focus on restorative justice, with a skit showing chaos in the aftermath of post-election violence. A young man steals a cell phone and a mob captures him and burns him. The thief's brother initially wishes for revenge but realizes this would continue the cycle of violence. Instead we see a courtroom scene, with a student portraying a judge meting out justice via the probation system.

---

1 Watch a brief photo-essay account of the whole adventure: *https://voiceofjsirri.wordpress.com/july-2017/journey-mercies-forum-theatre-outreach-in-east-africa/*

2 Watch a short video showing them playing together: *https://www.youtube.com/watch?v=mtyosnYdYPs*

Conflict can be a creative force, not just destructive—yet the primeval urge to avenge has been shown to elicit neural pleasure not unlike sweets or drugs. The brain twists the impulse toward justice into a thirst for revenge.

In this clip, former militia members are experiencing pleasure in play, while practicing shared leadership: *https://www.youtube.com/watch?v=pffSEPFkBOk*

Conclusion

What are the benefits of utilizing forum theatre in such contexts? Why not just hold a discussion? Many people are comfortable sitting and talking. However, some people's power and agency are limited when verbal language is the only way.

Forum theatre renders ideas vivid and tangible, like a thought experiment fully fleshed out. We can enact a choice hypothetically to see where it might lead. Members of the crowd can add their ideas: this becomes a vehicle for the collective imagination. Outsiders often supply a missing viewpoint.

Furthermore, when others witness your story, isolation decreases. Perhaps it is their story too, and sparks their own perspectives and memories, or their suggestions for change.

Theatre is a primordial art form that makes room for all of human experience. It is both pleasurable and practical, and its structures lend artistry and order when emotions run high. Forum Theatre, invented to foster social justice, offers an entertaining, edifying way to try out diverse possibilities in the aesthetic space, to heal and transform real life situations.

Mecca Burns

Mecca Antonia Burns is a registered drama therapist and board-certified drama therapy trainer. She runs a training program in Charlottesville Virginia to help drama therapists attain their credentials. Burns specializes in Theatre of the Oppressed and has led groups in Uganda, Kenya, Spain, and Romania as well as the USA. Visit *youtube.com/user/viewingpresence* for video documentation of these projects. Burns is the author of several related articles and book chapters, and she serves on the editing team for the Jana Sanskriti International Research and Resource Institute.

References

Boal, Augusto. (1979). *Theatre of the Oppressed*. New York: Urizen Books.

Boal, Augusto. (1995). *The Rainbow of Desire: The Boal method of theatre and therapy*. London: Routledge.

Burns, Beti, Okuto, Muwanguzi and Sanyu. (2015). The Domain of the Possible: Forum Theatre for Conflict Transformation in East Africa. Arts and Peacebuilding. *African Conflict and Peacebuilding Review*, Vol. 5, No. 1. pp. 136–151. Indiana University Press. *http://www.jstor.org/stable/10.2979/africonfpeacrevi.5.1.136*

Cohen-Cruz, J., & Schutzman, M. (2006). *A Boal companion: Dialogues on theatre and cultural politics*. London, England: Taylor and Francis.

Lederach, J. P. (2005) *The moral imagination: The art and soul of building peace*. New York: Oxford.

Lederach, J. & P., (2010) *When blood and bones cry out: Journeys through the soundscapes of healing and reconciliation*. New York: Oxford.

King, M. L. (1958). *Stride toward freedom: The Montgomery story*. San Francisco: Harper & Row.

Leveton, L. (2010). *Healing collective trauma using sociodrama and drama therapy*. New York: Springer.

Paterson, D., Burns, M., Sullivan, J. (2007). *Theatre of the Oppressed*. In A. Blatner (Ed.) *Interactive and Improvisational Drama*. Lincoln, NE: iUniverse.

Roberts, M. J. (2009). Conflict Analysis of the 2007 Post-election Violence in Kenya. New Dominion Philanthrometrics Journal. 1. http://www.ndpmetrics.com/papers/Kenya_Conflict_2007.pdf

Sajnani, N. (2009). Theatre of the Oppressed. In Johnson, D. & Emunah, R. *Current approaches in drama therapy*. Springfield, IL: Charles Thomas.

Schutzman, M., & Cohen-Cruz, J. (1994). *Playing Boal: Theatre, therapy, activism*. London: Routledge.

van der Kolk, B.(2015). *The body keeps the score: Brain, mind and body in the healing of trauma*. New York: Viking.

Using Action Methods in Men's Groups

Wes Carter

I need to preface my submission by stating that this is based mainly on my application of action methods used during the conduct of 8 day residential Men In Bali Retreats which I initiated in 2001. Since then I have conducted 38 separate Retreats in Bali for men, The Elders Way for men aged 50+ and A Man's Journey for men of any age, both of which are located and held in a Balinese village near Ubud in Bali.

My other introduction is that I have no formal qualifications as a group work facilitator/director; my qualifications are based on a desire to serve what I perceive to be a deficit in men's lives, qualifications earned by experience.

The group work in Bali involves many aspects, the first being the co-creation of a safe and confidential container in which the attendees are taken through a process of forming agreed protocols and declaring the group work space as "sacred." Men are asked questions like — "What do you want for yourself at the end of the Retreat?" in addition to "What are the barriers to change that will get in the way for you?" All responses are recorded and used throughout the program. Eight days and nights with a 'captive audience', all willing to enter into the mystery and beauty of being a man in a different environment, without their usual fall back family or friend support, is a responsible task and one that I take care to preserve.

My involvement in conducting men's groups emanated from my 40+ years of senior management in the automotive industry. Not only was my own life suffering from over work, too much alcohol, junk food and no exercise, I was a male doing male stuff with other males. We all followed the same well-worn masculine prescription to earn entry into the world of male compliance, work hard and successfully if you want to make it as a man.

Relationships were secondary to me and as a result of my ignorance and dedication to a falsehood, my 17 year marriage failed and my children suffered. (I have since remarried and completed 37 more years, this time with a lot more awareness of relationship dynamics and the absolute joy of maintaining an effective model of relating.) At that point I entered therapy to find out why I was on this path of self destruction. I did Transactional Analysis, Gestalt, Encounter groups, NLP, massage, body work, Psychodrama, Sociometry, you name it, and I was hooked into a different way of being.

I coupled my own personal discovery journey with wanting to recognise the patterns of the many men that I spent time with and how the parallel process of male socialisation played out in their lives.

In another life I would have been suitable Crusader material!

Donning my new found identity as a group leader, following many years of therapy and group work training attending the local Wasley Centre. I decided to organize a men's group, the first being a weekend residential affair with 10 paying participants, two of whom were Psychologists in training and a medical Doctor experiencing relationship problems—not a desirable selection of participants, and the first of my many baptisms of fire as a facilitator.

On reflection, I was then gainfully employed in the automotive industry and doing this part time group work with men. Naiveté, courage, humor and a 'can do' attitude, saw me through many years of organizing, participating and facilitating a wide range of themed men's groups without earning any money in return. I was being nourished from these attempts to be of valued service to mankind and that feeling continues to the present time.

Fathers, as a theme to work with men has always been the "easiest" to promote. Sit 10 men in a circle, co-create some simple group protocols then ask the question, "Describe your relationship with your Dad." Moving that question into action by asking the protagonist to introduce the group to his non-present Dad using a vacant chair and calling in an auxiliary to play the role and role reverse with the protagonist. All very basic group work, albeit powerful if the interchange is expanded to include other family members and the various roles they too played in the formative early years of the protagonist.

The process of warm up, contract with the protagonist (P) and the auxiliaries (A), scene setting, enactment, closure and sharing, being the necessary steps to take with any action piece.

My early shaping years conducting groups taught me about the real importance of warm-up, if the P is not fully engaged in the preparation of safety, confidentiality and apparent support from the audience of group members, then his entry into action becomes a trial for facilitation.

The "contract" to enter into action with both P and A also implies a contract with me as facilitator/director, I am there to be fully supportive of the P in his exploration of an issue he wants to attend, and to ensure the A's are safe in so doing. Depending on the "depth" and previous group work experience of the group, the contract also infers that I can challenge P rather than collude with his automatic responses to given situations.

A generalization here is that many men have an expectation that their "situation" will be fixed during this process of self-discovery. Warm-up and contract time are used to suggest to the P that we are not actually "fixing" anything, what we are about to do is to explore his issue in a manner that is different from one that is based entirely on theory. He will be invited into an action based description that enlarges his story and enables him to not only feel, but to perhaps gain an awareness of the origin of his reactions within the scene that he creates.

A one-off action based experience is rarely the completion; most men want to be involved further in the process and willing to learn from their new found awareness. When men sit as witness to an enactment, they are encouraged to raise their hands if that point in the scene is also part of their own life experience, in other words, they have been there too! That dynamic is also useful to support the P in the scene by referring him to the group that he is not alone in this dilemma.

With contract, warm-up and scene setting in place, the accompanying strategic inquiry questions have to then be relevant to where the P needs to go. I use the concept of exploration related to the circumstances he has described, P is asked whether he would be willing to explore that situation within the group and what would make it safe for him to do so? Auxiliaries are similarly invited to not only be supportive witnesses but be available for part of the action.

Initial scene setting or description of the significant time for the P usually requires much attention to detail to take P into a place of recall. At the same time, that process of relevant inquiry can serve as a supportive mechanism for the P to feel comfortable with where the exploration is headed. Remaining closely connected with the P, his every word, non-verbal cues, physical movement, any apparent unspoken fear and use of "props" is paramount for effective facilitation. It is within the subtlety of the interchange between P and the facilitator/director that keeps the action moving to a place where the other players emerge in the scene.

Closely watching and monitoring the P's responses during the initial scene setting, and during subsequent action, enables trust to be established, my experience in this regard is that the P will always correct me if my direction is not aligned with his reality.

Spontaneity with a "here and now" aspect of the unfolding drama, rather than me as facilitator holding any pre-conceived notion as to taking the P along possible alternative directions, is the key to an effective piece. Again, the response of P, when he is fully engaged in role usually flows and can be a time to check in with him as to how he is feeling here and now about what discovery moments he is aware of. I do this with the use of an "aside" question.

If the P is actually undecided or stuck during his scene, spontaneity in the form of a facilitated new direction, or even coming from one of the other A's involved, perhaps even a witness becomes part of my method. (Men usually apply themselves to a solution based response so again it requires advice to the whole group that we are not there to provide solutions to other men, we are part of an enabling process for the P, and each of us, to find his own direction within the drama action.)

There have been occasions with P and I being stuck during his drama, and unsure as to where to take the scene. Another contract question is then required with P, "would you be willing to . . . ?" The memory retention of other aspects of his original scene creation, interchange and role reversal with other A's, serve me as a reminder to perhaps be somewhat radical with offering an alternative exploration at that moment.

A radical example during a drama with an adult man, who had been sexually abused as a child, was to invite him to urinate on a pretend grave that was constructed outside in the garden bearing the name of the offending Priest who had since died. He and all the others took great delight in taking this unique action; it was a significant turning point for the P to take some charge of his life.

Yelling, wrestling, dance, movement, anything physical can be invoked to take P out of his stuck thinking. Men in general have a tendency to want to "understand" their confusion and make sense out of their situation which takes them into a state bordering on fear and sorrow. There have been many times at this point where a P has experienced a level of sadness reminding him of similar times in his life that have resulted in not knowing what to do. Close observation of the non-verbal clues are required here, as with the type of questions to ask. Significant breakthroughs occur when a radical direction is taken.

Instances in this type of situation, where the P is aware of his need/desire for change but is held back by his only known automatic response and unsure as to how to take on a new emerging role. With two A's in place, one being the familiar response and the other being the new role, action here takes the form of P being held by both A's with arms extended and a typical dialogue ensues using role reversal with each part of the P.

I use this as an example of a typical dilemma model, the P is "up on the cross' being pulled from both sides of his personality and perhaps not knowing how to make the next move. The P can be asked if there is anyone in the room who could take on the role of wise advocate for him. Some coaching here if P is not familiar with that internal role of wise person, he selects an A to take that role and another A to take on his role being held/pulled by both sides. With P now in the role of wise advocate/ambassador he is interviewed and asked what assistance or good advice can he offer to the A as himself? Role reversal many times to concretise his solution to the dilemma and then take him out of the scene and have the A's take on all the previous dialogue while P is invited to walk around that scene and view from a different perspective and perhaps coach/respond to the A's so that he is sure of his own strategies for change.

Finding closure of the drama and checking with the P as to whether this is a suitable time to end his work will now entail all of the A's being de-roled and taken back to their chairs by the P, suitably thanked for their participatory support and for me to ensure that they are not still carrying any part of their previous roles.

For the sharing, I then invite all of the audience to share with P, their experience of either being an A in in the action or witnessing the drama. I sit in a semi-circle with P facing the audience, and care is taken here to ensure that the individual audience response is not advice giving or a *post mortem* on what they have just seen. Instead, they are asked to share with the entire group in a non-judgmental and supportive response what feelings have arisen while participating or witnessing. Usually this is in the form of a similar experience that was evoked during P's drama. He is not alone in his search for meaning.

As facilitator/director I too share with him from my own personal experience and at the same time share with him and the group how I was managing the drama and what was happening for me while so doing. The action process is one of many during the eight days in residence, all leading up to each man making firm commitments to change and to be more aware of their own personal process and the effect that has in their lives.

The Men In Bali Retreats also include physical activity such as village walks with carrying back packs loaded with weight to represent the barriers to change that they have previously indicated. At different points of the walk they are requested to address one or more of the weights in a type of role reversal and make a statement or a spontaneous physical effort to throw off the weight.

Activities include working in pairs to address specific questions to share, rituals upon entry to the village compound, washing feet, hands and face rituals, guided meditation, a death and dying ritual for The Elders Way, a Balinese cultural experience of their "kecak and fire dance." All the men are asked to closely observe each other during the Retreat and write up a 'blessing and challenge' letter, suitably decorated, to be given out at the closing ceremony. This is to encourage men to be more observant and to write something really positive and supportive of the other men, a task that they would rarely undertake in their 'normal' life.

Another activity deals with unfinished business utilizing a small item or symbol/image or any representation of significant recall, something that no longer serves them on their journey through life. This could be about things, situations, memories, old hurts, resentments, unfinished business, personal behavior, a lost opportunity, a past mistake, a grievance, anything that is not yet dealt with, stuff that hangs around and continues to be deferred or ignored. Letting things go is an act of far greater power than depending or hanging on to. The men are taken across Bali to a Hindu Temple located in a cliff face, blindfolded and subjected to some minor hazards upon entry to the Temple, here they are invited to discard the item/s they identified the previous day by casting them into the sea accompanied by making a statement as to why they are doing this.

A wide range of different modalities, all based on abundance, care, good food, personal support, Balinese hospitality and service, are the corner stones for these unique programs for men. Action methods in men's group work also require courage, intuition and a touch of humor.

Wes Carter

Wes is an 81 year young Western Australian. Since 1980, Wes has been conducting personal development group work with men and women, he has listened to, encouraged, challenged, supported and guided hundreds of men. A pioneer of the Men's movement in Australia, he has committed his life to exploring and contributing to the wellbeing of people. A recipient of the Order of Australia Medal for his work in the field of men's health and wellbeing, his work has touched many hundreds of lives. From his deep source of life experience, he shares and facilitates action methods with rich, resonant compassion. Wes is absolutely committed; he brings humour, challenge, support, and life experience to this important work among men.

Circle of Values

Action Approaches in Indonesian Education

Mario Cossa

This article provides an overview of the first two years of a project using action methods in an educational setting in Indonesia. It was conducted at Campuhan College, in the village of Ubud on the Island of Bali. Campuhan College is a post-high-school program for Balinese youth that teaches English and computer skills combined with Leadership- and Values-Education. The author introduced staff to basic sociometric and psychodramatic techniques, with a special focus on the Social/Cultural Atom. He then worked with selected staff to integrate these, and other action techniques and philosophies into their program through regular, group sessions with students from the graduating classes of 2016 and 2017.

First Efforts in Bali

As a psychodramatist, drama therapist, and theatre educator, I have spent over thirty years working with youth in both therapeutic and educational settings. Most of my work has been in English-speaking, western countries. When I relocated to Bali in 2012 I was eager to see how action approaches to work with youth would translate into this particular Asian culture and setting.

Shortly after my arrival in Ubud, I was introduced to Wayan Rustiasa, the founder of Karuna Bali, a private, not-for profit organization that sponsors the programs at Campuhan College. He became excited by the idea of using action methods in service of both the educational and social goals of their program and we began formulating a plan of action.

Campuhan College draws post-high-school youth from all over the island of Bali. Although the tuition for a year seems modest by western standards, about US $1,000 per year, many students require scholarships to be able to enroll. The program itself is innovative in combining practical skills in English and computer science with more socially-focused skills in Leadership, and Values Education.

Balinese youth traditionally grow up in a community-based culture, living in multi-generational, family compounds in which there is limited personal space. Most Balinese are Hindu, a religious and cultural tradition rich in ceremony. This expresses itself in daily practices of gratitude, as well as frequent community rituals celebrating family events as well as seasonal recognitions, and connections to all aspects of life. One of the challenges for programs such as the one at Campuhan is to honor the richness of the culture while supporting contemporary youth in coping with increasingly western ideals and technology.

After getting to know some of the staff at Campuhan, I offered a three-hour training for them that introduced sociometry (the measurement of connections between and among members of a group based on various criteria) and sociodrama (the exploration, in action, of issues existing within a group). The staff was especially attracted to sociodrama as a way to explore both positive and challenging interpersonal interactions that arise with a group of about 25 students and 10 staff working closely over the period of a year.

I had worked with interpreters in other countries in the past, but this was my first time doing so in Indonesia. I was eager to see if and how the staff connected to working in action and whether these approaches were relevant within the Balinese culture.

One portion of the training mentioned above was an action demonstration of the adolescent brain and the changes that occur from the onset of puberty into the mid-twenties. Members of the training group enacted the different parts of the brain to explore the tremendous neurological changes that occur during adolescence. Participants seemed engaged and to be understanding the neurobiology involved.

I noticed, however, that one of the younger staff members was sitting back from the action and sketching on a piece of paper. I wondered if he was not following the concepts we were exploring, or perhaps just needed to be doing something with his hands to be able to pay attention. At the conclusion of the training he presented me with the drawing shown in Figure 1. I was astounded by the depth of understanding of the concepts we had explored in action and how he translated them graphically. Both graphic and performing arts are an integral part of the Balinese culture and working in action certainly seemed an effective way to go with this group.

Training Workshop for Indonesian Youth Workers

The following year Campuhan College staff organized a two-day training for youth workers from Bali and Java (the Indonesian island west of Bali) which attracted over 25 participants. The workshop was co-sponsored by The Asia Foundation, Values Institute, and World Interfaith Harmony Week. Additional

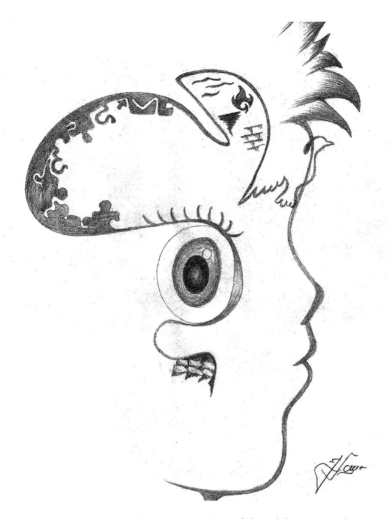

Figure 1 – An Artists Interpretation of the Adolescent Brain

funding was provided by private contributions from members of the psycho-drama communities in the USA and the UK.

The participants became excited as they learned and practiced basic principles of sociometry and explored the ways they could be used in schools, in community outreach programs, and in working with troubled families. Although sociometry, by definition, means the measure of connection between individuals in a group, we recognize that sociometric activities also help build new connections.

We focused on three types of sociometric activity, all of which can be easily learned and employed in educational settings. They were: *spectrograms, locograms,* and *step-in sociometry.* (Handouts were provided that had been translated into Indonesian. One that I used was my adaptation of *"Practical Sociometry—* Directing *Spectrograms* and *Locograms,"* by Herb Propper, PhD.)

Spectrograms measure a range or spectrum of opinion, feeling, like or dislike within the group about some particular thing or issue. They are constructed by placing two objects at a distance from one another, creating an imaginary line on the floor that represents the particular spectrum. Participants then place themselves at the position along the continuum that seems most true for them. It is like putting a typical questionnaire that uses numbers to represent the range from "agree" to "disagree" into an action format. A few examples of the end points of the spectrograms that were used were:

- I came a great distance/short distance to get here.
- I like western rock music a lot/not at all.
- I have a lot of experience/no experience with working with action techniques.
- I am generally comfortable/uncomfortable in a new group.

Locograms show a choice or preference of group members among three or more possibilities. *Locograms* are constructed by indicating a location for each choice by using an object (chair, scarf, *etc.*) Sometimes we label each location on a piece of paper to help the group members remember which location stands for which choice. Participants may stand directly at one location, between several, or even remain in motion between two or more locations. A few examples of the *locograms* used were:

- My favorite time of day is: morning, early afternoon, late afternoon, night time.
- I live closest to: Denpasar, Sanur, Ubud, Jakarta, Surabaya, *etc.*
- I work with young people in: a school, a community organization, a Banjar (local community) youth group, a health setting, *etc.*
- The greatest challenge to me in working with youth is: the young people themselves, the parents, the setting in which I work, the community, *etc.*

Step-in sociometry has participants stand in a circle. They are invited to make a statement that is true for them, *e.g.* "I like working with older teens and young adults best." Those who feel the same way as the speaker step into the circle as well.

As someone who has been facilitating these activities for decades I had forgotten how exciting they can be when encountered for the first time. Participants worked in small groups to practice facilitating and exploring ways that these activities could be used to build group cohesion, to help focus on commonalities in a group, to elicit possible group goals, and then assess how well the group was meeting the goals. Several days after the workshop, one of the participants sent me photos of her using spectrograms in one of her groups.[1]

The other major piece I introduced to this group was J.L. Moreno's concept of the Social/Cultural Atom (S/C Atom).

The S/C Atom is a map of the individual in relationship to the people (living and dead), organizations, cultural influences, *etc.* which impact on his/her life. It is generally drawn first on paper, and then may be put into action by having group members inhabit the various roles. It is a powerful tool for helping an individual explore their own sociometric connections and notice how relationships change over time.

Although often employed in therapeutic settings, one can use this tool in educational settings to enhance social/emotional learning and support students in gaining greater awareness of their interpersonal connections, both positive and negative.

Another use we explored was how a youth worker can gain insight into a student or member of a youth group, by stepping into the role of a particular youth and exploring that youth's S/C Atom. When we put the S/C Atom of a client of a youth worker from Jakarta into action, he discovered an important piece of information about how this youth had a much closer relationship with his drug dealer than with his father. This led the youth worker to realize that addiction was not the only issue for which this youth needed support.[2]

The workshop also utilized sociodrama and group discussion to explore the similarities and differences between various aspects of development for Indonesian adolescents at various ages and their counterparts in the USA and other western countries.

The group was divided into four subgroups representing early adolescence (from the onset of puberty to about thirteen years old), mid adolescence (from about thirteen to sixteen), late adolescence (from about sixteen to 19), and young adulthood (from about twenty to twenty-six; a period during which the final neural growth spurts of adolescence are reaching conclusion.) Each group presented a series of short scenes (sociodramas) showing how adolescents of their assigned age range relate to J.L. Moreno's *Universalia of Treatment*:

---

1 For a bi-lingual video (English and Indonesian) of a group of Indonesian Junior High School teachers learning these three techniques please visit *https://www.youtube.com/watch?v=TXUmdO5zSB8&t=30s* or go to YouTube and search for "Psychodrama Video: Intro to Sociometry Techniques."

2 For bi-lingual videos (English and Indonesian) of a group of Indonesian Junior High School teachers learning to conduct and evaluate a Social/Cultural Atom please visit *https://www.youtube.com/watch?v=8uzi4T1uZPk&t=8s* and *https://www.youtube.com/watch?v=TU6EQ_ELGa4&t=81s* or go to YouTube and search for "Psychodrama Video: The Social/Cultural Atom" and "Psychodrama Video: Working with The Social Atom."

Time, Space, Reality and Cosmos. This provided a foundation for exploring the differences between adolescent perception and adult perception, which led to small- and full-group discussion of the ways in which this understanding is useful within educational settings.

Scenes about *Time* demonstrated the phenomenon that the passage of time tends to be perceived as much slower for younger individuals, for whom a year is a significant percentage of their lives. This was quite similar to what one finds with western youth. Three months is perceived as a long-term relationship and having to wait for a week for something feels like forever.

Scenes about *Space* demonstrated a seemingly reduced need for personal space for Indonesian youth from both their western as well as adult Indonesian counterparts. Considering living situations which tend to be multi-generational with little personal space for children who often share a bed as well as a room, this was not surprising.

Reality scenes were similar to those I have seen presented by youth-worker groups in the USA; namely that the reality experienced by youth is both more subjective as well as more influenced by the perception of peers than for adults. That which adults see as misrepresentation or outright lying may often just be a skewed perspective on events, colored by strong emotional reactions.

The scenes focused on *Cosmos,* or the trans-personal awareness of youth, demonstrated a much greater connection to both an individual and collective expression of the spiritual in daily life than is generally true for most western youth. This was not surprising, given the degree to which Hindu and Muslim youth in Indonesia participate in family and community religious practices and ceremony that is significantly more a daily than once-a-week occurrence.

For a more thorough exploration of the relationship of adolescents to these four *Universals,* the interested reader is referred to Chapter One of *Rebels With a Cause: Working with Adolescents Using Action Techniques.*[3]

Following this activity, each of the sub-groups then reviewed a series of statements that tend to be true for western adolescents at each stage of development. These statements were further sub-divided into: physical, mental, emotional, personal (*i.e.* related to the emerging personality), and social development. Each group was asked to reflect on the statements and consider which of them also held true for Indonesian youth.

The interesting outcome of this activity was a consensus that physical and mental development were quite similar for both western and Indonesian youth, but that elements of emotional, personal, and social development occurred a

---

3 Cossa, 1996, Jessica Kingsley Press, London

bit later for Indonesian youth, especially for those from Bali whose life experience tended to be in a more collective environment (as mentioned earlier) than their western counterparts.

The Campuhan College Project – First Year

The workshop for youth workers led to a series of seven, action-focused group sessions that I co-led with some of the Campuhan College school staff over a period of seven weeks during March and April of 2016. These groups ended shortly before the students went off to engage in off-site, work practicum experiences, prior to their return shortly before graduation.

Finding the right language that could translate easily into Indonesian was one challenge that we addressed. It led to the use of the term "Motivational Arts" to describe action methods, and the *Circle of Your Life* to describe the Social/Cultural Atom. In translation it made more sense, and also allowed us to use the song from Disney's *The Lion King* as part of the introduction to the activities.

During that seven-session program we used the *Circle of Your Life* to explore the changes in interpersonal and cultural connections as students moved from a very community-focused life (living in their multi-generational family compounds) to developing more independence while at school. Change was dramatically evident between the depictions drawn by students to represent their lives before Campuhan (labeled *Past*), and the ones drawn to represent the time after seven months as students (labeled Present).

The *Present Circles* included the many important relationships that had been made among the students and between students and staff at Campuhan College. Additionally, the *Past Circles* tended to show little or no space between the student (represented by a circle for females and a triangle for males) and those surrounding them. (See Figure 2 for an example.)

The *Circles of Life* were put into action, with fellow students playing the various, roles and conversations enacted between the *Protagonist* (the person whose *Circle* was being enacted) and the people and other elements in their life. During this process we discovered that an increased sense of individual identity and claiming of personal space had developed, without diminishing the importance of the relationship to family and cultural values.

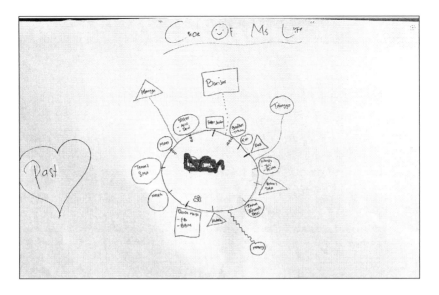

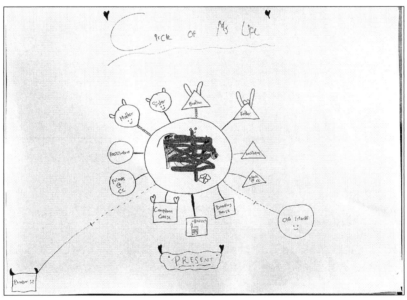

*Figure 2 — A comparison of the Circle of Life before coming to
Campuhan College (above), with the Circle of Life after being in the
program for seven months (below). Name is obscured for confidentiality.*

A particularly poignant moment during an enactment was with a young
woman whose father had died when she was very young. He still was placed
in a significantly close position in her *Circle*. During her enactment, which
was one of the first, students were still giggling a bit as their classmates were
selected to portray various roles.

Before asking her to pick someone to portray her father I shared with the group members that when we depict someone who is no longer alive, we are inviting their spirit to join us in the room to provide support and guidance. In that moment the tenor of the room went from that of somewhat uncomfortable giddiness, to genuine reverence. When the young man she selected to play her father stepped into the role, she embraced him and began to weep. Her tears were joined by those of most of the others in the room, both students and staff. This occurrence was certainly underscored by the Hindu connection to the sacred reality of the spirits of ancestors.

As we neared our final session we used Sociodrama to assist the students in exploring how they might integrate their family and cultural values with the more contemporary influences of technology and school. After a session in which students created their *Possible Future* Circles, we conducted a sociodrama in which the students were divided into seven different roles with about three students in each role. The roles were: the Campuhan College graduate about to leave for university in the USA, the members of their family, their ancestors, their friends from home, members of the Campuhan *family*, the Internet and world-wide-web, and social networking media.

During the drama the departing student received the blessings and advice from family and ancestors (the latter during a dream encounter), bid farewell to friends from home and from school, got some words of advice about not overusing from the world wide web, and then went off to face challenges at university.

During an encounter with *Surfer Dude*, played by the director of the drama, the student was being encouraged to spend a weekend before a major exam on a surfing holiday. The student was in a quandary, wanting to do well on the exam, but also wanting to build new relationships with American fellow students.

The trio playing the role of the student decided to use social media to connect with fellow students from Campuhan for advice. The conversation led to the decision to suggest to *Surfer Dude* that they postpone the surfing holiday until spring break. This character made a cameo appearance later in the drama when the student, now a university graduate and managing a hotel in Jakarta, had to tell family about having to work and not return home for one of the important Hindu holidays.

As I worked with the students during this first program year I was also training staff, who then could take over facilitation of many of the regular, group-session activities, as well as facilitating small groups using their native language to guide various action-based activities that I first demonstrated using an interpreter. Students and staff alike looked forward to our group sessions and participated with enthusiasm, honesty, and openly shared feelings. The closing session ran over time by a significant amount as appreciations were shared, and tears and laughter were both part of the celebration of the time we had had as a group.

The Campuhan College Project – Second Year

During the following year it was decided to hold monthly sessions over the entire school year. They began on the first day for the incoming students. In addition to working with the *Circle of Your Life* with the students, I met with staff before each session to discover concerns and how students were progressing since I had last worked with them. We would then co-create an outline for the coming session that could address concerns and reflect on where the students were at that point in their experience of the program.

One concern that was addressed using sociometric exploration was the tendency of the students to form into sub-groups or cliques that in some ways excluded those not part of the group. We created an *Action Sociogram* (a depiction of the various sub-groups created by having people cluster with those to whom they felt the most solid connection) and invited members of each group to celebrate and appreciate each other. Then we invited them to partner with someone from one of the other groups and spend time getting to know each other. This activity helped build new connections within the student body and developed a greater awareness that connections within a preferred group did not have to exclude the possible richness of knowing people from other groups.

One of the significant and original extensions of *the Circle of Life* that came out of working with the class of 2017, was the creation of *the Circle of Values*, a way of mapping the values that were part of the students' lives before coming to Campuhan, and exploring the ways those values were changing and growing as well.

The process began with a paper and pencil rendering of the students' reflection on the values that were important in their lives prior to their coming to Campuhan. In *the Circle of Life* one might indicate specific family members and specific friends. In *the Circle of Values* one would indicate the value of *Family Connection* or *Friendship*. As with the traditional *Circle* (S/C Atom), distance from the shape on the page that indicates self is an indication of how important these values are or were to the individual.

After completing *the Circle of Values* for the *Past*, students then completed their *Present Circle of Values*. I then demonstrated the process for taking these charts and putting them into action. I used a staff member, who was also a member of the original graduating class from Campuhan in 2008 for this demonstration.

Since we would be working in small groups of four, I had her select three colleagues to represent the three most important values she held before she became a student at Campuhan and arrange them in a sculpture around herself indicating the importance of each value by the distance that it was placed. Next came the opportunity to dialog with each of the values to explore further their importance to her as well as their origin in her life.

This was followed by a similar process for the three most important values in her life after having been a student in the Campuhan program. We then could explore how some values were still present but their position had changed, and how other values had emerged that were not present in the past.

After completing the demonstration, the students broke into their small groups, each with a Balinese facilitator and took turns exploring *the Circle of Values* in action and in their own language. For some, this meant using Balinese, instead of Indonesian. Although Indonesian is the official language of the country, most young people also speak the language of their island, which is different in many ways from Indonesian. Family members, especially older one, often do not speak Indonesian, or only in a limited manner, so Balinese may be the language of home and family.

One of the challenges in working in other cultures is to recognize the language differences and complexities that often do not translate directly from and to English. Having good interpreters is a must. Even with groups who are comfortable and conversant in English, it is generally important to conduct activities in the first language, as this allows a greater richness of meaning and expression of feeling.

Another challenge in working in the Balinese cultural environment is how to support students in developing roles for success in a modern world without losing the importance of their ancestral traditions and values. This application of *the Circle of Values* and the sociodramatic (group-focused) and psychodramatic (individual-focused) exploration that ensued really helped students meet this challenge. A similar sociodrama to the one described for the class of 2016 was also conducted as a culminating activity for this class, but the roles tended more to focus on the values expressed by the various character clusters.[4]

Although psychodrama and sociometry are often imagined to be used only in therapeutic capacities, they have enormous potential for use in education. It is exciting and challenging to be bringing these methodologies to Indonesia. I am indebted to my many trainers and colleagues in the field who have prepared me for this important task.

---

4 For a bi-lingual video (English and Indonesian) of the Campuhan College session during which the Circle of Values was first explored, please visit *https://www.youtube.com/watch?v=HxzFEtMPWQo&t=73s* or go to YouTube and search for "Sampler of Motivational Arts at Campuhan College." The video demonstrates the ease with which the Balinese teachers have learned to facilitate these action techniques and the enthusiasm with which the students participate in them. The video also includes brief interviews with several students who relate their experience of participating in these group sessions.

Mario Cossa

Mario Cossa is a Psychodramatist (Certified Trainer, Educator, Practitioner [TEP] by the American Board of Examiners), Drama Therapist/Master Teacher (RDT/MT, Certified by the North American Drama Therapy Association), and Theatre Educator who has traveled globally offering trainings, retreats, and workshops in the USA, Canada, the UK, South Africa, Malaysia, Indonesia, Australia, New Zealand, South Korea, and China. His primary trainer in psychodrama was Zerka Moreno and he is ever influenced and inspired by her work and passion.

He is a Trainer in the Therapeutic Spiral Model™ for the safe utilization of psychodrama with survivors of trauma and for using action methods to enhance post-traumatic growth. It was through Therapeutic Spiral International that Mario first became a figure on the international psychodrama scene.

Mario believes passionately in the ability of the Creative and Performing Arts to expand consciousness and to transform lives. He lives primarily in Bali, Indonesia, and has offered trainings for Indonesian youth workers for a number of years. His chapter in this volume is a testament to the living nature of psychodrama and the way in which its theories and methods impact other cultures and are, in turn, impacted by them.

For additional information or questions, please contact Mario at *mario@ dramario.net* or visit *www.dramario.net*

References

Blatner, A. (1996) *Acting in: Practical applications of psychodramatic methods in everyday life* (3rd ed). New York: Springer.

Clayton, G. M. (1994) *Effective group leadership.* Caulfield, Victoria: ICA Press.

Cossa, M. (2018, January 4). *Directions for Making a Social/Cultural Atom*, Retrieved from *http://www.dramario.net*

Cossa, M. (2018, January 4) *Psychodrama Video: The Circle Of Values From an Adolescent Perspective* Retrieved from *http://dramario.net/ psychodrama-video-the-social-cultural-atom-the-circle-of-your-life/*

Cossa, M. (2018, January 4) *Psychodrama Video: The Social/Cultural Atom (The Circle of Your Life)* Retrieved from *http://dramario.net/ psychodrama-video-the-social-cultural-atom-the-circle-of-your-life/*

Cossa, M. (2005) *Rebels with a cause: Working with adolescents using action techniques.* London & Philadelphia: Jessica Kingsley.

Cossa, M., Ember, S., Glass, L., and Hazelwood, J. (1996) *Acting Out: The Workbook—A guide to the development and presentation of issue-oriented, audience-interactive, improvisational theatre.* Muncie, IN: Accelerated Development/Bristol, PA: Taylor & Francis.

Moreno, J. (1994) 'Psychodrama moral philosophy and ethics.' In P. Holmes, M. Karp, and M. Watson (eds) *Psychodrama since Moreno: Innovations in theory and practice.* London: Routledge, pp. 97–111.

Moreno, J. L. (1993) *Who shall survive?* (Student Ed). Roanoke, VA: Royal Publishing Company. Sternberg, P. and Garcia, A. (1994) *Sociodrama: Who's in your shoes?* Westport, CT: Praegar.

Moreno, J. L. (1944) *The theatre of spontaneity.* Beacon, NY: Beacon House, Inc.

Resnick, M. D., Bearman, P. S., Blum, R. W., Bauman, K. E., Harris, K. M., Jones, J., Tabor, J., Beuhring, T., Sieving, R. E., Shew, M., Ireland, M., Bearinger, L. H., Udry, J. R. (1997) 'Protecting adolescents from harm: Findings from the National Logitudinal Study on Adolescent Health.' *Journal of the American Medical Association,* 278, 823–832.

Rohnke, K. (1989) *Cowtails and cobras II: A guide to games, initiatives, ropes courses, and adventure curriculum.* Debuque:Kendall/Hunt Publishing.

Sociodrama in Action

Ron Wiener

In our book *Sociodrama in a Changing World*,[1] 37 authors from over 20 countries described theoretical and practical aspects of sociodrama. I define sociodrama as a way to help groups better understand their situation and where appropriate to change it. To achieve its aims, sociodrama, as you will read, makes use of many action methods such as: spectrograms, doubling, role reversal, soliloquy, sculpting and role taking.

In this chapter, 10 sociodrama practitioners from 5 different countries describe different ways they have used sociodrama in their work. These include: in education, in organizational consultancy, in workshops exploring the present state of the world and in coaching.

Leader
Valerie Monty Holland

The company boardroom is not the usual working milieu for me. However, for the last 6 years I have been part of a team of coaches in the US supporting the delivery of a leadership program with account executives in financial services. Over this period of time, I have gained a reputation for helping people to move out of their comfort zones and into a space where they can lead.

Role naming is a good place to start. Many people do not see themselves as leaders and without that perspective and intention, becoming one is very difficult. There is frequently confusion between leader and manager as separate roles and an early task is finding different contexts in which each of those is the most appropriate role to play. Most of the people I coach must step into both of those roles (among others) on most days.

---

1 R.Wiener, D.Adderley, & K.Kirk (Eds.) (2011), *Sociodrama in a Changing World*, UK, Lulu

Even before we can name a role, however, the concept of playing a role needs to be explored. Many people hear 'role play' instead and their anxiety levels shoot through the ceiling. Some associate it with an act of pretending, an anathema to them as they strive for authenticity. When they understand the Morenian concept of a role repertoire that offers us a variety of genuine behaviors and actions to manifest, they are often palpably relieved from a quest for the true self. The search for the 'real me' occupies much time and leaves many angst-ridden when some inner hero refuses to emerge.

I describe a role as a set of clothes that we wear. We choose the most appropriate ones for the situation into which we are headed. Everyone wears those clothes differently even if they are the same items of clothing that someone else has. This explanation has helped people understand that we define our own roles and that they are not all of who we are.

It also points to the need for thinking or warming up before going anywhere. To further the metaphor—is it best to wear the suit or the jeans? This leads on to naming the most effective role for the next circumstance.

The title above refers to one of the first questions I ask my coachees—what kind of leader do you want to be? Choosing one or two descriptive words (sometimes three at a stretch!) is part of their ongoing exploration throughout the ten months we work together. Choosing the kind of leader they would like to be can take months of thought, experimentation and observation of others. Practicing roles in real life, experiencing the role relationships that evolve from meeting others in those roles and noticing the shifts is the stuff of action methods-based coaching.

And powerful stuff it is. In the past six years I have watched these leaders grow to take over regions, and the people they lead are now part of my group of coachees, a small legacy of a successful application of Morenian methods in corporate America.

Using action methods in working with a peer group in the field of Master of Educational Management
Dagmar Heinrich

The task for the group was to understand how over the past year they had progressed through Tuckman's (1965) stages of forming, storming, norming and performing. The peer group had 5 members.

The first task was to take a little object such as a broken toy car, a little wooden puppet, a very small superman, a paper with numbers on it, just things you might collect in a display case. They had to choose the object without looking.

Each person then role reversed with the chosen object. They then did a short presentation to the other group members using the object. After that, staying in the role of being the object, they met and greeted each other.

Then staying with the feelings that arose from the role reversal and subsequent feedbacks and meetings each person had 5–10 minutes to do a little painting: as the object or as some thoughts arising from the encounters.

The paintings became a medium for discussions to develop between the participants.

This was further developed after the a break where each person presented their painting, followed by discussion and feedback.

The group was then asked to create a sculpture exploring how they first met. When the sculpture was created, people's positions were replaced by their objects so that they could all stand back and observe what they had created. People were free to take photos and drawings of the sculpture. The final task was that they all together they had to do a painting about the Tuckman process. This lead to a lot of discussion, laughter and contentedness.

Using sociodrama/psychodrama
action methods in a non-therapeutic setting
Noelle Branagan and Sue Orton

In 2011 we facilitated a start up session for a multidisciplinary group of professionals looking to provide holistic support for families through divorce. In autumn 2017 the co-founders contacted us for help, as the now developing network was experiencing some tensions in it's functioning.

The processes of joining, collaborating and choosing coworkers across disciplines was unclear and was creating tensions around inclusion and exclusion. Their intention to collaborate effectively in the service of their clients was strong, however they had limited support or supervision for themselves.

Our contract was to support them in creating healthy and authentic communications, allowing individuals to contribute, feel valued and heard, and working together more effectively. We agreed to facilitate two ½ day sessions with the network. The first (A) to explore and discover the state of the network and their development needs and the second (B) to begin the development.

Attention to warm up is at the heart of action methods, in order to be able to work spontaneously and creatively.

Paying attention to our warm up allowed us to pay attention to the group warm up. We knew that this group would have its own dynamics and be new to Action Methods. These factors along with our contract, helped us listen to the questions for the group warm up such as 'how do we invite them in?' and 'what role are we warming them up to?'. This first session (A) would be a warm up to the second (B).

We will illustrate our use of three action methods in this non-therapeutic setting: the use of a continuum (A), the use of an object to assist in concretisation of ideas or situations (A) and mapping to illustrate situations and relationships (B). We offer a rationale, context and outcome for each.

Continuum in A

Rationale: After our warm up exercises we invited the group to build a continuum of when they first joined the network. This was to make evident the timeline of development of this group now and to explore their experience of joining it.

Context: Given the apparent struggles in relationships and the tensions around inclusion and exclusion, we focused on their first experience of the network. By bending the continuum line into a horseshoe everyone was witnessed by everyone as each spoke of their experience.

Outcome: This brought a real interest in listening to and being listened to. They heard things they hadn't heard before and that was important in terms of building an authentic environment for the work to come.

Offer and Invitation to take an object (or more) in A:

Rationale: They were invited to pick an object(s) to represent the network for them at this moment. Then to share their choices in pairs and then in fours. This was to broaden their awareness of their own and others experience of how the network is for them now.

Context: Having listened to and heard about each other's excitement when first joining the network in the continuum, the action of choosing objects and then sharing those choices with others was developing upon their genuine desire for this network to function more healthily. The use of objects created a space and focus outside themselves, to express what they found, was and wasn't working so well.

Outcome: This brought about a means for speaking about things hitherto unspoken. A real desire to become more able to be comfortable with being uncomfortable. It lead to the creation of a truly authentic sculpt of the network from the objects chosen.

Mapping out client process in B:

Rationale: We asked them to map out how initial client contact was managed in the network and the processes involved. As this was a known successful process we knew it would provide a 'safe' platform from which everyone would have the opportunity to witness and contribute as they felt fit.

Context: From the first session the group stated their need and desire to communicate more openly and effectively so we chose to do the mapping as a whole group reflecting in pairs as needed. This afforded explicit exposure of how layered and complex collaborative working can be.

Outcome: By mapping out the process they could all see, and tried to untangle, the complexities and look for solutions in a collaborative and authentic manner. More voices were heard that went on to brave naming of other more personal processes later in the session.

Non-clinical uses of Morenian methods
Diane Adderley

In order to make a living as a freelancer, I operate across a wide range of spheres: psychodrama psychotherapist, sociodramatist, life coach, supervisor, organizational consultant and business role play actor, Playback Theatre practitioner and accredited trainer. My internal model of how to work with individuals or groups is rooted in my training in Moreno's teachings, both psychodramatic and sociodramatic. Here are a few brief examples of non-clinical uses of his methods in my work:

Coaching in a Skype interview (use of surplus reality)
I was invited to interview (over Skype) for inclusion in an online resource for managers, T&D or HR departments to enable them to access consultants, trainers and coaches across the globe for corporate projects — a 'Find a Consultant/Coach/Trainer' website. I was asked to present, in ten minutes, a method I might use in a training or coaching context.

I'm currently very enthusiastic about using 'time-lines' so I invited the interviewer (who had expressed his willingness to be a guinea pig for the purposes of my presentation) to think about a project he was currently part-way through and perhaps a little stuck with. He chose the personal project of learning the native language of his partner and the country they were now living in.

Using a quantity of various pens and pencils he had on his desk, we concretised the time-line from where the 'project' began to its' present state of stuckness, marking important moments along the way. Using surplus reality, we then went into a future time (defined by him as two years hence), when he had completed his task.

I congratulated him on his success and invited him to identify the steps he had taken over the 'last two years' to reach his 'present' (in reality 'future') state of fluency. He was, after a moment or two, easily able to do so and we returned to present time reality with a ready-made roadmap of how he could achieve his goal. As a method to use in the time-honoured coaching model of 'Gap Management', I have yet to see the action time-line bettered. (By the way, I was successful in the interview and my guinea pig, when I last checked in, was putting his action plan into effect.)

RealPlay (doubling, mirror, role reversal)

I manage a small team of professional business actors, under the name RealPlay. We work in organizational settings facilitating small group practice in communication skills (influencing, negotiating, managing difficult conversations, handling conflict, coaching for managers, effective leadership *etc*.).

One of our models of work is to invite participants in group training sessions to share with the group a story of a 'difficult conversation' they have had, or are about to have. The actor then plays the role of 'the other' and, working with the storyteller, in their own role, we enact the encounter as it currently is perceived to be. The group, the actor and the facilitator all then participate in coaching the person in the hot seat to find other ways of influencing the conversation towards the desired outcome. Role reversal, doubling and mirror are all methods I use in this context, and have taught to the other professional actors in the group, to help the group participant understand the 'other', become aware of previously unidentified feelings and to 'see' their own behavior.

The sessions become, in effect, little vignettes which are frequently commented upon in evaluations: "the acting session was the best bit of learning for me—more next time please."

Organizational Training and Consulting

There are a million and one ways of using Moreno's work in this field, but I'll focus on just one here, which, in my view, is so often overlooked. T&D professionals may require a consultant to cram a program with 'models'. It thus appears that large quantities of learning are somehow taking place through the hours of chalk-and-talk or PowerPoint slides, and that the company is therefore getting a good ROI (Return On Investment, in business jargon).

To any Morenian, the crucial bit that may be squeezed out is Warm-Up, which needs and takes time and breathing space. Frequently, there is ambivalence (not to say downright resistance) at the beginning of a training event from some participants. The event may be on a topic an individual feels will not be relevant or purposeful for them but they've been told they 'have to' come. They may have been 'sent' by a senior, for their perceived knowledge, skills or attitude-based problems to be sorted out by an external trainer. There may also, simply be too much stuff in their in-trays to feel OK about taking a day out—the pile will inevitably have grown by tomorrow.

I am always keen to take time at the beginning of any organizational training event to warm-up the group, to bring participants into a positive resourceful state from which learning can take place. As I was taught by sociodramatist Ron Wiener, who I have learned from and worked with since the mid '90s, a key purpose of Warm-Up is to create a spider's web of connections between group members which can then hold and ground the sense of the group-as-a-whole being a safe enough space in which to experiment and learn. In my own practice, I endeavor to warm any group up to three states of awareness: to how they are in themselves, in this moment; to recognition and connection with each other; and to their purpose in being present.

I avoid like the plague the terrible word 'Icebreaker'—what image does that warm a group up to?!?! (I give credit here to Francis Batten for bringing this to my attention—be aware of the language you use and the warm-up it creates.)

Mostly, I use some form of Sociometry, Moreno's mapping of the group in space according to various criteria. I often include an exercise which will get individuals accessing a positive memory (*e.g.* "If this room was a map of the world, go to the place where you had an experience of feeling good in yourself that you could briefly share."). Once I've reached this place (maybe 20 minutes of up-on-your-feet action), I can lead people into defining what their purpose may be for the training from a state of positive self-awareness.

Now You See

Irina Stefenascu

32 participants attended a team-building session for the management team of a Romanian group of companies dealing with the production and distribution of dried food. One of the problems they had reported was that of very unclear roles. In the third session of working with them I focused on a cultural atom of one of the key positions: the production manager, M.

M. displayed a professional atom of 14 stakeholders. Using group members and doubling we explored the role of each stakeholder through three statements:

1. I am . . .
2. my relationship with M. is . . .
3. from you, M., I need . . .

Then M. took his place in the center of the atom and heard all the message. I then asked M:

"How is it for you to hear all these messages, M.?"

He replied: "Well, this is my work, depicted accurately."

For all of us around, it felt overwhelming.

I then asked all the actors to help M. to name the roles he needed to have to meet all those needs. M. validated the suggested roles. Meanwhile, I wrote each role on a piece of paper, with big letters.

After thanking all the actors and sending them back to their places, I put all the papers on the floor and ask M. to have a good look at them. Two-thirds of the papers were about providing information and reporting. It was obvious that it took quite a while to do all that on a regular basis. I asked M. which are the roles he got paid for. He picked a few pieces of paper with roles about planning, managing, organizing, following-up, *etc.*

"And what about the rest of them?" I asked.

"The rest I just do." He sighed. Then he smiled, took a straight position, spread his legs, looked around to all of his colleagues and repeated: "Yes, I have to do them."

Silence. The CEO jumped from her chair: "Now I see. You'll get an assistant! Or two!"

Applause, relief, satisfaction, lots of smiles and hope. I feel grateful.

Then the session ended with sharing.

Should I work again with the cultural atom with this size of team, I would ask the rest of the participants to go in the end to enlarge some of the roles—from single to collective characters—based on the similarity of the relationships / needs towards the central protagonist, so all participants are involved.

The cultural atom in a nutshell:

- Contract—to clarify the roles or to position a person / team / organization.
- Warm-up—to self, others, space, role naming, action methods, theme.
- The protagonist takes a central role on the stage.
- The stakeholders appear on the stage, with a clear identity and are arranged sociometrically in relation to the center.
- The stakeholders are presented as in the a-b-c above.
- The center defines and/or validates their own roles towards each stakeholder.
- The roles are named to define the function and the quality of the relationship of the center with each stakeholder.
- The roles get clustered in 3–4 big categories and there is a discussion about their utility / priority, *etc.*
- Sharing from role, then from experience and from the learning about the bigger systems we belong to.

Non-Therapeutic Uses of the Method
Arohanui-Grace and John Wenger

This article focuses on framing up a session and attending to the sociometry of the group; all part of the warm-up for a successful session. Creativity thrives and doesn't spiral into chaos when there are good boundaries. Framing headlines the content of the session and also sets boundaries within which exploration can occur freely and safely.

Dr. G. Max Clayton (1994) suggested four elements that bring about a coherent framework for the session that will ensue. We have successfully used this framing in a range of settings. The four elements are Purpose, Time, Structure and Credibility, applicable for planning and also expressed explicitly to the group at the very beginning of the session.

Purpose has most often come out of in-depth conversations with the sponsor of the work. These conversations allow us to stand in the shoes of someone who is looking for an outcome for their organization. For example, an HR Manager seeking to create a shift in organizational culture to one where so-called "difficult conversations" become a regular part of people's working lives.

Articulating purpose clearly and crisply with the group allows this to become part of the frame within which the work will unfold. Attending to the sociometry of the group early in the session is where we align the participants with the purpose and with each other in relation to the purpose. This is, of necessity, a director-directed warm up. A simple sociogram might achieve this: "Here is the purpose, where do you stand in relation to it?"

In our experience, alignment to purpose is essential to reduce anxiety and increase spontaneity. Often, in organizational settings, the structure of a training session takes the form of agendas with rigid time-frames, objectives and content. We have found that producing an agenda that looks familiar and which outlines themes to be explored has helped people to arrive expectantly, rather than fearfully. In the session itself, a simple description of how it will unfold provides enough structure that doesn't lead to a sense of being "unsafe," neither for the director nor the participants.

It is important to work to time. We make clear that we will take breaks at appointed times, finish at the appointed time and if necessary to over-run, we negotiate time extensions. This boosts trust and credibility. Credibility also comes about when we display, right from the minute we meet people as they walk in, that we have considered them in our planning. We have usually used role reversal in our planning process, to stand in the shoes of the sponsor and potential group members. As we meet them, we relate to them in ways which let them know that we already "get them."

We have found that a useful early sociometric exploration has come out of doubling what may be alive in group members, some of whom may not even want to be there. We have done this by placing some chairs in the action space, concretising a few of the roles that people may be warmed up to, but are possibly trying to keep hidden. This has been done in a light-hearted way and enabled people to authentically express dissatisfaction, discomfort or disgruntlement. This has also enabled people to consider alternative ways of warming up to participating in the session. We are enabling people to bring their full selves to the session. Then the issues they explore and solutions they eventually find as we move into sociodramatic enactments will be authentic and directly relevant to their work.

Beginning with sociometric explorations, we let people know that they are the subject of the workshop and that the content will arise from their real concerns, crafted around the purpose. The purpose is not the subject. For example, in a "Difficult Conversations" workshop, we have invited people to join a continuum based on the ease with which they enter into a conversation with a colleague or manager, and then invited them to express their experiences of these conversations. This early part of the session is about getting people to relate to one another and the purpose, and to increase trust that the solutions which may emerge are already within the group.

Part of our own warm up is trusting that everything is there before us in the room, awaiting on us as directors to produce them as they arise. As we continue to produce what is directly in front of us, spontaneity and creativity increases and we don't find ourselves as fixers of other people's problems.

Using Action Methods and Sociodrama
To Facilitate Dialogue In a 'For Profit Organisation'
T.T. Srinath

I was invited by the Human Resource (HR) Head of a large multi-national corporation having one of its manufacturing facilities in Chennai, India.

The brief offered to me by the HR Head on behalf of the President was, "The communication team is in my opinion doing an excellent job, yet there seems to be no acknowledgment of this within the organisation. Could we encourage the communication team to not seek endorsement yet self-appreciate?"

A one-day offsite was arranged where the nine participants of the communication team including its Head participated.

Through warm-up participants shared the 'moments of pride' they felt working in the current organization. The participants self-disclosed and acknowledged one another.

Following this the group created a spectrogram, with one end being 'we feel acknowledged and appreciated' and the other end being 'we are not being acknowledged.'

All nine participants positioned themselves along the continuum establishing their current thinking in the 'here and now'. Some participants voiced that the more senior members of the team seemed to have positioned themselves closer to 'we are not being acknowledged.'

The participants were also demonstrated doubling by the facilitator. This prompted a few participants to attempt doubling and alter-ego their colleagues.

Consequent to this experience the group formed a circle and those participants, who felt a compelling need to share, were invited to move towards the center. Two participants did so and each of them shared their story in brief. The rest of the participants aligned behind one of the stories.

The chosen story was 'we are being taken for granted because we are seamlessly working; our absence will reveal our importance.'

The teller of the story then described the characters involved in a few sentences. Participants were invited to take on roles, particularly those they thought they connected to. Four roles were described by the teller and after the participants had physically located themselves, the teller was asked to watch a conversation taking place among the role holders.

Doubling also happened with some of the observers coming in to alter-ego.

When the conversation among the role holders seemed to be reaching an impasse the drama was paused and the teller suggested an ideal situation that she would like see happen. The role holders were invited to enact her request.

Following the enactment there was sharing first from role by those who participated and then from personhood. The observers were then invited to share how the enactment had impacted them.

The storyteller finally shared and revealed as did the few who shared, from personhood, 'seeking acknowledgment was in some ways seeking approval and therefore as a team they would address the organization with data to establish their credential and not attempt to prove or justify their existence. This would establish that they were not seeking approval.'

A Workshop—Finding Hope in an Ever Changing World
Ron Wiener

In the blurb for the session I wrote: "Sometimes the news is so depressing that I turn it off, stop reading the papers and look for some form of escapism. So how and where do we find hope and optimism to combat the dark days?"

Ten people turned up in Manchester to explore the topic. We started with warm-ups—a sociometric exploration using wool to make connections followed by participants using objects to show the reason for their attendance. This was followed by sub groups creating a scenario where two of the group were producers tying to pitch a positive themed movie to a Hollywood mogul.

After a break, people using pen and paper laid out on the floor all the possible stakeholders in the action. They included: climate change, money, Putin , a homeless beggar, plastic, a Chinese diplomat, *etc.* People then worked in pairs to group the stakeholders. Staying in their pairs, people were asked to find the role they were most warmed up to and then to do some role interviewing of each other. People then took on roles and interacted with each other. There was then a sharing from role

Post lunch participants were asked to find a space in the room which they felt was right for them and their view of hope. People then shared how they felt and others responded. People were then asked to use the chairs to collectively build their vision of hope. The next task was to build a sculpture of hope using themselves. People did this and then shared from their position. One group member then led the others in the song by Jenny Goodman called 'ripples on the water'

> *I cannot change the world alone*
> *But you and I can cast a stone*
> *That ripples on the water (ripples on the water)*
> *Many ripples turn to waves*
> *That turn the tide to better days*

This proved to be very moving, There was then a final sharing.

Ron Weiner

Dr. Ron Wiener is a senior sociodrama trainer, and ex honorary President of the British Psychodrama Association, who awarded him a lifetime achievement award in 2008. He is also a community theatre director working on issues to do with ageing and dementia. He is the author of *Drug Taking among school children*; *Community Action the Belfast Experience,* and co-editor of *Sociodrama in a Changing World, The Handy Book of Unscripted Plays,* and many book chapters and articles. He also works as a supervisor and mentor in person and on Skype. Finally in semi-retirement, he enjoys lunching with friends and being a grandfather.

Dagmar Heinrich

Dagmar Heinrich is an artist, performer, and filmmaker. He studied in Zurich, Berlin, and New York and then studied psychodrama at the Swedish Moreno Institute with Anja Puhlmann and Dag Leif Blomkvist, with Zerka Moreno and Gretel Leutz. He learned at the Alfred Adler Institute that the painting process when it is accompanied can help to identify behavioural patterns, and discover new and creative solutions as well. You can contact him at *clandestine@bluewin.ch*

Sue Orton

Sue Orton has 30 years experience as learning coach and group facilitator. Her passion is to rekindle, encourage and inspire the facilitation of healthy communication and deep learning. Fellow of the Higher Education Academy. She balances her professional work with life as a weaver; it is a fruitful combination. You can contact her at *learning-in-action.com*, or *sue@learning-in-action.com*

Noelle Branagan

Noelle Branagan is an experienced group facilitator and psychotherapist. For over 25 years she has used Morenian Action Methods both in psychotherapy, and, in the design and delivery of courses and workshops for staff and management groups. Her expertise lies in facilitating personal and professional change and development, using these methods.

Diane Adderley

Diane Adderley started her working life after university as a professional actor and musician. She changed direction when she met psychodrama, playback theatre and sociodrama in the early 1990s. Jointly qualified in psycho- and sociodrama, she is a BPA Accredited Senior Trainer in the latter and an Accredited Playback Theatre Trainer. She earns her living as an independent practitioner, actor, trainer/consultant and coach, in both the UK and internationally. Co-editor and co-author of *Sociodrama in a Changing World* (2011, *lulu.com*). Lives in Manchester, UK. You can contact her at *diadderley@gmail.com*

Irina Stefanescu

Irina Stefanescu is a Sociodrama practitioner with BPA (2012), psychodrama facilitator with ARPsiC (2009), certified coach with Austrian Institute for NLP & NLPt (2009) and trainer (UK, 1997). Having her own company in Romania—FLUX Training and Consultancy, working internationally with organizations and individuals—Irina has been developing since 1996 the role of a learning partner. Traveller and dancer, learner and mentor, wife and mother, daughter and friend, citizen and colleague, Irina enjoys life every day. She can be reached at *irina.stefanescu@gmail.com*

Arohanui-Grace and John Wenger

Arohanui-Grace and John Wenger have been working together for 15 years. They trained together at the Auckland Training Centre for Psychodrama in Aotearoa/New Zealand. They have applied Moreno's methods in workplaces large and small, with groups ranging from factory workers to corporate bankers. They continue to write on those experiences. Grace is currently based in Christchurch, Aotearoa/New Zealand and can be contacted on *grace@graceworks.co.nz* and John is currently based in London, UK and can be contacted on *john@q-shift.com*

T.T.Srinath

T.T.Srinath, Ph.d., is an accredited sensitivity trainer. He lives in Chennai, India. He has done extensive work in Gestalt, Psychodrama and Sociodrama. He works in both the corporate and non-corporate sector, facilitating human interaction processes. He can be reached at *ttsrinath@gmail.com* and his website is *www.ttsrinath.com*

Section 4

Action Explorations in Personal Growth

H.A.P.P.Y!

Elders Improve Life With Improv!

Anne M. Curtis

Recently a nurse suggested I visit an elderly woman who had suffered a debilitating stroke. "She has some dementia and has lost the ability to speak. Would you be able to handle that?" she asked. "I am sure I can! I shall sing, mime, use fun props, and be colorful," I replied.

When I entered the room, the elderly lady turned her head toward me and seemed to understand that I was a friendly face. Her daughter was visiting, so I engaged her help. Knowing that the more senses one can involve, the better it is for neurological recovery, I gave the daughter a hot pink feather boa and an orange hat to wear. I donned a purple boa and my sparkly purple top hat. We teamed up for a happy song and dance to *Cabaret* that delighted the patient. Her eyes followed us and appeared alert.

We then began blowing "Healing Bubbles" as I sang, *Whistle a Happy Tune*. The daughter encouraged her mom to blow bubbles too by holding the wand close to her lips. We were both so excited when she actually began to purse her lips and blow. We rejoiced at this good sign!

As I played soothing Mozart music, I took out my "Magic Box" and mimed taking out the gift of a beautiful rose. The daughter and I pretended to fill the room with more and more roses, placing them in an imaginary vase on the bedside table. Her mother was very interested and reached for the "roses" we handed her. She seemed so engaged and relaxed as we repeated the word 'rose' with each rose we picked.

I went one-step further and drew a rose with crayons, writing and repeating the word 'rose.' Her daughter then asked, "What is that picture Mom? What did we get out of the box?" Her mother tentatively said, "Rose." Then she repeated it with greater confidence, "Rose!" What an awesome miracle!

I continued to pick "gifts" from the "Magic Box": a bird, sun, and rainbow. I then drew each picture and wrote the word. Each time, she was able to say the word! We were filled with awe!

We followed up with joyful reinforcement in the form of a "healing dance" pretending to tap dance to the song *Go Into Your Dance* from 42nd St. I left her holding the gift of a metaphorical "Healing Buddy" bear, a smile on a stick, and renewed hope.

The daughter filled in a survey and on the comment section she wrote simply, "The artist got my mother to speak again!"

I believe that the Action Explorations such as blowing bubbles, moving her hand to reach the imaginary gifts from the "magic box," listening to music, watching us dance and hearing our laughter, relaxed this frail elder enough to lower stress chemicals. The relaxation response helped her mind and muscles to regain the neurological pathways to speech, previously frozen by the trauma of her stroke.

I am grateful to be able to touch lives in this unique way! As a traumatic stress specialist, registered drama therapist, and actress, I am able to help people with the challenges that arise in their lives. My main focus has been uplifting people suffering from illness, crisis and loss in hospitals, elder care, hospice, and community support groups.

·   ·   ·

Most of the time I am not playing the role of a therapist, rather I am a creative, caring visitor who engages people with humor and playful expressive arts activities. I have been given the title of "Healing Arts Specialist" and, my favorite, "Director of Happiness!" For the purpose of this chapter, I will focus on my work with the elderly in various settings.

Jack Benny on his 80th birthday said, "Age is strictly a case of mind over matter. If you don't mind, it doesn't matter!" This statement sums up my approach to helping elders live with the difficulties they face. I use an approach that combines laughter and learning, metaphor and creative arts. The overall goal is to enhance quality of life by teaching and rehearsing resilience skills, in an enjoyable way, through Action Explorations.

I was originally a creative dramatics teacher. I used improvisational drama as a fun, active way to teach theatre skills to children. My classes also helped each child grow in mind, body and spirit. They learned social skills, self-control, spontaneity, problem solving, and communication skills. They learned how to develop empathy. "If I were that person in that situation, how would I breathe, think, move, speak and relate to other people?" They used their talents to help others, by entertaining the elderly.

Later, I adapted my creative drama teaching to help grieving children in the schools. The six-week grief education program helped children, who had suffered loss, to cope and begin to heal. It was important to make the program fun and active because they needed to be uplifted to continue their school day. I helped them understand and cope with their pain through metaphorical stories, puppets, props, art, music and movement. I juggled heavy and light content. I wrote my "Circles of Life" curriculum guide as a resource for teachers and grief educators.[1]

When I became a Registered Drama therapist and Certified Trauma Services Specialist, I coined the term *TraumaDrama* to describe my theoretical framework. Gradually my work became focused less on prescribed "therapy" and more on helping people of all ages to cope with the ups and downs of their life story. I changed the method to include a higher proportion of laughter and comedy techniques. The "H.A.P.P.Y!" method (Humor & Arts Prescription= Positive You) is based on the algorithm:

Metaphor + Expressive Arts + Humor = Stress Reduction + Heightened Resilience

1. **Metaphor:** Symbols address traumatic issues and teach coping skills while lowering stress. Metaphor creates a safe distance from the trauma and produces a positive shift in perception.
2. **Expressive Arts:** Creative, fun activities mindfully engage the creative side of the brain to lower stress chemicals produced by the *"Flight or Fight"* reaction. Reducing levels of stress hormones allows the logical side of the brain to become activated and begin to process difficult circumstances and learn resilience.
3. **Humor:** Laughter is a catalyst that breaks down resistance and builds positive attitudes. It replaces stress chemicals, such as cortisol, with endorphins (+ dopamine) to produce positive affect. Humor is a key resilience skill. *"Improve Life with Improv-a-Laugh"* is my unique technique for harnessing humor, as needed, to lower stress. This mirth method is based on studies that show the brain perceives a "faux" laugh as real and releases all the healing chemicals associated with real joyful laughter.

This theoretical model is a way to engage people of all ages and to help them with the comedy and tragedy, ups and downs, happiness and sadness, of everyday life. Everyone's life-story is a mix of the masks of comedy and tragedy that are the symbol of the theatre. I have used this active, playful method for over 25 years with all ages. Like Moreno, I have found that Action Methods are a life-giving gift to boost happiness for all humanity!

---

1   Curtis, A. (2001). *Circles of life: A creative curriculum for healing traumatic loss in childhood. Part 1 facilitator guide and part 2 children's book.* Self Published: ac_hearts@hotmail.com

"H.A.P.P.Y" harnesses metaphor, drama, creative arts and humor to address aging issues related to mind, body and spirit. Seniors need to be given permission to be playful and have fun. A Wall Street Journal article, by Clare Ansbury,[2] observes that many adults forget how to have fun. In the busy working years of adulthood, "having fun and being spontaneous-a key element of fun and play-gets lost. It's considered non-productive which makes some people feel guilty."

I give older adults permission to play by having them actually act out putting their "self-critic in time-out!" I help them to see that having fun is good for them.

Ansbury refers to a study of older adults and play that found, "playful older adults are psychologically upbeat: they are happy, optimistic, cheerful, joyful, positive, relaxed and enthusiastic individuals." This 2011 study by Yarnal, Careen and Qian, Xinyi created a research tool called an "Older Adult Playfulness Scale." This scale could be used to expand research on older adults and playfulness. I agree with their comment in the abstract "Limited research suggests that playfulness in later life improves cognitive, emotional, social, and psychological functioning and healthy aging overall."[3]

"H.A.P.P.Y!" techniques are designed to enhance verbal and non-verbal expression, movement, social skills, socialization, mood, motivation, resilience and cognitive function. My mission is to help people live well with the physical, mental, emotional and spiritual struggles that are a "normal" part of their everyday experience with the aging process. Creative arts and drama activities include breathing exercises, vocal practice, movement, pantomime, art, dance, singing and improvisational comedy. Playful metaphors link elements of each session together and offer participants a safe, novel approach to expressing difficult emotions.

The Arts and Human Development: Learning Across the Lifespan[4] has a section devoted to the arts and aging. The report cites studies that show many positive effects of dance, poetry, art and drama on specific quality of life issues faced by the elderly. For example, studies of an active theatre training group for seniors by Noice and Noice in 2004 & 2009 showed that the theater group had significant improvements compared to the two control groups in four of the five cognitive measures: immediate word recall, problem-solving, verbal fluency, and delayed recall. Noice and Noice suggest that the multimodal nature of theatrical engagement, which engages physical, cognitive, and psychosocial faculties, contributes to the positive effects of the intervention.

---

2 Ansberry, Clare, (2018) An overlooked skill in aging: How to have fun. WSJ, 6/5/2018.
3 Yarnal, Careen; Qian, Xinyi (2011) Older-Adult Playfulness: An Innovative Construct and Measurement for Healthy Aging Research *American Journal of Play*, v4 n1 p52–79 Sum 2011
4 This 2011 publication is free of charge at arts.gov, the website of the National Endowment for the Arts.

This National Endowment for the arts report concludes that:

> In older adults, arts engagement appears to encourage health-promoting behaviors (physical and mental stimulation, social engagement, self-mastery, and stress reduction) that can help prevent cognitive decline and address frailty and palliative care through strengths-based arts interventions. Prevention can have profound effects on individual quality of life and on the cost of healthcare.

I undertook a similar study with A. Mitchell MSW, LCSW, (2013)[5] Bringing interactive drama sessions to assist elders with Parkinson's, and their aging spouses, showed positive results. I continue to facilitate monthly sessions of *"Cheer>Up."* (Creativity, Humor, Education, Encouragement, Resilience, "greater" Understanding of Parkinson's.)

The level of participation in the program, despite the fact that some members have faced physical and mental decline over these 5 years, is further proof that Action Methods help people to cope and find greater happiness. I am able to show them that despite moving from walking, to walking with a walker, to being in a wheelchair, they can still have fun acting in improvisations, creating humorous skits and practicing coping skills. During the acting, these elders move, speak and show emotion more freely than they usually do. In turn this gives the caregiver/spouse a chance to have fun with their loved one in a safe, hopeful environment. Seeing a husband laughing with his wheelchair-bound wife, as they do a comic theatre exercise, is a heartwarming reminder of the resilience of the human spirit!

The aging population has many challenges. 80% of older adults have at least one chronic health condition, and 50% have two or more. Illness or falls lead to mobility decline, speech problems, loss of vision, hearing and independence. These stress factors impact emotional health. Depression is more common in elders who also have other illnesses like Parkinson's, heart disease, or cancer. Many elders are suffering from unresolved grief from multiple losses. They have lost their spouse, home and autonomy. Physical decline limits frail elders' ability to function independently.

Older adults are often misdiagnosed and under-treated. Healthcare providers may see older adult's symptoms of depression as just a natural reaction to illness, or the life changes that may occur as we age, and therefore not see the depression as something to be treated. Older adults themselves often share this belief and do not seek help because they don't understand that they could feel better. Offering "H.A.P.P.Y!" support to these at risk groups is a way to help in

---

5 Curtis, A. and Mitchell, A. (2013) Cheer>Up: drama therapy support groups for Parkinson's, *Journal of Parkinson's Disease.* Vol. 3, Suppl.1. p. 40.23

an informal recreational setting. "H.A.P.P.Y!" is re-creation through recreation! The method boosts people's HQ: Happiness Quotient! It allows their "inner child" to come out to play!

Music is one of the fastest ways to activate the creative side of the brain. I use music throughout my sessions as memory boosters, rhythm and movement catalysts and ways to introduce a theme. I also use music as background to enhance the mood or topic of an improvisational exercise or scene.

I often begin with a song to focus everyone's attention and raise their spirits. Songs that have positive lyrics and upbeat rhythm will encourage people to engage with clapping and other movement activities. For example, the song "Happy" (2013, Pharrell Williams[6]) is a great theme song for my groups. Sometimes I give people two paper plates to use as rhythm instruments. I have them discover all different moves they can do with the plates. It can also become a "mirror exercise" beginning with them mirroring my moves, then taking turns as the leader. This can be done as a whole group or in pairs. It always generates energy and laughter! They begin to breathe more deeply, move more freely, and become ready to look for happiness! How can anyone feel glum singing and moving to these "*Happy*" lyrics:

> Huh, because I'm happy
> Clap along if you feel like a room without a roof
> Because I'm happy
> Clap along if you feel like happiness is the truth
> Because I'm happy
> Clap along if you know what happiness is to you
> Because I'm happy
> Clap along if you feel like that's what you wanna do

In my role of "Director of Happiness" for seniors, my first objective is to address mental, emotional, social and physical issues associated with aging through the use of drama and humor. My second objective is to empower patients and caregivers by demonstrating Action Explorations to improve wellness, re-frame thought patterns, build resilience skills and live mindfully in the present.

Some elders are still living at home with family or professional caregivers. These are able to attend groups at Adult Day Care Centers or Support groups for health issues such as Parkinson's, Alzheimer's or Cancer. Senior Living Facilities are proliferating due to aging Baby Boomers. Many offer different levels of living arrangements. Healthy seniors begin in Independent Living, and then, when the need arises, they can transition to Assisted Living or the

---

6 Williams Pharrell (2013) "Happy", *Despicable Me 2*, Soundtrack Album, Backlot Music, Columbia.

residence's Health/Rehab. Center. Some offer in-house Hospice Care beds as well. My programs can help people in each of these stages.

The "Independent Living" elders have access to a wide range of activities. They are able to enjoy play-reading and improvisational drama classes. One such program is, "Acting For Life." Each group meeting has a different theme and theatre-training goal along with didactic handouts to reinforce the key points. For example my July session revolves around the celebration of "4th of July!" The theme serves to tie all the elements of the session plan together with planned segues to seamlessly move from one activity to another. I begin with warm-ups for body and voice. These include movement to music, singing, sharing memories and laughter exercises.

One of the main Action Explorations in this session was the creation of an imaginary Fourth of July Parade. The actors explored roles they would like to play and added costume pieces such as red noses for clowns and props like cheerleader pompoms! As facilitator I am constantly assessing the abilities and responses to the different levels of activity. The participants warmed up easily and, when it came time for the parade, everyone was relaxed, happy and energized. They enjoyed picking from the array of props. One elder, who is blind, found the session particularly enjoyable because improvisation can be done without having to read. The group wanted to share their acting and suggested going out into the lobby where people were beginning to gather prior to dinner. So I carried my boom box of parade music, and they paraded playing their chosen roles: clowns, cheerleaders, band members, baton twirlers, personalities on floats, *etc*. They spread their energy, joy and laughter to their impromptu audience! The lobby filled with an audience of smiling residents.

Afterwards, when I was alone, packing up my props, one of the actors returned with a friend saying, "You are not going to believe this! When we went out to parade around the lobby I was so into the acting, I completely forgot that I use a walker! I left it behind!"

To download an outline of the session plan, visit *bitly.com/AEcurtisA*

· · ·

Yes I have seen miracles happen! Einstein said, "There are only two ways to live your life: as though nothing is a *miracle,* or as though everything is a *miracle.*" I live my life as though Action Exploration and *"H.A.P.P.Y!"* are, indeed, miracles! I have watched in awe as people begin to re-create themselves and find their inner light. Even the frail elders who are bedridden can find some moments of happiness. Action Explorations also include guided imagery. Through narrative, music and words that stimulate the senses, I can take a patient in the health center to a far away place of their choice.

I remember going into a double room that had only a curtain between the patients. My first step in a bedside visit is to act as a friendly visitor, to assess their ability to interact, and openness to engagement in the arts. I liken this stage to audience members buying a ticket to a show. The "ticket" symbolizes their agreement to interact with me and explore creative expression. The man in the bed closest to the door had his wife visiting. We chatted together and they were pleased to have the healing arts visit. I checked the second man beyond the curtain, and he said he was sleepy and wanted to just rest with the curtain closed. I did various warm up activities with the first couple and then said, "I know you love it in this rehab facility, but if you could travel somewhere else, where would you like to go?" They started sharing how much they dreamed of going back to Ireland. I then proceeded to narrate an imaginary journey to Ireland. I ended with guided imagery of a visit to an Irish Pub, singing Irish songs and doing a comic jig. I then pretended to be an Irish barmaid. In an Irish brogue, I said, "Let me pour you some good Irish Stout. 'Tis surely good for yer health. In fact, 'tis better than whatever is in your IV bag!" Before we could drink our imaginary toast, a voice from the far side of the curtain shouted out with joyful energy "I'll drink to that!" So I, as the Irish barmaid, opened the curtain, and we all continued the interaction together! Irish jokes and more songs ensued. The change in affect was miraculous!

Stanislavsky,[7] who developed "Method Acting" said, "The most important thing is to build the life of the human spirit." He wrote that his " 'small truth' of physical actions stimulates the 'great truth' of thoughts, emotions and experiences . . ." He defined "action" as being "human behavior." He referred to an unbreakable tie between the physiological and psychological self.

We are mind, body and spirit. Physical Action for Stanislavski included gestures, stage movement and words. What an actor says and how he moves, shows meaning to the audience. Words conjure up images in the mind that, in turn, bring about emotional responses. Stanislavski taught ways to access the "subconscious through conscious means." The actor creates the inner experiences of the character, incarnates them and makes this creative process understandable to the audience.

This holistic view of the interaction between actions, thoughts and emotions helps us to understand why the arts can give people relief from stress. The man behind the curtain was listening to the words and his mind began processing the images. These positive images brought about a change in his brain chemistry, so that he became relaxed and ready to play. His toast to Irish stout was a metaphor for hope. As Shakespeare wrote, "The show must go on."

Resilience is the ability to bounce back from difficult circumstances in our lives.Aging brings many traumatic circumstances such as diagnosis of a serious illness or loss of a spouse. Studies have identified many traits of resilient people.

---

7   Moore S. (1960, 1965) *The Stanislavski System*, The Viking Press, U.S.A.

These traits can be learned. Action Methods, using the expressive arts and humor, provide a stress free way to discover and rehearse key coping skills. Frail elders who are living at home with a chronic condition such as Parkinson's or Cancer can benefit from attending support groups that use metaphor, improvisation, art, music, poetry and humor. Positive psychology has proven, what Stanislavski suggested, that the mind, body and spirit are connected in amazing ways. Creative activities help individuals to say "*yes*" to challenges "*and*" explore new ways to face them. The group members learn to make positive, practical choices that help them to feel and act "*as-if*" they are doing better! Recently the spouse of a person with Parkinson's said that her new watchword is "*Pretend.*" She spoke about how accepting her husband's downward physical trend, staying in the moment, choosing to look for joy, and acting "as-if" things are fine, helps her to stay upbeat and cope one moment at a time.

Actor training consists of a broad array of theories, methods & exercises to master vocal skills, physical movement, emotional expression and dialogue. These action methods are valuable tools to help with issues in the areas of speech, movement and socialization. Members of my Parkinson's group enjoy the challenge of doing improvisational warm-ups for voice and body and creating skits. The skits promote problem solving, communication and social skills. These aging actors engage fully in my "*Improv-a-Laugh*" method to produce "*faux laughter.*" They experience the effect hearty laughter has on their energy level and mood. Laughter makes them feel better, in part, because they get a critical boost of dopamine in the brain.

An effective way to engage people who are frail, disabled physically or have cognitive impairment is to engage their senses with interesting, colorful props and costume pieces. Wearing a hat, holding a prop, using a scarf, vest or apron as a creative costume, helps stimulate the brain and makes these more disabled elders feel empowered. Waving a blue streamer in a poem about rain, wearing a colorful hat for a musical number or holding up a sign, helps these frail elders to become a part of the action.

I recently did an interview about my Orlando Cheer>Up therapy to help Parkinson's patients and their caregivers for Orange TV's YouTube webpage at *Active Lifestyles Magazine.*[8] The video clips of a session clearly show the seniors, caregivers and Parkinson's patients, enjoying props and hats as stimulation for the action. In this video the action methods revolve around a Fall/Thanksgiving metaphor. Silk fall leaves, flowers and plants from my yard and pictures of autumn were used to focus everyone's attention on the theme. I then led them into discussion of autumn as a metaphor for changes in the seasons of our lives.

---

8 CHEER>Up: *https://youtu.be/oiZMGnoRJsk*

Warm-up exercises included large movement to use their arms and hands to dance like falling leaves. Silk leaves and scarves in fall colors were helpful props to initiate this movement. They imagined the scarf was a magical dancing scarf, pulling their hand and arm in a happy dance. Choral reading of a poem about fall and singing a fall song with gestures warmed up their voices. Later in the session, the seniors picked titles from a hat such as *"The Unexpected Guest"* or *"The Turkey Disaster"* to explore problems that can arise at holiday gatherings! A colorful array of props and costume pieces were laid out on a table for them to choose. Giving opportunities for group members to make choices is an important element of the method. Many seniors have limited opportunity to choose what happens in their daily lives. I try to mix ability levels in each group when they work on an improvisational scene. This allows everyone to participate at his or her own level of health and promotes a positive feeling of accomplishment.

Every month is a surprise! Surprise is an emotion that can be either positive or negative. When elderly persons suffer a lot of negative surprises, such as a chronic illness diagnosis, they need positive surprises to help create a balance. Metaphor takes their minds away from everyday stresses and creates a safe, fun narrative for social interaction. Studies have demonstrated that novelty stimulates the brain, promoting the growth of new neural networks. The novelty inherent in the metaphors and the improvisational drama is good for maintaining brain plasticity. Metaphors for sessions are always different. They include hats, masks, bridges, kites, kaleidoscopes, sports, illusions, superheroes, holidays and the butterfly: a powerful metaphor for change.

When the participants create and act in metaphorical scenes, they can explore difficult issues without anxiety. The study of neurology supports the use of stories as "powerful tools for the work of neural network integration at a high level." Dr. Daniel Siegel in The Developing Mind: Toward a Neurobiology of Interpersonal Experience (1999) wrote "Stories serve to bridge and integrate neural networks both in the present moment and through time."

For aging issues relating to Parkinson's, I use action methods based on improvisational drama and actor training. For elders with cancer, I use an interdisciplinary approach.

Victory Support Group's (VSG)[9] Mission is to enhance quality of life through the development of innovative creative approaches that build resilience skills, lower stress and provide a joyful respite experience for those associated with cancer. Session plans for VSG are unique, lively, empowering, educational and encouraging. Many support groups provide information about the disease and encourage sharing of difficult concerns. VSG takes a different approach! Victory

---

9 *www.victorysupportgroup.org*

gives group members a mini-vacation from illness! The focus is on joy! Each month explores a different healing theme or metaphor that weaves the creative activities together. Shared humor, drama, songs and artwork give a break from stress and empower people to make a positive shift in attitude. Victory sessions harness the healing power of "faux laughter" imagery, singing, visual art and poetry in order to lower stress chemicals in the brain and body. The support group empowers participants to face challenges by teaching stress-reduction techniques. Helpful handouts reinforce featured coping strategies.

Victory is an acronym for Vitality! Imagination! Creativity! Tenacity! Optimism! Resilience! You! Our ground rules are: Have fun in the present moment! Enjoy the process! There is no right or wrong way-only your way! Put your self-critic in time out, respect confidentiality and help one another feel better!

When we are faced with traumatic events such as cancer treatment, the "fight or flight" stress reaction readies the body for action-releasing adrenalin and glucose to create energy for physical activity. Action methods are effective ways to cope because they engage the creative side of the brain in a positive way. Creative activity lowers stress chemicals in the brain. The individual then becomes more relaxed and can begin to process challenging life circumstances in a logical manner, without the painful emotional component.

Victory was started at the request of an MD, who was facing cancer herself. This doctor found regular support groups, that simply discuss the illness, made her more anxious. What she needed was a place where she could be uplifted and learn to deal with difficult emotions. Doctors are taught to professionally distance themselves from the emotional side of illness, so they can concentrate on the science of healing others. However, when medical professionals are faced with their own life threatening illness, they need to find ways to acknowledge, experience, and cope with, strong, negative emotions. They need to explore other roles they play in life.

Members of Victory Support Group never know what surprise metaphorical theme awaits them! We begin with an introduction of the theme and the learning goals for the session. We take time to breathe, put our "self-critic" in "time-out," put aside burdens and use mindfulness techniques to focus on the "NOW." Creative arts warm ups for voice and body include songs with movement, choral poetry reading and short, fun, creative dramatics exercises. This leads into a visual art project. During the art we encourage conversation, reflection and the singing of happy, positive songs with a live musician. Sometimes we write a group poem, with each person adding lines then folding the paper so that only the next writer can see only one previous line. Poems are magical expressions of the emotions, goals and themes of the Victory session. It always causes a gasp of awe when we read the group poem as an empowering wrap-up of the Victory Group. Group members choose from a table of surprise gifts as a happy symbol of caring. Gifts reflect their need to choose to look for joyful surprises, in order to balance life's negative surprises!

One of my favorite sessions is the plan about *"Shoes We Wear and Roles We Play."*

A key learning objectives is to help elders choose positive roles. Instead of playing the powerless role of "sick-one" or "victim" they learn to choose powerful roles such as "hero, "problem-solver" or "survivor." So, I created new lyrics to *"These Boots are Made For Walking"* in order to engage the group in a metaphorical musical theatre number.

Members discussed and scribbled things they disliked about cancer on large paper banners. We did role playing movement exercises using pictures of shoes to stand and move as different characters. Then we sang the song, with live guitar music, mime and simple choreography. The musical number ended with a grand finale of marching all along the banners to stomp out cancer! It was a breathtaking, cathartic moment, a tribute to the power of Action Explorations to help lives and teach resilience skills.

(You can download an outline of the session plan here: *bitly.com/AEcurtisB*)

Participants' comments express how well *"H.A.P.P.Y!"* Action Exploration works:

> *"I feel fortunate and grateful to be in the Victory group! It is a break from the pain and suffering. I love the creative outlet."*

> *"Victory shows positive ways to increase our joy every day!"*

> *"My experience with the victory group is to gather with intelligent people, who have a shared experience of loss. Then I learn, through the process of art and activity, a means to rewrite the way I view myself."*

> *"I'm always happiest when I'm around other people expressing themselves. This group is a vacation from the pain!"*

> *"I always feel better when I leave than when I came in! I've been to many support groups, and this is the most amazing one! I learn that is never too late to play."*

Another member who participated for several years wrote:

> *I've been searching for positive energy to heal me, I found just that in Victory's Healing Arts Support Group. I've been fighting cancer for 13 years. I believe that stress is the main contributor of spreading this complicated disease. All the medicine in the world does not heal us from our own mental strife. Healing, I believe, is as much mental well being as is physical health. Victory support group brings out*

your inner child, delighting in the arts, leaving your inner critic outside in the dark, where it belongs. If you are looking for a support group that allows you to forget your disease for a little while, please join us; we have plenty of room for those who like to think outside of the box! This includes the caretakers dealing with a family member or a friend with cancer, you need laughter and healing, too!

I feel awed when I think about the added joy these "H.A.P.P.Y!" sessions give to people's lives. As facilitator of this group, I see healing miracles. I watch people transform from tired and depressed, to energized and hopeful. I see heartwarming interactions between fellow sufferers. I help an elderly couple enjoy creative activities and laughter together, a few weeks before the death of the spouse with cancer. I have the opportunity to uplift a new widow with action explorations surrounding butterfly imagery. The retired Doctor keeps a binder of all the didactic handouts. She told me that whenever she is having a hard day, she goes to the handouts and always finds something to help her with her anxiety and problems.

With playful "H.A.P.P.Y!" Action Explorations we can keep our spontaneous inner child alive, whatever our age! We can choose to say, *"yes"* to aging *"and"* look for joy in the present moment. Let us act *"as if"* we are grateful for each precious moment. Then we can joyfully say, *"Age is strictly a case of mind over matter. If you don't mind, it doesn't matter!"*

Anne Curtis

Anne Curtis, MS, RDT, CTSS is a Drama Therapist and Trauma Services Specialist who has brought the arts and humor to patients, caregivers and families in hospitals, hospice, senior living facilities and community support groups for over 30 years. Anne developed bedside visits and group interventions for all ages to lower anxiety and create hope.

Anne is facilitator and co-founder of Victory Support Group, found at *www.victorysupportgroup.org* Victory's mission is to teach resilience and help people focus on finding joy, despite challenging circumstances. This expressive-arts/therapeutic humor based support group for cancer patients, caregivers and family members is allied with Orlando/UF's Integrative Medicine Department.

Anne also assists Parkinson's patients and their caregivers, providing innovative support through Cheer>Up. This Drama Therapy based intervention was featured at the World Parkinson's Congress.

Anne Curtis' HAPPY programs (Humor Arts Prescription for a Positive You!) provide energizing interactive sessions to uplift seniors. Seniors engage in song, movement theatre games and art to stimulate mind, body and spirit. Author of Circles of Life: a Creative Curriculum for Healing Traumatic Loss in Childhood, Anne presents interactive lectures to universities, community agencies, and conferences. Her work has been featured in print, on radio interviews and TV: *https://youtu.be/oiZMGnoRJsk*

Anne played roles in over 100 performances at Sleuths Mystery Dinner Shows in Orlando as well as local theatres and recently appeared in several annual Maine Blueberry Festival Musicals. Anne is committed to using her creative talents to bring laughter and hope to uplift people and make this world a happier place!

References

Ansberry, Clare, (2018) An overlooked skill in aging: How to have fun. Wall Street Journal 6/5/2018.

Bailey, Sally D. (2010). *Barrier-free theatre. Including everyone in theatre arts-in school, recreation, and arts programs-regardless of (dis)ability.* Enumelaw, WA. Idyll Arbor Inc.

Brown, S.. with Vaughan, C. (2009) Play: *How it shapes the brain, opens the imagination and Invigorates the soul.* Avery. A member of Penguin Publishing Group (USA) Inc. New York.

Charidimou A., Seamons S., Selai C., and Schrag A., (2011) *The Role of cognitive-behavioral therapy for patients with depression in Parkinson's disease.* Parkinson's Disease Volume 2011 (2011), Article ID 737523.

Curtis, A. and Mitchell, A. (2013) *Cheer>Up: drama therapy support groups for Parkinson's*, Journal of Parkinson's Disease. Vol. 3, Suppl.1. p. 40.23

Curtis, A. (2001). *Circles of life: A creative curriculum for healing traumatic loss in childhood. Part 1 facilitator guide and part 2 children's book.* Contact: ac_hearts@ hotmail.com

Curtis, A. (1999). *Communicating with bereaved children: A drama therapy approach.* Illness, Crisis, and Loss, 7(2), 183–190. Thousand Oaks CA. Sage Publications.

Hanna G., Patterson M., Rollins J., Sherman A. (2011.) *The arts and human development: Learning across the lifespan. Framing a national research agenda for the arts, lifelong learning, and individual well-being.* National Center for Creative Aging. National Endowment for the Arts, Washington D.C., arts.gov

Huseman R, (2014) *Prescription positive. A great way to live... and live longer.* Equity Press. U.S.A.

Moore S. (1960, 1965) *The Stanislavski system*, The Viking Press, U.S.A.

Modugno, N., Iaconelli, S Fiorilli, M., Lena, F., Kusch, I., and Mirabella, G. (2010) Active theater as a complementary therapy for Parkinson's disease rehabilitation: a pilot study. *The Scientific World JOURNAL* 10, 2301–2312 DOI10.1100/tsw.2010.221

Real Life 101 TV episode 191, 2013–2014 Season. *Interview With Anne Curtis, Drama Therapist*. Available online at: RL101.com

Robbins J., (2002) *Acting techniques for everyday life: Look and feel self-confident in difficult, real-life situations.* New York, N. Y. Marlowe & Company.

Schwartz E., RN (2005) *Humor in healthcare: The laughter prescription.* Western Schools Inc. Brockton MA.

Sightings, T. (2015) *10 worries older Americans face: Individuals have different concerns than health and financial experts.* U.S. News & World Report, July 20th 2015

Schaefer, Charles E., editor, (2003) *Play therapy with adults.* J. Wiley & Sons. N.J.

Walters, Quincy J. (2018) *Improv comedy helps people with Parkinson's* TweetShareGoogle+Email Quincy J Walters / WGCU News 4/3/2018

Weisberg, Naida (Editor) and Wilder, Rosilyn (Editor.) (2001) *Expressive arts with elders: A Resource. Second edition.* Jessica Kingsley Publisher's Limited, London U.K.

Yarnal, Careen; Qian, Xinyi (2011) *Older-Adult playfulness: An Innovative construct and measurement for healthy aging research,* American Journal of Play, v4 n1 p52–79 Sum 2011

The Art of Play

Adam Blatner and Allee Blatner

The Art of Play is an improvisational dramatic approach we created in order to help adults reclaim their imagination and spontaneity. Around 1979, Adam (a psychiatrist and trainer of psychodrama) recognized that psychodramatic methods could and should be applied beyond the clinical context—that these techniques could help healthy people learn to enjoy themselves and life more fully. Allee (a creative arts professional) had a lifelong interest in promoting the fun of role playing characters. She had enjoyed role taking during her high school drama activities. Both of us became motivated to explore ways drama could enhance a greater sense of vitality for adults.

We decided that a supportive workshop structure using good group process procedures and offering people ample time and activities for warming-up would form the foundation for more challenging role playing. The central theme for the focus of our method was the concept of "play"—that natural and easy realm children continually pursue. Playing monsters, kittens, warriors and princesses is so easy and refreshing in childhood. As we explored many techniques from psychodrama, creative drama, sociodrama and the creative arts, we met other professionals who were interested in imaginativeness and spontaneity.

The Art of Play is a recreational form performed not for therapy but for fun and socializing. The method may be conducted in larger or smaller groups. A large group would be broken down into sub-groups of 3–4 people. The method can also be conducted in a group of up to 9 people without breaking into sub-groups if there is more than 2 hours—*i.e.* in a half or all day "play-shop" that allows time for most participants to play their own character. The method begins with various warm-ups, and then in small groups, one participant at a time is helped to play a character from his or her imagination. Another group member acts as a director and the other(s) take supporting roles. The goal is for the main player to explore what it is like to "be" the character "in role," experience the role's environment, state of mind, feelings, and relationships. No personal problems are brought to be solved, and the roles chosen are not to be viewed as expressions of a player's personality. The Art of Play is a social and recreational activity and its success rests in the leader's ability to establish and maintain an emotionally safe, relaxed group space.[1]

Background

By 1981, Adam Blatner had been working for fifteen years in the roles of child and adult psychiatrist as well as a psychodramatist. Adam recognized that the role playing process in psychodrama promised a greater potential than its application in clinical settings, where it was used to work on patients' problems. After a period of talking with Allee, his wife, and contemplating what was most dynamic about this method, he realized that the most energizing element in the process was the activity of role-taking itself—the essential component of children's natural, make-believe play. This insight was substantiated by the fact that both Adam and Allee retained a strong sense of the childlike, enjoying not only playing with their kids, but also with the toys the kids used – hand puppets, masks, make-up devices.

The idea for the Art of Play was stimulated at a Halloween party for adults, when Adam met a fellow costumed as an extra-terrestrial alien. Instead of just saying, "cool costume," and otherwise relating to the person behind the role, Adam related to the role: "Wow, this is an opportunity to learn something about life on your planet." Adam and the guy shifted into a kind of interview with an extra-terrestrial: "What do you folks eat? If I may be so bold, how do you have sex? What is your religious belief?" The fellow played right to the questions and improvised answers that were clever and amusing. Later, he said how much he enjoyed the interchange, and Adam, in turn, not only enjoyed the play, but the "aha!" clicked: Let's have people just enjoy the creation of imaginary roles!

Not long after the party, Adam and Allee experimented. They gathered about nine of their friends in a group room and warmed them up to characters that popped into their imaginations. Then they brought these characters forward and, using modified psychodramatic techniques, helped them to experience the dramatic potentials inherent in these character roles. There was no interest in the group members' actual lives, but only what is was like to be the character and what might happen next if these scenes were to be carried forward.

For example, on being asked to open their imaginations to whatever character "wanted to come through," John (all names are fictional) announced, "I am a steam roller." Adam, as director, facilitated the action by asking, "Can you show us your parts." "What is around you?" At some point, it was fitting for someone to be in the scene—a driver of an automobile in the steam roller's path. Another of the group was chosen and agreed to play that role. The director

---

1 An extensive treatment of this method, with related chapters on theory, sample sessions, applications, *etc.*, is described in our book *The Art of Play*. See "References," at end.

needs to balance the way the main player wants the scene to happen and the way the supporting player is inspired to spontaneously respond. The result is often an amusing interaction.

Several more workshops ensued. The ideas and techniques were refined and it was tried with different groups such as the staff of an alcohol rehabilitation program or a group of adults in a church community. It became clear that The Art of Play evoked a rich mixture of simple enjoyment and self-discovery. Group members reported that they didn't know they could be that spontaneous.

In 1985, the Blatners wrote this approach up in a privately produced monograph. A few years later, The Art of Play was published and marketed as a psychology book. Since then, it has been used by professionals in a variety of related fields, and this in turn inspired Adam to consider the broader reaches of drama, aside from its obvious benefits as a therapeutic modality. (In 1995, Gary Izzo also used the primary title *The Art of Play* for his book about theatre games and improv—he hadn't heard of our book.)

Benefits

Blatners' *The Art of Play* method offers associated benefits as participants discover the depth and pleasure that accompanies improvisation and the companionship that comes with sharing one's imagination with friends. Other benefits include the following:

- promotes role flexibility, spontaneity, imaginativeness, and recreation
- offers a pleasant form of "role relief" for people who use role playing for serious purposes, such as in education, therapy, social action, *etc.* Here's a way to enjoy the richness of character development for its own sake
- provides a wholesome participatory activity that can be enjoyed without needing expensive equipment, travel, and other special elements
- creates a method for personal development, cultivating the human potential, and redeeming qualities that may have been neglected
- makes it possible to recapture the magic of childhood, the child-like (not the child-ish) ability to be young at heart
- allows access to the joyful essence of drama without the hassles of scenery, rehearsals, the politics and economics of a production for an audience
- sets up a way to interact physically, in a friendly way, at the level of imagination, which makes for a kind of encounter that cannot be replicated by the realm of internet chat rooms, video games, and other media with a thicker technological interface

- builds group cohesion, warms people up for other drama activities, emphasizes the power of the here-and-now as an occasion for enjoyment
- sensitizes the mind to the more subtle cues of the creative subconscious by the practice of opening to imagination and inspiration
- develops the skill for playing with children, your own kids and grandkids

Method

It was felt that a group of about nine was optimal at first, but that was for group sessions that might last three or four hours. Later, while working with groups of between 30–150 people, and with time constraints at conference workshops so that the activity was confined to a 90–120 minute session, we found that it worked to have the participants work in small groups of three to five. This allowed people to take turns and enjoy the benefits of playing one of the three main roles in the method — protagonist, director, and supporting player.

The protagonist is the main player whose imagined character is explored. The director's role is to facilitate the optimal experience of the main player. The supporting player (equivalent to the auxiliary ego in psychodrama) takes any role that will help the main player enjoy his or her own character most fully. There may be one, two, or a few supporting players.

When children play, they tend to improvise from the viewpoint of themselves and their chosen role or character. It requires a bit of adult thinking to relinquish one's tendencies to be egocentric and instead to offer one's own imagination mixed with mature judgment in the service of either acting as a directive facilitator or as a true supporting actor who, for the duration of the enactment, strives to become what is most needed by the protagonist or main player.

Children at play cannot achieve this level of focus. They unconsciously compete even as they cooperate. The understanding that people will take turns in the various roles demands a capacity for mature time-binding and a temporary relinquishment of egocentricity. In this sense, the Art of Play offers adults an opportunity to enjoy many of the benefits of child-like play without some of the disadvantages of the subtle intrusion of competing desires.

After the group leader explains and demonstrates the Art of Play, people take to it relatively easily. The skills involved can be developed, so the more one enjoys using the method, the more one practices. The more skilled the participants become, the richer will be the ensuing enactment. Generally, each enactment requires about five to ten minutes. There are skill building and imagination-enhancing opportunities in being any of the three role positions, so it is best to allot enough time — at least 45 minutes for a small group, so that each member of a small group can experience the process from every position. Learning how to direct, facilitate, and draw out could be as much fun as being a main player who learns how to be led into his or her imagination.

The essential process involves a warming-up of the group, a moving into the beginning of the enactment in the small group, a further warming up of the main character, and then having that person play through the role, discovering its intrinsic potential for humor, poignant depth, and interesting variation. In general, there isn't much sharing or processing until after all the group participants have done their own enactments. (Remember, this isn't supposed to be therapy.)

The Warm-Up

It's best if a somewhat experienced person leads the group so as to be able to explain the techniques and engage in some activities that promote a sense of trust and playfulness. A variety of warm-up techniques may be used. For example, crayons are used to help keep people in a fun, childlike state of exploration. Images are supposed to be doodles. It's very hard to try to make a realistic or "good" drawing with a crayon! This art activity starts breaking down the sense that things have to be "right" or that there are people who are "talented" or "better" than others.

However, the choice of warm-up depends on the size and nature of the group, the past experience of the group members with drama or theatre games, and so forth. Some groups have already been exposed to improvisation, but for many, the process is brand new. This latter group needs a more gentle and prolonged warming-up as they have layers of inhibition about "showing off," "getting attention," "making a fool of themselves," and other cultural residues that accompany the general social role of behaving as if "grown up."

We often begin the overall process by singing some simple songs together. We use song sheets so that folks don't have to remember the words. The songs are fairly familiar, often popular tunes from Broadway musical shows. Depending on time, we might also introduce a simple dyadic exercise, "draw-a-mandala." Two people draw together, beginning with one making a circle on a piece of paper with a crayon, the other, using another crayon, adds a design element. They then take turns adding elaborations until it becomes an interesting little picture. The technique shows what simple improvisation can do in the realm of art.

Next we warm people up to the activity of role taking with an exercise called "the talk show host game." Working in pairs, the group members interview each other. One person plays the role of a television talk show host whose job it is to draw out the guest while the other person plays a surprise character. The roles chosen might draw from a variety of categories:

- someone with an unusual occupation
- a person from history–either a famous one, or one who lived out a recognizable role (this could also be a person participating in current events, or someone in the future)
- a mythical figure, or someone from the comics, literature, television, or other fictional source
- an animal (and beings that can not in ordinary reality speak English or even speak at all can, in pretend play, speak clearly and express themselves articulately, and often with great insight)
- a plant, something in nature, an inanimate object, even a spirit of some abstract principle
- a family member (but not of the player's actual real-life family)

People need not play characters of their own actual age or gender–they can easily be the opposite gender and a very different age. The interviews go on for about five minutes. The group leader calls "one minute to commercial break," then a minute later, winds up the exercise. "De-role and change parts." The one who had previously been the interviewer now becomes the guest, allowing a character to come through his or her imagination. The previous guest now becomes the talk show host and begins to interview and draw out the new guest. After another five to seven minutes, the group leader winds up the exercise and invites everyone to share who they were. "A very clumsy juggler." "A very, very stingy millionaire." "An angel trying to help a nerd." "A dog waiting in the car for its owner." "A street lamp in a big city . . ." and so forth. The characters mentioned are often amusing in themselves and stimulate others to imagine variations of their own. The more people say who their imagined roles were, the more they warm the others up to the essential fun of imaginative play. (The talk show host game is further described on my website: *blatner.com/adam/ pdntbk/talksho.htm*, noted also as a good exercise for developing a basic skill in spontaneity development and learning how to be empathic.)

We then break up into small groups to do the Art of Play method. One person at a time becomes the main player and his or her role or character is helped by one in the small group playing the director to expand that role into a scene and from that, making it a small story. The others in the small group play supporting parts. After about 5–10 minutes, the director helps draw the scene to a close, they de-role, and begin again. Now another person in the group becomes the main player, another person the director, and the remaining others the supporting players. Adults can take turns this way better than children can!

The director's artistic challenge is to help the main character discover and experience a culminating event for his or her role. The director should get the players up and moving, redirect tendencies to talk *about* the scene to action and dialogue *in* the scene — "Don't tell us, show us!" — keep the improvisation unfolding, and, within the time given, bring it to a close. Group members can then finish, de-role, and change parts. No analysis is needed, and generally, no processing. Occasionally, near the end of the session, some people feel they want to talk about ideas or insights they've picked up in the process.

The basic skills involved in The Art of Play are also the most basic theatre arts skills, and these are mainly learned by doing — more like learning to swim than learning by memorizing from a book. There's a knack to it that develops with practice, so the more one uses this method, the better one becomes. (This is true for most spontaneity-training exercises, theatre games, improv methods, and so forth.)

Accessing a Character

The imagination is rich. We all have thousands of potentially available roles derived from all of the images of our culture. These role elements can be mixed up in funny and often incongruent ways. We should recognize that the imagination is very subtly available as a fountain of these roles as ideas. This dynamic is more obvious in the dramas of our night dreams, but if we were to quiet our business-like focusing mind, these more playful possibilities can emerge while awake, also.

After breaking up into the small groups, the group leader has everyone become quiet to "get in touch with their character."

"Imagine you have a kind of dark room or empty dark stage, and slowly bring the light up. Just see who is sitting or standing there. Allow it to surprise you. *Become whatever it is.*"

Some folks will get their ideas immediately even before the group leader suggests these processes of natural unfolding of the creative subconscious mind. Others will get their character only later, after seeing who else in their group has come up with someone. Everyone proceeds at their own pace. The more you do the process, the more open is the flow of images. The process is spontaneous and informal. Sometimes the director needs to remind people, "The character you become need have nothing whatever to do with your actual life." This is to remind people that this is a recreational activity for the imagination, not therapy.

People are encouraged to imagine themselves more vividly in role. "What shape do you have? What kind of garment are you wearing? What object might you be holding? It might be a staff, a pipe, a harp, something else, or nothing. If you are an object: What are you made of? If you are an element such as water: Are you cold or hot?" Then, to move the character toward a story, "What or who else is in the scene?" As the main players warm up to their characters, the director assigns supporting roles to the others in the group. The characters may similarly be either animate or inanimate, such as a chair, the wind, a clock, trees, or the surrounding water.

Further Techniques

Part of the novelty of this approach is that it can be extended and deepened using the general range of techniques used in psychodrama.

Replay: A main character (*i.e.*, protagonist) is free to say, "I want to do this over," just to feel the enjoyment of the activity, or to vary the enactment in some way–a little or a lot. Some people might suggest a replay of a movement or scene element to deepen the main player's warm-up. For example, if a character would, in the course of a given scene, be expected to yell wholeheartedly, many people have not brought their voice skills up to a degree that over-rides their habits of inhibition and soft-spoken-ness. It's liberating to be coached and encouraged by the group to find their voice and learn to express a yelp, roar, cry of anguish, shriek of fear, and other full-throated expostulations.

Role Reversal: This technique is used in two ways: First, a character may take the part of the co-character for a short time just to illustrate to the person playing that supporting role how to behave. This generally involves not only what the other character says or does, but also how that role is performed, with what degree of vigor, emotionality, pace, or other variables. The other way role reversal is used is to offer the main character an opportunity to also experience the role of the other person or being in the scene either for understanding or just for a more complete satisfaction of the event. Children do this intuitively. You might have heard kids playing house and saying, "Now you be the mommy and I'll be the baby." In the Art of Play, grown-ups can also transcend the belief that just because they start a scene in one role, they are supposed to finish it that way, also.

Asides: This is the theatrical equivalent of the "voice over." The character turns his head to an imagined audience outside the circle of enactment and shares thoughts or side comments that the others in role in the scene pretend not to hear. Using this device, role playing can be deepened a level, including expressing mixed feelings, secrets, manipulations, and so forth.

Cut or *Freeze*. Just as movie directors can suddenly interrupt the play of a scene, so can the players. Derived from the movies about making movies in the 1940s, "cut" stops the action and prepares for a replay. "Freeze" in this era of video and DVD might also be called "pause." In the interim, some change, or comment is made, but then, when "action" is called, everyone continues as if nothing happened. Little kids call "time out" or, in my childhood neighborhood, "Kings X." The point here is also that the enactment need not be smooth, polished, and finished. There can be a kind of rehearsal, a groping, as the main player is helped to find what responses, counter-actions, shift in situation, might best bring forth the deeper sense and purpose of the character being played.

Integrating Other Dimensions

In addition to drama, some elements from art, poetry, singing, making music, drumming, dance and movement, using props like hats, puppets, masks, and various costuming devices, all can add depth to the overall process. As mentioned in the description of the warm-up above, we also use singing and improvisational drawing as aids.

Sometimes we warm up a group that is somewhat wary about this procedure just by talking about toys we loved as kids, or the kind of clubhouse, fort, or other protected special place we might have enjoyed alone or with others. There seems to be a real hunger for and delight in reclaiming these dimensions of imaginativeness.

Applications

The Art of Play method may be integrated as a warm-up or "cool-down" in workshops that also use other approaches mentioned in this book. It is a good technique for helping actors learn to improvise. Further, it can help them develop the characters they are to play by exploring aspects of those roles that may not be overtly expressed in the script. Many drama therapists use this method as a part of their training, as do some people involved in drama in education. It's a gentle introduction into some sociodrama or role playing, and may be used also as a kind of closure: The larger group breaks into groups of three to five, and they then take turns enacting a scene that would be the most satisfying, wonderful event, something imagined as happening five to ten years in the future. This event need not be something that has any real probability of happening. It might or might not. The point is to exercise the faculty of envisioning positive future events by offering an opportunity to enact them with the help of a few others.

Summary

Many more techniques and methodological subtleties can be elaborated that can deepen and extend the play. Like any good game, the more it's played, the wider the scope and more complex becomes the technique.

There are interesting benefits to this process, if one wants to utilize the component skills. In everyday life, many of these techniques are applicable. The authors in their own life at home occasionally weave in a variety of imagined "alter ego" roles. We may act like parent and child, commander and recruit, two kids playing, or letting our "shadow" complexes be expressed by acting like monsters or villains or pouty babies. The capacity for role flexibility increases, and we learn the phrases that communicate explicitly that we're playing and how we are shifting roles.

Another purpose for this method is that it offers "role relief." This concept recognizes that people can get subtly fatigued or bored or restless in playing the same outward roles in life, such as always being the considerate parent, the service-oriented salesperson, the obedient student. Why wait for Halloween or Mardi Gras to cut loose and let the other inner roles out, giving vent to the opposite qualities? We all need a general balancing process, relief from playing one role all the time.[2]

Our vision is that if more settings would include the Art of Play as a lubricating process, it could help retreats, workshops, and programs lighten up a bit. It is a method that brings many of the benefits of creative drama to adults, integrating sociodramatic methods so that grown-ups can reclaim their natural heritage of imagination and spontaneity.

·   ·   ·

Note: This chapter originally appeared in *Interactive and Improvisational Drama: Varieties of Applied Theatre and Performance*, by Adam Blatner, with Daniel Wiener (2007).

Adam Blatner

Adam Blatner, M.D., TEP, is a retired psychiatrist and Trainer of Psychodrama. He is a former Associate Professor of Psychiatry at The University of Louisville School of Medicine and Texas A&M University School of Medicine. Adam has written books and articles in the field of psychodrama, drama therapy and the creative arts in therapy. He is internationally recognized as an authority on the theory and practice of psychodrama. Adam has championed the place of the arts in healing and health for over 50 years through his writings, teachings at conferences and mentoring students all over the world. He is author of the basic text in psychodrama *Acting*-In, many articles and chapters, and the books *Foundations of Psychodrama*, *Interactive Improvisation*, and co-author *The Art of Play*.

Allee Blatner

Allee Blatner studied at The University of Texas/Austin and Carnegie-Mellon University. She was trained in psychodrama by her husband Adam, as well as in workshops with many other leaders in the field. For over 30 years, she

---

2 See the webpage supplement: *interactiveimprov.com/morewecanbe.html*

has led or co-led workshops and training seminars at colleges, hospitals and at national and international conferences. For 10 years, she and Adam taught a day-long class, "Practical Applications of Psychodramtic Methods," at the American Psychiatric Association annual convention. Allee is co-author with her husband, Adam, on their book *The Art of Play: Helping Adults Reclaim Imagination and Spontaneity.*

References:

Further quotes, observations, and references may be noted on the webpage supplement: *interactiveimprov.com/artplaywb.html*

Blatner, Adam & Blatner, Allee. (1991). Imaginative interviews: a psychodramatic warm-up for developing role playing skills. *Journal of Group Psychotherapy, Psychodrama & Sociometry (JGPPS)*, 44(3), 115–120, Fall, 1991. Available on website: *www.blatner.com/adam/pdntbk/talksho.htm*

Blatner, Adam & Blatner, Allee. (1997). *The Art of Play: Helping adults reclaim imagination and spontaneity.* (2nd ed.). New York: Brunner-Routledge. This book has extensive further references. (This book was first published privately in 1985 in a spiral-bound edition, then by Human Sciences Press in 1987. The present edition has been further updated.)

Blatner, A. (2002a). Psychodrama. In C. E. Schaefer (Ed.), *Play therapy with adults.* Hoboken, NJ: John Wiley & Sons.

Blatner, A. (2003). Singing for the Fun of It. *blatner.com/adam/level2/sing4fun.htm*

Noxon, Christopher. (2006). *Rejuvenile: Kickball, cartoons, cupcakes, and the reinvention of the American grownup.* New York: Crown/Random House.

Pink, Daniel. (2006). *A whole new mind: Why right-brainers will rule the future.* New York: Riverhead.

Enhanced Simulations Beyond Psychotherapy

An Introduction to Applied Improvisation Beyond Comedy and Before Therapy

Robert Lowe

Jacob L. Moreno was an Improviser before he was a therapist. Improvisation[1] is an ancient survival skill developed by all mammals, and probably other species. It is found first in the joyousness of play and playfulness. Improvisational Comedy has a distinct branch in the history of human theatre.

Applied Improvisation[2] is a maturing, formal field of study with a burgeoning professional consulting practice, in a growing global industry. AI is being successfully used in the areas of organizational development, all levels of education, personal development, business management, action-based consulting, disaster preparedness and relief, and the medical field.[3] Improvisation principles are being introduced in coursework in prestigious business, and law schools across America, and increasingly around the world. Literature in the field is expanding both in quality, and quantity.

Modern Improvisation as a "thing" is less than 100 years old, and a basic introduction is all that can be accomplished in a single chapter. You may find any number of statements that can make you tilt your head, and squinch your eyes in question. If this happens please look to the bibliography, and the growing body of literature for clarification.

---

1 The words Improvisation and their adjectives are capitalized as they are in my books in an effort to help formalize the images of the profession.

2 The terms, Applied Improvisation, AI, and Improvisation, will be used pretty much interchangeably.

3 Boynton, Beth, *Medical Improv: A New Way to Improve Communication (With 15 activities you can teach*, 2017.

.   .   .

This introduction begins with the passion of Improvisation, and by distinguishing Applied Improvisation from therapy. Terms of art will aid understanding, and a distinction will be made between AI and comedy.

We will touch on Improv as an Action Methodology and its illuminating back story, and we will discuss the major schools of thought and practice.

Mention will be made of successful Applied Improvisation practices, and some of the powers of Improvisation will be detail There are suggestions for putting Improvisation into work and play, deeper considerations, and specific steps about how to get there.

.   .   .

AI engages powers of craft, art, psychology, sociology, philosophy, and science. In 2000, my book, *Improvisation, Inc.: Harnessing Spontaneity to Engage People and Groups*,[4] was the first in North America to specifically detail using this methodology for working with business, organizational development, and human communication and collaboration, though there had been other books dealing with various aspects of the applications of Improvisation.

When modern Improvisation began, early in the 20th century, it was a subset of sociology and Improvisational Theatre. By mid-century the rise of a global movement had been seeded. There are distinctions from other forms in which improvisation techniques may be used that are needed to achieve a clear introduction.

The fields of simulation, Role play, Psychodrama, Sociodrama, psychotherapy, and Improvisation all have made distinguished contributions to the history of human development. Each has methods, and means, that are specific to their professions. Each with strengths and weaknesses that vary within their values, uses, and constraints.

Because of the durable histories of these unique systems of working with people, we can run into misleading understanding when the names of these fields are used while introducing applications of Improvisation.

When working beyond psychology, and outside the theatre, the terms "Role Play" and 'simulation" have taken on "brand" identity. A common thought when the term is used is, "Oh, I have done that before, so I know what this is."

A subtle reason to exercise caution in the use of these terms is a phenomenon which leads to something we call "script writing mind." This is ultimately the desire to control the moment, and usually appears in people who are new to Improvisation. It is a very normal response; an effort to get a leg up on what is going on. It starts with labels. "If I can name it, I can control it." The problem

---

4   Robert Lowe, *Improvisation, Inc. Revised 2017: An Applied Improvisation Handbook*, 2017, Atlanta, GA, RLJ Publications.

is that labeling tends to cover creative spontaneity. Effective Improvisation creates interactive practice in not labeling things.

An Element of Passion

When Improvisers describe the uses of this lovely art, the most consistent themes are in terms of passion, life change, love, and human connection. These are all factors that may be used by individuals, or groups of practitioners engaging in simulation, or Role Play, Psychodrama, or Sociodrama. At the same time there have been no global movements in these marvelous arenas. This is because these fields are used primarily as techniques, methodologies, tools, with education paths, and required credentials.

Improvisation is more than a technique operating through its own lens. First, it is a tool making tool. Then it is a personal and professional practice. It is a discipline that can take an entire lifetime to fully develop. Improvisation is accessible to all ages, and backgrounds.

One can approach Improv from a host of directions as: audience member, workshop attendee, as an independent troupe member, theatre troupe member, teacher, director, Artistic Director, or Program Manager. It can also be approached from the perspective of an Applied Improvisation student, practitioner, specialty program participant, developer, leader ('Autism Improvised', legal education programs, Medical Improv', *etc.*), or academician. In the industry we have at least one published Ed.D, and emerging Master's, and PhD programs around the world.

The available path to high level leadership runs from non-governmental service to business and corporate management, to local leadership, to global leadership, to genuine innovator, and to author. Among the most successful current professional practitioners there are individuals generating six and seven figure incomes, and new companies engaging growing numbers of employees.

Beyond this there is fame, fortune, and influence available in the entertainment and media industries. Stephen Colbert is a prominent Improvisation artist. Actor, author, Alan Alda has become an Improvisation educator in the world of scientists, and "Saturday Night Live" has a bully pulpit.

Following this growth and development are tens of thousands of children being introduced to Improvisation from elementary, and middle schools, through high schools, colleges and universities across the nation, and around the world.

•   •   •

Further distinguishing definitions may be helpful in considering this presentation of Applied Improvisation as a unique methodology. By my definition, simulations at the professional or formal levels, are technical events.[5] Among the highest examples are in training fields with airlines, and naval pursuits, space and ocean exploration, and fire and disaster control.

By this definition, Role Play in therapy, training, and organizational development can rarely reach the definition of simulation, except as in a technical setting such as having an Air Traffic Controller take the pilots chair in a real airline simulator. The developing field of Virtual Reality devices and programs is creating new considerations in this regard.

As this anthology is about action exploration outside the therapy fields, further comments regarding "Role Play" will be as used in business and organizational development, rather than coming from technology. The roots of Role Play here are in the theatre, Improvisation, and the work of Jacob Moreno. This model uses scenes and scenarios that prompt participants into taking part in a variety of "action explorations." These all occur in the mind, and in the interchanges.

As described by Adam Blatner,[6] Role Play is a venerated derivative of Sociodrama, and "It has been known as a method in education since the late 1940s, but there were enough problems with its use that it hasn't fully 'caught on.'" It has also been used in business and Organizational Development for nearly as long. This is the arena from which the "labeling" phenomenon most often arises. Adam Blatner also notes that "The most common problem with role playing is that of the leader not appreciating its essential nature: It is an improvisational procedure, and improvisation requires a feeling of relative safety."

·   ·   ·

Improvisation is a physical as well as a verbal activity; an engaging action method. It is not a thought process. It is the active embodiment of accommodation learning.[7]

As a fundamental survival form it is also a requirement of the ability to play. It is a major component of all interesting human conversation, and appears, now and again, in all art forms including: music, dance, fine art, sculpture, architecture, street theatre, and performance art. Applied Improvisation is a

---

5 My experience with simulators started as a four year old when my brothers let me "fly" an early Civil Air Patrol trainer. More formal training came with a U.S. Navy Officer Candidate School WWII ship convoy simulator, and with the first Navy OCS computerized battleship simulator, and with a number of Navy Fire Fighting School simulators.

6 Adam Blatner, "Role Playing in Education", *https://www.blatner.com/adam/pdntbk/ rlplayedu.htm*

7 Piaget's definition of a primary learning format.

wonder much like language, musical notation, and DNA. When its alphabet is understood whole worlds can be illuminated.

.　　　.　　　.

A delightful definition of Improvisation comes from *The Hitch Hiker's Guide to the Galaxy*.[8] A massive computer is asked the answer to the ultimate question of "life, the universe and everything." After 7.5 million years of calculation, the computer says, "The answer to the question of life, the universe, and everything is ... is ... 42!" It happens that in ASCII computer language code the number 42 stands for the asterisk symbol (*), which translates as, "Whatever you want it to mean," which is a great meaning for the "applied" part of Applied Improvisation.

The bottom line is that this common human survival skill is described today as the foundation, and philosophy of a global movement based in the most natural human balance between expression as a confident, vulnerable, genuine individual, and engaging as a vital member of a collaboration—wherein the aim is change, laughter, communication, safety, spontaneity, and the playfulness needed for survival and prosperity by advanced mammals on this delicate and complex planet of ours.

In its finest forms, Improvisation is most beautifully defined by the title of the great oral history by Jeffrey Sweet. Improvisation really is, *Something Wonderful Right Away*.[9]

AI vis a vis Therapy

Many have asked why I have kept my Improvisation at the level of humor and laughter in all venues. Improvisation works best when there is a safe working space for interpersonal development, and where spontaneity and creativity are primary factors. The conditions in the processes of Improvisation, can reach deeply into the individual psyche. Exploration into matters that are too serious can open tender issues that may not be able to be adequately supported in group gatherings.

The use of Improvisation as therapy is a very serious matter. Without the presence of a trained and credentialed therapist, and without a therapeutic contract, and appropriate support, and ethical systems in place, its use can be quite disturbing, and possibly dangerous. At the same time there is a resurgence of interest in Applied Improvisation by therapy practitioners. The Second Annual Improv & Psychology Conference will be held in 2019.

---

8   A Hitchhikers Guide first appeared on BBC Radio 4, 1978.
9   Sweet, Jeffrey, *Something Wonderful Right Away: An Oral History of The Second City and Compass Players*, 1978, New York, NY, Limelight Editions

Even with care taken regarding language, structures, guidelines, and environment, personal realities may be touched on, and the Professional Improviser (Applied Improviser, workshop leader, teacher, or director) must be aware of ramifications of the depth of this work, both for the individual, and for the gathering. This is also why I encourage foundational reading, as suggested by the bibliography.

The underlying, and saving truth is that laughter is its own healing wonder, which can clear problems as they surface, without specific intervention or intention on the part of the leadership. In the presence of laughter, we simply feel better to begin with. Laughter has long been known for its restorative qualities. Being in the presence of laughter generated by a collaborative human event is like being in an old growth forest on a sweet spring morning. Wholesome laughter can have the same effect as a deep embrace. The nature of good Improvisation is such that laughter is its constant companion, and laughter, with its varieties and intensity are a most amazing barometer, thermometer, and group analysis tool.[10]

When Improvisation is working, we begin to move in a new state of consciousness; a mindset in which our first instinct is to simply accept whatever is going on as an offer with which one is to become engaged. The added commitment is the guidance and support needed to use one's most genuine self and thus to help everyone involved to play together. The state, and the laughter become infectious.

Terms of Art

There is an emerging technical language in the field of Applied Improvisation, with terms of art, and of distinction that are important within the discipline.

Improvisation is the concept of using nothing except what is at hand and a set of relationship tools for generating spontaneity, creativity, communication, and unknown-unknowns.

The form is used in theatre, in comedy, in most music, dance, fine art, presentation art, poetry, creative writing, Zen pottery, parenting, and in simply being a human being.

Honesty refers to the convention that if one has thought of an idea before the current moment, or has used a line or idea before, it is no longer Improvisation.

Call Back is a term for a comedic technique used wherein someone refers to a word, or idea that was mentioned (or suggested by an audience call-out) earlier in the current performance or workshop. If not over-used, it pleases, surprises, and demonstrates that the players or participants are also listening all the time.

---

10   Improvisation, Inc. "Wholesome Laughter Leads the Way", Page 128.

Improv is an abbreviation for the entire field of Improvisation, or any part of it, or its general use in the world.

Improvisational Comedy Theatre is among the oldest, and newest forms of the theatre arts. Its modern form began in 1955 with "The Compass Players" in Chicago, Illinois. Its most ancient use being prehistoric.

"The Improv" is a franchise business name of a great number of Stand-up comedy clubs across America.

Impro is a word coined by Keith Johnstone to describe the altered state of consciousness which is active when a person, or group, or whole theater are engaged at the highest levels of possibility. It creates a palpable sensation. Somewhat akin to being "in the zone" in sports metaphors.

Side Coaching is the term for a technique taught by Viola Spolin where the director or teacher makes comments, from outside the playing area. The players are instructed to completely ignore the comments as they play. The comments are not intended to effect adjustment at the time offered. The remarks are intended to provide feedback, and to encourage more functional action.

Debriefing is an organized discussion about whatever just happened, whether following a show, during a rehearsal or workshop, with the group of participants, within any set in the group, or with individuals.

Rehearsal is a term often used by an Improv Troupe when working toward a public presentation. The work may include games to be played, and perhaps the players to be used in particular games, and the order of the games to be played, and sometimes the director or emcee is selected.

An Offer is any premise or situation presented by any participant, or observer.

Game s (*Exercises, techniques, forms, structures*) are all mechanisms used to advance scenes, and explorations in Improvisational theatre. Viola Spolin detailed many, and more are being invented all the time. For work with non-theatre people it is often best to use terms like exercises, techniques structures, and forms.

Sketch Comedy is normally sets of people presenting scripted work which is often developed using Improv methodologies.

Stand-up Comedy is normally one person telling jokes or stories with punchlines. This will be explored in detail below.

Applied Improvisation vis a vis Comedy

The entry of Improvisation into the realm of the serious is both inhibited, and advanced by its strong associations with comedy, which is often seen as the epitome of the not-serious. In the pursuit of Applied Improvisation, it is helpful to understand the development, growth, and range of Improvisational Theatre, and its relationship to comedy.

A distinction is to be made when refering to Stand-up comedy because it is only vaguely related to Improvisation. Stand-up has its foundations in jokes and punch-lines. Its history comes from ancient parodists, story tellers, and songsters, and thereafter primarily from Vaudeville, night clubs, and early television. While there are some interesting intersections with clowning, and Marionette, Improvisation and Stand-up do not share a history until recently, due to prominent cross-over players.

Improvisation for presentation has its origin as far back as the Etruscans to Oscans, and the "Fabula Atellana,"[11] with great later contributions through The Comedia dell'arte, (also known as "The Italian Comedy), best revealed by Pierre Louis Duchartre's 1929 work, *The Italian Comedy*; a truly magnificent presentation of the era. Theatre greats, Konstantin Stanislavski, and Berthold Brecht influenced early Improvisation pioneers. The practices and philosophies of the two arts are exactly opposite in many ways.

Stand-up comedy is usually a solo endeavor, Improv is almost always a collaboration. Stand-up is normally scripted; Improvisation does not work with scripting except in specialty formats. A Stand-up show can be repeated; an Improv show cannot. Stand-up depends on jokes and punchlines; Improvisation prefers not to use jokes at all. The goal of Stand-up is laughter; the product of Improvisation is relationship. Failure in Stand-up is called "dying on stage"; failure in Improvisation is called another chance to build something new out of thin air. A stand-up practitioner is called a comedian or a comic; an Improviser is called an Improviser. Both produce laughter, though for quite different reasons. Improvisation came from the desire to promote positive social change. Stand up is developing further in this direction.

Stand-up is as different from Improv as throwing pottery is different from oil painting. However, Improvisation is attracting a great number of stand-up comedians who are finding the skills of great value.[12] Many Improvisers will go through a period or course in Stand-up to strengthen individual presence and personal comedy timing. There are also, some great comedians who have come directly from Improvisation, including Robin Williams, Dave Chappelle, and Jonathan Winters.

Improvisation as an Action Methodology

Improvisation is both an old friend, and a newcomer to the world of serious methodologies. This action is what we call "Applied Improvisation." It is a complex, self-developing, and rapidly expanding system with structures, axioms, principles, tools, techniques, and patterns that can be actively applied to virtually any situation, in any venue, at any time, where people are engaging

---

11   See *https://prezi.com/oi4nmx4dtmsf/etruscan-and-oscan-theatrical-influences-in-rome/*
12   See the international work of the Applied Improvser Belina Raffy, and her development of "Sustainable Stand Up" comedy at *www.sustainablestandup.com*

one another. At the same time, the methods can gather huge amounts of infor-mation about the people, and dynamics involved in a gathering.

Before committing to an exploration into this young field it is good to understand that Improvisation is about taking action, and teaching action, and it is accomplished by guiding communal activity. As an explorer and leader in the field, after about a chapter of discussion, it is time to get up and do something about it.

The objective of this chapter is to introduce a doorway to what can be accomplished with Improvisation. After a basic introduction the next steps require showing up where Improvisation is happening, and immersing oneself in the practice, for at least a few hours per week, over a course of at least a few months. This is quite easily, and joyfully done, and it is pretty much a minimum investment if one wishes to use Applied Improvisation effectively while working with others, or oneself.

The first action step is to attend a live Improvisation show, or another, with the work of this anthology in mind if you have been before. The next action will be to take at least one set of introductory Improv classes leading to a showcase. These will almost certainly be available in your nearest large, or next to large, city or at a college, or university near you. Watching Improvisation on television has value, and is quite fun yet, it does not count as a live Improv show because, so far, almost all television work has been presented in edited form.

The next required action in this quest is reading. Most of the important published Improvisers, will be included in the guided bibliography at the end of this chapter. There is also an extended bibliography in *Improvisation, Inc.*, along with a work-in-progress historical timeline.

There is also great value in watching selected videos: TED talks, interviews, classic shows, and from related fields; with examples below.[13] These do not qualify as live performance.

If you are adventurous you may seek one (or more) of the 150 Improv Festivals going on in a given year, in any of 14 countries, on five continents, around our little globe.

Back Story

Improvisation and psychology share a developmental crossroad that leads through sociometry and sociatry therapies from the work, and play, of Jacob L. Moreno. He brought *Stegreiftheater*, "The Theatre of Spontaneity," to New

---

13   TEDx by Dave Morris *https://ed.ted.com/on/1wZorQmq*
Interview with David Shepherd, (history) *https://www.youtube.com/watch?v=t5wgtkgCH3A*
There is a Mike Nichols and Elaine May classic performance on YouTube: *https://www.youtube.com/watch?v=MYSijdiFPkY*
A fine demonstration of Aikido may be viewed at *http://www.dailymotion.com/video/x2ik3n*

York City around 1925 where he and his playmates read newspaper headlines, and immediately created scenes from the suggestions. This was long before he became seriously interested in psychotherapy. His work, still influenced by Improvisation, founded its own branch leading to the development of Psychodrama.[14] Adam Blatner tells us there are now more people engaged in Applied Improvisation than in Psychodrama, and drama therapies combined.

Improvisation continued its development through sociometry and into sociology, entertainment, and play. Serious Improvisation has a rich history leading to the inevitability of its applications. It was first a nearly magical delight, and then a technique, then a discipline, a field of study, a philosophy, and now a professional "practice,"[15] and a versatile action methodology.

Neva L. Boyd,[16] was a teacher and an academic authority on the games of children of Denmark and Norway. From the early 20th century, through the 1960s, Ms. Boyd was a professor at Northwestern University, and a lifetime resident of Gad Hills Center, and of Hull House in Chicago. She is credited with being a pioneer in the field of "hands on" Sociology. Among other wonders, Ms. Boyd introduced the use of games as rehabilitation therapy in Veterans Hospitals across the America.

Neva Boyd's student was Viola Spolin, who is considered the mother of modern Improvisational comedy theatre, for her explorations, her books, and her workshops, and for being the mother of Paul Sills, one of the founding members of the world's first modern Improvisation Comedy theatre in 1955,[17] and a co-founder of Chicago's "Second City Improv Theatre" in 1959.[18] Viola's work and heritage has led the branch of Improvisation for comedy and audiences.

Schools of Thought

I am currently aware of at least eight basic "schools of thought" that have been most influential in the ancestry, history, and creations of styles being used to guide our work and students.

---

14 Moreno, Jacob, *Who Shall Survive? Foundations of Sociometry, Group Psychotherapy, and Sociodrama*, 1934, Washington, DC, Nervous and Mental Disease Publishing Company

15 Professionals are generally referred to as Applied Improvisation Practitioners, Consultants, and Workshop Leaders. As of 2018 Credentialing, and certification systems are developing on a global scale.

16 Neva L. Boyd, https://socialwelfare.library.vcu.edu/people/boyd-neva-leona/

17 Coleman, Janet, *The Compass: The Story of the Improvisational Theatre that Revolutionized the Art of Comedy in America*, 1995, New York, NY, Alfred A. Knopf.

18 McCrohan, Donna, *The Second City: A Backstage History of Comedy's Hottest Troupe*, 1987, New York, NY, Perigee Books / The Putnam Publishing Group.

The premier schools come from the lives of Viola Spolin, Keith Johnstone, David Shepherd, Willie Willey, Del Close, and Charna Halpern. Influential guidance has come from Frost and Yarrow in the UK, and in the U.S. from The 2nd City Chicago, iO in Chicago, United Citizen's Brigade(UCB) in New York, from Sanford Meisner and from other independent teachers. There are also a huge, and growing number of formal Improvisational Theatres around the world, many of which have created unique variations. Large communities are driving this global development of Improvisational Comedy activity—which is effectively serving as an "undergraduate school" system for Applied Improvisation practitioners, and the most effective sources of opportunity, clientele, and causes.

The most wonderful thing about these developments is that each and every way; each path, each school, each AI provider, and each expression of Improvisation is a very best. Each formulation appeals to different and diverse assortments of people. Each way can take a lifetime of work, play, and study, and the gathering storm is spreading, and growing like individual flower species, to attract people of different viewpoints and emotional tempers, while each school is ultimately a facet of the same diamond.

The marvelous anthology edited by Adam Blatner, and Daniel Wiener, *Interactive and Improvisational Drama: Varieties of Applied Theatre and Performance*, captures no less than 32 examples of forms being used and developed in the use of this fine art.

· · ·

For nearly 40 years it has been my privilege to have observed impressive social development in people of all ages and backgrounds who have been exploring participation in performance Improvisation. Moreover, it has been my great pleasure to have watched the lives, and families of a great number of people being transformed by incorporating the tenants and practices of this truly sweet, and gentle action methodology into their lives.

The spirals of Improvisation and therapy are turning back on themselves again, as wonderfully introduced by Daniel J. Wiener in *Rehearsals for Growth: Theatre Improvisation for Psychotherapists*.

From here we see a bountiful, global blossoming of Applied Improvisation.

Successful AI Practitioners

Practitioners today are successfully using Applied Improvisation beyond obvious business and general communication applications such as team building, problem solving, and presentation skills development. New explorations include work with people in the Autism Spectrum, with Alzheimer's patients and their families, with negotiation teams in clinical, and hospital settings, with students of all ages and learning abilities, in language education, with people who have Parkinson's Disease, among drug abusers, among prisoners, in community building; with bullying issues in middle schools, in the work of disaster preparedness and relief in the Philippines, with the global work of the Red Cross/Red Crescent Climate Center,[19] and with Central American refugee children coming, battered, and unaccompanied, across the border into the United States. The list grows as the movement spreads like dandelion seeds upon the wind.

The presence of Improvisation in all its forms has experienced extraordinary growth during the most recent forty years. The expansion of Improvisational Comedy on video, and in clubs, and theaters, has introduced the basic joyous concepts to millions of people around the world which has made it easier to present the concepts to people, businesses, and organizations not familiar with the form.

Applied Improvisation, and Improvisational Comedy can be found all over the developed world, with more than 6,600 members of the international association known as The Applied Improvisation Network (AIN),[20] and another nineteen thousand in other online networks.[21] This past year has seen a growth in the number of professional conferences around the world as well.

Powers of Improvisation

It has long been recognized that we may experience an entire family in a home, a city in a single neighborhood, all life in a strand of DNA, all of thought in a single moment, and the universe in a drop of water. We have been told by explorers of the quantum fields that the center of any atom is in a relationship with the center of all atoms.

An extension of this reality is told by a story about the founder of the revolutionary martial art of Aikido. His name was Morihei Ueshiba, and he was called O Sensei.[22] When asked how he was able to gather vast power in his just over five-foot tall body. It was reported that he said, "I connect my hara (the center of balance of the human body) to the center of the Earth, and let the Earth do the work."

---

19   Pablo Suarez, *http://www.climatecentre.org/about-us/our-people*

20   See *http://appliedimprovisation.network/*

21   A Google search of Facebook sites offers an introduction to the field: "Improv for Humanity", "Improv Orchestra", United Atlanta Improv", "Impro Improv Improvisation Theatre", "My Improv Addiction", "Fans O' Fun", "Improvisation theatre groups for players worldwide", "Atlanta Improv Documentary", "Improvisation as Meditation", "Improv Spirit", and "Mindful Improvisation."

22   "O Sensei" means honored teacher. Stevens, John, *Invincible Warrior: A Pictorial Biography of Morihei Ueshiba, Founder of Aikido*, 1997, Boston, MA & London, Shambhala Publications, Inc

We connect our consciousness to physical and emotional realities engaged by the concepts of time and attention that are encouraged by the practices, and then we let Improvisation do the work.

·   ·   ·

As being shown by this anthology, every skill-set, and all studied practices have practical applications in varieties of circumstances. From the world of building, we get such wonderful success wisdom as, "Cut to shape, hammer to fit, and paint to match." This kind of clarity can work wonders, from dealing with organizations, to creating colored paper art. Carpenters, and those who use saws tell us to, "Measure twice. Cut once," applying directly to anything with permanent, dire consequences.

From running we get persistence, from music we get rhythm, manual dexterity, and emotion; from study we get focus, perspective, organization, and action; and from any "practice" or training we get discipline, embodiment, internal measurement, ritual, craft, art, science, discovery, invention, and more. While it is true that anything can be made to apply to any-thing. Improvisation is particularly flexible and facile in its universal application.

·   ·   ·

A deep power of Improvisation lies in the fact that the essential skills are natural to most mammals, and intrinsic to surviving in an uncertain word. The early methods in this skill development are referred to as play, curiosity, exploration, and practice being in ever changing relationships, with ever changing realities.

Another of the powers comes from the fact that when used in its optimal wonder, it operates simultaneously on all levels of experience: thought, imaginary, emotional, physical, verbal, vibrational, electromagnetic, metaphysical, and spiritual included. Each of these levels can be accessed, and used, to influence the others. The structures of the processes prompt participants to keep moving between various levels of experience, and eventually to the ability to do so in daily life.

The magic, for me, is that one does not need to know that all of this is going on for the benefits to inure to the participants. The "games" are fun. The engagement with all of it is fulfilling and satisfying. It calls on me as an individual, and as a member of a collaboration to imagine and achieve an enlightenment, change a life, educate a workgroup, delight an audience, and to be part of a global movement all at the same time.

Putting Improvisation to Work, and Play

A first, most important value in Improvisation is its great simplicity. It is a fun, activity centered practice, founded on as many (or as few) as 25 simple guidelines, In less than an hour we can teach half a dozen best practices, and a few "games" that will allow almost anyone to engage any-one, or any gathering in the activities and exploration of this art.

The learning of any five to fifteen key principals will allow a conscious, diligent and playful person to work effectively with others in any venue, from the home, to the streets. to the community, to the classroom, to the stage, to the boardroom.

With 25 or more of the "exercises, techniques, forms, or structures" mastered, with any of a number of good books in hand (see the bibliography), and with a generous heart, one can begin to teach the craft/art/philosophy/science of Improvisation for play, for personal development, for community and issue activism, and as a profession. Remember, as noted above, an immersion in the activity of Improvisation is truly necessary for the best use of this work.

·   ·   ·

As with all great endeavors 90% can be learned within a year or so of gentle, laughter-filled wonder. The other ten percent, and more complete understanding, will take the rest of one's life.

The foundational source of Improvisation is in the complexity of mind, including the conscious, unconscious, subconscious, semi-conscious, altered states of conscious, the unknown unknown, and the over-mind.[23] Each of these complex and interactive aspects of perception, contain implications in the work of Applied Improvisation that can be accessed, and used in a nearly universal set of venues.

We demonstrate natural unconscious, or semi-conscious improvisation in many unplanned, usually physical activities such as walking quickly over uncertain ground, or making our way in the unfamiliar dark, walking in a crowd, or talking with a stranger. Subconscious reactions are often triggered by new experiences of human engagement in the playfulness. Clear, grounded consciousness is developed for effective listening, which allows us to accept as offers, new information, and interchanges that generate unexpected, unplanned responses. The responses generate new information and interchange. This cycle helps us to maintain the sense and presence of our most genuine personal self, in current time.

In Improvisation we teach folks to adopt an attitude, and a verbal response to new information in the form of the words, "Yes, and . . . ." This discipline creates a commitment that requires accepting what is offered, and offering some new information or element to the interchange, which when accepted with "Yes, and . . . " begins an exchange cycle. Engaging thus, with the guidance of

---

23   de Chardin, Pierre Teilhard, *The Phenomenon of Man*, 1959, New York, NY, Harper and Row Publishers.

an Improvisation Leader, allows individuals and groups to activate exceptional interpersonal connections, and to generate delicious levels of communication, creativity, spontaneity, and collaboration.

We live in a world of multileveled rhythms. In good Improvisation there is a simple rhythm based on the "Yes, and . . . " personal exchange.

> *"Hi there. I'm Adam."*
> *"Yes, and I'm Eve."*
> *"Yes, and you are the Moon."*
> *"Yes, and you are the Sun."*
> *"Yes, and we are the world."*

Dealing with the fire of Improvisational Creativity will almost always look and feel somewhat disorganized. This is partially because creativity at this level produces truly new things that have not yet been labeled and categorized. Goal orientation in an Improvisation activity generally limits the scope of the process, and of the promise of the event. As we begin to heed, and engage in Improvisational guidelines, frameworks, feedback, and tracking devices such as debriefing, we begin to understand that disorganization within can generate reorganization on the outside, without the need for "scripted" intervention.

Experience has shown us that we can achieve greater outcomes, and discover the communications and connections needed for people to meet specific ambitions which can be more perfectly articulated, with the insight gained during the Improvisation event.

We find an equilibrium in Improv that comes from a reality that our minds, and experiences seek to create equivalents, and familiar patterns. While there are direct correlations between what we think, and what we are doing; between what we believe is going on, and what is happening in reality, these relationships can be easily twisted askew and made subject to the whims of our massive neuro-electric system, and wave fields. When we engage in professionally guided AI events, the relationships can also be acknowledged in the presence of light, collaboration, joyfulness, and safety, and thus allowed to work with the same kind of unexplained influence as gravity.

The human electrochemical system works, whether in imagination, or reality, much like any of the four fundamental physical powers of nature: weak nuclear force, strong nuclear force, electromagnetic force, and gravitational force. Our mental/physical systems create field events, in which relationships, and changes occur, creativity bends space, and enlightenment is generated by forces functioning at a variety of angles in response to one another.

The action field of Improvisation can be described in terms of multiple sets of vibrations. We are made of vibrations, and we live as compound-complex waves, that interact with each other in noticeable patterns. Our available sound waves interact in very physical multi-harmonics, as with a symphony orchestra, or sonic boom. Rhythms, natural and otherwise, do wondrous things with each other, and with our own psychological and psychic senses. We talk of these wondrous vibratory patterns in terms of "environment," and "atmosphere." We use words describing feelings, and emotions to explain events and places: "It feels comfortable here." "It feels safe here." "That feels funny."

Deeper Considerations

For a long time, I considered myself to be capable of speech. The skill developed before I even knew what it was. Then I began the study of speech, and human communication, and have spent 55 years in the wonder that all the possible thoughts that can be expressed, in the English language alone, have yet to be even touched by the available combinations of 26 letters, and 14 punctuation marks. Applied Improvisation works like this. It is not possible to exhaust the range of any of the forms or structures.

For a long time, I walked, and danced, polkas and shoddishes, waltzes and Tangos, two steps, and the hora, thinking, without thought, that I knew how to walk and dance. Then I discovered the divine martial art of Aikido, where my teachers taught me the concept of *maai*, being the perfect distance between my center of gravity, and the centers of gravity of all people and things with which I can interact as a conscious being.

I have spent 40 years learning how to transport my weight, and physical design through our pervasive gravity field, in dynamic relation to other moving bodies: people, falling things, doors, cars, cats, and more of the unknown unknown. I still did not really know how to dance. Then I met Judith Greer Essex who opened the portals of Improvisational Dance, and my body being took flight in the freedom of the structure, just as a bird does with the structure of her wings. Awareness of these elements of physicality are fundamental to the uses of high level Applied Improvisation.

For a long time, I sang, and played instruments, thinking I knew how to make music. Then Jonathan Glazier introduced me to the work of Harry Partch, which introduced me to the infinite number of intervals, and the endless combinations of sound available in a single octave, and the capacity of the human ear to hear so much within such a small range of sound vibration. This led to variable tuning intervals, and whole new modes of music, not based on a 12-tone scale;[24] music extending into the nature of chords and multileveled harmonics. Attention to personal and group harmonics advances deep Improvisational life and group changes.

For a long time, I thought I understood rhythm; that I knew how to keep time with the music. Then came Improvisation and I was delighted to discover

---

24   Partch, Harry, *Genesis of a Music: An Account of a Creative Work, it's Roots and it's Fulfillments*, 1949, New York, NY, De Capo Press.

that rhythm is not to be understood at all; it is to be felt in the beat of the heart, the tap of the toe, the sway of the whole body, the motion of the people, places, and things brought to our attention when we are engaged in "Impro."

.   .   .

Everything is always revolving between giving and receiving, which is a highlight of Improvisation. Our world provides the perfect exercise with our breathing. As we breathe in we take in our portion of oxygen which has been exhaled by our planets generous plant life. As we breathe out, we exhale a share of carbon dioxide which is chemical food for our interdependent benefactors.

We cannot take in, nor expel, more than some certain maximum of breath, we can, however, breathe unevenly. We tend to hold, or misuse, our breath when faced with uncertainty or perceived difficulty. It is interesting to know that the patterns are about evenly split between holding after an inbreath, or after an exhale, or in rapid or uneven breathing. Each of these responses creates imbalance. The imbalance will show up in the actions of the body, mind, and spirit, and in the relations of any gathering.

Rhythmic interchange is fundamental to a most powerful aspect of Improvising in all its forms. It provides real time practice in expressing our own, genuine, vulnerable, human individual self, while working in true, deep, fast paced collaboration with others, with our participants, with audience, with cohorts, neighbors, families, and even with ourselves, and the day we seem to be living this day.

The way we feel and move creates wave patterns which we can generate, or moderate—both within our bodies and minds, as well as in and around our environments. Applying these realities to Improvisational gatherings encourages the appearance of true spontaneity, the search for which was a primary motivator for Jacob Moreno.

.   .   .

Time manipulations provide a marvelous aspect of working with Improvisation. We can conceptualize our experience within time; that is within the present moment, or outside time; that is recalling the past, and beyond time; that is considering the future. We tend to operate in mixed time frame perception with past, present, and future all engaged at once.

Applied Improvisation suggests that when one needs to consider and make plans, it is best to set aside private moments, and to do whatever works best to orient oneself to current time. When speaking of current time, we mean jet pilot current time, marathon runner current time, new mother presence, as well as *Be Here Now*[25] current time. In this state, one can be aware of the past, and mindful of the future, yet not emotionally, or culturally attached to either. It is a lovely state of mind in which to Improvise, to make plans with a world of possibility, creativity, and spontaneity as part of the very structure of the doing.

These steps can also be taken for a clear review of the past, accomplished in current time, as well as with fussing over the future done in current time consciousness. Improvisation forms provide active practice in being engaged with others while in a current state of mind.

The practices required in becoming aware of the power of the current moment are all excellent for developing public presentation, stage, interpersonal communication, and public Applied Improvisation muscles. The positive effect on one's personal life is a collateral wonder.

Each of these time manipulation activities can be done as a personal practice, or as a group game. Each can be done with, or without context. Each will be productive and fun in a direct ratio to the strength of our commitment and enthusiasm. These, along with the developmental suggestions above, will often bear completely unexpected fruit.

Getting There

Small, successful, incremental steps toward the *Impro* generated, creative-collaborative state of consciousness and action, is important when working with Applied Improvisation. Having complete faith in the small set of moments we experience as "now" requires macro-understanding, and micro-action that will achieve extraordinary results. The little, moment by moment things we do, add up to the results we achieve. Only in magic, and genuine inspiration does a whole thing simply appear out of nowhere.

Another perspective that assists the use and development of AI is created by framing Improvisation activity, in terms of analog and digital flow patterns. These depend on the density of the focus of the leadership, and of the gathering. This is the same language that reveals light, indeed all electromagnetic activity, as the action of waves, and as physical photon packets, at the same time, depending on focus.

Imagining works wonderfully in an analog, free flowing state of mind. Action seems to work best as a digital event; doing this, or in making that; though the action of an artist, or a craft person can be both simultaneously. General processing (organizing, prioritizing, matching) is usually a cross-over as with a Venn diagram, and seems to work best when one is switching rapidly between the two perspectives, with attention paid to the rhythm of such a thing. When hard planning is the task, (blueprints, business plans, agendas, logistics),

---

25   Baba Ram Dass (Dr. Richard Alpert), *Be Here Now*, 1971, San Cristobal, NM, Lama Foundation.

it seems that a clearly digital, measurable, and visible mindset, works well. Then when implementing action, it is often more effective using an analog-waveform approach; engaging and accepting others, and unknown, or unexpected factors with fluidity and the commitment to add material (melody), and vibrations (harmonies) as inspired in balanced Improvisational Symphony.

This duality is also present in our language. The noun is a photon, and the verb is a wave. Being able to see the world around us as both, at the same time, is the nature of "comedic awareness." Timing, with its penchant for upsetting, or creating balance, is at the center of Improvisational mirth. The speed at which laughter generating timing operates is faster than the speed of thought and translation into language. It must come directly from the spinal cord to the vocal cords. Going through the brain takes too long, though the brain is there, as a watchtower, playing with time, space, and perception, while wielding a veritable pharmacy of hormonal and environmental influences. Developing these skills, and skill sets is worthy of long consideration, and lifetime practice. Such awareness can also be vital to living a rational life.

It has been my experience that, whether or not humor, and timing skills have been been developed through nature, nurture, or study, they can be learned by almost anyone who will engage diligently in a group practice that requires being completely in the present moment, and is accompanied by love, light, laughter, and joyfulness, or, as we say in the business, by engaging joyfully in any of the number of paths leading to personal Improvisation, and discovering the essentially infinite applications available with this newcomer to serious Action Methodology.

·   ·   ·

We are rightfully concerned by realities of cause and effect, which is a good thing, up to the point that we begin to try too hard to control both sides of the equation through the process of discovery. When practitioners ask how I "make" certain things happen, my response is that, "It is not mine to 'make' things happen'." Mine is to encourage the appearance of an *Impro* state of consciousness, as suggested by Keith Johnstone.

Though the state of mind varies with miscellaneous human communication factors, there are simple steps that help in achieving the appropriate mindset.

- Let go of the past and the future, and actively pursue staying in the current moment. (Unless the process is a true review as discussed above).

- Try to listen with the whole sensory system (we have at least seven senses[26]). This requires listening to understand, and to be changed, and to engage with, rather than to merely react to what is being heard.
- We must offer our personal presence as an example of the commitment to accept everything and everyone, at current face value, with the promise to add something to the moment. ("I'm going to shoot you!" "Yes, and when you miss, it will be a great boon to more life than one.")
- Do this while being mindful of breathing, posture, personal space, odd influences, and being thankful for the miracle of human beings working and playing together.
- We must then be prepared to present what we are doing for public view, engagement, interchange, response, feedback, and anything else from which we can learn.

With this frame of mind, we can collaborate equally in the dozens of immediate little decisions that are required to create action. When this state is engaged by the largest number of participants, wonderful things happen by themselves.

There are, as noted, maybe as many as 25 guidelines that help in the presentation and development of Improvisational Skills. Here are some that I like.

Show up. Be present. Listen. Give and receive in equal measure. Say, "Yes, and . . . ", Do not fear failure. Strive to be honest. Strive to be yourself. Look for real things. Move around physically. Go for relationships. Go for details. Help one another. Have fun. Play playfully. Go for love, light, laughter, and joy. Have more fun.

· · ·

"As the Improvisation movement spreads around the globe, I see in the progression, the lowly dandelion. *Tarasacum Officinalis,* which comes from the Greek words for 'disorder' and 'remedy'."

In her appearance she seems to be little more than a flat weed in the grass. On closer inspection it is discovered that her roots are nutritious and health giving, and her leaves a fine tea, and even wine do make.

Then up she sends a spindly stalk to a sort of funny looking, simple yellow flower; able to light up the under-chin of a child, creating laughter, then shared again, and again.

Suddenly a breathtaking ball of faerie fluff appears, for just a moment, before a puff of air sends flying its seeds of 'Yes, and, I *am* listening to *you*',

---

26   The traditional five, plus, at least, a kinesthetic sense, and others.

floating, disbursing to seed again wherever there is enough love, light, laughter, and joy to encourage bliss."[27]

·   ·   ·

For the simple sake of the fun and the wonder, it will be a good idea to watch Bobbie McFarren and "The power of the pentatonic scale," available on YouTube.[28]

Here begins the action part.

Robert Lowe

Robert Lowe is an internationally known Improvisation elder, and founder, of Improvisation Incorporated, a pioneering educational consulting firm. His clients have included AT&T, Georgia Pacific Corporation, The Southern Company, and Medtronics, Inc., among many others.

In Atlanta, Georgia he is known as "The Godfather" of Improvisation, as founder of the first Improv Comedy Troupe, the first Improvisational Comedy Theatre, and the longest running college or university Improvisation program in the Southeastern U.S. He taught in the Communication department at Georgia State University for 13 years.

His book, *Improvisation, Inc.: Harnessing Spontaneity to Engage People and Groups*, published in 2000, was the first full work on the subject in North America. It has been translated into Arabic, and was revised as *Improvisation, Inc.: An Applied Improvisation Handbook*, in 2017.

Robert is the author of *Happy Vernday Birthcox: Revolution, Evolution, and an Uncommon Commune* (1970, 2015, Atlanta, GA, RLJ Publications), and *The Greater Number: A glimpse of our universe and sort of everything in it* (2018, Atlanta, GA, RLJ Publications).

You can contact him at *Rlowe46@outlook.co* or at the web site: *atlantaimprovdocumentary.org*

References

(*in recommended reading order*)

Alda, Alan, *If I Understood You, Would I Have This Look on My Face?*, 2017, New York, NY, Random House.

Spolin, Viola, *Improvisation for the Theater*, 1963, Evanston, IL, Northwestern University Press.

---

27 Improvisation, Inc. "Epilogue" p. 244.
28 See *https://youtu.be/ne6tB2KiZuk*

Keith Johnstone. *Impro, Improvisation and the Theatre*, New York, NY, Theatre Arts Books, 1979.

Boal. Augusto, McBride & McBride, Tran., *Theatre of the Oppressed*, 1985, New York, NY, Theatre Communications Group.

Nachmanovitch, Stephen, *Free* Play: *Improvisation in Life and Art*. 1990, New York, NY, Jeremy P. Tarcher/Putnam.

Belgrad, Daniel, *The Culture of Spontaneity: Improvisation and the Arts in Postwar America*, 1998, Chicago, IL & London, The University of Chicago Press.

Jackson, Paul Z., *The Inspirational Trainer: Making Your Training Flexible, Spontaneous, and Creative*.1998, London, UK, Kogan Page, Ltd.

Lowe, Robert, *Improvisation, Inc. Revised Edition 2017*: *An Applied Improvisation Handbook*, 2017 (originally subtitled *Harnessing Spontaneity to Engage People and Groups*, Jossey/Bass-Pfeiffer. San Francisco, 2000), Atlanta, GA, RLJ Publications.

Koppett, Kat, *Training to Imagine: Practical Improvisational Theatre Techniques for Trainers and Managers to Enhance Creativity, Teamwork, Leadership, and Learning*, 2nd Ed., 2013, Sterling, VA, (First Edition 2001), Stylus Publishing.

Ryan Madson, Patricia, *Improv Wisdom: Don't Prepare, Just Show Up*, 2005, New York, NY, Bell Tower, imprint of the Crown Publishing Group, division of Random House.

Blatner, Adam, Ed. with Daniel J. Wiener, *Interactive and Improvisational Drama: Varieties of Applied Theatre and Performance*, 2007, New York, NY, Lincoln, NE, Shanghai, iUniverse, Inc.

Dudeck, Theresa, and Kaitlin McClure, *Applied Improvisation: Leading, Collaborating, and Creating Beyond the Theatre*, 2018, London, UK Methune.

Frost, Anthony, and Ralph Yarrow, *Improvisation in Drama*, 1990, London, UK, The Macmillan Press, Ltd.

Wiener, Daniel J., *Rehearsals for Growth: Theatre Improvisation for Psychotherapists*, 1994, New York, London, W.W. Norton and Company.

Johnson, Steven, *Wonderland: How Play Made the Modern World*, 2013, New York, NY: Riverhead Books, an Imprint of Penguin Random House LLC.

Duchartre, Pierre Louis, Randolph T. Weaver, Tran., *The Italian Comedy. The Improvisation, Scenarios, Lives, Attributes, Portraits, and Masks of the Illustrious Characters of the Commedia Dell' Arte*, 1929. New York, The John Doubleday Company.

How We Use Action Explorations to Enhance Our Relationship

Adam Blatner and Allee Blatner

We find action explorations helpful when applied informally outside of the bounds of psycho-therapy. This article explores how we actively use 'surplus reality' in our own relationship for over 40 years. This article outlines techniques of using play to expand understanding of an issue, compassionately respond to one another and provide new perspectives on disagreements. Illustrated examples of seven of these methods can serve as tools for practitioners to add to their therapeutic repertoire when working with couples, and more importantly, as a way of enhancing their own interpersonal life.

Our marriage is a teamwork endeavor that integrates our personal and professional backgrounds as a psychodramatist and assistant as well as husband and wife. Both of us have backgrounds in the arts and also therapy. We have conducted workshops on psychodrama and the applications of dramatic techniques in psychotherapy at many conferences over the last forty years, as well as integrating these practices into our married life. By being open to being corrected in the spirit of playfulness, we strengthen our co-creating of our interactions with one another. This practice fosters mutuality and helps turn disagreements into a process for working out more satisfactory solutions. It makes life more fun and turns problems into adventures that are more like puzzles to be solved, and yet neither person knows what the outcome will be!

Our article is intended to share information from us—as two practitioners—about how action methods can be applied in everyday life. Therefore we make no effort to present this material in a scholarly fashion. We offer these ideas as if you were watching a demonstration video of vignettes from our relationship.

Drama therapists and other expressive arts therapists will easily recognize in the following scenes how the techniques can be applied in therapeutic settings as strategies for clients. Our hope is that readers also will be motivated to consider the usefulness of this approach in normal, healthy relationships and furthermore to use them to help enhance the vitality and health of those relationships.

The primary theoretical background of our work resides in the core texts of psychodrama and drama therapy. The underlying premise in both of these approaches is that exploring our problems using enactment is more effective, faster and more amenable to self-recognition, revision, or resolution than is solely verbal discourse. Solutions to problems then become a process of exploring various possible actions, simulations, role taking past experiences — all in the context of experimentation without blame.

Working tentatively while trusting the process one still expects miscommunication and misunderstanding. The methods described below help to detect, clarify and adjust these tensions as they are occurring.

Background

Adam has been involved in psychodrama since 1966, became a trainer, educator and practitioner of psychodrama (TEP) and has written several books and many chapters and articles on the subject. Allee joined the field a decade later, has led groups using creative arts methods and also has written about applications of psychodrama. We have found over the years that action methods and the domain of 'surplus reality' facilitate our creating a more authentic, congenial and fun relationship with each other in our everyday lives together. That is, what we teach we have also brought into our personal lives as an everyday practice. We would like to share some of them in this article.

The term "surplus reality" needs to be clarified for those unfamiliar with the term. The founder of psychodrama, Jacob L. Moreno, MD (1889–1974), created this term to signify the context used in an enactment in which participants choose to act 'as if' Ideas and actions take place in a space/time that exists only in the imaginations of those involved in the play. The scenes can involve things that have not happened, may never happen or could never happen. It is also the place in which new or modified roles can be rehearsed and revised.

We each like living imaginatively and find that our married life allows us to apply roleplaying techniques to not only solve interpersonal problems but even more to enhance the enjoyment of our relationship. We live in an ongoing state of the unspoken invitation to improvise, which is similar to the ease of make-believe play of children. We have discovered that learning to consciously return to these natural and innate abilities of imagination opens up great potential for adults. We wrote a book and teach about this: *The Art of Play: Helping Adults Reclaim Imagination and Spontaneity.*[1]

Much of the time we behave quite ordinarily, and yet just below the surface there is a mutually agreed upon attitude that our life is open to improvisation. There is a continual rising and falling of play. We do not have to say this to each other explicitly every time. It is indicated by our facial expressions, voice tones, our body language, *etc.*

"Action Explorations" as a process also is our ultimate first-aid-box for interpersonal conflicts. Problems become a creative challenge that each of us can grapple with, knowing that we have resources. Stepping back from a disagreement and consciously choosing a certain technique can lighten up the negativity of the situation and make a resolution more doable.

Come Play with Me / Warming Up

Before we begin to explain in more detail the various techniques we use, it is important to note the need for warming up; it is foolish to assume that someone is warmed up for spontaneous action at every given moment. Taking some time and having chances to make mistakes, learning verbal and nonverbal cues, works best when done playfully—which is what we do. If the other is being too pushy or running ahead with the action, we say, "Let me warm up to this." Continuing to try actions and behaviors without any sense of failure is the key. Each of us acts as a coach to help bring the other towards the focus or scene we are envisioning.

Considering that we both know that warming up occurs gradually, we do not expect each to be ready for play or problem solving right off. The most obvious reason is that one of us may be involved in another task. Adam might say, "I can't do that right now." Allee may then ask, "When do you think we can?" There is an expectation of trust between us that we will take one another seriously and give an answer that the other can count on, and when the other is ready there will be help with the warming up.

For example, if the invitation is to an imaginative play episode, it might unfold as follows:

> **Allee:** Are you ready now? I remembered this funny thing and want to play it out with you.
>
> **Adam:** Sure, but let me warmup.
>
> **Allee:** Quack, quack! We're ducks.
>
> **Adam:** What?! I'm not sure what we're doing?

---

1 Blatner and Blatner 1996

Allee: Oh, right . . . I'm a duck down on the creek, and . . .

Adam: Wait . . . Where are we?

Allee: The creek downtown where we go to watch the ducks.

Adam: Oh, yes. And how they all swim by us going, "quack!"

Allee: Yes, and it's getting dark.

Adam: Okay, and now we're (as ducks) starting to go to the bank to settle down for the night.

Allee: . . . and all of us are announcing to each other, "quack quack quack" . . .

Adam: (*joins in*) quack quack quack quack quack!

(They both find the imagined scene humorous and start laughing together.)

This simple example involved Allee helping Adam warm up by stopping her own role playing to describe the scene. Then she again needed to go out of her role and address the process to orient Adam to where the action was taking place. Caring about having both of us onboard encourages our practicing going in and out of reality with ease and without judgment. This nurtures a sense of trust and safety between us as players for future enactments and further fun.

Breaking a Stalemate / Doubling

There are times when people are at a loss for words. Perhaps after a discussion Allee might be withdrawn and quiet. Adam wonders whether something is wrong. Initially he simply asks, 'Is something wrong between us?' Allee might answer, 'I don't think there is anything wrong'. Adam notices the tentativeness of her answer and says, 'You've been unusually quiet after our discussion about going to that movie with our friends'. Allee is still tentative, 'Oh, I'm willing to go'. Adam then suggests they explore it further and Allee agrees.

Adam will use doubling to clarify his hunch that things are not okay for Allee about going to the movie. As you see it unfold in the following example, doubling is a technique that can help a person become clearer about their thoughts, feelings and preferences. The person who doubles is imagining, 'What might it be like if I were in that situation?' The double then speaks as if they were the other person while making suggestions. The double, it must be understood, is only guessing and always stays open to correction. The goal is to keep offering suggestions to help the other person to figure out what is going on.

This is a powerful technique. When doubling is done with a close friend or partner, it must be done with extra kindness, respect and integrity. The double chooses to put their own agenda 'on hold' and to step outside of the real discussion (or argument) to enable the other to obtain a more authentic response, even if it ends up being one that might go against the preferred outcome of the partner.

A high value in our relationship is to help one another to be more honest about individual preferences. We do not want to foster or perpetuate discomfort, but rather to live more congenially with each other. It is understood that the one doing the doubling does not know for sure and is always open to correction. Our goal is that we would rather help clarify and better understand each other than 'win'.

Another point: Being witnessed counts! It makes what is said or done 'real'. The mind has a peculiar tendency to disqualify as a bit unreal that which has not been witnessed, at least with some temperaments.

Let us imagine this technique unfolding in the following situation:

> **Adam:** Thank you for agreeing to explore what might be bothering you.
>
> **Allee:** Okay, although I'm not really sure what it is.
>
> **Adam:** I'll start by doubling for you and saying what I think might be going on when I imagine being you.
>
> **Allee:** Okay, and I'll correct you if you're wrong.
>
> **Adam:** Well, you started being kind of withdrawn after you agreed to go to the movie. If I were you I might be wondering, "Do I really want to go with these people?"
>
> **Allee:** They are your friends more than mine, and I don't have much to talk with them about.
>
> **Adam:** I'm still you: "And it seems the three of you go on about people you've known and stuff that I have no relationship with" (*Changing from doubling*) How close is this to your feelings?
>
> **Allee:** You're doing a good job. Everything you say is true but I still have this feeling that who they are isn't it (*Sighs*).
>
> **Adam:** Well, what about the movie? Do you want to see this movie?
>
> **Allee:** I think I do. Everyone's talking about it.
>
> **Adam:** If I were you I might want to say, "I don't care what people are saying! It isn't my kind of movie."
>
> **Allee:** That feels closer to the truth, but I could see it anyway since you want to go.

Adam: Might you be wanting to say, "Adam, I really don't want to hurt your feelings, but really there isn't any reason why I want to take the time to see this movie"?

Allee: Oh I don't know. (*Sighs*) I love being with you and I don't want to hurt your feelings but that last thing you said is closer to the truth. Could you go without me?

Adam: I don't want to. But I also don't want you to be miserable.

Allee: I wouldn't be miserable, but I just feel like it's such a waste of my time. I'd rather do other stuff if you could go without me. How important is it to you?

Adam: Probably a '2' (*see next paragraph below*). As I said, I don't want you to be bored. I hate being bored and wouldn't want you be. I can go without you even easier since my friends are going.

Allee: Oh, what a relief! Thank you so much. I didn't even know what was bothering me.

You will notice another technique in this dialogue: the use of a number to quantify our preferences. 'Yes' or 'No' is often too exclusionary. So statements such as (a) 'I don't want to but if you want to' or (b) 'I'd like to but if you don't want to' are followed by 'how important is it to you?' These are then submitted to our informal grading system of 1 through 5. The answer to question (a) above might be It's only at a '2' and for (b), 'I'm at a "4" for not doing it'. One has to trust one's partner to be honest in checking their own preferences. The whole point is to move towards greater clarity of each person's intentions, for opportunities to negotiate and possibly one person will want to override their own preference in order to make the other happy. When this is done with integrity it can help decide things more quickly and make gestures of giving in to another's preference even more sweet since it is being done explicitly.

What I Would like to Hear You Say / Role Reversal

We use role reversal to facilitate an ease of loving and appreciating one another. We never wait around for the other to say 'just the right thing'. It is terribly sad to hear people talk about how someone 'never said what I wanted to hear' or 'what they said was so lame — how could they think that was good enough?!'

Role reversal is the technique of speaking as if you are the other person. Like doubling, this is another powerful action method from psychodrama. It also requires the person with whom you are using this technique to have the right, freedom and to understand that they are expected to correct you. We have adapted it in our relationship for the specific purpose of hearing the words that help us feel appreciated, loved, understood right when we need to hear them. We do not expect the other—or anyone else, for that matter—to know what is the perfect thing to say to us.

The following scenario illustrates how this application of role reversal unfolds:

Allee: Thanks for taking the car for servicing.

Adam: Didn't you notice that I had the tires rotated too?

Allee: No but thanks for that, too.

Adam: I don't think you realize what went into making the extra trip to the tire people.

Allee: Probably not, but thanks.

Adam: You seem distracted and just mouthing "Thanks." I'm not feeling very appreciated for that tire business. You were the one worrying about the tires!

Allee: I really am happy with what you did. What would be nice for you to hear me say?

Adam: Well let me see . . . I know that you said you'd do the service appointment but now when I see you also did the tires too, I really appreciate your initiative and extra effort.

Allee: That's really true and now I see that it was extra special.

Adam: Thanks for helping me feel that you saw the extra work I did for us.

Here is another version of the same scene and an impasse has been reached:

Allee: Actually I don't agree. The tires are a part of regular service of the car. In honesty, I can't say that.

Adam: But what's wrong that you can't say what I really want to hear?

Allee: When I do that task I often do what you call 'extra' as just part of the whole service.

Adam: I didn't know you always do it. For me it was extra, I was tired and pushed myself so that you wouldn't have to go back and do it later.

Allee: Oh! Well now I see where you're coming from. Yes. Sure. I can say it with even more appreciation, since you went out of your way to save me a trip.

Our intention is to create more harmony and ease in living ordinary life together and loving one another. We deal with the frictions as challenges to our use of psychodramatic methods in service of kindness and appreciation. We employ these techniques consciously, intentionally, explicitly.

Taking it Over Again/Replay

Being able 'to take it over' right in the moment is a freedom that we enjoy using whenever necessary. Usually it has to do with saying something that we want to say in a kinder and nicer or less harsh and crude way. Replay or taking things back relates to living as if one is in an ongoing rehearsal; as Wiener noted, growth can be facilitated by treating interactions as if they were happening in rehearsals rather than performance (1994).

Replay is such a liberating technique interpersonally. If one of us has offended the other, the offended one can immediately say 'I don't like what just happened. Let's take it over and here's the way I want you to say it this time . . . .' We can use role reversal to show the other person how we want it done and then have them play it that way. This can continue until it feels right to both people. This avoids devolving into a blame game. The goal is to have a happier result and to restore our goodwill towards one another. We can also use replay to expand on something fun that we are doing in imaginative play or to explore other possibilities in serious discussions. We weave it constantly throughout our interactions to clean up mistakes and misunderstandings.

Parts of Oneself / The Empty Chair

In psychodrama, the empty chair is used to speak to someone else not present or to yourself in order to get some role distance in order to clarify your feelings. There are situations where many empty chairs are set up to talk with many different people or to examine many parts of oneself about a concern.

Most of the time we use this technique for the latter reason: to help clarify our mixed and often contradictory emotions. Normally we do not use actual chairs but rather positions in the room. We express this ambivalence by saying: 'Part of me feels . . . but another part feels . . . ' or 'One part of me wants to do this . . . another part doesn't want to . . . another part says I should . . . ' The power of this method lies in the ability to get the muddled thoughts or feelings out into a more workable context. We help one another when using the empty chairs to explore the different parts by asking questions, directing each other to talk to different parts, drawing out the voices, thoughts, feelings, concerns associated with each part or to be an engaged witness if one of us is directing our own exploration. In this last case it is valuable to know that there is someone who has heard you. A postexploration sharing and discussion is then added.

The many parts of self technique in psychodrama is similar to what Richard Schwartz (1992) later developed as Internal Family Systems Therapy (IFS).

Here is a selfdirected exploration using empty chairs and followed by a shared discussion:

Allee: Adam will you take some time with me later today while I explore a decision I have to make?

Adam: OK. How about this afternoon?

Allee: That works for me. Thanks.

(*After some time*)

Adam: Okay, now I've got time to work with you on that decision. Are you ready?

Allee: Yes. Let's go into the living room where there will be space for empty chairs because I have a number of parts of me that are babbling in my head and I need to sort them out.

Adam: Great. I'm here to help.

Allee: OK. The topic is this job I have as a Simulated Patient at the Medical School.

Adam: Thanks for giving me an orientation to the subject.

Allee: I want to do this myself just to get the different voices out of my own head but I really need you to hear me and then give me your opinions at the end. OK?

Adam: Sure.

Allee: So here I'm going to put the part of me that loves helping the medical and nursing students. (*Chair 1*) Next to it is the part that loves my supervisor and knows she needs me and values my abilities. (*Chair 2*) Those two are pretty clear. (*Walks around the room thinking*) OK.

So then there is the part that has to memorize the scenario of who I am, my ailment, what I can and can't disclose to the students and the strict requirement that I can't do any improvisation. Stick to the script! I hate that!

Chair 3/Allee:: (*stomps around thinking*) . . . and the part where I have to grade the student on how they did from my role as a simulated patient and tell them good first then bad in front of all of the other students and their supervising physician—totally yucky—I hate that too because there's no chance for the two of us to talk about the encounter and I have to say something "bad" that they need improvement on even if I think they're perfect because they're just students and obviously aren't perfect . . . yet. Ha! As if any doctor, any person, ever is?!

Chair 4/Allee:: (*sighs heavily, voices an expletive and walks loudly around the room. Then gets up*) All right, I want to talk with these parts!' (*walks to one place in the room*)

Chair 3/Allee:: Do the script! It's how they learn and keep it all the same for each student. That's the protocol! Just literally get with the script!

Allee: I hate tight scripts . . . I've vowed to *never* do them again! I believe in improvisation and working things out in the here and now even if it's in front of an audience but never, ever again for me . . . not performance!

Chair 3/Allee: What?! So you're too good to do something you obviously can do to help these students but you're just too opinionated to do?

Allee: I am not opinionated. This is a huge, major lifestyle choice that has taken me years to align with. I don't believe in any scripted theatre for myself ever again. I feel like a dishonest, uh, lying whore!

Chair 3/Allee: Well just forget it then. Obviously, you won't do it even to help these great young people.

Allee: But I want to so much and I'm good at it but . . . I come home and loathe myself. I go through the actions but hate myself afterward.

Chair 3/Allee: I think you've made it clear that you pay a big price to be a good actor. Only you can weigh whether you want to balance the toll it takes versus the help you give.

Allee: Yes. That's very true . . . the big price I pay in the days afterward and how I feel about myself. I'm not myself around my family and friends too because I feel so disgusted. It even affects my body and loss of appetite. Also I'm so tense and anxious in the time before the next "performance." It's just not worth it. But it makes me sad to think of quitting. I need to add another Chair that's for grieving the loss of this job and opportunity (*Chair 5 is added*) . . .

The enactment continues with Allee exploring the grief with Chair 5 and talking to the Supervisor Chair 2 about quitting, which includes considering lying to the person to cover up her rather enigmatic and eccentric real reason for leaving.

Allee uses Chair 5 to express grief about the loss of the relationship with her Supervisor. She comes back to Chair 3 to admit that it is a blow to her pride that she also no longer has the stamina to endure the anxiety associated with scripted performance. Again she goes to Chair 3 as her process unfolds to criticize the banality of the script itself and how she could write something much better. This insight leads her to Chair 5 to share her grief at getting older and losing the sharpness of her memory.

As can easily be seen, this is an amazingly effective method for bringing forth an extensive number of 'parts of oneself!' Because we have had a lot of training and practice we can flow into an enactment and navigate many aspects fairly quickly. The method itself elicits one feeling after another. Having a director to help with this process is ideal for deep exploration, although Allee, as an experienced practitioner, did not require Adam's involvement beyond his serving as witness.

Let us conclude this example with the following interchange:

> **Allee:** So I'm going to quit and now I feel very clear about my choice and the tradeoffs. It was good to have the Chair 5 to help me grieve. I'm definitely out of the mess in my mind and emotions. Thank you.

> **Adam:** It has really helped me to understand what you've been going through because you haven't been your usual self for several weeks. It never really came up specifically till now. I think you did a really good job and getting the different parts out and having them speak.

> **Allee:** I know we say this to one another after something like this but I really need to have you be there as my witness in order to concretize these mixed feelings and thoughts.

The goal is to achieve a sense of sincere selfdisclosure. We realize that one part of us feels countermanded by other parts that disqualify, dismiss or in other ways offer counterarguments.

So the way we use the empty chairs encourages us to go ahead and say it all, knowing that we can then explicitly add another part of ourselves in a chair that expresses an additional point of view or even offer a counter-view.

Role Relief / 'Herb' and 'Tracy'

To give ourselves a break from having to constantly be our normal selves we have intentionally adopted subpersonalities whom we call Herb (for Adam) and Tracy (for Allee.) One term associated with this kind of activity is role relief, which is used when someone consciously chooses to engage in behaviors that are 'out of character' with what is commonly expected. It is a variation of what in psychodrama is called 'the multiple ego technique'. We also call it 'the many parts of self'. In fact, Herb and Tracy represent much simpler parts of us, persons with limited cognitive ability. Adam and Allee have performed at high levels of educational standards, and this conscious shift into subpersonalities offers much-needed 'role relief'. First, Herb and Tracy really like to do mundane tasks that need to be done. For example, Herb does dishes and laundry, and he says 'I like to help.' Tracy does bookkeeping, vacuuming, and likes to take out the trash. So when the traditional roles that we play become too hard to maintain we choose to regress as role relief. We become less complex and more dependent personalities. In ego psychology, this is called 'adaptive regression in the service of the ego'.

When we shift into being Herb and Tracy we enjoy the rich delights of being two people with simple jobs around the house. Herb and Tracy live with two adults, Mr and Mrs Blatner, who take care of all of the adult responsibilities. The Blatners have created what we call 'The Home for Assistance in Living' (a takeoff on 'assisted living'). They never think about or worry about money, buying food, car upkeep or anything outside of their simple duties. These they do cheerfully and are just happy to help the Blatners, who take total care of them and never make them go out into social settings, such as the grocery store, or driving on the freeway.

This side story relationship has been going on for a number of years and provides an alternative lifestyle within which to enjoy and explore other aspects of ourselves. We imagine that Herb has taken classes in his 'workshops' that allow him to advance his skills such as learning how to properly hang up different kinds of clothes after he has put them through the dryer. Herb allows Adam to delight in his limited abilities and celebrate them without any concern that there are other things to do or achieve. Herb's world is very simple and satisfying. Similarly, Tracy affords Allee a context within which she can relinquish the pressures and expectations of her normal life and be contented with Tracy's simple chores within the home. Moreover, Tracy does not like 'going out' because it overloads her with sensations and choices. The backstory on Herb and Tracy is that met at a 'workshop' on 'how to live independently' and fell immediately into an inseparable friendship. Tracy demanded that she be allowed to stand next to Herb when they're in the same room. Unfortunately they did not successfully graduate into independent living, and thus they were placed with the Blatners. They love one another and thus they were thrilled when the Blatners said they could have the same bedroom.

By cocreating these role relief characters we can express our simpler selves in this new relationship where interpersonal expectations are greatly reduced. We have created role flexibility between us, so that when we need to be Adam and Allee we are competent to play those roles, and yet when we want to relax into a simpler life, we can become Herb and Tracy.

Performing for 'Them' / Surplus Reality

A number of years ago, our son came home on a visit and remarked, 'Gee Pa, it's just hit me being away and coming back, that for your being a psychiatrist, it's pretty weird that so many things in this house aren't real'. We all agreed with a laugh! Indeed, physical props, hand puppets and stuffed toys are abundantly visible and available to serve as stimuli and co-characters to our ongoing imaginative enactments.

Sometimes we play to them as if they were an audience. We might call out: 'Look everybody!' This reminds us that we are in role. Because they are not a real audience we have no concerns for putting on a great show. We declaim, as if we were giving speeches: 'Everybody, everybody!' A particular puppet or stuffed animal might be addressed: 'Apricot Flopsy would agree with that!' (She is an apricot-coloured bunny hand puppet with floppy ears.) This helps to emphasize our point and bring 'to life' one of the available characters.

Our use of surplus reality might be compared with a line from the Beatles' song 'Penny Lane' that goes something like this: 'In the roundabout a pretty lady is selling poppies from a tray, and though she thinks she's in a play, she is anyway'. In other words, imagining that we have an audience makes it at once more real, more fantasy, more emphasized and more malleable to our shifting inspirations.

We both share a view of our cosmos as a place that contains a consciousness or mythic intelligence that is benevolent and with which we are constantly cocreating. We imagine that there is a 'cast' of angels or other beings with which we make our affirmations more vivid. Moreover we invite this transpersonal realm to play with us. Thus through our own imaginations we can open to the flow of spontaneity, a dimension highly valued by Moreno and now by each of us.[2]

In addition we'd like to honor the vast genius of Moreno's own imagining, and note that he has hypothesize a realm he called "metapraxie." We have written about this as a dimension from which spontaneity draws its unending flow.[3]

2 Blatner and Blatner 1996
3 Blatner & Blatner, 1988

We envision it as a 'place' before form actually arises, whether that be in visual art, language, music, dance, *etc*. Each person can access this fountain of creativity. By using the concept of 'surplus reality,' whether we are involved in psychodrama, drama therapy, or the other expressive arts, we can offer everyone a context within which they can explore and expand their lives into more health, freedom, creativity and fun.

Summary

We not only enliven our individual lives but continually cocreate our married life around a group of action methods. By looking at our relationship as an ongoing improvisation, a perennial rehearsal process, we are able to create a deep harmony with one another. We add a measure of the mythical, storytelling play to stay connected with the cosmos. Action methods (many derived from psychodrama) have practical applications quite aside from psychotherapy. These techniques are powerful forms of applied imaginativeness, an extension of 'what if . . . ?' to clarify situations, resolve differences, create kinder and more loving relationships and to cooperatively play with life together.

We envision it as a 'place' before form actually arises, whether that be in visual art, language, music, dance, *etc*. Each person can access this fountain of creativity. By using the concept of 'surplus reality,' whether we are involved in psychodrama, drama therapy, or the other expressive arts, we can offer everyone a context withing which they can explore and expand their lives into more health, freedom, creativity and fun.

To look at this from another viewpoint, what we do is in some ways to employ 'constructivism,' a post-modern perspective.[4] We are consciously playing fast and loose with levels of reality, but we are always open to renegotiating with one another. This is crucial: there is a pull to reach closure to support one's own beliefs, but we know that we must resist that tug and remain receptive. We hope that readers will be inspired to adopt and adapt these action explorations approaches in their own lives.

·   ·   ·

Note: This chapter originally appeared in *Drama Therapy Review*, February, 2019 (Volume 4, Issue 2). Reproduced with permission of Intellect Ltd, through PLSclear.

---

4 Neimeyer 1998

Adam Blatner

Adam Blatner, M.D., TEP, is a retired psychiatrist and Trainer of Psychodrama. He is a former Associate Professor of Psychiatry at The University of Louisville School of Medicine and Texas A&M University School of Medicine. Adam has written books and articles in the field of psychodrama, drama therapy and the creative arts in therapy. He is internationally recognized as an authority on the theory and practice of psychodrama. Adam has championed the place of the arts in healing and health for over 50 years through his writings, teachings at conferences and mentoring students all over the world. He is author of the basic text in psychodrama *Acting-In*, many articles and chapters, and the books *Foundations of Psychodrama*, *Interactive Improvisation*, and co-author *The Art of Play*.

Allee Blatner

Allee Blatner studied at The University of Texas/Austin and Carnegie-Mellon University. She was trained in psychodrama by her husband Adam, as well as in workshops with many other leaders in the field. For over 30 years, she has led or co-led workshops and training seminars at colleges, hospitals and at national and international conferences. For 10 years, she and Adam taught a day-long class, "Practical Applications of Psychodramtic Methods," at the American Psychiatric Association annual convention. Allee is co-author with her husband, Adam, on their book *The Art of Play: Helping Adults Reclaim Imagination and Spontaneity*.

References

Blatner, A. (1987), *Creating Your Living: Applications of Psychodramatic Methods in Everyday Life* (privately produced monograph).

Blatner, A. & Blatner, A. (1988). The Metaphysics of Creativity as Reflected in Moreno's Metapraxie and the Mystical Tradition. *Journal of Group Psychotherapy, Psychodrama & Sociometry, 40* (4), 155 163.

Blatner, A. and Blatner, A. (1996), *The Art of Play: Helping Adults Reclaim Imagination & Spontaneity*, 3rd ed., New York: Brunner/Mazel (1st and 2nd ed. from Human Sciences Press).

Blatner, A. & Blatner, A. (2018). *How we use action explorations to improve and enhance our relationship*. Drama Therapy Review, 4(1), 71–81.

Neimeyer, R. A. (1998), 'Social constructionism in the counselling context', Counselling Psychology Quarterly, 11:2, pp. 135–49.

Schwartz, R. (1987), 'Our multiple selves: Applying systems thinking to the inner family', http://www.hakomiinstitute.com/Forum/Issue10/OurMultipleSelves.pdf

Wiener, D. J. (1994), *Rehearsals for Growth: Theater Improvisation for Psychotherapists*, New York: W. W. Norton.

Section 5

Action Explorations in Spirituality

Bringing the Scriptures to Life with Bibliodrama

Patrick T. Barone

Like psychodrama, the word "bibliodrama" carries with it certain connotations that are neither helpful nor accurate. For this reason a better phrase for whatever this thing is might be "participatory storytelling," a phrase that is perhaps more intrinsically accurate because, also like psychodrama, bibliodrama is a group process, a co-creation of the surplus reality that exists within the white fire, a concept explained at length below. The master metaphor for this form of participatory storytelling begins with you as a story facilitator. What happens within the bibiodrama framework is the telling of a story together, as a group. The group begins their storytelling within the framework of the black fire, which is the text of the Scripture that's been handed down. Because there is also a tremendous amount that has not been made explicit in these stories, the group will use the Scriptural text only as a starting point and the facilitator will invite the group members to begin to think about and then to explore what's between the lines of the text. This is the essence of the process of co-creation, which in turn is the essence of this work.

Nevertheless, while the term "participatory storytelling" may be more accurate, the more technical term bibliodrama remains useful, and so it may be helpful to consider the root word *biblio*, which comes from the Greek *biblion*, meaning book. Hence, when we use the word "bibliodrama," we are most often referring to dramatization of the written word. This small "b" bibliodrama may derive from any secular text. This chapter however will address and describe capital "B" Bibliodrama because the texts drawn from are non-secular, and include, but are not necessarily limited to, the Hebrew Torah, the books of the Prophets, the Wisdom Literature and the Christian texts. Consequently, capital

"B" Bibliodrama is a text-based experiential approach to Biblical interpretation.[1] Accordingly, Bibliodrama is a form of exegesis that may involve a dramatization that can take many forms, anything from that which is totally improvised to that which is fully scripted.

Some authors have posited that the first Bibliodrama's were actually psychodramas from biblical text.[2] This type of Bibliodrama is a form of story exploration and interpretation that loosely uses the tools, methods, and techniques (often called "interventions") of psychodrama. These methods are applied to the exploration of Biblical stories in small groups of participants. Depending on the environment and the facilitator (in psychodrama referred to as the "director"), Bibliodrama can evoke psychological transferences and projections as participants feel their own "stuff" being triggered by the relationships described in the text.[3] A middle-aged woman, for example, begins to look back on her own motherhood with a sense of deep trepidation as she embodies the Eve of Genesis 4 who has just learned of the fratricide that has taken place. Hence, the Bibliodrama mirror is at work, and this mother's own story is reflected back into the ancient text. In this way Bibliodrama can be an excellent warm-up to the personal work of psychodrama. However, while the form of Bibliodrama described in this chapter has been influenced by psychodrama, it begins and ends with the text. The goal is for participants to gain insight into the deeper meaning of scripture, and see how their personal stories are reflected in the meta-stories described in the sacred texts. The goal is not to evoke in participants the deeper meaning that may thereby be revealed within one's own psyche. Nevertheless, Bibliodrama can be highly evocative as psychodrama remains as the tap-root from which it is nourished. This is particularly true because Bibliodrama relates to the involvement of not just the mind, but also, through various forms of movement, the body. Nevertheless, while psychodrama training and experience is helpful, it is by no means essential or even necessary. This is not to say that experienced psychodramatists cannot or should not use Bibliodrama precisely for this additional purpose, something the author has found to be particularly satisfying. The point is that the further exploration of this mirror piece is not central to the core tenant and purpose of Bibliodrama.

Other authors have suggested that Bibliodrama started in the 1970s in Europe as a reaction to the staid traditional forms of scripture interpretation that then existed.[4] This movement is survived today by a very active European

---

1 Krondorfer, B., Martin, G. *Body and Bible; The Origins of Bibliodrama and its Special Interest in the Text*, p. 85, Trinity Press International (1992).

2 Krondorfer, Pg. 87.

3 The Bibliodrama term for these transferences is "mirror," which in this context has a meaning different from the psychodrama intervention of the same name.

4 Krondorfer, pg. 86.

Bibliodrama group, which is particularly vibrant in Germany, Sweden, Denmark, Netherlands, and Finland. Each have their own, albeit similar, style and method of interpretation. It is worth noting that the Europeans call what is described in this book "Biblilog," while reserving the word "Bibliodrama" for the form that prevails in Europe.[5]

Another form of Bibliodrama, this one from South Africa, is a play script based on a story found in scripture. This is perhaps the least spontaneous form of Bibliodrama as the "actors" are reciting memorized lines written well before the performance. One such play is entitled "He is risen! A play based on Acts 1:1–12." From the School of Biblical Sciences, Potchefstroom Campus of North-West University in South Africa, this script has all the markings of a typical dramatic production, and includes a description of the set, props, scene, *etc.* It is also designed explicitly for evangelical purposes.

There is still another precursor to this form of Bibliodrama, and that is the Jewish Midrash. After the destruction of Jerusalem and the Temple, during the rabbinic period, Midrash was thought of as a way to discover the hidden meanings within the Torah. In this context though, the term Midrash refers to a highly authoritative form of biblical exegesis by ancient Judaic authorities.[6] Bibliodrama too is a form of exegesis, but one that most often takes place in groups of participants with varying degrees of scriptural acumen.

This list of Bibliodrama's precursors and influencers is almost certainly not exhaustive and undoubtedly many other forms of Bibliodrama probably exist. What is common among them is that they allow participants to experience and explore the scriptures in way that is much different from and perhaps more enriching than a rote reading of them. It is also a mind/body experience. It is also worth noting that while Bibliodrama can be a deeply spiritual and religiously rewarding endeavor, it does not necessarily have proselytization as its goal, and many find participation to be simply an interesting intellectual exercise.

This chapter will explain, discuss and suggest a single form of Bibliodrama that first arose in geographic isolation from the rest. It is the author's modification of a form of Bibliodrama originally devised and heavily influenced by the work and writings of Dr. Peter Pitzele. As is more fully described below, this particular form of Bibliodrama might be thought of as non-traditional Midrash. In this context it is interesting to note that some have theorized that the Gospel of Matthew was written in the style of Jewish Midrash literature meaning the author was not writing about historical events. According to this theory, this Gospel sets forth an imaged commentary or interpretation of the Old Testament texts. Though this thoroughly discredited view is undoubtedly

---

5 *http://www.bibliolog.de* (last checked 3.12.18).
6 Neusner, *What is Midrash? And a Midrash Reader*, pg. xi. University of South Florida (1994).

offensive to some Christians and Jews alike it does help to demonstrate the point. Also, this particular form of Bilbiodrama is not beholden to any specific religion, sect or principle. Instead, if there is a goal at all, that goal would be to personalize the scripture. To synthesize modern life with ancient scripture, and to allow participants to consider a new way to interpret and internalize the written narrative.

More broadly it might be said that Bibliodrama has as its aim the movement of an individual from simply reading to instead deeply experiencing the scriptural narrative, including the characters, settings and themes of the texts, and to do so in a unique and different way. Thus, while the Bibliodrama set forth in this chapter was informed by psychodrama, it nevertheless is not personal and does not have as its purpose any sort of personally therapeutic goal. The only exception to this is the understanding that Bibliodrama has a way of removing the toxicity that some may feel toward a God they may conceive of as a distant, judgmental, and retributive despot. Bibliodrama has a way of removing this view and replacing it with one of a loving God with whom one is invited to have a personal relationship. Additionally, one does not have to be a Biblical scholar to facilitate or participate in a Bibliodrama. The ability to carefully read the relevant Scripture is the only essential skill. The facilitator of Bibliodrama will nevertheless benefit from a thorough working knowledge of the Biblical Texts. Finally, it is worth noting that while Bibliodrama has exclusively been explored in groups, most recently, the author has begun developing a new form of Bibliodrama intended to be used between just two individuals as a form of pastoral counseling. This is an exciting expansion of the methods and techniques described in this chapter.

The Development of This Form of Bibliodrama.

The style of Bibliodrama described in this chapter is the author's adaptation of a form that was developed by Peter Pitzele, who earned his Ph.D. in English and American literature from Harvard, and later also trained in psychodrama with Zerka Moreno. He thereby become a psychodrama TEP (trainer, educator and practitioner) and eventually worked as a clinical psychodramatist.

Peter started to experiment with an early form Bibliodrama when, in the early 70's, he was asked to stand-in and teach at a Rabbinical Seminary. Because Peter had taught at Harvard, he was very comfortable in the classroom, but seminary instruction was a new experience for him. At the time he had no life orientation that involved the Torah and had never been to a seminary. So, he decided to simply be spontaneous and to thereby draw from both his primary training in literature and his secondary training in psychodrama. Peter further honed this form of Bibliodrama while teaching at the Union Theological Seminary, the Institute for Contemporary Midrash, and the Jewish Theological Seminary.

This form of Bibliodrama is a kind of Biblical exegesis or literary interpretation that lends itself to more than one explanation. One of these involves an incorporation of the belief that the Hebrew Bible was born from a fire of many different colors. Of these many colors, the written page includes the "black fire" and the "white fire." Metaphorically, the black fire is comprised of the immutable and transcendent words that exist on the printed page whereas the white fire is comprised of the "blank" spaces between those words. Bibliodrama exists, is drawn from and is an exploration of these white spaces. This white fire stokes Bibliodrama's reification of the Scriptural surplus reality. It is the imagined place where the real and the unreal co-exist. The white fire becomes the reality within which the stories and the characters within them continue to live and play in the here and now. It is the place where participants are introduced to and may interact with anyone from Abraham to Zachariah.

Perhaps a more nearly complete understanding of the style and purpose of Bibliodrama can be obtained by thinking of it also from the perspective of non-secular comparative literature. To that end, a reading of Chapter one of Mimesis is instructive. In this chapter, the book's author, Auerbach, compares a classic example of western literature, that being the Odyssey, with the Old Testament. This comparison and contrast involves the premise that in western literature the author provides much detail about the characters involved, the way they look, their backgrounds and information relative to their motivation, and often, descriptions of their inner thought life. Little is left to the imagination. To utilize the metaphor, in western literature there is, most often, very little white fire. The Old Testament authors on the other hand, are nearly always terse. The reader is provided with only fragments of a character's history and motivation. Rarely do we read of a character's internal dialog. Some Old Testament stories, such as the 17 verses of Cain and Abel, are so terse that they are composed primarily of white fire. In the introduction, Edward Said describes Auerbach's comparison of western literature with the Old Testament this way:

> On the other hand, Auerback's consideration of the Abraham and Isaac story in the Old Testament beautifully demonstrates how it "is like a holding of the breath . . . the overwhelming suspense is present . . . The personages speak in the Bible story too; but their speech does not serve, as does speech in Homer, to manifest, to externalize thoughts — on the contrary, it serves to indicate thoughts that remain unexpressed."

Thus, one purpose of Bibliodrama is to explore, that is to "externalize," these inner thoughts of the characters that remain unexpressed. That is, to make said what is otherwise left unsaid. This is another way of thinking about the "white fire" exploration in Bibliodrama. For this reason, the older books of the Bible might contain more opportunities for exploration than later, more modern books, which often contain more details regarding a character's actions and motivations. On the other hand, a beginning Bibliodramatist might be overwhelmed by the sheer volume of "white fire" contained in the more ancient stories.

Said continues as follows:

> [*There is an*] *externalization of only so much of the phenomena as is necessary for the purpose of the narrative, all else is left in obscurity; the decisive points of the narrative alone are emphasized, what lies beneath is nonexistent; time and place are undefined and call for interpretation; thoughts and feelings remain unexpressed are only suggested by silence and the fragmentary speeches; the whole is permeated with the most unrelieved suspense and directed toward a single goal (and to that extent far more of a unity), remains mysterious and 'fraught with background.'*

So again, this form of Bibliodrama, helps to externalize, that is, bring to the foreground, those parts of the biblical narrative that are otherwise left in obscurity. Also, to make expressed the otherwise unexpressed thoughts and feelings of the biblical characters. Hence, a Bibliodramatist's task is to facilitate a co-created "filling-in" of these empty spaces.

Bibliodrama as a Form of Midrash

This form of Biblical exploration is essentially a modern-day expansion of the Jewish tradition of "Midrash," which is a kind of Biblical storytelling. The Hebrew root word for "Midrash" means to investigate. Midrash is a synonym for the English word "exegesis." Midrash is a Jewish form of exegesis of the Torah that has existed for centuries. Between the first and the seventh centuries, a Judaism took shape around the conviction that at the biblical Mount Sinai God revealed to Moses the Torah, or revelation, not only in writing but also orally. This oral Torah was formulated and transmitted in memory and was handed on from prophets to sages until it was written down as the Mishnah. Alongside this, there was an effort to reread scripture, that is, the written Torah, and the result was Midrash compilations.[7]

Faced with an unredeemed world, Jewish sages read Scripture as an account of how things were meant to be, not how they were in the perceivable world around us. Because the perceivable world does not testify to God's plan, Scripture serves as a metaphor for how things are meant to be and Midrash shows

---

7 Neusner, *What is Midrash? And a Midrash Reader*, Pg. 43, University of South Florida (1994).

how the Judaic sages mediated between God's Word and their own world.[8] In Midrash, there is a constant interplay and ongoing exchange between everyday affairs and the Word of God in the Scriptures. "What we see reminds us of what Scripture says—and what Scripture says informs our understanding of the things we see and do in everyday life."[9] "The God of Midrash is a God close to men's expectations, sensitive to experience and memory, who brings about, through His intervention in history, the 'recognition' of His kindness."[10]

The word Midrash refers to three types of exegesis; Midrash as (1) parable (2) paraphrase and (3) prophesy.[11] Thus, a person may perform exegesis by producing a Midrash of a scripture verse. In other words, a critical interpretation of the verse. One may also say that "life is a Midrash on scripture," meaning what happens in everyday life imparts meaning and significance to Biblical stories and characters.[12] Midrash may refer to a particular paragraph or unit of exegetical exposition. When individual Midrash are combined into a cohesive whole the result may collectively be referred to Midrash. An example of this might be a Midrash addressing the Book of Jonah. Putting the three together in summary form, Midrash can refer to a (1) a process, (2) a unit of exegesis resulting from the process, (3) or a compilation of the units derived from the process.[13]

There are three elements to Midrash; (1) exegesis, (2) starting with scripture, and (3) ending with community.[14] Bibliodrama might be thought of as a form of Midrash because it incorporates all three elements. Bibliodrama is a critical explanation or interpretation of scripture that "ends in community" in that it is co-created by the participants in the Bibliodrama. By participating in the Bibliodrama, group members are offered the opportunity to see Scripture as a metaphor for how things are or should be in their lives. Participants might also gain a better understanding of how Scripture is related to the things they see and do in everyday life.

This form of Bibliodrama offers a compellingly method of exegesis where the interventions of psychodrama are combined with the Midrash investigation.

---

8   Neusner, P. 48.

9   Neusner, pgs 102, 103.

10   Rojtman, *Black fire on White Fire; An Essay on Jewish Hermeneutics, from Midrash to Kabblah.* University of California Press, 1998, pg. 44.

11   Neusner, pgs. 8, 9.

12   Neusner, pg. 8.

13   Neusner, pgs 8, 9.

14   Id.

The White Fire and Black Fire of Bibliodrama

Midrash is often a quite literal commentary on the Torah, but it can also be a fanciful. An example of this would be a Midrash about creation where "all the letters of the aleph-bet clamored and begged, 'Create the world through me!'"[15] In His act of creation, God brings forth order out of chaos through the divine attributes of His Wisdom, His Spirit and His Word. This fanciful Midrash expands on what is found in Genesis where the Word is called on to "found and speak the world."[16] For example, in Genesis verse 9, we find "Then God said, 'Let the waters under the heavens be gathered together into one place, and the dry land appear'; and it was so." The Gospel of John begins with the sentence "In the beginning was the Word, and the Word was with God, and the Word was God."

This Word of God is often referred to as "fire." For example, referring to Mount Sinai, Deuteronomy 33:2 we see that "From His right hand came a fiery law for them." And from Jeremiah 23:29 "Is not My word like a fire? says the Lord." The ancient rabbis believed that the Torah the Holy One gave to Moses was given to him from white fire inscribed by black fire. It was fire, mixed with fire, hewn from fire and given by fire.[17] The black fire refers to the printed letters, the white fire to the spaces between and around them. At the origins of speech, this white space was fire, mingled with the black fire of letters; "the Law that God gave to Moses was written in black fire on white fire."[18] Both fires are to be read and interpreted. The black fire refers to what the Torah says, the white fire refers to what the Torah means.

An underlying precept of Midrash, particularly Rabbinic Midrash, is that nothing in the Bible is superfluous. If things are repeated or left out, if there are gaps and ambiguities, if there are what appear to be needless expressions, these all exist for a reason. Additionally, everything in the Bible is interrelated somehow. In the modern lexicon the Bible is heavily hyperlinked. It has been suggested therefore, that the white fire that is interspersed between the letters of black fire should also be counted as letters.[19]

In Bibliodrama we begin with the black fire. The white fire is co-created, by the group, with the assistance of the Bibliodrama facilitator. Bibliodrama is an exegesis of the "letters" of the white fire, and is a Midrash that first brings the black and white fire together and then delivers both into the experiences of everyday life.

---

15   Sherman, *The Outstretched Arm I*, Vol. 2, Issue 2., Fall 1999/5760

16   Rojtman, *Black fire on White Fire; An Essay on Jewish Hermeneutics, from Midrash to Kabblah*. University of California Press, 1998, pg. 9.

17   Verman, *The Torah as Devine Fire*, Vol. 35, No. 2, 2007.

18   Rojtman, pg. 3.

19   R. Margoliot, Hamikra Vehamesorah (Jerusalem, 1964) p. 46.

Selecting a Text and Creating an Outline:
How to Read Bibliodramatically

With this background and history, it is now time to look at the steps involved in creating a Bibliodrama. Since we are starting and ending with text, creating a Bibliodrama begins with a selection of Text, and this will often arise out of one's personal interest in a specific story, character or theme in the Bible. At this point it is helpful to pause and consider the definitions of two words as they are used and apply to Bibliodrama; the window and the mirror. Both are heavily at work in this form of action exploration and group story-telling. The mirror is that part of the ancient story that reflects into our own life, and evokes our own parallel story that is then reflected back through our own role-play. The window is the part of another's story evoked as they play the same role. The window is how you are thinking about what others have said; your contemplation of it in the context of your comparison to your mirror.

Since this is the case, thought should be given as to why a particular text has such personal resonance. This is the mirror piece applicable to you as the facilitator. Is the text compelling because of some unresolved past relationship or some other form of hurt, habit or hang-up? If so, then perhaps you should consider doing some personal work around these issues? If you are drawn to a story of forgiveness perhaps you are currently working through forgiving others or being forgiven by them. It is helpful to have an awareness of this so that one's own story does not become imprinted on your facilitation of the Bibliodramatic work.

Once the text is selected, you begin by fully embracing your selection. It may be helpful to read what others have said about this text and to understand its context within the broader narrative. This is important because as the facilitator you will be chief storyteller, and good story telling requires a large breadth from which to draw. Furthermore, to read Bibliodramatically is to read slowly and imaginatively; to read between the lines and even more to read between the words. It is through a consideration of the missing parts, the gaps and ambiguities inherent in this literary style, that we find the stuff of Bibliodrama. Begin to think through the unexpressed and the unanswered questions posed regarding the characters in the text. What is unexpressed is one form of white fire, and presents various possible entry points, *i.e.*, those spaces through which you and the group participants can step into the text. Very broadly speaking, each of these entry points are referred to as "role-moments" by Pitzele.[20]

Consider for example the previously mentioned story of Cain and Abel in Genesis chapter four. This amazing story consists of only 17 short verses yet

---

20   Pitzele, *Scripture Windows, Toward a Practice of Bibliodrama*, second edition, Ben Yehuda Press, 2019, Teaneck, New Jersey

in its subtlety we find vast meaning that is nearly incomprehensibly profound. Much of its profundity comes from all the white fire—what is left out. Consider verses 2–5:

> *Abel took care of sheep. Cain worked the ground. After some time, Cain gathered some of the things he had grown. He brought them as an offering to the Lord. But Abel brought the fattest parts of some of the lambs from his flock. They were the male animals that were born first to their mothers. The Lord was pleased with Abel and his offering. But he wasn't pleased with Cain and his offering. So, Cain became very angry. His face was sad.*

By contrast, Malachi chapter one, verses 6–8, likewise address the subject matter of Cain and Abel and the appropriateness of the sacrifice. Here we have what looks much more like a script:

> *"A son honors his father. A servant honors his master. If I am a father, where is the honor I should have? If I am a master, where is the respect you should give me?" says the Lord who rules over all. "You priests look down on me. "But you ask, 'How have we looked down on you?' "You put 'unclean' food on my altar. "But you ask, 'How have we made you "unclean?"' ' "You do it by looking down on my altar. You sacrifice blind animals to me. Isn't that wrong? You sacrifice disabled or sick animals. Isn't that wrong? Try offering them to your governor! Would he be pleased with you? Would he accept you?" says the Lord who rules over all.*

Both stories offer much to the Bibliodramatist yet the Cain and Abel story is so sparse, it contains so much that is unanswered that the sheer number of possible entry points is itself intimidating. There are so many entry points to the text that one runs the danger of stepping in and then falling right out again!

Once you've carefully read, pondered and contemplated a text, you may begin by taking an inventory of what characters and things exist, either explicitly or implicitly. Each character or thing offers an entry point through which you can facilitate a stepping into the white fire. These entry points offer an opportunity for the participants to step into the cracked leather, dust-covered sandals of a Bible character. Looking at Cain and Able, your inventory may include the brothers, Adam and Eve, God, the sheep, the field, the crop(s), the ground that "opened its mouth" to receive Able's blood, the offerings themselves, the sin "crouching" at Cain's "door," the final breath of Able, and then perhaps by implication, the birds or even Angels flying overhead as celestial witnesses. Your imagination is the only limitation to whom or what can be enrolled and concretized during a Bibliodrama.

Once you have a list of possible characters or roles, your next step will be to consider the context of the story. What do we know about the history? In exploring the Cain and Abel story for example we know that Adam and Eve just ignominiously left the Garden of Eden. How does this fact impact their decision to have children, and what guilt might they carry for the very fact that this fratricide occurred? How were their hopes and dreams shattered when they learned of the death of Abel and the banishment of Cain? As transient empty-nesters, what is their thought process as they decide to have another child? This is the very essence of creating a Bibliodrama, to think of the characters as real, modern day people, who, just like you and me, have a past and who experience life no differently from us. As you begin to contemplate this, what questions do you have? Being curious, what do you want to know? While you may begin with the why question, you want to phrase your group prompting such that it will allow them to enter the feeling place. You may want to know why Eve decides to bear again and this might lead to many different questions. A role moment from what we've just explored might be, to the group, "Eve, allow yourself to imagine the moment that you've decided to have another child (pause) now, tell us, what is this moment like for you?"

As was intimated above, role moments may involve objects, and these role moments can be incredibly rich entry points. Genesis 4, verse 10 provides: The Lord said, "What have you done? Listen! Your brother's blood is crying out to me from the ground." Here we have two possible roles, the blood of Abel and the ground which, in verse 11, has "opened its mouth to receive your brother's blood from your hand." This is a very provocative image, and an excellent entry point; "you are the ground of the field beneath Cain and Able. What sound do you make as you open your mouth to receive Abel's blood?"

Conducting the Bibliodrama

It is useful to give some thought as to the environment within which your work will take place. Will all of the participants be seated and relatively unable to move about, as with a seated congregation in a place of worship, or will you be working in an open meeting space within which you can create a space to designate as your "stage?" Your work space will dictate how you are able to invite participants to join you and step into the work you will be doing together. The time available will also impose limits on what you are able to do with your group. The group's faith orientation may also play a part, and finally, your experience level combined with that of your participants, will also impact your work.

The Bibliodrama will consist of three parts, the warm up to action, the action phase, and the cool-down phase, where the group will review and process what has occurred and share with the group what they learned.

Warming up to action

In life we have a "warm up" for many of the important tasks or events of our lives. In the morning we may warm up to our day by drinking coffee while reviewing our "to-do" list. We may then warm up to a task on the list by beginning to envision our engaging in and completing the task. Emotionally imbued events such as weddings often have very long warm-ups, that may include both tradition, planning a wedding, and self-reflection as we ask ourselves "how will my life change with the marriage of my daughter?"

Group members will come to the work in different phases of warm up as it relates to the Bibliodrama. Some may walk in cold, having never read the text, and having given little thought to the work, while others may be very "warmed up" to the subject matter or to the event more generally. Your first task then will be to re-align the group process so that group members are more closely in agreement relative to their readiness for action.

As with other aspects of your Bibliodrama, the way you warm up your group will depend on many factors. When presenting at a place of worship you may have very limited time, and the group warm up will have been led by and transpired to completion before you have first approached your group. It may only involve a short introduction by the worship leader. On the other hand, if you are working with a new group and have the luxury of time and space, then you may wish to consider more formalized warm ups that will allow group members to begin bonding with one another and thereby help the group begin to feel safe, ready to share, and more willing to deeply immerse themselves in the various roles.

Because most group members will have some measure of anxiety, and since the amount of anxiety in the room will be inversely proportional to the amount spontaneity or creativity, it will be good to help the group release some of their anxiety. A good way to start is to offer an introduction. Explain who you are and at least in general terms, what you are going to be doing together. Be sure to explain that all group members have total control over their level of participation. They may participate frequently, or not at all. They will always have the option of not participating and they should know that their non-participation will be respected.

If you do have the luxury of a large open work space and when the participants have an understanding of the type of group work they will be doing, then a simple exercise from psychodrama that can easily be employed here is called the spectrogram. This involves designating two related factors that are usually opposed, and then designating these factors on opposite ends of a straight line. This allows you to "measure" criteria in the group. For example, you may want to determine how familiar the group members are with the story you are going to explore. If so, your two "poles" might be "I know this story so well I could write a book about its meaning" and "this is the first I've ever heard of this story." You designate a straight line across the floor and ask group members to place themselves along this imaginary line according to the criteria. The authors will be on one side, the novices on the other and those who are between the two poles will place themselves on the line wherever they belong. In a more traditional setting, simply going around the group and allowing them to introduce themselves and briefly describe why they decided to attend might be a good option.

Another purpose of the warm-up is to help make what is covert in the group overt. From the perspective of psychodrama this is group sociometry. Since all group members will be experiencing some form of anxiety about the work in which they are about to engage, a warm-up regarding anxiety is useful. On one side of the line is "I have no anxiety" while on the other, "I have so much anxiety I almost didn't come today." After group members have made their selection, be sure to invite each person to tell the group why they are standing in the spot they selected. This will further enhance the group connections and will serve also to decrease anxiety.

Reading the story together, or in turn by verse, is another effective form of warm up. It might also serve as a good segue to the action phase where you will be inviting group members to take on roles and step into the story. An alternative to the group reading is for you, as the group leader, to become their story teller. This way you can quickly summarize a longer story and focus on the aspect of the story you wish to explore. Good story telling is trance induction, and this trance helps to allow a suppressing of the ego, which in turn, allows a deeper role-taking experience. A combination of the formal reading, followed by the storyteller's introduction to the role moment, can be a most effective warm-up. Once you've completed your warm up, you are ready to move into action.

Moving into action

The type of action methods available to you will be limited by your level of experience and training in various transferable action methods such as Playback Theater or psychodrama. The introductory action level, which is not to say simple, or unrewarding, occurs when you invite the group to collectively step into a role by asking them a challenging question and waiting for them to provide an answer. A few examples of this have been given earlier in this chapter. Looking again at the Cain and Abel story, you may wish to explore the obvious theme of sibling rivalry accordingly: "I'd like you to imagine that you are Cain as a child, and your brother Abel has just come into the world. For the first time in your life you realize that your mother no longer belongs you alone. What is this moment like for you?" At a different point in the story you may ask the group to consider; "Abel, how does it make you feel when you learn that God has 'failed' to look on your brother Cain's offering with respect?"

There are many more advanced action options, and these might include having two characters speak to one another. You may wish to give Cain and Abel a chance to work out their differences in the afterlife. To begin this encounter, you might set two chairs, facing one another, in your work area. Ask members of the group to sit in a chair thereby taking on the role of the occupant. With the chairs now filled with a Cain and an Abel, you may ask one to begin the conversation, perhaps with something like: "Cain, your brother Abel has asked you to join us today, do you have any idea why he's brought you here?" Allow Cain to answer, and this will begin an extemporaneous conversation between the two characters.

Case Study:
Adam and Eve; The Fruit of the Poisonous Tree

After determining the text you will utilize for your Bibliodrama it is important to slowly read the text several times. Consider the context and mindfully listen to the questions that arise for you as you examine the white fire. Who is present in the scene described, either explicitly or implicitly? Where does the scene take place, imagine what the landscape looks like, and what other objects, persons or animals may be present or close by. Begin to compile a list of these things. For example, looking at 3 Genesis 1–19, we first encounter a serpent, and we know Adam, Eve and God are all present in the scenes described. We also have a tree, and a piece of fruit. Are there insects or other animals present, and can any other beings be imagined in this scene? Is Adam carrying a staff? In Bibliodrama each of these non-human things can be anthropomorphized and reversed roles with as a role moment. Each may also offer a different perspective into what's happening, thereby adding significant richness to the Bibliodrama. Finally, each character or thing offers participants a potential opportunity to step into the Scripture, not in one's own shoes, rather, in the "shoes" of another.

Considering your audience, what role moments appear to have the most potential? Said differently, which have the most white fire? Using this as your guide, and by way of example, let's start with Eve. Reverse roles with Eve, and in that role imagine looking around the Garden. What information might you have to share about what you "see" as you perceive this place in which you exist; information that is not in the text? Have you been to this place before? Have you beheld the tree? The fruit? Have you ever encountered this serpent before? What have you been doing, from the time of your creation until now? Do you ever get bored? What is it like for you as you stand here, (first person present tense) looking at this tree? Why are you here alone? Does Adam know you're gone? How did you learn about the forbidden fruit? The text does not answer this question, and yet you tell this to the serpent when he first begins to tempt you. The serpent does not tell you to share the fruit with Adam, why do you make this choice? What do you know of death? What do you think God meant when He told you if you ate of the fruit you would die?

Now, reverse roles with the tree, have you met Eve before? How long have you been here, in this place? Do you have an understanding of who God is? How do you feel when Eve is in your presence? What is it like for you as you listen to the serpent speak to Eve? If you could speak to Eve what would you say?

Adam certainly has his own perspective of what's happened and what is happening. With the exception of the moment the apple is shared with him, the Scripture provides the reader with very little information about where he is before, during and after these events, and prior to his denial in verse 10 he says nothing. In other words, there is plenty of "white fire" as it relates to his role. Thinking of the context, what do you want to know that Adam can tell you? For example, to the role of Adam; why did God say that it was not good for you to be alone? When you are in the Garden, are you always with Eve? Who told Eve about the fruit? Do you see Eve eat the fruit? (If so) what is it like for you as you watch Eve eat the fruit? When Eve offers you the fruit, why do you say yes?

Once you have compiled a list of roles and a list of possible questions, the next step is to assemble it all into a cohesive whole, one that will flow from beginning to end. Consider the amount of time allotted to you and consider how long each role moment may take to complete. In part this will be a function of the number of participants, the amount of participation, and the way you facilitate each role moment.

With experience, you might also consider more complicated or sophisticated combinations of role moments. In the Garden scene we have a tree, a serpent, Adam, Eve and God. How are each of them arranged in the scene? Asking group members to create a physical space and placing themselves into it is called a sculpture. Sculptures can further deepen the participant's experience of literally feeling as if they are part of the scripture rather simply reading it. Encounters between two characters in the Bible are also exciting possibilities. After being thrust out of the Garden, what might the conversation between Adam and Eve sound like? Encounters are not necessarily confined by time. Would Adam have anything to say to Cain? These more advanced forms of Bibliodrama should not be attempted until the facilitator has much experience with directing many different role moments from many different stories with many different audiences. Additionally, Bibliodrama books and workshops are available to help you learn and practice new Bibliodrama skills.

Facilitation Through Interviewing and Echoing

After you've introduced yourself and described Bibliodrama to the group, it's time to begin your action. Start with your first role moment. "Eve, allow yourself to imagine that you are in the center of the Garden, what is it like for you as you stand here looking at this tree?" The question hangs there in the silence and as the facilitator your anxiety may be begin to peak. You may even find a parallel process happening, as Eve perceives the tree perhaps she too is feeling a similar anxiety arising out of the unknown. Sure enough, as the participants begin to think about this question, and begin to imagine themselves as Eve, out of the silence, the first brave participant will eventually offer a response. As the facilitator you must always thankfully and fully embrace what is offered. Otherwise, participants will feel discouraged, and the group's spontaneity will be quashed. Remember, there is no agenda, no correct interpretation, and no right or wrong answers. It is important that you demonstrate your gratitude to the participant, and to do this by carefully honoring what is said. You do this by repeating their words back and emphasizing what has been offered. This form of facilitated listening is in this context called "echoing" and is a way for the facilitator to assist group members in more fully "voicing their parts."[21] As Eve the first participant may say, in response to the question about encountering the forbidden fruit: "it's scary." To help the group understand the importance to role-taking of speaking in the first person present tense, the facilitator may offer "I feel scared," to which the participant will respond "I feel scared by this tree." In response the facilitator may offer the echo statement; "Yes, it's scary because this is a new experience for me." The participant who said "it's scary" may then continue with the dialog, and incorporate the echo, "I've been here before, but I'm scared because I've never thought about eating the fruit, and for some reason in the moment I feel drawn to it." Another participant may then offer a different perspective; "I'm not scared, in fact standing here in the presence of this tree makes me feel powerful" to which you may respond "yes, it's as if I am somehow joining in the power of the tree, we are somehow joined together." Your responses echo what has been offered, but also offers an elaboration that helps deepen the experience for the participant and for the group as they process what is taking place. Remember also that the mirror and window is always at work. As you elaborate, you are always thankful for the participation while simultaneously being careful to neither correct nor attempt to guide the participants to what you think is a more appropriate interpretation of the text. Exercise caution and be mindful that there may be what you believe is an academically correct interpretation as well as a second interpretation that you think is correct because of your own transference. Be mindful of what is coming up for you in this work, and be forever willing to bracket this transference in service to the group. This is a group process, and there is no right and wrong. Your being ever open and appreciative to what

---

21 Pitzele, pg. 42.

is offered by the group will create safety, help move the action along and will invite others to join in.

Once a participant has accepted a role the facilitator can also enhance the participant's embrace of the role with thoughtful questioning. This is similar to but also different from echoing, and involves the facilitator interviewing the role-taker by asking questions of the character, being careful to always encourage the participant to answer, in first person present tense, in role. In a Bibliodrama from the Book of Ruth, the character of Ruth might be interviewed relative to the scene in which the story takes place. This scene-setting will allow Ruth to become more fully enveloped by the Bibliodramatic trance. You may ask Ruth, in first person present tense: "Ruth, I'd like you to look down at your feet and tell us what type of shoes you are wearing?" If the answer is "I don't know" then you may cajole the participant to use their imagination and remind them that there's no right or wrong answer. "I'm wearing sandals." Always embrace the answer positively; "Yes, and are these new sandals, or are they old and worn?" As you question Ruth, consider moving for the periphery to core, such that you begin with factual thinking questions while moving progressively to questions involving more emotionally-based questions. Ruth, what are you thinking as you bring the wheat and barley home from the field? This mixed question invites Ruth to move from the head to the heart. A question about the heart may follow, such as "what are you feeling as you are lying in the bed of Boaz?"

A note on playing God

The Bible is replete with conversations between God and people. Even if no conversation takes place, it's fair to say that the entire text concerns God's relationship to and interaction with people. Naturally then it should occur that God might play a "part" in Bibliodrama. If the role of God is being considered, then the facilitator must be sensitive to how participants might view this role. Some might consider it sacrilege. Even those more open to this role might feel trepidation at the thought of playing God. Because the first rule of Bibliodrama is that all participants are always free to say "no" to any request made of them, if a person expresses any form of resistance, then the facilitator may either gently explore the resistance, or simply allow this participant to pass altogether. Also, participants can always opt-out. Nevertheless, as the leader, thought should be given to the preferences, assumed or known, of all participants, and if it is possible that even one person might object to this embodying of the incarnate, then this God-role should be left unexplored. Also, when God does play a part, role reversal can be very helpful. As the name implies, role reversal occurs when the players of two different roles reverse with one another. The person playing Abraham plays God, and the person playing God plays Abraham. This psychodramatic tool allows the person playing Abraham to respond to him or herself in the role of God. This is particularly helpful when a question is asked of God by a different character. Role-reversal allows the participant asking God the question to become God who then gives the answer. Role-reversal is also appropriate when a person, in role, feels ashamed or otherwise disciplined by the God role. The role reversal will allow a working through of his or her shame and may provide a deeper insight into the fuller nature of a forgiving God.

Concluding the Bibliodrama

Once the action had begun it is not always easy to determine how and when to end. Provided you have created a comprehensive outline of your Bibliodrama before you have begun, you will have an idea of what the last role moment will be, but that's not the same as deciding where to end. Bibliodrama is most often co-created group work, and therefore, you should always be willing to abandon the "script" if favor of the place the group's spontaneity takes you. You should always follow rather than lead the action. However, it's always good to leave when the action "balloon" is still full. If all the air has been drained out so too will be the energy of the group. Be sure and leave the role moment during a time of excitement and activity. Knowing the difference between too much and too little will come with practice. Also, be aware of the fatigue of empathy that takes place while facilitating and roll taking. Be mindful and caretaking when it comes to the needs of the group and the energy levels you are able to both produce and perceive.

Closing, de-roling/sharing/reviewing/confidentiality

Once the action has ended it's important to always leave time for closure. Undoubtedly participants will have been impacted, sometimes deeply, by what has taken place, and it's important to allow the group members to share with one another what the process was like for them. Also, to share what they learned about the story and perhaps too what they learned about themselves. In the process of closure there are several steps to consider. First, the participant's taking of Bibliodramatic roles is often a powerful experience. The role enters the body and has the potential to "stick" unless the participants are invited to de-role, meaning leaving the role behind, stepping out of the skin of the character and back into one's own skin. This is an essential part of closure. At the conclusion of the Bibliodrama ask participants to de-role by saying "I am not [character's name] I am [participant's name]." This de-rolling can be accompanied by a gesture, a physical taking off of the skin of the character, such as unzipping the role, and climbing out of the character's skin, while saying "I am not Ruth I am Joanne." Participants may use their imagination relative to how to de-role, or you may simply ask them to "stand up, shake off the role, then sit back down as yourself again, and state your name to the group."

As part of the closing, you may wish to allow participants to say a final word to, or pray for the characters. This sharing is done not from the role of the character but rather from one's own role. One way to do this is with the empty chair. Place empty chairs in the room for each character and invite participants to give their final goodbyes. Pitzele also suggests a closing exercise where, as facilitator, you ask participants to close their eyes, and imagine that all the characters "we have brought here from the Bible are returning home." Have the group open their eyes, hold up a Bible and then tell the group that the characters have all "gone home" back to their place in the Bible.[22] In this time of Bible phone apps, you might instead hold up your phone, but this has less power than an actual book. Also, you might designate an empty chair as representative of the Bible, tell the group that this chair is the Bible, or a portal back to the Bible, and suggest that the characters are all returning "here" pointing to the chair.

Participants can now be asked to share what the experience has been like for them. It's important to explain the parameters of sharing. These include that sharing is not an opportunity to critique how a role was played by another person, or to offer advice, but rather, to share only what the experience was like for them; what did you learn about the story we explored and what, if anything, did you learn from the experience about your own story?

Before ending your work with the group explain to them that the process of Bibliodrama typically unfolds over a period of time during and even after the work is done. Invite participants to review the work and the story with you after the Bibliodrama, or to contact you outside the group for further discussions. This is an important part of accepting the role of Bibliodrama facilitator.

As has been stated, Bibliodrama is not designed as or intended to be therapy. Nevertheless, the mirror is always at work, and participants will begin to see their own stories as being reflected in the Biblical narrative, and vice versa. During the Bibliodrama participants might share something personal, including their feelings, or something about their own lives, with the larger group. When this happens, it is important to protect the confidentiality of the group and of the individual by seeking a pledge from group members. Explain to the participants that during the action or sharing group members have shared things with the group that they may not wish be shared outside the group. For this reason, group members are told that they may not discuss others participation in the Bibliodrama with anyone, including family or friends. They may discuss their own experiences, their own learning and interpretations with anyone they wish, but they may not disclose to anyone outside the group anything shared

---

22 Pitzele page 204.

by other participants about their own feelings or their own stories. Be sure to have each person acknowledge this before ending.

A note on the healing aspects of Bibliodrama

Those of us raised with a spiritual tradition at home can often ascribe some level of toxicity to whatever it is that we associate with or think of when we contemplate this compilation of books often referred to as the Old and New Testaments. Also, through the ages, religion has sometimes been used, by some people, as a source of control. And, some people brought up in certain faith traditions may associate with the Bible strong feelings of shame, guilt and judgment. For many these feelings from childhood have left trauma scars that are deeply entrenched. Additionally, while the soap-box standing, placard wearing, Bible thumping, fire-and-brimstone preacher may bring some to God, such an approach to the Biblical texts causes many others to flee.

In order for the Bible to be no longer viewed as the nidus of our internalized shame, guilt and judgment and thereby to be utterly transformed into place where one finds healing, inclusion and inspiration, one must be freed from the ways it's been made toxic for them in one's past. It's as if a spiritual piece of us is snagged on a bramble bush. In Bibliodrama the enactor has the opportunity to recreate the past, and to correct this trauma, thereby changing their spiritual history such that there is a disentanglement of the spiritual snag from the bramble, thereby allowing one to move more freely in the their spiritual life.[23]

Once it is has been so cleansed, the Bible can the Bible can instead become a nidus for wisdom and wellbeing. Consequently, in its ideal form, Bibliodrama can serve as a powerful way to cleanse the Bible of this past trauma and/or toxicity so that the Bible can anew become a repository for the surplus reality of one's life-experiences — a place for us to see our lives reflected in the master archetypes presented in ancient stories and scriptural characters.

Once transformed, the Bible becomes a life-affirming, life-giving medium — one that gives greater meaning and guidance to our lives while simultaneously allowing us to better understand the world and our place within it. This spiritual trauma-repair and toxic cleansing comes not just from the catharsis of a deep character enactment, but also from a freeing of the imagination, and in the ability to redo a scene from one's spiritual past in a wished-for way. This healing often simply comes from the role-playing where participants allow, by accident or design, the Bible characters to do the healing. In this idealized way the Bibliodrama facilitator can take on the role of spiritual healer, and in the end, the Bibliodrama group offers not just a place to experience the Bible, but

---

23 Gracia, A. & Buchanen, D.R. (2000). Psychodrama. In P. Lewis & D.R. Johnson, (Eds.). *Current Approaches in Drama Therapy*. Springfield, IL: Charles C. Thomas Publishing, LTD., at pg. 174.

also a place of respite and healing where one becomes vulnerable to one's own life experiences and spirituality.

Patrick Barone

Patrick Barone, J.D., C.P., P.A.T., is a Michigan trial lawyer and author who began experimenting with Bibliodrama in 2010 while training to become a Board-Certified Practitioner of Psychodrama. Since this time, Patrick has trained extensively in Bibliodrama with his friend Dr. Peter Pitzele and currently leads Bibliodrama workshops designed to facilitate subject matter competency and to inspire personal and spiritual growth. Patrick has also presented and taught Bibiodrama at the American Society of Group Psychotherapy and Psychodrama's annual conference.

In 2014 Patrick co-founded the Michigan Psychodrama Center with Elizabeth Corby, Ph.D., C.P., P.A.T., and together they provide a wide variety of workshops and training opportunities, including week-long and weekend intensives. They also co-lead a bi-monthly psychodrama therapy group, and a once monthly psychodrama training group, and regularly co-lead Bibliodrama workshops.

Patrick also uses psychodrama and sociometry infused methods in the courtroom, in his role as a business consultant and when teaching trial skills. Finally, he introduces law students to psychodrama in his capacity as an adjunct professor at the Western Michigan University/Thomas M. Cooley Law School.

For more information about Bibliodrama training and workshops, business consulting, or to register for personal growth or psychodrama training opportunities, please visit *michiganpsychodramacenter.com*. Mr. Barone can be reached directly at *baronep@outlook.com*.

Souldrama®

The Need to Develop our Spiritual Intelligence

Connie Miller

Today Spiritual Intelligence is considered by many to be the most important of our intelligences and has the power to transform our life, civilization, the planet and the course of history.[1] How do we move from immature ego-driven behaviors to more mature higher self-driven — from competition to co-creation? How can we develop the ability to hear the voice of our higher self, to understand and transcend the voice of our ego, and to be guided by profound wisdom and compassion? How can the group be used to provide the corrective therapeutic factor to reframe trauma and move people past the resistance in their own lives toward their higher purpose and reunite them with their Spiritual Intelligence?

Souldrama® is an experiential group method that aligns all three of our intelligences, the rational, emotional and spiritual to move past the resistance in our lives, reunite the ego and soul and ignite our spiritual intelligence.[2] Multiculturally, it crosses diversity by putting spirituality into action within the group promoting cross-cultural growth and understanding through connection, creativity, and spontaneity. This new holistic group action model was published as a new action model for the 12 step recovery program.[3] As an international program, it has been presented many times for psychologists and faculties in Indonesia, Holland, Portugal, Brazil, Lithuania, Greece, Italy, Latvia, Holland, England, India, and Mexico. This article relates the seven experiential stages of Souldrama as a holistic experiential cross-cultural action model for group therapy.

---

1 Buzan. 2002. p.xii

2 Miller, 2008, 2010

3 Miller, 2013

"My soul you-are you there? I have returned, I am here again. I have shaken the dust of all the lands from my feet, and I have come to you, I am with you. After long years of long wandering, I have come to you again . . .

Should I tell you everything I have seen, experienced, and drunk in? Or do you not want to hear about all the noise of life and the world? But one thing you must know: the one thing I have learned is that one must live this life. This life is the way, the long sought-after way to the unfathomable, which we call divine.

There is no other way; all other ways are false paths. I found the right way, it led me to you, to my soul. I return, tempered and purified. Do you still know me? How long the separation lasted! Everything has become so different. And how did I find you?

How strange my journey was! What words should I use to tell you on what twisted paths a good star has guided me to you? Give me your hand, my almost forgotten soul. How warm the joy at seeing you again, you long is avowed soul.

Life has led me back to you. Let us thank the life I have lived for all the happy and all the sad hours, for every joy, for every sadness. My soul, my journey should continue with you. I will wander with you and ascend to my solitude."

—Carl Jung, *Red Book*

We are all agents of change. The task of this generation is to cut through the illusion that we live in separate worlds. Today, if we want to change systems, we have to change human behavior; however, human behavior is not so readily changed. The primary responsibility of a real leader today is to change the motivations that drive behavior, enabling people to achieve real transformation. The only way the world can be transformed is for individuals to make changes in individual levels of consciousness.[4] A truly intelligent person is not one who can merely memorize words and numbers; it is someone who can relate "intelligently" to all the opportunities, simulations and problems provided by the environment. We can develop our rational intelligence with the internet and computers by ourselves; we can access our Emotional Intelligence by ourselves; however, we cannot develop our Spiritual Intelligence alone for the key words here are to relate and to interact.

---

4 Miller, 2010

Today people are looking globally to find a sense of meaning, social and spiritual connectedness. To do so requires the development of the capacity for creativity, and that in turn involves the integration of language, rationality, perception, intuition, emotion, imagery, and the felt sense of the body in action. In other words, we need to balance the left hemisphere of the brain, or our rational intelligence, which deals more with language and reason, with the right hemisphere or our spiritual intelligence, intuition, imagery, emotion, and action, bridging the gap between the right and left hemispheres by working through the expression of our feelings, our emotional intelligence. It is then that we can awaken our higher purpose and create spiritually intelligent leadership.

Research in creativity in the last century has shown that both left- and right-brain functioning are needed for optimal mental flexibility, especially that which has to include considerations of human relationships, morale, motivation, and a sense of team spirit or community. Souldrama is one holistic method that balances our rational (left brain), emotional (feelings) and right brain (spiritual intelligence) functions. There are lots of techniques to work through resistance. Some work well. Others do not work at all. As mental health professionals, we address the psychological aspects of a client's problems but largely overlook the significance of their spirituality. That is because spirituality was not part of our training and we tend to think of spirituality and therapy as mutually exclusive—a kind of church-and-state mentality.

However, spirituality is not a synonym for religion. It is an energy that defines the way we view our world. Moreover, when we access this energy, it empowers us with self-faith and courage to resolve problems and move ahead. This action-oriented multidisciplinary training system adds a psychospiritual element to psychodrama called Souldrama, a process that aligns the ego and soul to enable us to reach our higher selves by incorporating the new model of spiritual intelligence.

Souldrama® is a new transpersonal psycho-spiritual action technique that aligns ego and soul and incorporates the new concept of spiritual intelligence to enable us to reach our higher selves. This process combines mind, body, and spirit to create therapeutic energy within a group process. By doing this, the soul becomes a co-creator in a person's life, and this is the soul's mission: co-creation.

Souldrama is an adjunct to psychodrama for treating such issues as co-dependency, depression, addictions and low self-esteem. By incorporating spirituality into the therapeutic process, Souldrama helps people to overcome these blocks to a happier, more fulfilled life. Through myth and metaphor, the client goes through seven stages of faith or spiritual development into higher states of consciousness. Through the spark of spirituality, the clients can overcome problems ranging from relationship and prosperity problems to reach the higher purpose of their soul.

Spiritual intelligence allows a human being to be creative, to change the rules and to alter situations. It addresses those who feel that something is missing in their lives. When we ignite our spiritual intelligence, we learn how to go on a personal journey to embrace spirituality, develop intuition and bring it into our everyday lives for the ultimate fulfillment of serving others. Rational intelligence asks "What can I get?" spiritual intelligence asks "How can I serve?"

Investigations have shown that the more spiritually intelligent we become, the more the childlike qualities of innocence we have, such as cheerfulness, joyfulness, spontaneity, enthusiasm, and adventure.[5] Spirituality is an essential component of a holistic approach to life and work. It finds expression in creativity and all forms of the arts.

SQ involves connecting and understanding others. It is about how we behave—how we make decisions and act—in the everyday, stressful world of interacting with difficult people and situations.

Levin (2000), in her book *Spiritual Intelligence: Awakening the power of your spirituality and intuition*, theorizes spiritual intelligence as "a marriage of spirituality and intelligence."[6] Miller describes spiritual intelligence as an alignment of the ego and soul.[7] Spiritual development involves regularly shedding our old roles, the competition to be clever, attachments, and identities to make room for expansion into a larger perspective and identity.

Human beings grow spiritually by repairing the bond with his/her soul following disconnection, in other words realigning the ego with the soul. Healing that split is the process of integration, individuation, self-actualization, transformation. Inner resources such as innocence, trust, spontaneity, courage, and self-esteem were lost, stolen, or abandoned in traumatic moments early in our personal history. Retrieving the inner resources that coped with those traumatic events restores our connection with the soul.

Souldrama as an experiential transpersonal group process takes us through seven stages of growth or transformation, each stage building upon the other, aligning our ego and soul and balancing all three intelligences, IQ, EQ, and SQ. The seven sequential doors of Souldrama indicate the seven intrinsic qualities needed to comprise our spiritual intelligence[8]: Faith, Truth, Compassion, Love, Humility, Gratitude, Inspiration. The rhythm of human development, including spiritual development, involves regularly shedding our old roles, competition to be clever, attachments, and identities to make room for expansion into

---

5 Buzan. 2002. p.xii

6 Nasel, 2004. p.67

7 Miller, 2007, 2008, 2010, 2013

8 Ibid.

a larger perspective and identity. Thus, we move through the doorways of our rational intelligence challenging ourselves to regain faith, trust, and truth and clarity of our higher purpose. The ego surrenders itself to an unknown force that carries it into an infinitely expanding world so that we can become co-creators with God. The doorways to our Emotional Intelligence require us to move through the forgiveness and love to develop compassion and unconditional self-love.

The strength of character, resilience, determination, deep trust all come from repair of disruption in an intimate relationship, not through eliminating any disruption. Likewise, the growth of the human being spiritually is achieved through the repair of the bond with his/her soul following disconnection (miscoordination). "Trauma acts to increase spiritual development if that development is defined as an increase in the search for purpose and meaning."[9]

Spiritual Intelligence (SQ) is defined by Wigglesworth, C. (2012) as the ability to behave with wisdom and compassion, while maintaining inner and outer peace (equanimity), regardless of the circumstances. The quality of wisdom includes knowing the limits of our knowledge and includes values such as courage, integrity, intuition, and compassion.

Levin (2000) proposed the development of spiritual intelligence requires a change in perception and perspective (involving one's intuition), which provide a new basis for motives and intention that consequently shape behavior. Levin suggests that the development of SQ requires the recognition of our interconnection to all of life, and the capacity to utilize perceptual powers beyond the five senses including our intuition, which is seen as another level of consciousness and intelligence beyond analytical, linear, and rational thought.[10] Spiritual maturity, she suggests, is characterized by concern for the common good and involvement in the well-being of the greater whole.[11]

Ken Wilbur (2000) writes about a process of psychospiritual development that we are all going through, both as individuals and as members of a historically located culture. The three broad sections, the pre-personal, the personal, and the transpersonal, can be related to the three broad phases used in Souldrama that are necessary to access our spiritual intelligence: the rational, the emotional, and the spiritual. Each of these phases, both in Wilbur's model and in Souldrama, are sequential and depend upon the development and completion of the previous phases. The three phases are separate, and in each, we have to revise our notions of who we are and what kind of person we were.

Wisdom is the ability to look through a person when others can only look at them. Wisdom slows down the thinking process and makes it more

9 Decker, 1993, p. 33

10 Amram.2009. p.45

11 Nasel, 2004. p.67

organic; synchronizing it with intuition. Wisdom helps us make better judg-
ments regarding decisions and makes us less judgmental. Wisdom understands
without knowing and accepting without understanding. Wisdom is recognizing
what's important to other people and knowing that other people are of the
utmost importance to you. Wisdom is both a starting point and a conclusion.

Besides logic and language, we need a method to integrate the realms of
intuition, emotion, imagination, and the subtle but profound feelings of the
body in action, doing rather than just passively watching and hearing. The use
of action methods in a group is a holistic process, integrating many dimensions
of life; engaging in action methods promote thinking and living more holisti-
cally. Action methods can help generate types of thinking that reflects greater
mental and emotional maturity and flexibility to move from the past to reach
for a more promising future. When action methods are added to the group
process, it dissolves passivity and focuses the consciousness of the members
on their interactions, which in turn channels and enhances the energy within a
group. Instead of just verbalization, action methods help participants become
more present more aware and more conscious. Consciousness makes our interactions intentional and gives greater visibility to our inner worlds and greater
energy to our words. Action also helps to clarify our thoughts and feelings by
providing internal and external feedback. Action is international—it is worth
a thousand words and crosses all cultures; it counters cultural tendencies to
compartmentalize and judge others.

No matter where we live, a large and essential part of our spiritual journey
is the power and the fellowship of the group. Our need to talk, interact and be
with each other is part of our development. One way to be sensitive to others
and make our intentions conscious is to examine ourselves in relationship to
others. A group is one of the most feasible methods for initiating, improving
and evaluating connections.

The dramatic nature of psychodrama builds group cohesion and support.
Souldrama gives structure to the transformational process that aligns and
balances the rational, emotional and spiritual intelligences, removing the
blocks that keep us separated from our divine selves. During this process, group
members begin to hold one another responsible for their behavior. Meanwhile,
participants also begin to recognize their responsibility for change. By taking
responsibility, individuals become empowered—a critical step in personal
transformation. The group focuses on involvement, belonging and aspects of
relationships. Being in a group brings up concerns about ethics, conscience,
and awareness of one another.[12] There is a feeling of justice because of the
love of someone else or an ideal. This aspect of justice of conscience is the
basis of love for one another and makes us human with the ability to reflect,

---

12 Miller, 2010

create, and form boundaries. These qualities counter cultural tendencies to compartmentalize and judge others. Our families of origin were not necessarily a chosen group. The idea of good group cohesion comes from giving people choices.[13] When we make poor choices, we need therapy, or we learn what we need to for our soul to grow.

J.L. Moreno, the father of group psychotherapy, believed that what is learned in action must be unlearned in action and what is learned in a relationship, must be unlearned in a relationship. This goal of undoing problematic patterns of thinking, feeling and behaving through the vehicles of action and relearning new, more adequate ways of experiencing and expressing the self in a Psychodrama is the action methodology for the science of action. Often it is described as a laboratory for learning how to love, where the patient's inner world can match the outer world. It is a place where love and acceptance of the worst aspects of ourselves can be discovered, where we can experience our humanity and learn how to be compassionate toward others.

Zerka Moreno (1965) has described the group as the "double for life," saying that group consciousness reflects the spiritual and moral ideals of society and is the foundation of our society's rules and laws. In a group, we expose our darker sides and experience the cathartic effect of being re-admitted to the group. J.L. Moreno believed that there is no authority than what comes from the entire group itself; each person of the group is the therapeutic agent of the other. Within the environment of a supportive group, members can share feelings with others and realize their experiences are universal to all humans. Group members are fully accepted despite their weaknesses, feelings of shame, and isolation subside. Transformational group methods like psychodrama facilitate the revelation that others have similar problems thereby reducing isolation and alienation.[14]

Research into the phenomenon of SQ reveals the fact that spiritual intelligence allows collective thought or wholeness in thinking. Consequently, those who employ this particular type of intelligence do not just focus on themselves as the basis for deciding on particular decisions. Instead, they would consider the effect that their actions have on other persons. This type of intelligence makes individuals aware of the fact that they are connected to other human beings. It also highlights the fact that there is a bigger picture at play.[15]

As we come together and work together to awaken our higher purpose, we bring the focus of our attention on truth, beauty, love, and service and delve deeper into that awareness. To realize our highest potential, we must be

---

13 Z. Moreno, 1965
14 Miller, 2010
15 Sisk & Torrance, 2001

sensitive and compassionate to other people.[16] Spiritually intelligent people behave with love, wisdom, and compassion. Wisdom is the highest stage of development of the intellect (head). Compassion is the most elevated stage of Emotional Intelligence (heart). The group behavior which results from such highly developed holistic model leads us forward to our Spiritual Intelligence and helps us to become good spiritual leaders that can lead with an inner calm.[17]

Zohar and Marshall (2000) claim that spiritual intelligence is cultivated through the soul and not the brain. Spiritual intelligence can heal one's wounds and complete a person's being. Spiritual intelligence surpasses the conscious mind and goes beyond the ego. This sort of intelligence has nothing to do with what society or culture dictates. Instead, it advocates tapping into our intuition and our deep of sense of meaning.

It is imperative for those who plan on cultivating spiritual awareness to look deeply into themselves.

Buzan (2002) introduced ten ways to enhance SQ including:

- Getting the 'Big Picture.'
- Explore Your Values. Your values and principles determine your behavior and have a massive effect on the probability of your success in life.
- Your Life Vision and Purpose. With a clear and defined purpose, your life will gain meaning and direction, and you will become healthier, stronger and more confident.
- Compassion: Understanding Yourself and Others
- Give and Receive. Encompass charity and gratitude.
- The Power of Laughter. Laughter is a vital quality of Spiritual Intelligence, and benefits us in many ways, including reducing stress levels and generally leading to a more cheerful and happier life.
- Onward to the Child's Playground. Investigations have shown that the more Spiritually Intelligent you become, the more the childlike qualities of innocence you will have;[18] and also cheerfulness, joyfulness, spontaneity, enthusiasm, and adventure feeling increases in your life.
- The Power of Ritual. Rituals provide stability and opportunity for regeneration and strengthens a sense of connection with oneself and others.
- Peace. Cultivate your inner peace through the practice of techniques such as contemplation and meditation.
- All You Need Is Love![19]

---

16 Miller, 2010
17 Wigglesworth, 2006
18 Buzan. 2002. p.xii
19 Ibid, p.xvii

Sternberg writes in his book *Successful Intelligence*: Successfully intelligent people realize that the environment in which they find themselves may or may not be able to make the most of their talents. They actively seek an environment where they can not only do successful work but make a difference. They create opportunities rather than let opportunities be limited by circumstances in which they happen to find themselves. Zohar and Marshall (2000) claim that spiritual intelligence is cultivated through the soul and not the brain. Spiritual intelligence can heal one's wounds and complete a person's being. Spiritual intelligence surpasses the conscious mind and goes beyond the ego. This sort of intelligence has nothing to do with what society or culture dictates. Instead, it advocates tapping into our intuition and our deep of sense of meaning.

Today we look for our individual and collective experience as we have created it and search again for the meaning of life. We must take a page from within our therapist tool-box and look for ways to recreate ourselves. I believe our creativity holds the key to our life dream, purpose, or calling. I, like many others, have placed many obstacles between my creative gifts and myself. Creativity, for me, is critical to success in that it is the ability to manifest what has real meaning and purpose for us. When creativity is shut down in childhood to stay safe, we remain in jobs and relationships that we have outgrown, that no longer serve us. When we learn to listen to the inner voice of our spirit as opposed to the internalized critical voice, we can follow the voice that leads us toward fulfilled, creative lives. That voice is difficult to hear if we are struggling with learned beliefs, trying to control the outcome of situations and enmeshed in expectations of the way things "should" turn out.

Consequently, the concept of spiritual intelligence is quite viable because it is the only type of intelligence that allows us to derive a sense of life fulfillment.[20] We want to be happy, we all want to be loved. Can we be successful if we are not truly happy? I would argue not and that a balance of IQ, EQ and SQ are necessary for a happy and prosperous life.

Connie Miller

Connie Miller, ACS, MS, TEP, LPC, NCC is the owner and founder of both the Spring Lake Heights Counseling Center and the International Institute for Souldrama®. A highly sought-after speaker, trainer and workshop presenter, she has been practicing individual, marital, family and group psychotherapy for adults and children for over 25 years.

Connie is a trainer, educator, and practitioner of group psychotherapy and psychodrama and is renowned in her field as a trainer of action methods, innovator, author, lecturer created Souldrama in 1997, which is a seven-stage

---

20 Gardner, 1999

process of spiritual transformation that integrates psychology, spirituality, and creativity enabling individuals to move forward in their lives, especially after years of therapy.

Connie has written two books and many articles. She is the creator of the new action model for the 12 step recovery program and recipient of the T. Duffy ACA and ASGPP award for innovation and creativity. Her work published in numerous professional journals and several languages. Her most recent publication, *Starve the Ego: Feed the Soul*, is published in four languages. All profits go to a scholarship fund for training psychologists and pastoral counselors in Indonesia.

Connie has guest-lectured at universities, professional conventions, and conducted workshops in England, Italy, Greece, Portugal, India, Italy, Indonesia, Brazil, Portugal, Holland, Lithuania, Lativa and throughout The United States. To schedule an appointment with Connie or to request information about upcoming workshops, email *connie@souldrama.com* or visit *souldrama.com*

References

Amram, Y. (2009). *The Contribution of Emotional and Spiritual Intelligences To Effective Business Leadership*. Doctoral Dissertation, Institute of Transpersonal Psychology, California, Palo Alto.

Buzan, T. (2002). *The power of spiritual intelligence: 10 ways to tap into your spiritual genius*. Australia: HarperCollins.

Gardner, H. (1999): *Intelligence Reframed: Multiple Intelligences for the 21st Century*; New York. Basic Books.

Jung, C.G. *The Red Book: Liber Novus 2009* Published October 7th 2009 by W. W. Norton & Company (first published 2009).

Levin, M. *Spiritual Intelligence: Awakening the Power of Your Spirituality and Intuition*. Hodder and Stoughton.

Miller, C. (2000). The technique of Souldrama and its applications. *The International Journal of Action Methods*, 52, (4), 173–186.

Miller, C. (2007). *Psychodrama: Advances in theory and practice*. In C. Baim, J. Burmeister, M. Maciel (Eds.), Advancing theory in therapy: Psychodrama, spirituality and Souldrama (pp. 189–200). London: Routledge Press.

Miller, C. (2008). Spirituality in Action. *Journal for Creativity in Mental Health*. Volume: 3 Issue: 2 ISSN: 1540–1383 Pub Date: 7/31/2008. Taylor Francis Group.

Miller, C. (2010). *Starve the Ego: Feed the Soul: Souldrama: Ignite your spiritual intelligence*. Self Published. Lulu.com.

Miller, C. (2013) *Integrating Two Models for the Treatment of Addictions: Souldrama®️ and the Twelve Step Recovery in Action.* (To be published April 2013 by Taylor and Francis) The Journal for Groups in Addictions.

Moreno, J. L. (1971). Psychodrama. In H. I. Kaplan, & B. J. Sadock (Eds.), *Comprehensive group psychotherapy* (pp. 460–500). Baltimore, MD: Williams & Wilkins.

Moreno, Z. (1965). Psychodramatic rules, techniques and adjunctive methods. *Group Psychotherapy*, 18, 73–86.

Nasel, D, D. (2004). *Spiritual Orientation in Relation to Spiritual Intelligence: A consideration of traditional Christianity and New Age/individualistic spirituality.* Doctoral Dissertation, University of South Australia, Australia.

Sisk, D.A. and Torrance, E. P. (2001): *Spiritual Intelligence: Developing Higher Consciousness.* Buffalo, NY. Creative Education Foundation.

Wigglesworth, C. (2012) SQ21: *The 21 Skills of Spiritual Intelligence* (New York: Select Books, p.7.

Wilber, K. (2000). *Integral Psychology: Consciousness, Spirit, Psychology, Therapy.* Boston, Ma: Shambhala Publications.

Zohar, D., & Marshall, I. (2000): *Connecting with our Spiritual Intelligence* New York, Y.Y.: Bloomsbury Publishing.

Creative Realization Techniques

Saphira Linden

In this chapter, the application of action simulations and practices in Psychodrama and Drama Therapy are discussed in relation to various populations and goals. First, the process of conducting a spiritual retreat for self-realization is presented. Next, theater games programs with special needs students in the Boston schools are described. Out of that work, a participatory musical theater experience was created for the same population. Our theater company also worked with theater programs addressing racial unrest by bringing together high school adolescents from Boston and its suburbs and enacting their issues about ancestral immigration. Next, examples of using creative self-realization methods with executives and managers to resolve conflict in their organizations are discussed. Finally, the process of creating theatrical pageants to generate unity consciousness and encourage tolerance between religions, ethnicities, races and cultures using Drama Therapy and Psychodrama techniques is presented.

All of these programs are informed by a transpersonal or spiritual perspective that centers on seeing the strength rather than the pathology of a person, family, organization, or community. Our goal is to shift all whom we work with, including our theater casts, from their limited, conditioned sense of self to who they really are in their essential self. The core principles that have guided this work can be found below.

12 Principles of Transpersonal Drama Therapy and Psychodrama

1. Assuming Health Rather Than Pathology
2. Shifting One's Identity from a Limited Sense of Self to the Essential Self

3. Embodying/Roleplaying the Therapeutic Issues
4. Making the Unconscious Conscious through Symbolic/Metaphorical Approaches
5. Working with Archetypes
6. Embracing Love While Holding All Emotions as Sacred
7. Creating a Sacred Space
8. Fostering an Experience of Interconnectedness and Unity
9. Seeking Mastery Through Self-Discipline
10. Achieving Balance
11. Identifying and Achieving Our Life Purpose
12. Creating Life as a Work of Art

Guided Alchemical Meditation Retreat

For thousands of years, spiritual seekers have engaged in retreats using a variety of meditation practices. They have often lived in seclusion, doing self-realization practices handed down by their teachers. Some traditional eastern retreats involve sitting on a mountain top, or in a cave or hut, for 40 days, repeating a mantra thousands of times each day, while eating very little or fasting. The retreat discussed here uses practices from various meditative traditions that have been adapted to western culture. Most often retreatants leave their ordinary lives for a period to go deeply within and do meditation practices offered by the retreat guide. The goal is to concentrate on one's inner life and experience realizations that enhance one's life in the world. We present here an example of a retreat that integrates traditional meditation practices using breath, sound and light, methods drawn from Psychodrama and Drama Therapy, dream work, music, journaling and drawing. The retreatant involved was a woman who was confronted with a variety of serious emotional and physical life challenges at that time.

Integrating Transformational Embodied Arts into Spiritual Retreat

In the early '70s, I studied Psychodrama with its founders, JL and Zerka Moreno, and learned Sufi meditation practices with Pir Vilayat Inayat Khan, head of Sufi Order International. All three teachers created forms and practices for students to work with, while at the same time they often broke their own rules, working intuitively and spontaneously. They gave me permission to experiment, explore as a theater artist, and work intuitively and spontaneously with all of the methods I was studying. I was also trained to work with dreams by Jungian analysts for many years. I was inspired to integrate all of these disciplines in working with clients, seekers, retreat guides, clergy, and therapists in training, as well as students, executives, and theater artists. I have been honored to facilitate numerous retreats and trainings based on these multi-faceted transformational processes.

The Sufi alchemical retreat process was developed by Pir Vilayat based on principles from the ancient alchemists. The first three stages include Hindu and Buddhist practices to take people into a state of unity consciousness. The next three stages, based on the practices of western religious traditions, bring retreatants back into their everyday lives with new perspectives.

During an alchemical meditation retreat that I took in the Alps, I had a dream that revealed some challenging relationship issues and psychological patterns that needed to be dealt with. This pivotal learning experience motivated me to begin to integrate psychological depth work with classical meditation practices when guiding people on retreats.

· · ·

The following is part of an exchange between the author as retreat guide and the retreatant, both during the retreat and also in reflecting on it after its conclusion. This account includes some of the practices that I offered during the 28-day Sufi alchemical meditation retreat, and their results.

It is my feeling that every retreat guide, like every therapist, brings to their work what they know how to do best and what they are guided to do in the moment. Based on my initial interview, in which the retreatant described bouts of depression, panic attacks, and marital disruption, I felt that the best approach would be to help her go into a deep exploration via an integration of meditation practices, dream work, and adapted creative arts modalities to work on the root causes of these conditions.

I asked the retreatant what her hope was for the retreat.

> **Retreatant (R):** I felt like my whole life was a mess. My goal was to find out what it was in myself that was creating all this pain. I sensed the way to get through this was to get away from everything and sink into the retreat process and let it do what it was going to do because I was completely overwhelmed.

> **Retreat Guide (RG):** "Let us call on the guidance of the ancient goddesses, as well as the masters, saints and prophets of the great religions, so that the feminine will come into the healing process as well." The retreatant was also directed to enter the consciousness of a spiritual guide with whom she felt closely attuned. Thus we created the sacred container for the retreat process.

I suggested that she try to remember one or two dreams every night. She told me that she has rarely remembered any dreams, but she would try. Interestingly, every single night she remembered one or two dreams. I found that helpful because the dream images often referred to some part of herself that was asking to be heard and revealed what was going on in her psyche. Dreams also give clues about pacing and about what she was actually ready to address. The dreams became a guiding light as I integrated the meditative retreat practices with the processing of the dreams—using writing, drawing and other creative arts to get at what the dreams revealed. The retreatant's inner guide and life challenges emerged at this time. As the dreams and the other practices continued, powerful healing and transformation occurred. It was quite wonderful to have the dreams guide us on how to best work in the context of the sacred vessel of the retreat.

Integrating Psychodrama's Role Reversal Practice into the Retreat

The retreatant was guided to explore the dream images through the "active imagination" process of Carl Jung. In this process, the dreamer has a dialogue with the images, and we then added the Psychodrama and Drama Therapy techniques of enactment and role reversal to see what would emerge by embodying those images, thereby revealing more inner material.

> **R:** What amazed me during this process was that I learned there is no such thing as a nonsense dream. Left to my own devices, I never would have figured out the significance of these dream images. But you encouraged me to dig through the symbolism and find what my unconscious was really telling me. Every dream turned out to be pretty profound, even the ones that seemed trivial on the surface.

I encouraged the retreatant to share her earlier family challenges: "Why don't you say a little bit about what you were dealing with in your family system from early on?"

> **R:** My father was an untreated raging alcoholic. He was extremely violent. While I did not get the brunt of his anger directly, I witnessed a lot of it with regular beatings of my mother and my brother. We had to lock our doors on a nightly basis to get away from him and his violence. One night, when I was nine, he pounded down a solid oak door with his fists in order to gain access to my room. I experienced an emotional white out. I was actually too frightened to feel fear. And certainly, underneath the fear is anger and a sense of invasion. I remembered exactly what happened, but I just didn't feel anything about it

at all. Intellectually, I knew this dissociation was at the root of the depression and the panic attacks and the somatization I was experiencing. I was also diagnosed with multiple sclerosis earlier, and while it has been fairly benign in my particular case, there were still issues I had to deal with as well. So that's the background that I came to you to help me heal.

One of the exercises that you gave me was to draw my father, but to draw him abstractly, energetically, to uncover different feelings about him. That was relatively easy, but writing about him was harder. Writing about his good qualities turned out to be a very short list. Then came the button-pushing qualities; this was a very long list, but it felt good to make it. Then I had to own as a part of myself both these good and evil qualities, a process of learning to embrace my own shadow. I had to embrace it and transform it by consciously exploring his personality traits inside of me, feeling more empowered to dis-identify with his rage and its effect on me and move ahead in my own life. This was not a comfortable exercise, but the benefits have been immeasurable. A lot of energy goes into unconsciously holding something we dread at bay. This exercise freed up that energy to be used for other more productive purposes.

As Marion Woodman, the extraordinary Jungian analyst, said, "It is important to deal with the rotten foundations so that the jewel that is hidden underneath all that debris can truly manifest." That's the jewel of our essential self, our soul qualities, that cannot be tarnished. Emphasizing this source of strength helps people to change their identity from their limited, abused sense of self to who they really are. Like with our retreatant, when this doesn't happen, it can hinder a person from being successful in her life, in work and in relationships.

The retreatant faced many obstacles that made it difficult to live in balance. Different arts exercises were given, supported by ancient breathing and sound practices, while sitting and walking, to help balance her energy. Sacred music and movement helped inspire meaningful realizations to come forth during the retreat. Poetry writing helped to concretize the retreatant's experience, while allowing unconscious material to surface. These practices allowed us to clear through issues and discover and explore the multi-faceted dimensions of her essential self. As the retreatant was aware and motivated to work on herself as part of the retreat process, she had several authentic self-realizations.[1]

Role reversal was also used in the following practice:

---

1 Linden, 2013

The Ideal Mentor and Nemesis Meditation and Simulation

The retreatant was directed through a meditative visualization process to enter the consciousness of an ideal mentor. This being may have qualities of the spiritual guide she had chosen earlier, but she was asked to approach this exercise freshly, and to visualize no one who she actually knew. To think about what that ideal mentor might say to her is a good exercise. But to actually enter into the body, heart, soul, and consciousness of that being can be much more profound. I encouraged the retreatant to draw the image she received in meditation, concretely or abstractly, to list the qualities of this ideal mentor, and then to embody this mentor and "role reverse" with that being and offer guidance to herself in the role of her mentor. This approach helped her to get in touch with her own wisdom self and view her challenging issues with a broader perspective.

The second part of the practice was to visualize her nemesis. Again, this is no one that she knows. She was invited to draw the image of that being from the meditation either concretely or abstractly. Again, she was instructed to list and draw the personality traits of this nemesis, and to embody this being as well, as a way of holding both the ideal and the shadow aspects. Then the retreatant had a dialogue between them. This helped the retreatant to own her source of strength, including the less apparent positive power she developed in response to her father's abuse of power.

> **R:** Prior to the retreat I was feeling really stuck creatively. The energy was flat and colorless, just like my feelings about what had happened in my past. But I found a single practice in the last days of the retreat to be the climax of a very long process. That experience broke the dam and opened my creativity. It was on the 26th day. I was repeating a powerful sound practice with movements attached to it, and my mind was flip-flopping all over the place. Unexpectedly, I felt an energy around me and a voice said, "Try to stay with it." So I went deeper and deeper into the sound and movement, and I began having this image that was like a dream only I was very awake. I walked into a cave with a man by my side. I saw a two-year-old baby who was chained to the wall of the cave. The cave was very dark and enclosed. He unchained the baby and brought her out into the light. She wasn't crying. She was emaciated and very close to death. And he just held her. It was at that point I started to cry and cry. That baby he was holding was me.
>
> The man walked back into the cave and I followed him. He held up a lantern and I could see children of all different ages chained to the walls of this cave. It occurred to me that every

time my mother was beaten or there was a traumatic event in my house another child was chained to the wall of the cave. They all started calling to me and crying and saying, "Feed me! Love me! Take care of me!" I turned to the man and asked, "How am I supposed to do this? There are so many of them! Where do I even start?" The man answered, "Write about them. Write about every single one. It's time you gave each child her voice."

It was through that process that I began to feel all of the feelings that were too overwhelming to feel when I was a child. I had spent twenty years taking retreats and had been through years of psychotherapy, and all that was to get to exactly this place. As of this writing, after exploring and reconciling who each of these traumatized children were inside of me, my marriage is now on solid ground. I'm falling in love with my husband all over again. I'm taking flying lessons and he's my flight instructor. The panic attacks are history. The depression is gone, and I feel much more integrated and whole and more of who I am than I ever was before.

RG: In this retreat model, the key is being able to get to what's below the surface consciously through engaging the practices that are designed to lead toward self-realization: meditation, breathing methods that help balance energy, intoning phrases selected by the retreat guide to mirror and manifest particular qualities in the retreatant, and practices with light that connect the retreatant with her inner light. These practices catalyze images and memories to arise and, combined with other creative modalities to generate movement in the psyche, help to surface hidden elements of the psyche.

Working with the self is a life-long work. Retreats can be a wonderful vehicle for going inward deeply and integrating new insights and life lessons. Through this process, we can become clearer channels to bring through our highest, most meaningful intentions in our individual beings, in our relationships, and in service to our family, friends, and wider communities.

Special Needs Students in The Boston Schools

The Boston school system at the time of our involvement was beset by problems. In the midst of that dysfunctional system, an incredible woman teacher and program director named Ruth Love created several special needs programs in the elementary schools. We were invited into these school programs as an experiment. We asked the head teachers to give us their students with learning disabilities, physical disabilities, language barriers, emotional disturbances, or lack of motivation from parents to work with. We got the students out of their seats and created theater games based on the cognitive material that teachers were required to work with that semester. We created dramatic structures that allowed each challenged student to feel creative and masterful, and have fun too. With this approach, these "special" young people were learning in an embodied way, with all of their senses, and the teachers told us that they were learning more effectively.

As theater artists, we were inspired by these students and how we could make a difference. Part of the training for us as facilitators involved doing role reversals to get into the shoes of the students—body, mind, heart and soul. Like a spiritual guide, she embodied love always with her students and with us, and she really listened to the students and related to their strengths with perseverance, kindness, intuitiveness and belief in them. Here is what Ruth wrote about what happened:

> *Theater Workshop Boston has developed workshops in theater related disciplines for 140 students with special needs and for 30 teachers and others in the J.J. Hurley school. The personnel of Theatre Workshop Boston were sensitive to the entire spectrum of the realities involved. Their individual and combined educational preparation (advanced degrees in several fields), their experience in the classroom, in theater arts, and in personal discipline became increasingly impressive as those credentials were discovered to be alive in the people themselves.*

Inspired by the need for effective healing and educational play for the special needs students and their families, TWB created a participatory musical play called *Sunsong*.[2] The play addresses family dynamics using Family Systems theory. Definitions and descriptions of technical terms by family therapists David Kantor and Barry Dym are included in the script. One foundational concept in Family Systems theory postulates that if the child is seen as the one having the problem, one has to look at and work with the whole family system to improve the situation. *Sunsong* translated that principle into a therapeutic musical play about a family whose communication breaks down. The company also used a healing breath practice in working with the children based on the elements in nature.[3]

The play is designed to involve all the children who come to the performance, along with eight actors. At the outset, the children are guided through

---

2 Linden, Sonneborn, 1976; see References
3 Khan, 1926

a physical warm-up accompanied with original music.[4] Later in the play, every-one is led through a musical circle dance while singing, ending with: "Feel that love, follow that love, into the center of your heart."

When the children first enter the theater lobby, they are guided to draw each of their family members on paper before coming into the performing space. This is an adapted "social atom" exercise from Sociometry, a discipline within Psychodrama.[5] Based on what the children draw, the actors assign each child to one of the four element breath environments (earth, water, fire, air). Four actors in full-body costumes play People Puppets — mother, father, sister, brother. They perform on their knees to be at the same height as the children. The other four actors play Element Guides, each in one of the four elemental environments created in an open space. The Guides concentrate internally on the element breath attunements they learned beforehand, while working with the children in their elemental environments externally.

The family of People Puppets perform a humorous but believable scene, where the communication breaks down between the family members, and the sister and brother make their way to the element groups. The groups of children in the four environments create healing gifts in the form of songs, dances, stories, and rituals to help the puppet sister and brother go back to their parents and help to transform the dynamics in their family.

Over time the company learned that many children and their parents who participated in the play were inspired to interact differently. I recall meeting a child who participated in the play when she was four years old, now in her twenties, who still remembered the play vividly and who said that it continued to inform how she relates to her family. Also, as theater artists, we learned that we can create theater for healing, for transformation, and for education on deep levels.

One parent wrote:

> The children were loosening up and a beautiful spontaneous expres-sion was beginning to develop out of the structure of the play. As a parent, I felt very warm watching my children interact with the others. They were opening up, growing and learning in a very nat-ural way. Sunsong was much more than a short Saturday afternoon entertainment. Everyone there had been transformed. I witnessed a very vivid enactment that had shaken rigid parts of myself. All the parents in the audience seemed recreated in some way.[6]

---

4 Sonneborn, 1976

5 Dayton, 2005

6 Eivers, 1975

High School Theater Arts Programs to Address Racial Unrest

Our theater received a grant from the government to develop theater arts programs bringing urban (mostly African American and Latino) and suburban (mostly Caucasian) high school students together to do a theater project. We worked with socio-dramatic scenarios to explore what it might have been like to come to the U.S. through Ellis Island. Each student made a passport for one of their ancestors; then, in the drama, some were rejected by Ellis Island officials at first and some were accepted right away. The ones who were rejected had to wait in line for some time before being accepted. Students playing their own ancestors who were accepted, were placed on an assembly line, and some became artisans. One actor portrayed Mother Jones, who enacted a scene of a factory assembly line, passionately opposing labor injustices. The adult actor-facilitators played scripted roles, while also expressing improvisational responses to the scenarios based on what the high school students were enacting. Since the families of all the urban and suburban students had been immigrants, they found a natural commonality. Through this enactment, they had genuine experiences of being interconnected and were motivated to see the "other" in new ways.

Teacher Training Programs

We also developed other creative arts teacher training programs where Drama Therapy and Psychodrama modalities were introduced. The teachers were invited to create lessons that used creative arts and meditation techniques related to their curricula requirements in the current semester. We started these sessions with different approaches and discussed how the principles of meditation, quiet moments, tuning to their breath, and creating sound/music moments could be introduced to help students be more centered and productive. We then introduced different creative arts and demonstrated how to create lesson plans using these different art forms. It has been proven time and again and supported by neuropsychology research that people learn best and heal from trauma more effectively through embodied experiences. For example, Bessel van der Kolk[7] demonstrates that students, and others, more effectively experience a lesson, as well as heal from trauma, via a participatory theater game or a movement discipline that involves their whole body and all of their senses. This is why participatory plays are more effective learning experiences than proscenium plays (actors on a stage, audience in seats). When teachers have an experience of creating a lesson using embodied exercises, often first in a supportive training group, they are more likely to continue to work that way on their own.

---

7 van der Kolk, 2015

Organizational Consulting

The president of our theater's board of directors, Dr. George Litwin, involved me and others in our company in his work with top Fortune 500 companies. He was an active spiritual seeker, beginning with his professorship in the Social Science department at Harvard with Timothy Leary and Richard Alpert (Ram Dass), where they did controlled experiments with LSD. George suggested that we refashion the creative learning programs that we developed for students and teachers for corporate executives, who he felt would greatly benefit from our approaches to learning. He designed a comprehensive program called "Managing People" for all levels of management, at one of the largest banks in the world, and had been called in to help deal with a major personnel and financial crisis. The whole IT department, run by a Vice President who managed hundreds of people, went belly up when he decided to transition people jobs to computers and other technology, with no regard for all the people who would lose their jobs. George invited me into a private meeting with him and the VP. My role was to make the point that "Managing People" means that it is important deal with feelings and learn to empathize with the people that work for you.

I was not sure how I could help, but when the VP said, "George, I don't know how this happened," I asked him to talk about what had happened. After hearing his story, I spontaneously placed my hand on his heart. That one action said it all. He was stunned, and then got very quiet, and sheepishly said, "Oh, yeah." Then George, with compassion, helped him understand more about the situation and did strategic planning with him to remedy the situation in his department on many levels.

Later, our theater company was brought in to create a film about a similar situation in another country, where people were being replaced by machines, to be shown to 5,000 vice presidents around the world. The film catalyzed discussion, role plays, and other active leadership training exercises with other Vice Presidents at the bank, to demonstrate the importance of managing people with empathy, empowering them while helping them get other jobs or whatever they needed to move on, including financial assistance.

In a new start-up software company in California, one of the three founders was a spiritual seeker, who had participated in one of our Transformational Theater workshops. He knew we also worked with organizations and asked if I would consult with them as they were about to go away to have a strategic planning meeting. I asked, "Do you share the same vision?" He thought for a moment and said thoughtfully, "I don't know." I was invited to guide the partners in a brainstorming session via teleconference. We began a meditation process and visioning exercise with music, after which I asked them to draw their vision and create a short poem about it. They had been instructed to bring music and drawing materials. After each founder shared their individual vision with all of us, they were guided to create a shared vision together integrating the three images they had drawn. I explained that the visioning process uses their right brain and helps balance out the left-brain strategic planning process. They were pleased to discover how their vision drawings and poems complemented each other. Later, as their first company employees were hired, I was brought in to take them through the same process. In this way, each person could own the mission of the company, inspired by this shared creative process. This company became very successful.

In a radio marketing company, we worked offsite with the marketing personnel to develop the marketing plans for their own company. They were taken through a step-by-step process to brainstorm ideas, in small groups, for the company's future success. Each group was invited to create a mini-drama that expressed the ideas of each group member using music, drama, movement, costume pieces and props that we brought. Then each group creatively expressed their marketing ideas through dramatic enactment for the larger group.

In working with two real estate companies who wanted to merge, there were two co-owners in one of them who were in constant conflict. A spontaneous role reversal was guided with those two partners, where they were asked to express the feelings of the other. When they recognized how hurtful they were being to each other, that was a game changer in being able to go forward in the merging process. (See John Maxfield's recommendation in References.)

Theatrical Pageantry to Inspire Unity Consciousness

A series of theatrical pageants were developed with the guidance of a meditation teacher with whom I studied. It was my responsibility to develop the rehearsal process to realize our mentor's inspiration and script, while engaging all involved in a process of self-realization. The largest and most public of these pageants, *The Cosmic Celebration*, the unity of the human family, evolved over an eleven-year period in many cities in the U.S. and Europe, involving casts of 350–400 people in each city, with diverse racial and religious backgrounds. Participants were given roles that reflected a soul quality associated with a source of strength that they would express through the pageant. These roles included masters, saints, prophets, angelic beings, goddesses, and archetypal "people in life" enacting challenges human beings face. The cast was taken through spiritual practices to develop their characters more authentically. They were asked to embody and physicalize the being they represented through sounds and gestures, as would be done to develop any character in a play. They were invited to have a dialogue with this character as a guide, as was done in the retreat process described earlier. The player-seekers held these roles as inner concentrations through a two-month rehearsal process as the production unfolded. In this way the named soul quality was awakened and strengthened through the pageant rehearsal process as well as the performance itself.

Conclusion

In this chapter, we have discussed the efficacy of integrating meditation and other spiritual practices with Psychodrama, Drama Therapy, Transformational Theater and other creative arts modalities in the service of self-realization, healing, educational successes, organizational change, and other kinds of transformational learning, with a variety of populations. In the end, we ultimately work to inspire the people we serve to create their lives as beautiful works of art.

The author would like to acknowledge the superb professional editing assistance of Shams Kairys (shams@writingway.com).

Saphira Linden

Ms Linden, RDT/BCT, TEP, LCAT, Director, Omega Transpersonal Drama Therapy Certificate Program/Professional Psychodrama Training, Boston, since 1999; trained with Jacob and Zerka Moreno, Psychodrama founders; adjunct faculty several universities, institutes. Honored with ASGPP "Fellow" award, Gertrud Shatner life achievement award., "given by NADTA since 1993, in recognition of distinguished contribution to the field of drama therapy in education, publication, practice, and service." Earlier, "NADTA's first Teaching Excellence award "in recognition of outstanding dedication to education in the field of drama therapy through teaching and mentorship."

As Artistic Director of Omega Theater/Theater Workshop Boston, (since 1967), created and produced numerous award winning original plays, arts events including The Cosmic Celebration, transformational theater pageant, U.S, Europe, 11 years. Developing participational theater for young people/families as educational—transformational experiences, subject of half hour PBS film, in series Artists In America. Has trained hundreds of professionals in arts, mental health, education, pastoral service, organizational development.

Ms. Linden has been a leading pioneer in Transformational Theater and Drama Therapy, Transpersonal Psychotherapist;Sufi meditation teacher/guide, since 1971; Management Consultant; founded Omega Arts Network: Transformational Artist-healers globally; has a Boston private practice; the author of numerous articles/chapters about her work, she envisioned/edited the comprehensive anthology *The Heart And Soul Of Psychotherapy: A Transpersonal Approach Through Theater Arts—Drama therapy, Psychodrama and Transformational Theater*, Trafford Publishing, 2013.

Contact her at the Omega Transpersonal Drama Therapy Certificate Program and Professional Psychodrama Training, *http://www.omegatheater.org*, or at *info@omegatheater.org*

References

Dayton, T. (2005), *The Living Stage*, Health Communications, Inc., Deerfield Beach, Florida

Eivers, R, (1975), *Sunsong: A children's play in which they play at lighting up the world*

Khan, H.I. (1979), Art: Yesterday, Today and Tomorrow, *The Sufi Message of Hazrat Inayat Khan*

Linden, S, ed, (2013). *The Heart and Soul of Psychotherapy: A Transpersonal Approach Through Theater Arts*, Trafford Publishers, Bloomington, Indiana

Linden, S, Sonneborn, (1976), Sunsong: Om Company, Theatre Workshop Boston, New Plays for Children, Rowayton, Connecticut

van der Kolk, B., (2014), *The Body Keeps the Score: Brain. Mind, and Body in the Healing of Trauma*, Viking, New York

Section 6

Expanding Therapeutic Uses of Action Explorations

Author's Note: Although the primary emphasis of this book is on the non-therapeutic applications of action methods, we decided to include several chapters that address the use of action explorations in a clinical setting. This is because each of the following three chapters focuses on a different issue that is also relevant to working with individuals and groups.

This section begins with a detailed description of how one psychotherapeutic approach has not only been successfully enhanced with action methods but also offers opportunities for extension beyond therapy into helping and healing many areas of human life. The next chapter reminds us that when helping people to expand their imaginative and creative qualities it is important to recognize the pervasive underlying experience that many people have had around the theme of "shame." Another valuable resource for any group leader is the knowledge to recognize individuals with lowered interpersonal/social abilities. The chapter on the new formulations about Autism Spectrum/Asperger's Disorder highlights various issues for these people.

Positive Psychology and Psychodrama

Phoebe Atkinson and Nancy Kirsner

Positive Psychology is the study of the conditions that contribute to wellbeing and flourishing. It is evidenced based and its research and practices provide a powerful scientific foundation. The field has credibility and utility. Positive Psychology interventions (PPI) are strategies to increase wellbeing all based in research. These include: activating positive emotions, harnessing strengths, developing positive relationships, building psychological and social capital, pursuing mastery, utilizing flow states and developing purpose and meaning.

Psychodramatists and Sociometrists have the experiential skills that can be deployed to concretize and maximize these evidence based tools. Psychodramatists are uniquely positioned with an action methodology that informs and empowers experience. Action based interventions go beyond writing and verbalizing. As Psychodramatists, we can 'pay the Positive Psychology work forward' in powerful and unique ways. We can capitalize on our training and bring the Positive Psychology Interventions into a full expression of embodied learning.

This was in evidence when, during a lecture based on Positive Psychology training, Nancy observed the confusion around a segment of the teaching related to Jeffrey Schwartz's (2011) work on distorted brain messages and negative self-talk (a.k.a. *neuronal gossip*). As a psychodramatist Nancy thought, "too much talk without action." She corrected that limitation during her presentation later that day. Nancy's paper bag hand puppet, *Critical Rat*, made her Positive Psychology debut. In a quick action vignette, Critical Rat declared, "Who do you think you are?" as Nancy demonstrated how one's negative self-talk could be visually represented. This modelled the defining charge for all psychodramatists: *"don't tell me . . . show me!"*

History

The historical roots of Psychodrama, Positive Psychology, and Positive Psychotherapy have overlapped for nearly 50 years (Tomasulo). Beginning with the human potential movement of the 1960's, led by great pioneers such as Abraham Maslow and Carl Rogers, there has been a focus on finding the good within and understanding what makes life worth living. While these early years drew a wide range of thinkers and writers and produced many self-help books, there lacked a substantial empirical base to guarantee any academic rigor or sustainability.

A long period of time has elapsed and the past two decades have finally yielded a more contemporary evidenced based field of Positive Psychology, fathered by Dr. Martin Seligman. As APA President in 1998, Dr. Seligman initiated a charge to study what is best in people.

Benefits of Positivity

Plain and simply put . . . the findings from the field of Positive Psychology deserve our attention. Positive Psychology researchers study Positive Emotions, Character Strengths and Meaning. As an applied science they have created a variety of 'interventions' intended to increase overall wellbeing, motivation and resilience.

Some of the threads of research have to do with:

- Ratio *of* positive/negative emotions
- Engagement and flow and its impact on activities and relationships
- Strengths awareness and greater sense of meaning
- Health and wellbeing motivation
- Self Determination and Choice
- Developing skills of resilience
- Altruism/Belonging — connecting to a larger community

Positive Psychology and Psychodrama: A Perfect Fit (Nancy's Reflections)

Positive Psychology and Action methods fit together like hand and glove. Both share a common humanistic view of mankind as having everything within to live an authentic rich life. As practitioners, we can mindfully cultivate the core conditions for growth and can encourage the 'actualizing tendency' within our clients as they grow into their *possible selves*[1]—having a full role repertoire: satisfying roles to play, positive relationships and experiencing a healthy mind-body connection. Psychodramatists have a myriad of tools that explore and

---

1 Markus 1986

anchor behaviors. In Psychodrama this is called role training—the process of applied practice as one acquires new cognitive and behavioral strategies (roles).

Positive Psychology and Psychodrama are also inherently teachable, accessible and practical as practices everyone can learn. While there are experiential exercises in Positive Psychology (interventions), the additional skills of a Psychodramatist can deepen the experiential aspects as it impacts affective, behavioral, and cognitive domains while witnessing and sharing the experiences within the client and/or group.

Here are some of the parallel concepts in Positive Psychology and Psychodrama:

Positive Psychology	Psychodrama
Social Psychological	Social Psychological
Humanistic Existential Theory Responsibility Choice, Social Responsibility	Humanistic/Existential theory— Co-Creation Choice Social Responsibility
Living in deep connection with ourselves, each other and our Planet	A deeply human and co-created process between man and the Godhead
A science of Happiness & Wellbeing	A life of ultimate spontaneity/ creativity—A Full role repertoire
Cultivating Positivity, Flow, Resilience	Warming up to spontaneity and Creativity S/C Theory
At every moment we have a Choice Here and now Growth throughout lifespan	In Vivo—all done in here and now— Protagonist makes all choices Growth throughout lifespan
Our brains co-regulate together	Tele intuitive knowing—can be trained—Sociometrist awareness
Possible Selves /Best self-narratives	The self develops through the many roles we play
Mindfulness is a practice, Skills can be learned and cultivated	We live in action—Role Training Behavioral practice Rehearsal for living; roles can be trained
Permission to be Human Self-Compassion Theory	Aim for adequacy; a good enough response
The power of the word Words create reality/set intentions Personal storytelling for connecting	Re-storying our narratives for healing Help people tell their story
Savoring (past present future)	Zerka: 'Everything should be experienced 3 times' (Actual, surplus reality, change-redo)

Psychodrama, Sociometry, and Mindfulness

Mindfulness—the state of focusing awareness on the present moment while calmly acknowledging one's thoughts, feelings, and body sensations through a lens of nonjudgement—is innate to change. Psychodrama at its core is a mindfulness practice. It turns reality into surplus reality and slows it down to be felt, examined, recrafted, or responded to in new ways that the linear passage of time does not allow. Sociometry, the science and research branch of Psychodrama, is about making mindful social choices: *i.e.*, who do I choose in each moment and for what role? Conscious, mindful choices (role and person specific) make for a good enough life of wellbeing.

Example: Scene Setting and Mindfulness

In Psychodrama there are basic steps: Warm up, select and contract with a Protagonist about their drama, and then set the scene before beginning. Scene setting concretizes the protagonists' internal and external world in sensate detail using all 5 senses (visual, auditory, kinesthetic, smell, taste), asking:

- Where does this story take place?
- Describe in detail the people, what to you see around you?
- What are people wearing?
- What's the temperature like?
- Are there any smells?
- How do you feel walking in the sand?

This brings the teller and the audience into a shared reality. We have been invited into the Protagonists' intrapsychic theater which now exists through scene setting right before our eyes. This creates a shared mindfulness in action which is the rich playground psychodramatists' love to co-create with protagonist and audience alike. Our basic tool of Scene Setting is in and of itself, a rich mindfulness technique and experience—as we play and co create in the here and now and notice the new. It can stand alone in its power to engage, enrich, savor, and inform.

Here are some suggestions for scene setting prompts:

Your room as a child; the family table; a favorite birthday or holiday celebration you would like to revisit. As a Director, slow down, be very curious and interested. Get as many details as you can, and use auxiliaries where possible to represent objects, furniture, pictures. Using auxiliaries allows for easy feedback of narrative description to the Protagonist that furthers the instillation of the sensorial, emotional and verbal aspects of the scene.

Positive Psychology Action Interventions

This Chapter specifically explores three well known positive Psychology interventions using action methods from Psychodrama:

- The Values in Action (VIA) Character Strengths with the Segura Strengths Clusters Mat
- Gratitude in Action: Create A Bucket full of Gratitude! Be a Bucket Filler; and
- The Language of Positive Emotions in Action—The Ten Positive Emotions

The VIA Character Strengths and Action Methods

Our character strengths (CS) represent our best core qualities that endure over time. Our top five strengths are called signature strengths. With knowledge of our strengths we can be more deliberate and align ourselves to improve our levels of engagement, productivity and happiness. Because of our Negativity Bias (Baumeister) most of us have a tendency to focus on our weaknesses seeing them as more important for our growth. Findings in the strengths' literature have shown that It is actually the opposite. It turns out that people who focus on their strengths are disproportionally more engaged and successful! (VIA research) than others.

Strengths Workshop

This workshop was designed to teach the VIA (Values in Action) character strengths in action. Prior to the workshop all participants took the free VIA survey.[2] The *Segora Strengths Clusters™ Mat*[3] provided visual-kinesthetic enhancement to the experiential teaching.

Experiential / Action Teaching – Learning Objectives:

- For participants to begin a paradigm shift by learning and speaking the language of strengths; moving from 'wrong to strong'.
- Use the VIA teaching model of aware, explore, apply
- Locate, identify and apply your top five signature strengths through story
- Doing a 'walk-about' on the Mat to increase strengths awareness by naming the strengths, reading the definition and sharing examples from real life experiences. Do as many as time allows

---

2 *http://www.viacharacter.org/www*
3 *https://www.strengthclusters.com*

- Construct and amplify generative narrative practice using the VIA and Action techniques

After a brief introduction to the Via CS, dyad partners were created through a fun candy matching exercise (courtesy of Dr. Bill Wysong). Dyads got to know each other by telling "Best Self" stories. Everyone had a list of the 24 VIA strengths as they listened. Instructions were to notice all their partner's strengths throughout the telling of their story. Upon completing the story, listeners did "strength spotting" naming all the strengths they heard. The teller also names their strengths. Both dyad partners complete this.

Working on the Segura Strength Clusters Mat

Training and teaching the VIA character strengths has been enhanced by the creativity and design genius of Giselle Segura. Giselle is an alumnus of the *Certificate in Positive Psychology* and her final project birthed the colorful *Strength Clusters Mat* which brought clarity, playfulness, and kinesthetic action dimensions and possibilities that the printed VIA survey did not elicit. The Mat is multi-sensory and activates different learning pathways that are visual, colorful, playful and kinesthetic.

As Psychodramatists we jumped on the Mat and let the VIA action begin! On the Mat, individuals did a strength's *'walk-about'* using their top five signature strengths. Starting by locating their #1 strength on the Mat, people shared how this strength showed up in their daily lives or how that strength was useful. Signature Strengths are core to who you are and show up easily for us. When several people are on the Mat a natural sharing begins—"we both have Love for #1"—folks connect and hug. When bigger groups of 8 or more (a family or a team) share the Mat, sharing begins spontaneously—"I'd like more of that strength." The character strengths start interacting naturally, as they do in actual life. The colorfulness of the Mat invites a playfulness that reminds many of the game Twister.

The questions you can ask are many:

- What is the 'go to' strength you can always count on?
- What's your favorite strength?
- What's a strength friends and family count on you to have?
- What strength(s) would you like to grow and have more of?

Character Strengths and the Appreciative Lens

While the first layer of learning about Character strengths is individual, you learn about your own; their richness lies in their application towards having an appreciative lens toward others' with different character strengths. When couples, families, and teams explore and navigate the tension of their different character strengths on the Mat, it provides a positive language that shifts' one's perspective.

In this work, the director elicits narrative stories from individuals, which can be followed with a psychodramatic vignette that concretizes the differences and explores the shifts in perception and action that are possible. All of the skills of Psychodrama — role reversal, doubling, mirroring can help individuals explore their use of character strengths in relationships. Let your curiosity and compassion direct your questions to everyone on the Mat so that a full exploration of top strengths emerges. As director you will facilitate some application however much emerges spontaneously from the participants through interaction on the Mat.

The group ends with individuals sharing what they learned about their own and others CS. As well, asking individuals about how they might apply this in their lives and work helps them to consolidate their learning and translate their insights into next steps as they continue to live into their strengths.

Gratitude in Action: Filling our buckets

Gratitude and Appreciation are core elements of Positive Psychology research. Expressing gratitude is often awkward and thus it goes unexpressed. Gratitude as the 'heavy hitter' of the positive emotions and is also one of the 24-character strengths related to wellbeing. Gratitude has been most researched by Dr. Robert Emmonds (Gratitude Works). Creating a practice around gratitude is one of the most expedient ways to boost your wellbeing. *Gratitude Is Its Own Reward,* and it gives everyone — giver and receiver — a lot of bang for your buck! Gratitude interventions can be amplified through the use of action methods. In 2017 Dr. Dan Tomasulo was honored with the Innovation Award for the Clinical Division of the International Positive Psychology Association for his Virtual Gratitude Visit(VGV).

Experiential Action Learning on Gratitude

This activity includes use f sociometry, priming warm ups, group interaction, and a creative art activity as a unique, meaningful, and fun way to translate Gratitude into a visible form that all can easily do and share.

Learning Objectives:

- Learn the significance of gratitude work/research in the field of Positive Psychology
- Create, fill buckets as vehicles to express gratitude into visible forms to see and speak easily
- Cultivate/Practice expressing gratitude in the moment; face to face

Supplies:
Small colored plastic buckets (6″ diameter and 5″ deep), colorful small paper, pens, markers, stones, seashells, stickers, colored pipe cleaner. Printed assortment of Gratitude Quotes/Poems on attractive paper to hang on walls for Warm Up.

Action of Workshop

This workshop was given on the last day of an ASGPP Conference. Last days are frequently sparsely attended and Nancy was delighted to have over 20 people and several pairs of long time colleagues in the room. The workshop began by inviting participants to quietly mill around the room. Twenty Gratitude quotes on pretty paper lined the walls of the room. Participants were to select a quote and 'pair and share' with someone about their choice. We did a sharing with the larger group after the dyads. Then we read out loud the book, *Have You Filled a Bucket Today?* by Carol McCloud. This book is often used for teachers, parents and kids—for teaching children to love and give to others—in other words: to be a bucket filler!

Instructions for Bucket Filling

Fill your own bucket with your expressions/symbols of gratitude; and put something in the buckets of 5 others in the room. Or you can fill your bucket for someone you have not expressed Gratitude towards in your life. Allow around 20″ and leave instructions open so people feel free to create their buckets in ways meaningful to them.

The creating and delivering phase took around thirty minutes. Next, invite folks to begin giving and receiving from the buckets to each other and expressing their Gratitude and specifically what it is about. The instructions to 'be specific' about expressing Gratitude are important. For example, "I am grateful to you for the fact that every time I see you I get the warmest smile and hug. You seem genuinely happy to see me. From the quietness of the bucket filling time, the group became alive with close connection, warm looks and smiles.

Gratitude Worked its Magic in the Final Group

The whole group came together to share what the experience was like for them. How was this experience for you ? Was it easier to express or receive Gratitude? What did you learn about yourself and Gratitude?

Sharing in the large group was very powerful. The connection, love, attunement, and depth of sharing was deep as most people had known each other many years, there were three dyads of longtime friends. They expressed things to each other they had never said before; loved ones and mentors no longer with us were also mentioned. Two group members were new and I was concerned that they might feel isolated. Not so ! Members of the group had been in workshops with them over the prior Conference days, and had 'Gratitude Gifts' for them as well. I re-learned the power is in the group.

The timing of the workshop, the last day and last session which could have been a deterrent—actually turned out to be a gift. People were able to integrate their time together over the days. Participants expressed that it was a wonderful way to consolidate their conference experience and end feeling deeply seen and appreciated.

The Language of Positive Emotions in Action: The Ten Most Frequent Positive Emotions

Historically, little or no emphasis or research looked at the Positive Emotions. Most of Psychiatry and Psychology studied negative emotions as related to disease and diagnosis. While Seligman's later work (1975 onward) focused on the use of positive interventions, it was the not until the groundbreaking work of Dr. Barbara Fredrickson that Positive Emotions were demonstrated and linked as significant to our very existence, not just our happiness and wellbeing. Frederickson was one of the first researchers that Seligman enlisted to join in the emerging field of Positive Psychology.

The Ten Positive Emotions (PE)

Dr. Fredrickson's first research explored the nature of the ten most common Positive Emotions: joy, love, gratitude, awe, serenity, interest, hope, pride, amusement, and inspiration. This 'Positivity' research established an evidenced based foundation for the impact of positive emotions on the brain's power to think and be creative. These ten emotions are the focus of much research and it has been discovered that experiencing these on a regular basis broadens people's minds, builds their resourcefulness, increases resiliency and achievement, facilitates connections with others—helping individuals become their Best Selves. Positive emotions help us have a bigger picture and increase social awareness. They soothe, regulate, and calm us. Each positive emotion has its own action tendency (act hunger) and these mechanisms are important for our very survival.

As with most of the positive psychology interventions, use of positive emotions can be developed through practice. A large part of experiencing our positive emotions is cultivating the capacity to slow down; being open minded; and choosing to really take in the many micro-moments of our lives.

The Neuroscience and Kinesiology of Positive Emotions

Fredrickson has studied in depth the brain science behind Positive Emotions. It turns out that positive emotions are fleeting and have a "light valence." Dr. Rick Hanson describes positive experiences as "Teflon-like"—they are here and gone. Without a practice of mindfulness actively savoring, slowing things down and installing them (Hanson calls this 'taking in the good') . . . these 'micronutrients' can be missed and likewise the opportunity to really integrate them into our whole being. In contrast, negative emotions (depression, anger, fear) are stronger with a 'heavy valence'. They can be characterized as being Velcro-like as they stick and continually draw in our brains' attention. While they were once needed to protect us and be vigilant for our very survival, now we could call them, 'the bully in our brain'. In neuroscience this is called "the negativity bias." (Baumeister)

Learning Objectives for Positive Emotion (PE) Action Workshop

- Utilize "you at your best stories" to practice spotting positive emotions in yourself/others
- Create a PE Social Atom—who? which PE evoked?
- Enact a vignette—you at your Best, Precious Moment—PE double to amplify.
- Practice slowing down, savoring, double, mirror, echo (Savoring = noticing precious flowers in our garden—Dr. Rick Hanson).
- Use the PE worksheet P/N together (Positivity ratio P/N)

Materials Needed:

Names of Positive Emotions/Definitions. Print the names of the 10 Positive Emotions in large letters on regular 8½ by 11″ paper. Letters should be easily readable. I like to use attractive paper and I laminate the paper so that I can reuse the sheets. You can type the definitions of the emotions on the back of each card.

Positive Emotions Sociometry

- My "go to" positive emotion, easy and natural for me?
- Which PE supports you the most?
- Which is your strongest PE?
- Which PE do you want to grow that would help you in your life?
- Ask participants to sculpt, make a motion, or a sound for each of the positive emotions.

During sociometry (mostly locograms), all of the positive emotions were on large index cards on the floor. When folks responded to Sociometric prompts, they were asked to read aloud the definitions on the back of the cards. Everyone had their turn at speaking one or more times. Interaction and examples are invited.

Dyads

Best Self stories were shared with a partner. The listener noted the PEs either directly expressed/or inferred. After this was completed by both partners, we shared and noticed our barometer of PEs. How had the experience effected them? (Director notes Frederickson's concept of the upward spiral that is created as Positive Emotions are ignited during the exercises).

Positive Emotions Worksheets—Warm Ups to Action

- Depending on time available, you can choose which worksheets to use
- The Ten Positive Emotions: Where? With who? How? Rate1–10
- The Positivity Ratio in Action P/N: Who? What?

The Positive Emotions Social Atom

Everyone drew a PE Social Atom naming the people that evoked PEs. Who? What activity? What PE? From this experience a Protagonist can be chosen or someone can volunteer.

PE Social Atom in Action — this follows the traditional instructions with the Director taking time to slow down the action, with a PE double to amplify and savor all PE's. Enrole at least 3 individuals in their atom.

Prioritizing Positivity and Group Sharing

The group ended with everyone in the audience sharing and noting which PE they wanted more of in their life. Frederickson's theory of *'prioritizing positivity'* was woven into experiential exercise through directors' questions about how? when? and frequency? Frederickson's research illustrates that over the long term, people that *prioritize positivity* have more positive experiences which leads to more spontaneous positive thoughts. She suggests that with intention, these positive thoughts can be linked to behaviors that are good for us.

The research encourages us to deliberately select situations each day where we are more likely to experience positive emotions. A closing micro-Intervention suggested by Dr. Fredickson and colleagues (2014) can be offered as part of any workshop using the concept of 'prioritizing positivity.' Frederickson notes: "*Instead of wishful thinking about the future, put actions on today's to-do list that bring you joy.*"

You can download examples of these diagrams here: *bit.ly/AEfrederickson*

Phoebe's Reflections—Standing on the Shoulders of Giants

As stated above, positive psychology has been gaining momentum because of the research of visionary Martin Seligman as well as many others. Positive psychology studies the conditions and processes connected to the optimal functioning of people, groups and institutions.[4] Moreno also took a positive approach to helping individuals. Like practitioners of positive psychology, psychodrama practitioners follow Moreno's teachings and seek to encounter people where they are and assist them in contacting and developing the best that is within them (Moreno). The theme of hand in glove as mentioned above . . . and/or finding commonalities within the two fields continues to excite and engage me.

One of the early researchers in the field of positive psychology Sonja Lyubormirsky (2011) wrote in her book *The How of Happiness*: "the premise of positive psychology—that it is as important to investigate wellness as it is to study misery—has reached the mainstream." Positive psychology as an applied science uses *interventions* which are are simple strategies that seek to increase wellbeing. These interventions all based in research attempt to: *enhance positivity; increase engagement; and further a sense of meaning.*[5]

Psychodramatist and positive psychologist Dan Tomasulo writes that the positive psychology movement is all about savoring and flourishing. Here follow some reflections as to some of what has informed my thinking as a sociometrist and psychodramstist—as I've used key findings from the field of positive psychology—with 'savoring' and other evidenced based interventions—in order to create generative communities.

Enhancing Positivity: Use of Positive Emotions to Generate Positive Affect

Earlier in the chapter the work of Frederickson was discussed and her groundbreaking work which focuses on the role of positive affect (positive emotions, positive moods and positive attitudes) and correlation to increased energy, enthusiasm and engagement. As has been shown by work on the *Negativity Bias*—negative emotions seem to be stronger than the positive.

Therefore, cultivating awareness as to the why and how of positive emotions is a cornerstone when working within the field of positive psychology. Frederickson has coined the term *positivity resonance* which she defines as shared micro moments of positivity that individuals can experience in their daily interactions. As a Sociometrist use of positive emotions—can be a powerful tool to activate and seed many micro moments of positivity—activating the positive affect within a group at any stage of group formation.

Frederickson has shown that positivity is associated with the expansion of physical, social, and psychological resources. Frederickson in describing her *Broaden and Build Theory* states that *"positive emotions broaden an individual's momentary mindset, and by doing so help to build enduring personal*

---

4 Gable, Haidt, 2005
5 Seligman 2018

resources" . . . thus encouraging resilience and strengthening an individual's capacity to cope with adversity.[6] Questions and prompts can be shaped connected to each of the positive emotions. When working with groups, these can be woven in to turn on the social engagement brain and help individuals find their commonalities as they orient to a new group setting. Strategic use of PEs can be utilized at the beginning of a meeting and/or can be used to close a meeting on a high note!

Individuals experience the broaden and build effect within themselves as well as experience increased cohesion as a group. Frederickson's research suggests that people who regularly feel positive emotions are lifted on an 'upward spiral' of continued growth and thriving. As group and team facilitators we can ignite a *groups' upward spiral.* Each person's positive emotions can become helpful to others through the phenomenon of *positive emotional contagion.* When the group facilitator highlights the positive emotions of pride, gratitude or appreciation for example, this can broaden people's mindsets. When we are experiencing positive emotions we have more 'behavioral flexibility' and this allows us to build 'intellectual and psychological resources.'[7]

When considering sociometry for either large or small group encounters, I refer to what Dr. Rick Hanson calls highlighting the '*ordinary jewels*' (Re-Wire for Happiness). Suggested criterion for exploration might be connected to sharing examples of experiences in order to activate positive emotional states related to: joy, hope, love, interest, pride, amusement, serenity, gratitude, inspiration or awe—the emotions connected to the science of positivity. Layering in prompts using the positive emotions can prime any group and can promote mutuality and an incremental build of pro social connections—increasing the likelihood of experiencing both the ME and the We. This can also enhance a sense of belonging and group efficacy.

Increased Engagement—Tapping into Strengths

The study of character strengths grew out of the question researchers were asking, namely: '*what is virtuous character?*' Developing 'virtuous character' and working with character strengths are key concepts in positive psychology. As in the prior section, regarding use of the *Segura Strengths Mat*—strengths work with a team is a powerful intervention. Strengths awareness mobilizes the inherent capacities within an individual and their team. When we listen to strengths stories for instance, we are pulling out of the conversation the things a person holds dear and listening for the important aspects of a person's orientation as per what motivates them to take action. Increased awareness of an individual's strengths can lead to greater engagement and this also relates

---

6 Frederickson, 2009
7 Frederickson, 2003

to meeting a core need of mastery/competency and contribution. When developing strengths language within a group it can be impactful to use the intervention of '*me at my best*' stories where the facilitator asks the participant to share a story related to when this individual has been at their best.

Possible Selves (1986) is a concept rooted in social psychology and aligns with role theory in psychodrama. When a person describes a best self-story, the facilitator can amplify what is strong (through use of a double) and elevate the story through the lens of character strengths. This helps the individual with their own self-perception as the role and character strength become illuminated within a context which then can be generalized as a resource in other settings. *Selves* exploration is foundational for use with action methods. Action oriented practitioners have the methods to amplify and bring to life all aspects of best self-stories and can act as a mirror of hope as a new aspect of an individual is in the process of becoming. When we hear stories of human goodness—we are elevated as Haight (2003) suggests. When we witness others at their best—we are all lifted up and inspired. Yalom's (1998) therapeutic factors can also be brought in and heightened when a skilled facilitator can bring their awareness of character strengths and positive emotions and how these relate to group learning. As Frederickson and others have shown, micro moments—occasions related to strengths awareness and strengths development—can build incrementally and become resources—as a team leader (or peer) can use the skill of 'strengths spotting' within their team.

The same intervention of spotting strengths can be directed at oneself—as individuals are taught to self-appreciate and notice what has gone well in their day and how a strength was used. There is abundant research on strengths which shows that focusing on signature strengths can increase wellbeing. Appreciative Inquiry founder David Cooperrider says "*we must study what gives life to a system and use that to paint a picture of the future.*"

One of the founders of the VIA Character Assessment Chris Peterson called for researchers to consider that the focus of research and interventions not only be applied to individuals but also to enhance larger community settings. Helping individuals and groups build awareness of their strengths shines the light on the 'positive core'. Strengths work and *best self-stories*—linked to a practitioner's knowledge of role theory—can create a powerful foundation for both individuals and group—when looking at themselves—and the groups and communities they are a part of. This can lead to a virtuous cycle as relates to sociometry and the concept of co-creation and choice.

Further a Sense of Meaning

Researchers' continue on the quest in psychology as relates to the overarching question: what makes life worth living? Positive Psychology researchers have sought to contribute to the field and to move the discussion along by empirically examining the different facets of life associated with meaning. Humans need to make sense of their world, find direction for their actions and find a sense of worth in their lives. As a TEP, in my first year in the *Certification of Positive Psychology*, I recognized the possible intersection of the two compatible fields as they both touched on coherence (making sense); motivation (direction); and worth and belonging (significance). Questions related to these facets of life initially drew me to psychodrama. Since 2011, I have been exploring how these two field can complement each other. As a trainer and practitioner of psycho-drama working in a positive psychology oriented educational setting, I've had the unique opportunity to introduce the Science of Sociometry into both design and application and have been blessed with working on a team with exceptional colleagues who are dedicated to building connections within a learning com-munity and welcoming information regarding systems interventions and the strategic application of sociometry. I've tapped the science of sociometry along with foundational concepts from group psychotherapy and team effectiveness and action methods, along with the science of positive psychology and have seen and felt the lasting positive impact these interventions have had on both students and faculty. We've accelerated team effectiveness using the broaden and build theory. We have elucidated a sociometric consciousness and the tenet of co-creation throughout the course design which has helped to accelerate connections and create the conditions for flourishing teams both in the faculty and amongst the students and alumni.

In Summary—Vines Woven Together

Psychodramatist and Positive Psychologist Dan Tomasulo (2017) has likened positive psychology, psychodrama, and positive psychotherapy as 'three strands of a braided vine which have been woven together since their begin-nings.' Positive Psychology researcher, Alex Linley (2006) has written: '*positive psychology can prosper through integration, rather than whither through isolation*' and for several decades, Blatner (2000) has written that psychodramatists have a variety of therapeutic orientations as Moreno's triadic system is readily compatible and adaptable to most modalities.

Seligman (2013) has written about the concept of 'prospecting' as part of a proposed framework called: 'navigating the future'. Prospecting has been identified as a core organizing principle in animal and human behavior. This orientation includes activating the hope circuitry and imagining the future. Prospecting is a 'forward looking framework' (similar to future projection) that stimulates mental activity about future possibilities. Seligman's writing sets the perfect stage for psychodramatists and sociometrists who—using their tools of time lines or future projections—can activate the hope circuitry and help others 'dream again'.

Blatner, along with Linley, call out for practitioners to explore opportunities for integration and expansion. Blatner has gone in new directions writing this book, applying Psychodrama in service of other fields rather than merely psychotherapy. It is an exciting time for practitioners trained in action methods—we are in the front row. There is a growing interest in evidenced based positive interventions with their focus on improving the lives of individuals and communities—healthy applications of Psychology. In this article we have given examples of how we have integrated best practices from both fields into our work.

These ideas are snapshots of creative growth which emerged from our explorations in the intersection of positive psychology practices and action interventions. We are filled with gratitude for all of our trainers who inspired us. We have stood on your shoulders as we have shaped our work in the world.

Nancy Kirsner

Nancy Kirsner, Ph.D, TEP, CPP, MFT, OTR has experience as an Occupational Therapist, University Assistant Dean/Professor, Marriage and Family Therapist, Trainer, Educator, and Practitioner of Psychodrama, Sociometry, and Group Psyhotherapy (TEP), a Certified Positive Psychologist, a Forensic Consultant and over four decades in private practice in Miami, Florida. Nancy is the current President of the ASGPP (American Society of Group Psychotherapy and Psychodrama) and as well is Editor of the Psychodrama Network News (PNN). Nancy loves and values people above all else and has a passion and whimsy for translating learning into Action Methods.

You can contact her at *www.positivepsychologyworks.com*

Phoebe Atkinson

Phoebe Atkinsonis a Licensed Clinical Social worker (LCSW), a Fellow of the American Society of Group Psychotherapy and Psychodrama (TEP) and is a Board Certified Coach (BCC). She holds a Certificate in Positive Psychology (CiPP) from the Whole Being Institute (*wholebeinginstitute. com*) and serves that work forward as a member of the teaching faculty. Phoebe is a psychotherapist and coach in private practice where she uses experiential training methods to help groups and individuals gain personal insight, influence and effectiveness. She is passionate about creating flourishing teams and using the science of positive organizational scholarship to promote positive leadership and create thriving organizations.

You can contact her at *www.psychodramacertification.org*

References

Baumeister, R. F., Bratslavsky, E., Finkenauer, C., & Vohs, K. D. (2001). Bad is stronger than good. *Review of General Psychology, 5*, 323–370

Blatner, A. (1987) *Foundations of psychodrama: History, theory and practice*. New York: Springer.

Catalino, L.I., Algoe, S. B., & Fredrickson, B. L. (2014). Prioritizing positivity: An effective approach to pursuing happiness. *Emotion, 14*, 1155–1161.)

Emmons, R. (2007) *Thanks! How practicing gratitude can make you happier*. New York: Houghton Mifflin Company

Frederickson, B. (2009). *Positivity: Top-notch research reveals the 3 to 1 ratio that will change your life*. Harmony Press.

Gable, S. L., & Haidt, J. (2005). What (and why) is positive psychology? *Review of General Psychology, 9*, 103–110. doi: 10.1037/1089–2680.9.2.103

Emmons, Robert. *Gratitude Works*. 2013. Wiley: San Francisco, CA

Haidt, J. (2003). Elevation and the positive psychology of morality. Flourishing: Positive psychology and the life well-lived, 275, 289.

Hanson, R. (2009). *Buddha's brain: The practical neuroscience of happiness, love and wisdom*. Oakland: New Harbinger Publications

Hanson, Rick. (2013) *Hardwiring Happiness*. Crown: NY

Linley, A. (2006) *Positive Psychotherapy: Past Present and (possible) Future*.

Lyubomirsky, S. (2007) *The how of happiness: A new approach to getting the life you want*. New York: Penguin Books.

Markus, H., & Nurius, P. (1986). Possible selves. *American Psychologist, 41*, 954–969.

Moreno, J.L. (1978) *Who shall survive?* (3rd ed.) Beacon, NY: Beacon House.

Neff, K. (2011) *Self-Compassion: The Proven Power of Being Kind to Yourself*. William Morrow.

Ryan, R. M., & Deci, E. L. (2000). Self-determination and the facilitation of intrinsic motivation, social development, and well-being. *American Psychologist, 55*, 68–78.

Schwartz, J., Gladding, R. (2011) *You are not Your Brain*. Penguin Group. New York. NY

Seligman, M. E. P. (1999). The president's address. *American Psychologist, 53*, 559–562.

Seligman, M. E. P., & Csikszentmihalyi, M. (2000). Positive psychology: An introduction. *American Psychologist, 55*, 5–14. Seligman, M. E. P., Steen, T. A., Park N., & Peterson, C. (2005).

Seligman, M. E. P. (2011). Flourish: *A visionary new understanding of happiness and well-being*. New York: Simon & Shuster.

Seligman, M.E.P., Rashid, T., & Parks, A.C. (2006). Positive Psychotherapy. *American Psychologist*, 61, 774–788.

Martin E. P. Seligman, Peter Railton, Roy F. Baumeister and Chandra Sripada Navigating Into the Future or Driven by the Past *Perspectives on Psychological Science* (2013) 8: 119 DOI: 10.1177/1745691612474317 Sage Publications

McCloud, Carol. *Have you Filled a Bucket Today: A guide for daily happiness for kids.* 2006. Fern Press, Northville, MI.

Seligman, M., Rashid, T. (2018) *Positive Psychotherapy: Clinician Manual.* Oxford University Press. New York, NY.

Tomasulo, D. *Action methods in group psychotherapy.* (1998) Taylor & Francis. Ann Arbor, MI

Tomasulo, D. *Beautiful Thinking in Action: Positive Psychology, Psychodrama, and Positive Psychotherapy* (unpublished manuscript)

Tomasulo, D, Virtual Gratitude: *https://www.youtube.com/watch?v=Vkk_Db_3Jww*

Healing Shame and Developing Healthy Shame in the Imaginal Realm

Sheila Rubin, with Bret Lyon

My work these days and for as long as I can remember has been teaching about the emotion of shame. Shame heals through the restoration of the interpersonal bridge. Due to the special nature of shame, it cannot be worked with in the same way as the other primary emotions. Special care needs to be taken to work with shame in specific ways. We have created our work to help therapists understand how to avoid getting stuck in the shame freeze with clients or following them down the endless shame vortex.

When clients get stuck in shame, the most powerful and useful way to help them get unstuck may be to activate their imagination. The Imaginal Realm offers another way to access the incredible resilience and scope of the human brain. In the "imaginal realm," logic and time are fluid and flexible. What actually happened can be explored and changed. What was stuck in the cognitive realm can be reexamined and shifted. Shaming situations from the past can be revisited and resolved.

And the most curious thing about shame is that when a person is actually feeling it, frequently there is shame about having it. So often a person may feel shame and then have shame about the shame! That is where we come in. Shame is called many names, the inner critic, perfectionism, shyness, low self-esteem. And places shame can show up is when a person speaks of feeling embarrassed or not good enough or not fitting in. Someone who feels like an impostor is feeling shame. Someone who is putting themselves down is feeling shame, or having a shame attack. When someone says "I feel stupid" or "I feel stuck," it is often a sign of shame. Shame can get passed down in families.

The Purpose of Shame

Shame has a developmental purpose. We are socialized through being shamed. Every society uses shame to socialize. The issue isn't whether a society is using shame, but how it is using it. Shame is a primary emotion and the action tendency is to hide and pull away. Shame is there to protect us and keep us out of trouble by following society's rules and being aware of those around us. And understanding this can be vital in understanding our relationships, ourselves and the world more deeply.

Definitions of shame

Gershen Kaufman in "Shame the Power of Caring" wrote that "Shame is the rupture of the interpersonal bridge." Understanding this can also help with the restoring of the interpersonal bridge through caring and empathy and connection through witnessing. Brene Brown's definition of shame, "Shame is the intensely painful feeling or experience of being flawed and therefor unworthy of love and belonging." And Bret Lyon had identified shame as a combination of a primary emotion and a freeze state.

In the *Eight Keys to Safe Trauma Recovery* (2000), Babette Rothschild notes that "shame, quite simply, tells us that something is amiss"[1] and that "Rather than discharge, as an example in yelling or crying, shame dissipates, when it is understood or acknowledged by a supportive other. More than any other feeling, I find that shame needs contact to diminish."[2] Rothschild describes a process for deciding when to address shame, understanding the value of shame, apportioning shame fairly, and sharing shame.[3] In *The Transforming Power of Affect* , Diana Fosha wrote, "Over time the stirring of a visceral conclusion is drawn whereby any stirring of emotion (that is, core affective experience) comes to automatically elicit anxiety or shame . . . which becomes a spur to institute protective strategies."[4]

Reactions to shame

Because shame is the most painful of all emotions what we see and experience is mostly not shame but the reactions to shame. The nervous system reacts by attacking the self, attacking another, denial or withdrawal. *Shame and Pride*, Nathanson (1992). We teach the skill of "counter shaming."

Gershen Kaufman who identified shame as, "The breaking of the interpersonal bridge," also spoke about countering the shame through kind words, offering connection, and in certain instances even countering the shame with

---

1 p. 87
2 p. 92
3 pp. 98–100
4 Fosha, 2000, p.104

careful teasing—not too much because that can be shaming as well. In our work the phase one drama therapy games that provide rapport building and an experience of joining together. When a person has so much shame we have to counter it. Warm greetings, a kind voice, connection and care can be count shaming. We try to be curious about it.

Working in the Imaginal Realm

Because shame is an embodied belief "that there's something wrong with me." We need to be able to work with shame outside the body and a little beyond our thinking mind. Moreno's tele is a great place to go for shame work. I call it working in the imaginal realm. This is a place where imagination can open to something creative.

When people are stuck in shame often the most powerful way to get it unstuck is to activate the imagination. In the imaginal realm, logic and time are fluid and flexible. What actually happened in life can be explore and changed. What was stuck in the cognitive realm can be re-examined and shifted and shaming situations from the past can be revisited and resolved. We can explore the critical voices that may be remembered from childhood and/or childhood scenes that may be running an internal shame dynamic.

In a chapter about Psychodrama by Antonia Garcia and Dale Richard Buchanan in *Current Approaches in Drama Therapy* by David Johnson and Renee Emunah:

> Moreno believed that the self emerges from the roles we play. He postulated that when people learn a new role, they follow a particular pattern of role development. The arc of the learning curve begins with role taking and proceeds to role playing and role creating.

> "Dysfunction occurs when a person has a lack of either social roles or psychodramatic roles and function is seen as having a balance of both." First a person can't imagine a certain role, so I tell them a story about someone who had that role. Then I may suggest a conversation that that person may have. Moreno wrote that in order to develop functionally each of us must first be doubled as newborns. So much of the work I do in the therapy session is about mirroring the client.[5]

Healthy shame is like a new role for the person to try on and explore. We can use imagination by saying what did you want to say to the person and we can replay it through a role play or through a waking dream.

---

5 p. 43

Understanding Shame

Shame is a primary emotion. The role of shame is to warn us and protect us. Our nervous system shuts down and we actually lose cognitive ability when we are feeling ashamed. Two indicators of shame are confusion and stuckness. Shame can freeze both mind and body. Shame is so difficult to see and cope with because it often hides behind other emotions. Shame, like of its functions is to protect us by lowering our emotional intensity and capacity to act. It is important to differentiate healthy shame, which can help us pause and rethink, from toxic shame, which can produce paralysis and leave a person so frozen that he or she is incapable of action and clear thinking. Healthy shame can lead a person to take responsibility for his or her actions, reassess, and make changes.

Healthy Shame

While toxic shame can be bad for a person, healthy shame can actually be very helpful. We identify several elements to healthy shame. First the pause that the withdrawal reaction to shame can give a person. This is a time have compassion, then to assess and reassess did we misunderstand is there something that I did? There is the taking of responsibility. Then there is the humor which having a little humor can have give a little distance from the shame. Then the seeing the big picture. There is a precision to understand in the role of shame and how to make repair if possible.

John Amadeo in *The Authentic Heart* writes that shame can be instructive and that "properly acknowledged shame and guilt can open a doorway to understanding how you've hurt someone."[6] While excessive or toxic shame can keep a person in denial, "shame overload paralyzes your capacity for clear introspection." He says that, "No growth is possible without some small amount of shame."[7] This small amount of shame is what we call healthy shame. And it is different from the all pervasive toxic shame by being helpful rather than harmful. The healthy shame tells us what to do and how to repair.

Daniel Hughes in *Attachment Focused Family Therapy* writes about why shame may be a central factor in development of pathology and a deterrent to getting help: "First, shame places one in a fog, hidden from potentially significant others, actively avoiding the exposure to another who could provide — through intersubjective experiences of acceptance, understanding and empathy — a pathway toward both affective regulation as well as self-awareness.

---

6 p. 64

7 p. 65

Second, shame prevents the development of the ability to reflect on and make sense of one's behaviors and subjective experiences."[8]

In the *Eight Keys to Safe Trauma Recovery* (2000), Babette Rothschild notes that "shame, quite simply, tells us that something is amiss"[9] and that "Rather than discharge, as an example in yelling or crying, shame dissipates, when it is understood or acknowledged by a supportive other. More than any other feeling, I find that shame needs contact to diminish."[10] Rothschild describes a process for deciding when to address shame, understanding the value of shame, apportioning shame fairly, and sharing shame.[11]

The Role of Shame

Understanding the role of shame is vital. Shame is here to protect us. It is an emotion that tells us when to pause and pull back and reassess. It has a developmental role as well: to slow down the process and use the imaginal realm to have a different experience.

Adam Blatner expounded that psychodrama offers a place for replaying scenes of the past, expressing feelings now that have not been expressed, and for opening new possibilities for the future. "Individuals are invited to engage more authentically in activities that increase their sense of being alive."[12]

Case Example

Once I was working with a woman who was feeling very lost in her life. She wasn't sure if she even wanted to start a new job or a new relationship. I asked her what her picture was when she imagined getting a new job, and all she could picture was what happened in her last job: her co-worker and even her supervisor putting her down. I asked her what picture she imagined when she thought about a new relationship and she couldn't even imagine that; she just kept saying over and over, "The last one wasn't very good, so there must be something wrong with me." I realized that her hope and creativity and emotion was frozen.

One day she came into the session with a dream. In her dream, she was seeing friends from long ago. I asked her how it was to see those friends from long ago. She said, "There must be something wrong with me because they stopped being my friends." I said, "It sounds like when you want to move forward, you get these thoughts that there's something wrong with you." She

---

8 p. 184
9 p. 87
10 p. 92
11 pp. 98–100
12 Blatner, 1988, p. 85

said, "Yes," looking down. Case note—when a person looks down often it is because they are feeling shame.

In order to externalize her feelings in the moment so I asked her to draw what it felt like inside when she had that thought. Instead of choosing any of the brightly colored chalk, pencils, or markers, she picked the blackest black and slowly covered the whole page with it. I said, "Wow . . . That's really something. No wonder you can't move forward." I am witnessing and naming her stuckness. So, I asked how it was to draw her picture like that and to have it so black and to fill the whole page. She seemed encouraged by my support and said, "There's more." So, I asked her to draw the "more." And then there was a whole other level of black on top of the black.

It was very black, kind of take-your-breath-away black. So I wanted to acknowledge the darkness so she wasn't alone with it. Then I brought in play. We started playing with this picture of the blackest black. First we positioned it right in front of her, then slowly I moved it until it was all the way on the other side of the room. We began a process of acknowledging this black from the different distances. When it was far away from her, at one point she started to feel a little bit of hope. When it was a certain distance from her she began to have a tiny shift. Then she remembered a tree she used to climb back when she was a tomboy, before she started wearing skirts and having to act "right." I had her draw the image of the tree and then I had her feel the sensation inside of her of the tree supporting her, back when she was a tomboy. Slowly we began to work with this symbol of protection. The tree would protect her from the blackness. When she started to have thoughts that there was something wrong with her, she could imagine sitting in the arms of tree and the tree saying to her, "It's okay. You're going to be okay." This is counter shaming and resourcing.

A while after that she had another dream that she brought in. This dream was about the boss who had put her down. We worked on symbolism and talked about the different roles in the dream and worked in the Imaginal Realm with the psychodrama technique of surplus reality and Jungian active imagination. Surplus reality is an extension of ordinary reality where we can use imagination to have a conversation with someone as we wish we could or to complete something we wish we had been able to complete. We can call on support from memories, TV, movies or dreams. With my client, I suggested bringing in images that might protect and support her. She imagined the boss and then imagined a serpentine monster coming up and wrapping its tentacles around the boss, who was trying to run away. The monster was saying, *"Listen to her."* Then we brought her into the picture. She was eventually able to say to her boss, "I wrote those reports but you put your name on them." And then we brought me into the picture. I named what was going on and said to the boss, "That shamed her." Then she said, "I felt discredited. I felt like I didn't exist." And so, I said, "She felt like she didn't exist and that was shaming to her." Finally, she got to say what she meant to say all the time! Eventually I had her go back into the scene. This time the boss said, "I'm so sorry, I didn't mean to shame you."

When later I asked her to do another drawing of how she felt, instead of the blackest black of her original picture, she used all these different colors—orange, blue, yellow—and the image was kind of like a butterfly. I asked her what the butterfly was about and she said, "I'm feeling a lot better today. Lighter." I told her that the butterfly is a symbol of new direction and transformation and, some people believe, resurrection—coming back to life again. For her it was a powerful symbol because there was movement, color and lightness. Even though the real boss in real life had not apologized, even though the situation hadn't actually changed in reality, she felt very different inside. Instead of "There's something wrong with me" she was able to realize there was something *right* with her. As she healed from the constriction of all-pervasive shame, her life force energy came back to her. And she now was able to go out on job interviews and eventually get a job that she loved. Even though the work with her was just in my office, we were working with her imagination. We were able to work with the shame so that it wasn't holding her back anymore. She was able to be different in the world.

At one point she asked, "Do I need to call my ex-boss and tell him what an a**hole he was?" I asked her if she needed to do that or if she felt different enough from the work we had done that she didn't actually need to tell him anything. And she realized she was fine and didn't need to do it.

The Imaginal Realm is a place where I can gently guide the client if the shame is all-pervasive, when their thoughts or their body is stuck. By leading them through an expressive arts, creative drama therapy artistic process, I can help them find a different role they have inside. In the case of this client, she was stuck with the automatic thought "There's something wrong with me." CBT seemed to work in our early sessions but would not correct her automatic thoughts "something's wrong with me" and core belief about her worthlessness when she was out in the world. So I added some drama therapy to increase the effectiveness of CBT. When we challenged her automatic thoughts she would try on the new belief of "There's nothing wrong with me," but then she'd feel embarrassed because she didn't actually believe it and didn't want to admit that. So she hid her shameful thoughts from me during the session— more shame to hide. By working in the Imaginal Realm, we were able to bypass that part of her that was judging her and keeping the shame so stuck. I was working with the introjects in the client's imagination, which is more effective than working directly with her issues out in the world when there has been all pervasive shame.

Using imagination: This is Winnicott's "play space," this is Moreno's "Tele," it's the Jungian Imaginal Realm, Psychodrama's "surplus reality" . . . By guiding a client skillfully into it and then out of it back to their life, we can heal their shame in the Imaginal Realm and give them back roles to re-incorporate into their life, including roles that they've never had before. This woman eventually chose to become a big sister and mentor for kids (tomboys). She found her next job with delight and anticipation and enjoyed her new role of survivor rather than victim.

- Externalize shame so that it can be worked with directly.
- Work with roles, parts and shame-based introjects.
- Access strength, resilience, inner resources and role repertoire.
- Find a deeper understanding by working with objects you already have in your office.
- Utilize imaginal techniques to give the shame back, so that it stays in the Imaginal Realm.

Psychodrama

Created by J.L. Moreno and written about by Adam Blatner wrote about the multidimensionality of experience and the multiplicity of roles. Blatner (2000) wrote in Foundations of Psychodrama that sublimation is a healthy defense mechanism and the way many people hide parts of themselves. He explained that an activity would be avoided if it was associated with vulnerability. Therefore, "Immature behaviors will be retained if no support is given for the gradual and pleasurable acquisition of the new role.[13] He expounded that psychodrama offers a place for replaying scenes of the past, for expressing feelings now that have not been expressed and for opening more into more possibilities in the future. "Individuals are invited to engage more authentically in activities more authentically and that and an increased sense of being alive"

Shame-shifting—we are shifting from toxic shame to healthy shame.

Brene Brown, in I thought it was just me suggests we work with shame by four elements: understanding triggers, practicing critical awareness, reaching out, and practicing courage in a culture of fear.

This is toxic shame. This is the voice of the inner critic that puts a person down no matter what they do. There is also healthy shame which helps us to set boundaries and know what is right for us. Shame is different in each society. The developmental purpose of shame is to help us fit in. It also protects us.

The Shame Continuum

There is a continuum of shame that goes from shyness and embarrassment on one end to feeling awkward to feeling unseen, all the way to humiliation and exile on the further end. I read the first words, "shyness, embarrassment, social

---

13 Blatner, 2000, p.84

anxiety, there's something wrong with me." And I ask the group for some other words they have felt or heard that belong on this list. "Feeling flawed, invisible, feeling like an alien, stuck, isolated, don't fit in, not wanted, can't do anything right" says the group. In a lecture group, I write on a board and we discuss.

Exercise: Circle of strengths and shame

In order to work with this emotion, I like to identify and name positives and supportive things about each person. This is counter shaming to begin in the positive place if they will go there.

In an experiential group, I could do a little psychodrama circle by having everyone stand in a circle and I name one positive thing that people say about them or something that they like about themselves. They step into the center and I ask who else has hears something similar. And then shame like "shyness" and everyone who feels that way steps in the center. We can go through many of the feelings. Then I have students name other feelings on the embarrassment/shame continuum. Then a bit of psychodrama and put these feelings on a line and have everyone take their place where they feel most comfortable, a place that is familiar to them. We name a time they felt stuck or isolated. As the group hears others feel this way, there is usually a lot of relaxation. Shame thrives in secrecy. Shame heals by sharing secrets. The first secret is that we all feel this way at some times. This is the beginning of developing trust as we begin to move forward.

Exercise: "More than one mirror"

In the day to day experience of being alive and feeling and communicating clearly, there are moment to moment challenges and things to attend to. Sometimes a person may look into an inner mirror and think, "I can't do this." Or "something's wrong with me." I help them explore where they feel stuck and eventually invite them to try on a new mirror. I have an exercise that has to do with two mirrors. First we draw them on paper, exploring the inner feelings and the shame feelings and when they occur. I have an actual mirror with room behind for someone who is a double to give a true mirror.

Exercise: "Pillow" Put the toxic shame on the pillow to eventually find the healthy shame that can guide her

A woman who just divorced a man who was lying to her about his many girlfriends and hookups. She has survived the divorce and lives in a new city but every time she goes on a date when she starts to get interested in the guy, she suddenly starts to eat a lot of baked goods. When I have her tune into her body she says feels icky in the pit of her stomach. I have her put project this feeling icky from her stomach onto a pillow on to the chair and we talk to the pillow.

Healthy Shame: An Example

I want to write the most about the concept of healthy shame. Most shame that people experience is toxic and terribly uncomfortable. To have even the concept that it could play a role toward growth. "Being embarrassed at being uncovered or found out is not the same feeling as genuine shame. Shame is one of those mechanisms that makes a person think twice about doing something wrong in the first place. Moreover, a person who truly feels ashamed is certainly not likely to do the same things over and over again with no compunction."[14]

Some people have trouble accepting a complement for a job well done. Here is something from my article about the Golden State Warriors, June 2016, "They Won Again, Did Healthy Shame Contribute to the Golden State Warriors Success?"

Although I must admit I was never a basketball fan until a few years ago, I did watch the Golden State Warriors win the NBA championship yesterday for the second time in three years! When my husband first told me about an amazing 3-point shooter by the name of Stephen Curry, I immediately noticed Curry's smaller physique and graceful, dancer-like movements that allowed him to navigate his way through members of the other team in a very different kind of way. As my husband explained the game to me, I began to see the advantage of Curry's 3-point shots from far across the court, compared to the 2-point shots that most players compete for. I was impressed by the teamwork and spirit of cooperation by the Warriors, who live up to their motto of "Strength in Numbers."

A couple years back I read an article about Stephen Curry who shared about his father, a basketball star who also served as his mentor, and how he told him that because he was a smaller weight and size, he must excel at shooting baskets, otherwise no coach would even give him a second look. Curry spent the next few years slowly developing, working and finding his own way to shoot baskets. I believe this is a good example of growth coming from healthy shame. He had a choice: He could give up, and let his size keep him from succeeding, or he could step up and work hard to find his own journey as a player. Thankfully, he used the inspiration from his father to find something in himself to improve his skills on the court. He never gave up, and instead of feeling sorry for himself, he found his own path to shooting and winning. That same article also featured another amazing shooter, Draymond Green, who went through a time where he could have given up, but did not. Instead of getting stuck in a place of shame, he focused on what he could accomplish. Both of those men choose to overcome obstacles and find success on the court.

Is there a new paradigm for masculinity? Have those two award-winning players, part of an amazing team, found a way to work together to show everyone

---

14 p.37

that you don't need to be "overly muscled" and play "hero ball," which usually leaves the other team members behind? They work as a team in a collective, cooperative way, and are encouraged by Coach Steve Kerr to play to their own strengths. *And it works!*

I found myself watching and enjoying the entire series! And as I observed other teams starting to make 3-point shots, I realized Stephen Curry had demonstrated it was possible. He was comparable to the guy who broke the 4-minute mile, which inspired others to do the same. I feel as if I am watching a new spirit of cooperation filled with endless possibilities from this Oakland-based team that is changing basketball throughout the United States.

Using imagination: This is Winnicott's "play space," this is Moreno's "Tele," it's the Jungian Imaginal Realm, Psychodrama's "surplus reality" . . . By guiding a client skillfully into it and then out of it back to their life, we can heal their shame in the Imaginal Realm and give them back roles to re-incorporate into their life, including roles that they've never had before. This woman eventually chose to become a big sister and mentor for kids (tomboys). She found her next job with delight and anticipation and enjoyed her new role of survivor rather than victim.

In dipping into psychodrama, I want to acknowledge Jacob Moreno and his wife Zerka Moreno, who created psychodrama. Thank you also to Adam Blatner and Eva Leveton and Sylvia Israel from whom I learned directly about psychodrama and surplus reality.

Active Techniques from Drama Therapy and Psychodrama.

Drama Therapy—the intentional and systematic application of drama and theater processes to achieve psychological growth and change in a child or adult and deeper connection in the couple or family. This can lead to increased access to deeper feelings, ability to communicate feelings to the spouse or partner, increased connection, and ultimately increased access to imagination, spontaneity, intuition, play and creativity. Today we are using projective as well as expressive processes.

- Help client experience a series of successes (counter shaming).
- Separate shame from other emotions.
- Use objects or processes to externalize shame.
- Use projective or embodied methods to explore where the shame came from originally.
- Symbols or objects to express feelings—can be used for exploration or externalization to get beyond words, or beyond thoughts. "Can you show me something in the room that can be a symbol for show shut down you feel when you hear criticism?" "Can you choose a pillow to represent the feeling, or the shame?"

- Role-play "Can you show me what happened last night when you came home?" Role-plays can get deeper to the core of what is happening because they are embodied and experiential. The person can play both parts or the therapist can play one part, or there can be an empty chair.
- Role Reverse "Can you play your father? What might he say to you now?" Often empathy can be reached by playing the role of another person.
- Introduce a Protector
- Finding optimal distance from the client's shame to work with it

Sheila Rubin

Sheila Rubin, LMFT, RDT/BCT, is a registered drama therapist and a board-certified trainer through North American Drama Therapy Association (NADTA), adjunct faculty at John F. Kennedy University's Somatic Psychology Department. She is an alumnus and has taught for California Institute of Integral Studies' Drama Therapy Program. Her expertise, teaching and writing contributions have been featured in numerous publications, including six books. She is a president emeritus of San Francisco CAMFT and the Northern California chapter of NADTA.

Sheila has delivered presentations and workshops across the country and around the world, at conferences from Canada to Romania. Her expertise, teaching, and writing contributions have been featured in numerous publications, including six books. She has developed therapy techniques integrating somatic and expressive modalities to work with the all-pervasive shame and trauma that underlie eating disorders, addictions and toxic family dynamics. She offers therapy through her private practice in Berkeley and consultation to therapists over Skype.

For more information on Healing Shame workshops, certification and private therapist consultations visit *HealingShame.com* or *SheilaRubin.com*.

Bret Lyon

Bret Lyon, PhD, SEP, BCC is a Healing Shame trainer and Board Certified Coach. He co-created the Healing Shame – Lyon/Rubin method and is the Co-Director of the Center for Healing Shame, offering workshops for therapists in many cities in the U.S. and Canada, as well as online. Bret has been a teacher of Somatic and Emotional Mindfulness for over 30 years and holds doctorates in both Psychology and Drama. He is certified in Focusing and Somatic Experiencing® and has trained extensively in Reichian Breathwork. Bret has a private practice in Berkeley, CA.

References

Amadeo, J. (2001) *The Authentic Heart; An Eightfold Path to Midlife Love*, Canada, John Wiley and Sons

Blatner, A. (1988). *Foundations of psychodrama: History, theory, and practice.* New York, NY: Springer Publishing.

Emunah, R. (1994). *Acting for real: Drama therapy process, technique, and performance.* New York, NY: Brunner/Mazel.

Fosha, D. (2000). *The transforming power of affect: A model for accelerated change.* New York, NY: Basic Books.

Garcia, A. and Buchanan, R. (2009) *Psychodrama* in Johnson, D and Emunah, R. (2009), Springfield, IL: Charles Thomas Publishers.

Graham, Linda. (2013). *Bouncing Back: Rewiring Your Brain for Maximum Resilience and Well-being.* Novato, Ca.: New World Library.

Hughes, D. A. (2007). *Attachment-focused family therapy.* New York, NY: Norton & Company.

Johnson, S. (2005). *Emotionally Focused Couple Therapy with Trauma Survivors; Strengthening Attachment Bonds*, NY, NY. The Guilford Press.

Kaufman, G. (1974). *On shame, identity and the dynamic of change.* Paper presented at the annual meeting of the American Psychological Association, New Orleans, LA. Retrieved from http://files.eric.ed.gov/fulltext/ED097605. pdf

Kaufman, G. (1992). *Shame: The power of caring* (3rd ed.). Rochester, NY: Schenkman Books.

Nathanson, D. L. (1992). *Shame and pride; Affect, sex, and the birth of the self.* New York, NY: W. W. Norton & Company.

Rothchild, B. (2000) *The Body Remembers, The Psychophysiology of Trauma and Trauma Treatment.* WW Norton and Co, NY, NY

Rubin, S. (2007) *Self revelatory performance* in *Intercalative and Improvisational Drama; Varieties of applied theatre and performance*, ed. Blatner, A. Universe

Rubin, S. (2015) "Almost Magic: Working with the Shame That Underlies Depression; Using Drama Therapy in the Imaginal Realm", in *The Use of the Creative Therapies in Treating Depression*, Brooke, S and Myers, C Thomas Publishers, Springfield IL

Schore, Allen N. *Affect Regulation and the Origin of the Self: the Neurobiology of Emotional Development.* 1994 New Jersey, Laqrence Eribaum Assoc. Publishers.

Psychodramatic Techniques for Neurodiverse Individuals

Carol Feldman-Bass and Jonathan N. Bass

We were meeting the couple for the first time. Their marriage had been rocky almost from the start. She was exuberant, emotive, and wanted emotional engagement. "I want my husband to be my partner. I want him to challenge me." He was quiet, meek, and saw himself as "easygoing." No matter what his wife wanted, he could accept it as "fine." Beneath this façade, he was terrified of his wife's frequent displays of anger. As a consequence, he made every attempt to please her by acquiescing to her wishes. He quickly let it be known, to us, that he preferred to avoid confrontation. In the midst of the session, we asked the wife to show us an example of the problem. She set the scene. She had returned home from a medical consultation where she was told that she would have to undergo a procedure. She showed us how she entered the kitchen and asked her husband, "How do you want me to pay the bill? Do you want me to pay over time or should I pay the entire bill at once? Which credit card do you want me to use?"

The husband replied, "You can pay it all with the green card."

The wife felt furious, hurt, and frustrated. "You see, that's all he said. He didn't want to know anything more." When we explored why she felt injured she responded, "I just came back from the doctor's office. I wanted him to ask me about what happened. I wanted more feeling from him." We asked the husband about his response. "I just want her to be happy. She asked me about how to pay for it so I gave her an answer." In the language of Psychodrama, the wife expected her husband to, spontaneously, reverse roles with her, appreciate her position, and act empathically. Her husband, lacking that capacity, being rigid and concrete, and being fearful of her rage, was unable to do so. The interaction drove one more nail into the coffin of this couple's marriage.

High Functioning Autistic Spectrum Disorder (H.F.A.S.D.), previously termed Asperger's Disorder, is a psychiatric disturbance characterized by significant limitations in the capacity to read the verbal and non-verbal social cues of others. One might think of such individuals having a deficit in interpersonal emotional intelligence or a "social learning disability." Like many psychiatric difficulties, people with High Functioning Autism or Asperger's Disorder fall along a spectrum with respect to social awareness. At one end are individuals who have the capacity to role-reverse intra-psychically and do so, spontaneously, with little difficulty. They are experienced, by others, as being "sensitive," "intuitive," and "insightful." At the other end of this spectrum are those with Asperger's Disorder who have far more difficulty reversing roles and are less likely to do so spontaneously. This often leads to the perception that they are aloof, distant, insensitive, lack empathy, and are incapable of taking the perspective of others. Distributed between these poles are the remainder of the population who have various degrees of social abilities. Other cognitive disabilities, such as dyslexia, are treated by providing a child with both academic accommodations and educational remediation. Given the similarity to learning disabilities, the question might be raised as to what forms of remediation might be made available to assist individuals with "social learning disabilities" or Asperger's Disorder.

As described by Apter (2003), "Psychodrama is a therapy of relationships, where the person can explore and try to reconcile various parts of his life (past, present or anticipated) . . . Supported by a qualified psychodramatist, an individual can experience his/her roles (be they frozen or not), without any hazards, through games, plays, or actions and add spontaneity and creativity." Here, the action is to "explore and reconcile various parts of life" while the goal is to "add spontaneity and creativity." Chimara and Baim (2010) state that, "Psychodrama can, for example, help people to better understand themselves and their history, resolve loss and trauma, overcome fears, improve their intimate and social relationships, express and integrate blocked thoughts and emotions, practice new skills or prepare for the future." Here, the actions are largely intra-psychic, *i.e.* to understand one's self, overcome fear, resolve loss, express and integrate thoughts and emotions. Only the goal of improving intimate and social relationships involves a real time "other."

In his paper entitled, "A Concise Introduction to Psychodrama, Sociodrama, and Sociometry," Herb Propper states that, "In psychodrama the focus of the action is the life of an individual and uses as the basis of action the personal roles and life story of an individual." But what if the individual's difficulties are relational in nature and not intra-psychically derived. What if the inherent problem that occurs is neurobiological and developmental and is not derived from traumatic events (although difficulties in social situations may be, in and of themselves, traumatic) and they do not evolve from systemic dysfunction at home, at work, or at school (although the individual's issues may have profound effects in these areas). Specifically, we speak of individuals on the Autistic

Spectrum and, in particular, those with High Functioning Autistic Spectrum Disorder (HFASD) and Social (Pragmatic) Communication Disorder (SPCD). The DSM V[1] identifies two specific problem areas that are characteristically seen in this population and which create significant social difficulties. These include "Persistent deficits in social communication and social interaction across multiple contexts" such as:

- Deficits in social-emotional reciprocity, ranging, for example, from abnormal social approach and failure of normal back-and-forth conversation; to reduced sharing of interests, emotions, or affect; to failure to initiate or respond to social interactions.
- Deficits in developing, maintaining, and understanding relationships, ranging, for example, from difficulties adjusting behavior to suit various social contexts; to difficulties in sharing imaginative play or in making friends; to absence of interest in peers.

A related component seen in individuals with these disorders is the inability to take the perspective of others. Baron-Cohen has written extensively about this difficulty, which he refers to as Mind Blindness. Baron-Cohen (1995) Hence, one might see HFASD and SPCD as disorders in which the capacity to relate to others *i.e.* to have a successful "Encounter" is impaired. A central element listed above is the "failure of normal back and forth conversation." This capacity, which is so difficult for individuals on the Autistic Spectrum and those with SPCD, is captured by Moreno in his thoughts about "Spontaneity" as a part of the "Encounter." "Spontaneity operated in the present and was an unconservable energy that propelled the person toward an adequate and appropriate response to a new situation or a novel response to an old situation. Spontaneity required a sense of timing, imagination, appropriateness and the ability for an organism to adapt in a rapidly changing environment."[2]

It is our belief that all successful communication is spontaneous and that to have an effective "Encounter" requires successful communication. Taken from the world of Improvisation, the interchange must always be, "Yes, and." The ability to help people with HFASD and SPCD to acquire these skills and to be spontaneous would seem to us to create a greater degree of social flexibility and social relatedness.

As "Psychodrama is a therapy of relationships" (Apter, N., 2003) the question may be raised as to whether the techniques of Psychodrama might be utilized effectively to address problems in social communication and enhance one's capacity to see the other's perspective. Central to J.L. Moreno's theories

---

1 *The Diagnostic and Statistical Manual of Mental Disorders 5th ed* (DSM 5); The American Psychiatric Association, 2013

2 J. L. Moreno, (1946, 1985); Hale, (1985)

was the concept of the "Encounter." He described the "Encounter" as, "extemporaneous, unstructured, unplanned, unrehearsed, it occurs in the spur of the moment . . . it is the experience of identity and total reciprocity; but above all psychodrama is the essence of encounter."[3] This description of the encounter lies in stark contrast to what is seen in individuals on the Autistic Spectrum who are often rigid, highly structured, repetitive, and limited in their capacity to engage in fluid reciprocal conversation with others. Moreno, speaking of the essence of the "Encounter" speaks to the issue of being able to take the perspective of another. In a graphic and moving description of the process he writes:

> *And when you are near I will tear your eyes out*
> *and place them instead of mine,*
> *and you will tear my eyes out*
> *and will place them instead of yours*
> *then I will look at you with your eyes*[4]

The available literature on the use of Psychodrama with people on the autistic spectrum is scant. Of the few articles that are available, most use the terms Drama Therapy and Psychodrama interchangeably but from the reading the intervention that is employed appears to be Drama Therapy. Only two articles speak specifically to Psychodrama. Li, J. et. al. (2015) is a single case study involving a severely autistic child. The methodology involves dramatic scripts to shape small appropriate social interactions. The child is lead "hand over hand" and there is no spontaneity achieved. The second is an unpublished paper describing how one might implement psychodramatic techniques within a public school setting to develop and generalize appropriate social skills with children who have Asperger's Disorder.[5] The authors write about the use of psychodramatic techniques with this population although they provide no evidence to suggest that they have employed this method and make no statements about its efficacy.

In this chapter, we shall describe how one may utilize many of the techniques employed in Psychodrama to ameliorate deficits in social communication while enhancing the capacity to take the other's perspective in individuals who have HFASD and SPCD.

---

3 J.L. Moreno (1969, p. 9)

4 Moreno, J.L. (1914) *Einladung zu einer Begegnung Part 2* (p. 3)

5 Munir, S, Scholwinski, E, and Lasser, J, unpublished.

Scene Setting

"The body remembers what the mind forgets. If it didn't, none of us would breathe, walk or ride a bike." —J.L. Moreno

It is my experience that Scene Setting, used as a singular tool, may help persons who lack social awareness understand very specifically how and when a social disconnect may happen. The individual's active recreation of the visual details of the event: In what room did the event occur? What was the layout? Where were all the individuals in the scene standing and sitting? As the individual recounts these details they use scarves as markers establishing the distance between themselves and all the other individuals and significant objects in the scene. Scene setting, without dialogue, can show an individual the physical elements that may exist in a social disconnect. This "seeing and feeling" as the individual creates the scene may be enough to spark social awareness.

A high school student, who is over six feet tall, could not understand why his approach to talking with a girl in his class was not successful. Using scarves, he recreated the scene in which he sauntered into his math class and went directly toward her. Before he began to speak, I asked him to stop and just look around at what he had created. Did he notice anything? He examined the scene and realized that he was both standing a little too close and looking directly down at the top of the young lady's head. In order to replicate, for him, the feeling of being literally "looked down upon," I had his father stand on a chair and stare down at his head. The boy jumped up and said, "That doesn't feel good." He had never considered that his physical height could have had a negative impact on his social relationships. Now he had questions. Was he being intimidating? Was he making someone uncomfortable? Should he have sat before speaking? Simple scene setting can bring immediate awareness of one's physical presence in a room with others. With practice, this permits the individual to have an improved sense of body placement within the social setting.

Concretization

Individuals who have HFASD often have significant difficulty when asked to use language to quantify their own feelings and behaviors. Even when provided a verbal Likert Scale, they have difficulty making an assessment of their internal state and the questioner is often met with "I don't know," a look of confusion and, if the individual is pressed, he may become frustrated and angry. Concretizing the task, by using markers, often results in clear responses gladly given.

I frequently make use of scarves to create the same Likert Scale saying, "The scarf at this end is 'I'm so sad I can't get out of bed. The scarf at this end is, 'I'm perfectly fine'. Take this third scarf and place it where you are today, in school, at home, *etc.*" Concretization, using props, is a direct outflow from improvisation. In working with individuals who have HFASD, using objects to represent the position of objects in a scene, a quantity, or another individual plays a critical role in the work, particularly work with individuals. This is often the case when the person is talking to others or a part of himself.

Sociometry

> "Sociometric explorations reveal the hidden structures that give a group its form: the alliances, the subgroups, the hidden beliefs, the forbidden agendas, ideological differences, the 'star' of the show."
> —J.L. Moreno

For us, the use of Sociometry is extremely important in running action based skills groups. For people who suffer from HFASD and other social disabilities, there are often unverbalized feelings that they can never be a part of any group of neuro-typical peers. In addition, the social skills groups in which these individuals have previously participated have often been comprised of peers who were neurologically more impaired. Comments we hear from individuals who have HFASD include, "No one understands me. I'm alone. I'm not normal. Why is everything easier for everyone else? Why do I always get it wrong? There is no one else who is as damaged as I am. There is no one out their like me."

It is precisely to address these feelings that Sociometry is such a powerful tool. Effectively, it helps individuals to see that they are not alone or unique. Groups work best when there is a significant degree of homogeneity in terms of member's strengths and limitations. This permits the group participants to sense that there are others like themselves. A degree of trust is also a critical element in developing these groups as no authentic group interactions may occur without a sense of group trust. Would these feelings of aloneness change if those same feelings were authentically shared and felt by other members of the group? Through the simplest of Sociometric structures, "sameness" and "acceptance" can be established.

We begin a group by making use of Spectrograms to measure where people are in the moment. We watch where each group member places him/herself measuring social fears, goals, and anxieties. More often than not the group finds itself "clumping" together on the same point on the Spectrogram rather than being scattered. Individuals often experience disbelief that their feelings of inadequacy are shared by the other members of the group. Asking group members to place themselves along a spectrum which represents various self-percepts quickly results in individuals beginning to trust the process and the other group members. I am "not alone" is what the Sociometry can prove. Using other Sociometric tools we continue the "joining" process. The increased awareness of "sameness" encourages spontaneity, closeness, and trust amongst group members which will become central elements in developing an awareness of others' feelings. It also leads naturally into Role Reversal and Doubling.

In a group of young men working towards negotiating the world of dating, Sociometry was very effective in helping them to realize that they all experienced similar frustrations, desires, and questions. In one case a young man was shocked that he was in a group of "peers" who not only understood his frustrations but also had personally experienced them. The criteria question for the Spectrogram, how each member saw themselves in relation to the others, was a basic measurement of "What is your level of experience with dating?" One scarf was "none" while the other was "expert." The young men placed themselves somewhere between the two scarves. Most were grouped close to "none" while Dave placed himself closer to "expert." I asked each young man "why?" they placed themselves where they did. Dave listened carefully to each explanation. "I don't know what to say." "How do I flirt?" "How should I ask people to meet both on-line and off-line?" After each answer I asked the group who related to that particular response. All, including Dave raised their hand. He clearly related more to the questions and concerns of the others rather than being an "expert." Eventually, I asked Dave why he placed himself where he did. He explained it had always been safer to claim "expertise" rather then explain his difficulties and risk ridicule.

Doubling and Role Reversal

Moreno's primary thesis is that the "Encounter" is the heart of human relationships. People who suffer from social awkwardness, HFASD and SPCD are portrayed as having difficulty experiencing deep interpersonal connections. It is our observation that using the psychodramatic techniques, Doubling and Role Reversal, help to reveal to others the existence of emotional awareness and enhances the ability to connect. These techniques also help individuals who have HFASD to develop a clearer understanding as to why their actions or words are misconstrued and why certain words or actions have a negative impact rather than the expected positive one. Role Reversal also teaches alternative ways to approach a situation in order to achieve a positive outcome.

Reversing roles with her employer, a young woman experienced why her blunt direct approach for asking for a raise would be heard as a "demand" rather than the merit based request she thought she was presenting.

The social awkwardness that is characteristically seen in individuals with HFASD creates the impression that they are incapable of having the deep emotional connection or understanding seen in neuro-typical individuals. Through this method, those with perceived social deficits are able to demonstrate to the "other" that they are capable of having deep emotional commitment. Historically, it has been the way that these feelings and emotions are expressed that cause social disconnect.

A couple, where the husband had been diagnosed as having Autistic traits, explored a scene where a particular issue had put a huge strain on the relationship. The wife did not understand her partner's reactions to the situation which she experienced as callus and dismissive. His words and actions were an unreasonable and hurtful response to her need to be close to her extended family. Her perspective was that, due to his Autism, he could not understand her requests and he did not understand how she could not see that he supported her.

The scene chosen happened in their kitchen where she was complaining about the location of their summer cottage. The cottage was on a campground that was seasonally occupied by this couple's extended family. Going to this campground yearly had become an important tradition for both husband and wife. Each family owned an interest in this vacation community but not a specific cottage. Each summer these identical cottages were randomly assigned on a first come first served basis. That summer the wife was extremely unhappy with the location of the family's cottage. It was not near her parents or other relatives. The scene went back and forth, eventually ending with his leaving the room with a final response of, "Just sell it already!" From the wife's perspective, the scene was evidence of his inability to read and understand her emotional dilemma. She took his, "Just sell it!" as dismissive and simplistic. She wanted him to understand the nuance of her feelings and, "Because of his Autistic traits he can't." He did not understand why his response was heard as dismissive or why she did not understand the motivation behind his words. As the argument continued, the husband became more rigid and stuck to his answer as "right" and she became more emphatic that he, because of his diagnosis, would never be able to understand. I directed the couple to take the role of the other and the scene was replayed, roles were expanded, maximized, minimized, verbal tone and physical actions were reenacted as precisely as possible. In order to evoke, in both, the affective experience of the self and the other, it is critical to be as specific as possible doing the scene work. Towards this end, it is helpful to concretize important elements of the re-enactment.

After the scene had been done multiple times, both partners were asked to give an "inner monologue" based upon their own role. Fully experiencing himself from his spouse's perspective he was able to speak with a full understanding as to how his actions and exasperated tone caused her more emotional distress instead of diminishing it. He was quite appalled at his own behavior and completely understood why she perceived him as dismissive. Words alone had not had an impact. He had been told repeatedly about his "tone" and "attitude" but had never understood. It was his full immersion in the role of his spouse and the replay and role reversal that gave him an insight he previously did not appreciate.

What about her? Her monologue from his role was, from his perspective, completely inaccurate. As her husband, she spoke about, "If we sell it she won't bother me anymore, I won't have to hear it, why does she care so much, she is being ridiculous."

The "Double" is an invaluable tool when working with individuals with High Functioning Autism. For these people, it is critical to make the "covert, overt." It has been my experience that, as humans, we base our relationships on the quality of our social interactions. If we perceive another as lacking the necessary skills to be in a relationship, then our experience is that there is no relationship or the relationship is faulty. The difficulty with reciprocal gaze and the often delayed response to verbal cues frequently leaves those who live or work with individuals who have HFASD with the experience that they are not responding adequately. From Moreno's perspective, there would be a problem engaging in the "Encounter." For a person on the spectrum The Double is the voice that is never heard and when heard often not believed. The conserve has become that this population has no inner voice.

Reversing roles with his spouse gave the husband insight into how he sounded and acted on the topic of the cottage. What, however, had motivated the husband's final statement, "Just sell it"? It was not said out of self interest as his wife suspected. The accurate Double was, "I love you and I hate seeing you this upset. Let's get rid of the thing that causes you pain." The error was that he jumped over the verbal statement of love and went straight to the action that would stop his wife from being upset. Had the verbal statement of caring been expressed by him in the moment, it might have changed the negative tone of the conversation. He was amazed that his partner "did not know" the reason for his initial statement. She was amazed at the Double.

We have seen examples of how some of the individual elements of Psychodrama are employed in working with in couples and groups where one or all of the members have HFASD. The following is an illustration as to how each of these techniques are combined in working with an individual within the context of a group.

Paul was a 16 year old boy who participated in one of my teen groups working on enhancing social skills. He had been diagnosed with HFASD and had marked anxiety and severe Attention Deficit Hyperactivity Disorder (ADHD). He managed his ADHD symptoms through athletic activities such as competitive and non-competitive sports. Sitting left Paul feeling as if he would "jump out of his skin."

One morning, Paul told the group that he wanted to work on his competitive behaviors as he had some thoughts that this might be getting in his way socially, but he was unclear as to why. I asked him to share an example drawn from his personal experience. Paul described playing Ultimate Frisbee. It was a favorite activity, permitting him to burn off excess energy and help him deal more effectively with his ADHD and anxiety. It was also one of his strategies for making social connections. The problem was that Paul took the game quite seriously. The other peers with whom he played were in the game solely for fun. Ben, was one such team member. Not particularly physically adept, he frequently dropped passes and could not keep up with the game. With each dropped pass, Paul became increasingly frustrated and his shouts at Ben grew louder and louder. Ultimately, he would have to leave the game to "take a run" as a means of managing his feelings. Often, after he had regained control, he would return to an empty field.

Paul had joined my group because he wanted to make "real" friends. He thought these Ultimate Frisbee pick-up games would be the perfect vehicle. He was aware of his competitive nature but had no idea how any of these feelings or behaviors were experienced by the others. His intensity was off-putting and, while the other kids agreed to play, the game did not translate into meaningful friendships. Paul told the group that he knew that Ben was a nice person and that there was no reason to be angry as there was nothing at stake in losing. In fact, he always thought of Ben as a possible friend.

To help Paul, we created a space in the room to be the "field" and Paul picked one of the other group members to be Ben (Scene Setting). A Koosh ball replaced the Frisbee (Concretization) and Paul and the other boy recreated the moment when the Frisbee was dropped. Paul yelled, "Ben!" with the same volume and tone as expressed in the story. Standing behind Paul I said, "Damn it Ben! You're a terrible player. Why do you always have to drop it? Why aren't you any good? You shouldn't be in this game." (The Double) I took Paul's internal and unsaid emotional experience and made it external and available for Paul and the group to hear. I asked Paul if my Double felt correct. Shocked, he said, "How did you know what I was thinking?!"

I then asked Paul to reverse roles with Ben and replay the scene. Now Paul was the one who dropped the ball and the other child yelled angrily, "Oh, Ben!!" When Paul heard how angry he sounded he was appalled. (Role Reversal/ Development of an empathic response)

I looked at Paul and asked for Ben's inner monologue.

As Ben, Paul responded, "Holy shit! Paul is really angry with me and I don't know why. It's a pick-up game. It's supposed to be fun. Maybe I shouldn't play anymore?"

I reversed Paul into himself and I asked, "What do you think of what you said as Ben?" He responded, "I guess that's not really true. I think he would still want to play even though he's mad at me. He would just avoid me."

From his own monologue in the role of the other, Paul began to began to appreciate that his demeanor was experienced by others as being very aggressive. (Learning to take the other's perspective)

How does Paul change his pattern of responding with anger when he is feeling competitive? I use role training starting from the perspective of the other.

"Okay," I said. "Who can Double the role of Ben? Say out loud what you think he or anyone might be thinking and feeling when Paul sounds that angry." It is very important for the group to be the main source of the Doubling. It pushes them to think about how actions, tone of voice, and body language can affect any relationship. It also permits empathic understanding to grow within the group. It is very hard for anyone to Double, to try to understand and express the feelings and thoughts of another, that is to take "the other person's perspective." This is an essential problem for individual with HFASD. The capacity to Double implies the presence of the capacity for empathy.

We replayed the scene over and over, the toss, the drop, the "BEN!!" Following each "BEN!!" each young man said aloud what he though Ben might be feeling (Doubling). Some of the Doubles were, "Why is is Paul so mad?" "I thought this was supposed to be fun?" "Why is Paul taking this so seriously" "I'm not coming back next week."

As he took it all in, Paul's eyes filled with tears. The "problem" was clear and now the question was how to fix it. Paul wanted Ben to try a little harder in the game and, hopefully, to become friends. Unfortunately, he had no idea as to how to accomplish this. We returned to the scene and began the process of "role training," the process of learning how to develop new behaviors. Paul realized that his "usual response" did not get him what he wanted. He had to learn what the role of "understanding friend" meant and how to embody it. This had never been his norm. We did this in action with the entire group playing a collective Ben. Paul threw the ball, Ben dropped it, and instead of yelling his usual, "BEN!!" I asked the group, "What are some different ways Paul could address Ben?"

Members of the group tried alternative approaches such as, "Hey, Ben, don't worry, it's only a game"; "Hey, Ben, maybe you should be on the other team"; and "Hey, Ben, why don't you just watch?" After each new response I asked everyone, "From the perspective of Ben, would that work?" Ultimately the response that felt the most comfortable and achievable was some version of "Don't worry" and "Would you ever want to get together and practice?" Paul left the session promising to use this different approach during the next game and report back to the group. The following session, Paul reported to the group that he tried the new approach and felt less angry and actually enjoyed practicing with Ben, "but he still dropped the Frisbee."

Individuals with HFASD and Social Pragmatic Communication Disorder struggle with "the Encounter." Their rigidity, difficulty with social and emotional reciprocity, problems with taking the perspective of the other, and difficulty sharing in imaginative play with others leaves them isolated and alone. While Moreno developed Psychodrama and its associated techniques to help individuals explore the "Encounter" both internally and externally, these same techniques may be utilized to help individuals with HFASD and SPCD to develop more effective social capacities and to develop their ability to understand the other's perspective while developing the capacity for empathy.

Carol Feldman-Bass

Carol Feldman-Bass, JD., is a Psychodramatist and the owner and founder of Social Dynamix. Social Dynamix is a unique program designed to help Neurodiverse individuals with social and communication difficulties become more spontaneous and socially successful. Carol's individual and group programs are a combination of Psychodrama, Improvisational Theater and Carol's natural Spontaneity.

She received her Juris Doctorate from Boston University and is a graduate of the Hudson Valley Psychodrama Institute. She has advanced trainings and certifications in DBT in Action, CBT in Action, Psychodrama for Couples and Families, Positive Psychology, and Sociodrama. She is the first practitioner to use, and is an expert in, the use of Psychodrama with persons with Autistic Spectrum Disorder (ASD) and has written and presented on the topic on both the East and West Coast. She incorporates Improvisational theater and comedy into all of her individual and group work. Carol has been a professional Improvisational actress in New England for over 15 years.

Jonathan Bass

Jonathan Bass, M.D., is a child and adolescent psychiatrist whose wide interests have taken him throughout the United States. He received his BA, Cum Laude from the University of Rochester and his M.D., Cum Laude from the University of Maryland School of Medicine. Following six months working, as a physician, with members of the Southern Cheyenne and Arapaho Nations in Clinton, OK, he completed residency training in Pediatrics at the Harbor U.C.L.A. Medical Center in Torrence, Ca. Further exploring his interest in Psychiatry, Jonathan completed residency training in Adult Psychiatry at the Massachusetts Mental Health Center and fellowships in Child and Adolescent Psychiatry, Psychosomatic Pediatrics, and Developmental Disabilities at Boston Children's Medical Center.

He has served as the Director of Child Psychiatry at Boston City Hospital and the Director of Child Psychiatry Training for the Boston University School of Medicine where he was an Assistant Professor. Interests in Psychopharmacology lead to work at the McLean Hospital as a staff psychopharmacologist and work using microdoses of medication to treat anxiety and other disorders, particularly in the Autistic Spectrum population. He has received training in Psychoanalysis at the Boston Psychoanalytic Society and Institute. Presently, he has been exploring the use of action based methods in treating children and families. He works collaboratively with his wife, Carol.

References

Apter, N. (2003). The Human Being: J. L. Moreno's vision in psychodrama. *International J. of Psychotherapy.* Vol 8 #1 pp 31–36.

Chimara, C. and Baim, C. (2010). *Introduction to Psychodrama.* Workshop for IASA Conference, Cambridge.

Baron-Cohen, S. *Mindblindness: An Essay on Autism and Theory of Mind.* Cambridge, MA: MIT, 1995.

Feldman-Bass, C. Unique Interactive Style of Learning Can Reduce Social Anxiety. *Autism Parenting Magazine.* Issue 75, 2018

Li, J. et al (2015). Using psychodrama to relieve social barriers in an autistic child: A case study and literature review. *International J of Nursing Sciences.* V 2, Issue 4 December 2015, Pages 402–407.

Moreno, J.L. (1914) *Einladung zu einer Begegnung Part 2* (p. 3)

Moreno, J. L. (1969). The Viennese origins of the encounter movement. *Group Psychotherapy,* 22(1–2), p.9.

Moreno, J. L. (1985). *Psychodrama Vol. 1. (7th ed.).* Ambler, PA: Beacon House.

Munir, S, Scholwinski, E., and Lasser, J. *The Use of Psychodrama Techniques for Students With Asperger's Disorder* (Unpublished)

Propper, Herb *A Concise Introduction to Psychodrama, Sociodrama, and Sociometry,* asgpp.org/pdf/psychodrama.conciseintro.pdf

The Diagnostic and Statistical Manual of Mental Disorders (5th ed; DSM 5; The American Psychiatric, 2013)

52988773R00200

Made in the USA
Columbia, SC
09 March 2019